Vladimir Nabokov and the Poetics of Liberalism

Vladimir Nabokov and the Poetics of Liberalism

Dana Dragunoiu

NORTHWESTERN UNIVERSITY PRESS / EVANSTON, ILLINOIS

Northwestern University Press
www.nupress.northwestern.edu

This book has been published with the support of the Andrew W. Mellon Foundation.

Printed in the United States of America.

10 9 8 7 6 5 4 3 2 1

ISBN 978-0-8101-2854-5

The Library of Congress has cataloged the original, hardcover edition as follows:

Dragunoiu, Dana.
Vladimir Nabokov and the poetics of liberalism / Dana Dragunoiu.
p. cm. — (Studies in Russian literature and theory)
Includes bibliographical references and index.
ISBN-13: 978-0-8101-2768-5 (cloth : alk. paper)
ISBN-10: 0-8101-2768-7 (cloth : alk. paper)
1. Nabokov, Vladimir Vladimirovich, 1899–1977—Criticism and interpretation. 2. Politics and literature. 3. Liberalism. I. Title. II. Series: Studies in Russian literature and theory.
PG3476.N3Z636 2011
813.54—dc22

2011000507

∞The paper used in this publication meets the minimum requirements of the American National Standard for Information Sciences—Permanence of Paper for Printed Library Materials, ANSI Z39.48-1992.

To my family

Vladimir Nabokov, aged seven, with his father in 1906

Across the vacant lot in darkening dust
I glimpse a slender hound with snow-white coat.
Lost, I presume. But in the distance sounds
insistently and tenderly a whistling,
And in the twilight toward me a man
comes, calls. I recognize
your energetic stride. You haven't
changed much since you died.

—Vladimir Nabokov, "Evening on a Vacant Lot"
In memory of V. D. N.

Freedom of spirit! All the breath of humanity
lies in that conjunction of words.

—Vladimir Nabokov, postscript to the Russian edition of *Lolita*

Contents

Acknowledgments

This book's debts are many. The project benefited from the generosity and expertise of scholarly communities in Canada, New Zealand, the United States, and Russia. I am grateful to Rick Asals, Russell Brown, Patricia Brückmann, Melba Cuddy-Keane, Elizabeth Harvey, Linda Hutcheon, Ralph Lindheim, Fred Wilson, Sarah Wilson, and the late Michael Dixon from the University of Toronto for nurturing the project during its earliest stages. At Princeton University, the project developed further under the wise and patient guidance of Michael Wood, and then benefited from Caryl Emerson's generosity and erudition. Lively discussions with Mary Esteve and André Furlani of Concordia University, Montreal, furnished me with astute suggestions for improving the book's third chapter. At Carleton University, Matt Brillinger and the inimitable and much missed John (Jack) Healy did the same for the second chapter.

International scholars from a variety of disciplines (met at conferences and sometimes never met at all) placed their time and expertise at my disposal. I owe special thanks to Frances Nethercott and Randall Poole for spending long hours away from their own work responding to my queries, reading chapters, and offering valuable advice. Arnd Bohm, Linda Groves Gerstein, Kurt Johnson, Christine Korsgaard, Ralph Nelson, Brian Owens, Olga Voronina, Andrzej Walicki, and Alla Zeide similarly took time away from their busy schedules to answer my questions. The book has also benefited from discussions with Thomas Dilworth, Erwin Rosinberg, and Gwen Walker. My anonymous reviewers supplied me with inspired and inspiring criticism that helped me improve the book in more ways than I can recount. I am deeply grateful to Mike Levine for his enthusiasm and support throughout this undertaking, and to Paul Mendelson for editing my manuscript with patience, grace, and perspicacity. Anne Gendler shepherded the manuscript through its final stages with thoughtfulness and expertise. Dmitri Nabokov has kindly and generously furnished me with the photograph of his father and grandfather that graces page vi.

Far-flung Nabokovians played a pivotal role in nurturing the project.

Evgenii Belodubrovskii, Julian Connolly, Galya Diment, Charles Nicol, and Zoran Kuzmanovich responded with unstinting support and enthusiasm to requests for advice and information. Two Nabokov scholars, in particular, have had a profound influence on my work generally and this project in particular. Stephen Blackwell has provided sustained encouragement, and shared his vast erudition and critical acumen throughout the project's long gestation. His judicious responses inform the book at every level. Through many discussions and by way of his own luminous example, Brian Boyd worked hard to teach me the meaning of scholarly generosity and intellectual integrity. I am deeply grateful for his bracing criticism, tireless guidance, and unflagging support over more than a decade.

I trust that my readers will never doubt that all faults and errors in the book are exclusively mine.

Stephen Crook and Anna Culbertson (New York Public Library's Berg Collection), Pertti Hakala (National Archives of Finland), and Carol Leadenham (Hoover Institution Archives) guided me expertly through their collections. Special thanks go to the library staffs at the universities of Toronto, Auckland, Princeton, Concordia, Carleton, and Windsor. Patricia Paquette and Christine Taylor (Carleton University) and Graham Staffen (University of Windsor) have provided me with tremendous help by tirelessly tracking rare documents to their hiding places. I am also deeply grateful to Natalia Khomenko for her patient and enthusiastic assistance in translating numerous Russian documents. Research fellowships from the Social Sciences and Humanities Research Council of Canada and from Concordia and Carleton Universities have been critical for the project's development and completion.

I owe the greatest debt to the members of my family, and thanking them here in no way assumes that this debt can ever be repaid. My late grandparents, who pretended to understand no language but Russian, are ultimately to blame for the project. With great effort and at enormous personal cost, my mother always and everywhere made certain that nothing was impossible. Words are too poor to thank her in the terms she deserves; my only consolation is the hope that she knows the depth of my gratitude. Graham provided me with boundless fatherly indulgence, unfaltering encouragement, and scholarly support over many years. Kyra and Howard made possible many days in the company of books and my laptop. My husband and colleague, Andrew Wallace, has read the book countless times and unstintingly placed at my disposal his many scholarly gifts and inspired ideas. The justly impatient Harry and Sasha have ensured that the happiest of memories will always be entwined with the process of writing the book. I look forward to reading one day their "books."

Note on Transliteration and Translation

This book follows a simplified version of the standard Library of Congress system for transliterating Russian. Exceptions include Nabokov's own transliterations of names (Chernyshevski, Fyodor, Tanya, Innokentiy, Sergey), familiar Russian names that have acquired fixed English spellings (Soloviev, Tolstoy, Dostoevsky, Bely, Kerensky), and spellings canonized by others (Dmitri, Gennady). For the sake of simplicity I have dropped the Russian soft sign from all personal and place names (Gogol, Aikhenvald, Smolnyi). To provide the closest approximation to Russian pronunciation, I have opted for "Piotr" instead of "Petr," and "Semion" instead of "Semen." Whenever a Russian given name has a common English counterpart, I have used the English equivalent ("George" instead of "Georgii," "Michael" instead of "Mikhail"). However, bibliographic references preserve a simplified version of the Library of Congress transliteration to aid those readers who wish to consult these sources. Stand-alone Russian terms are given in the nominative, not in declension. Quoted materials translated by others remain unaltered; all other translations are mine.

Abbreviations

A	Vladimir V. Nabokov, *Ada or Ardor: A Family Chronicle* (1969), in *Novels 1969–1974,* ed. Brian Boyd (New York: Library of America, 1996), 1–485.
BP	Sergey N. Bulgakov, "Basic Problems of the Theory of Progress," in *Problems of Idealism: Essays in Russian Social Philosophy,* ed. and trans. Randall Poole, foreword by Caryl Emerson (New Haven, Conn.: Yale University Press, 2003), 85–123.
BRR	Judith Elin Zimmerman, "Between Revolution and Reaction: The Russian Constitutional Democratic Party, October, 1905 to June, 1907" (Ph.D. dissertation, Columbia University, 1967).
BS	Vladimir Nabokov, *Bend Sinister* (1947), in *Novels and Memoirs 1941–1951,* ed. Brian Boyd (New York: Library of America, 1996), 161–358.
CPR	Immanuel Kant, *Critique of Practical Reason* (1788), in *Practical Philosophy,* ed. and trans. Mary J. Gregor (Cambridge, Eng.: Cambridge University Press, 1996), 133–271.
CR	Gleb Struve, "The Cultural Renaissance," in *Russia Under the Last Tsar,* ed. Theofanis George Stavrou (Minneapolis: University of Minnesota Press, 1969), 179–201.
DBDV	Vladimir Nabokov and Edmund Wilson, *Dear Bunny, Dear Volodya: The Nabokov-Wilson Letters, 1940–1971,* revised and expanded edition, ed. Simon Karlinsky (Berkeley: University of California Press, 2001).
Def	Vladimir Nabokov, *The Defense* (1930), trans. Michael Scammell in collaboration with the author (New York: Vintage, 1990).
DRT	Alexander Vucinich, *Darwin in Russian Thought* (Berkeley: University of California Press, 1988).

EI — Randall A. Poole, "Editor's Introduction: Philosophy and Politics in the Russian Liberation Movement," in *Problems of Idealism: Essays in Russian Social Philosophy,* ed. and trans. Randall Poole, foreword by Caryl Emerson (New Haven, Conn.: Yale University Press, 2003), 1–83.

EIPL — Pavel Novgorodtsev, "Ethical Idealism in the Philosophy of Law [On the Question of the Revival of Natural Law]," in *Problems of Idealism: Essays in Russian Social Philosophy,* ed. and trans. Randall Poole, foreword by Caryl Emerson (New Haven, Conn.: Yale University Press, 2003), 274–324.

FB — Vladimir Nabokov, "Father's Butterflies: Second Addendum to *The Gift,*" trans. Dmitri Nabokov, in *Nabokov's Butterflies: Unpublished and Uncollected Writings,* ed. Brian Boyd and Robert Michael Pyle (Boston: Beacon, 2000), 198–234.

FPP — Terence Emmons, *The Formation of Political Parties and the First National Elections in Russia* (Cambridge, Mass.: Harvard University Press, 1983).

Gi — Iosif Hessen [Gessen], *Gody izgnaniia: Zhiznennyi otchet* [*The Years of Exile: An Autobiographical Account*] (Paris: YMCA, 1979).

Gift — Vladimir Nabokov, *The Gift* (1963), trans. Michael Scammell with Vladimir Nabokov (New York: Vintage, 1991).

Gl — Vladimir Nabokov, *Glory,* trans. Dmitri Nabokov with Vladimir Nabokov (New York: McGraw-Hill, 1971).

GMM — Immanuel Kant, *Groundwork of The Metaphysics of Morals* (1785), in *Practical Philosophy,* ed. and trans. Mary J. Gregor (Cambridge, Eng.: Cambridge University Press, 1996), 37–108.

I — Richard Pipes, introduction to *The Provisional Government,* by V. D. Nabokov, ed. Andrew Field (St. Lucia, Australia: University of Queensland Press, 1970), ix–xiv.

IB — Vladimir Nabokov, *Invitation to a Beheading* (1959), trans. Dmitri Nabokov with Vladimir Nabokov (New York: Vintage International, 1989).

L — Vladimir Nabokov, *Lolita* (1955), in *Novels 1955–1962,* ed. Brian Boyd (New York: Library of America, 1996), 1–298.

LE — Immanuel Kant, *Lectures on Ethics,* trans. Louis Infield (Indianapolis, Ind.: Hackett, 1963).

LL	Vladimir Nabokov, *Lectures on Literature,* ed. Fredson Bowers (San Diego, Calif.: Harvest, Harcourt, Bruccoli Clark, 1980).
LPRL	Andrzej Walicki, *Legal Philosophies of Russian Liberalism* (Oxford: Clarendon, 1987).
LRR	William G. Rosenberg, *Liberals in the Russian Revolution: The Constitutional Democratic Party, 1917–1921* (Princeton, N.J.: Princeton University Press, 1974).
MD	Michael Wood, *The Magician's Doubts: Nabokov and the Risks of Fiction* (London: Pimlico, 1994).
MEC	Vladimir I. Lenin, *Materialism and Empirio-Criticism: Critical Comments on a Reactionary Philosophy* (Moscow: Progress, 1973).
MM	Immanuel Kant, *The Metaphysics of Morals* (1797), in *Practical Philosophy,* ed. and trans. Mary J. Gregor (Cambridge, Eng.: Cambridge University Press, 1996), 363–603.
NA	Brian Boyd, *Nabokov's "Ada": The Place of Consciousness* (Christchurch, N.Z.: Cybereditions, 2001).
NB	Kurt Johnson and Steve Coates, *Nabokov's Blues: The Scientific Odyssey of a Literary Genius* (Cambridge, Mass.: Zoland Books, 1999).
NP	Raymond Pearson, "Nashe Pravitel'stvo? The Crimean Regional Government of 1918–19," *Revolutionary Russia* 2, no. 2 (1989): 14–30.
NpKv	Maksim Vinaver, *Nashe pravitel'stvo (Krymskiia vospominaniia 1918–1919 g.g.)* [*Our Government (Crimean Reminiscences 1918–1919)*] (Paris: Imprimerie d'Art Voltaire, 1928).
OB	Vladimir Nabokov, "On a Book Entitled *Lolita,*" in *Novels 1955–1962,* ed. Brian Boyd (New York: Library of America, 1996), 293–98.
Onm	Vladimir Vernadskii, "O nauchnom mirovozzrenii" ["On the Scientific Worldview"], *Voprosy filosofii i psikhologii* 65 (1902): 1409–65.
P	Galya Diment, *Pniniad: Vladimir Nabokov and Marc Szeftel* (Seattle, Wash.: University of Washington Press, 1997).
PF	Vladimir Nabokov, *Pale Fire* (1962), in *Novels 1955–1962,* ed. Brian Boyd (New York: Library of America, 1996), 437–667.

PG	V. D. Nabokov, *The Provisional Government*, in *V. D. Nabokov and the Russian Provisional Government, 1917*, ed. and trans. Virgil D. Medlin and Steven L. Parsons (New Haven, Conn.: Yale University Press, 1976).
PHK	George Berkeley, *The Principles of Human Knowledge: The Works of George Berkeley, Bishop of Cloyne*, ed. A. A. Luce and T. E. Jessop (London: Thomas Nelson, 1948).
Pnin	Vladimir Nabokov, *Pnin* (1957), in *Novels 1955–1962*, ed. Brian Boyd (New York: Library of America, 1996), 299–435.
Pp	V. D. Nabokov, "Plotskie prestupleniia po proektu ugolovnago ulozheniia" ["Carnal Crimes According to the Criminal Code Project"], *Vestnik Prava* [*The Law Bulletin*] 32, nos. 9–10 (1902): 129–89.
QS	Stephen H. Blackwell, *The Quill and the Scalpel: Nabokov's Art and the Worlds of Science* (Columbus: Ohio State University Press, 2009).
Rg	Daniil S. Pasmanik, *Revoliutsionnye gody v Krymu* [*The Revolutionary Years in the Crimea*]. Paris: Imprimerie de Navarre, 1926.
RL	George Fischer, *Russian Liberalism, from Gentry to Intelligentsia* (Cambridge, Mass.: Harvard University Press, 1958).
RLC	Frances Nethercott, *Russian Legal Culture Before and After Communism: Criminal Justice, Politics, and the Public Sphere* (London: Routledge, 2007).
RRRI	Christopher Read, *Religion, Revolution and the Russian Intelligentsia, 1900–1912: The Vekhi Debate and Its Intellectual Background* (London: Macmillan, 1979).
SL	Vladimir Nabokov, *Selected Letters, 1940–1977*, ed. Dmitri Nabokov and Matthew J. Bruccoli (San Diego, Calif.: Harcourt, Brace, Jovanovich, 1989).
SLL	Richard Pipes, *Struve, Liberal on the Left, 1870–1905* (Cambridge, Mass.: Harvard University Press, 1970).
SLR	Richard Pipes, *Struve, Liberal on the Right, 1905–1944* (Cambridge, Mass.: Harvard University Press, 1980).
SM	Vladimir Nabokov, *Speak, Memory: An Autobiography Revisited* (1967), in *Novels and Memoirs 1941–1951*, ed. Brian Boyd (New York: Library of America, 1996), 359–635.

Sm — V. D. Nabokov, "Soderzhanie i metod nauki ugolovnago prava" ["The Science of Criminal Law: Contents and Method"], in *Sbornik statei po ugolovnomu pravu* [*A Collection of Articles on Criminal Law*] (St. Petersburg: Tipografiia Tovarishchestva "Obshchestvennaia Pol'za," 1904), 1–23.

SO — Vladimir Nabokov, *Strong Opinions* (London: Weidenfeld and Nicolson, 1974).

Td — V. D. Nabokov, *Tiuremnye dosugi* [*Prison Reflections*], *Pravo* 34 (August 24, 1908): 1812–21; 35 (September 2, 1908): 1867–78; 36 (September 7, 1908): 1914–27; 38 (September 21, 1908): 2012–20.

TT — Michael Karpovich, "Two Types of Russian Liberalism: Maklakov and Miliukov," in *Continuity and Change in Russian and Soviet Thought*, ed. Ernest J. Simmons (New York: Russell & Russell, 1967), 129–43.

Vdv — Iosif Hessen [Gessen], *V dvukh vekakh: Zhiznennyi otchet* [*Two Centuries: An Autobiographical Account*] (Berlin: Speer & Schmidt, 1937).

VNAY — Brian Boyd, *Vladimir Nabokov: The American Years* (Princeton, N.J.: Princeton University Press, 1991).

VNRY — Brian Boyd, *Vladimir Nabokov: The Russian Years* (Princeton, N.J.: Princeton University Press, 1990).

ZP — Stephen H. Blackwell, *Zina's Paradox: The Figured Reader in Nabokov's "Gift"* (New York: Peter Lang, 2000).

Vladimir Nabokov and the Poetics of Liberalism

Speak, Father

> From the very start, History seems to have been anxious of depriving [my father] of a full opportunity to reveal his great gifts of statesmanship in a Russian republic of the Western type.
> —Vladimir Nabokov

> The history of Russian liberalism has been sadly neglected.
> —Michael Karpovich

IN 1920, DURING HIS FIRST YEAR as an undergraduate at Cambridge University, twenty-one-year-old Vladimir Nabokov participated in a debate hosted by Trinity College's Magpie and Stump Debating Society. His argument in favor of Allied intervention in Russia was an act of ventriloquism that saw him presenting as his own words a lecture that his father had written and delivered under the title "Soviet Rule and Russia's Future" a few months earlier at King's College, London.[1] Returning to the scene of that debate years later in his autobiography, Nabokov viewed the event as a minor disaster: "the (victorious) apologist was a man from *The Manchester Guardian;* I forget his name, but recall drying up utterly after reciting what I had memorized, and that was my first and last political speech."[2]

Forced into exile by revolution and civil war, the young, aristocratic Nabokov lifts from his father an argument that was dear to both of them. And yet, as he looks back on the event through the frame of his memoir, he is eager to cast the debating fiasco as a last look down a road not taken. He dismisses the speech as an anomaly, a youthful indiscretion on the part of a man more comfortable celebrating his "supreme indifference" to sociopolitical concerns.[3]

Nabokov's characteristic reluctance to engage in political advocacy and debate is striking not only because his own life had been so calamitously affected by political events, but also because two of his novels are fundamentally committed to portraying the brutality of unrestrained political power. *Invitation to a Beheading* (*Priglashenie na kazn'*, 1938) and *Bend Sinister* (1947) depict versions of the regimes that forced Nabokov to flee Russia, then Germany, then France. Unrestrained political power claimed the life of his brother Sergey, who perished in a Nazi concentration camp; vicious political partisanship led directly to the death of his father, who died trying to disarm a right-wing assassin bent on shooting a longtime friend and political colleague.

Nabokov's act of ventriloquism, his unequivocal assertion of intellectual kinship between father and son, would never again be so embarrassingly and transparently staged before the public. But the kinship itself was no illusion. His father's political and ideological commitments play a decisive role in organizing the concerns of Nabokov's overtly political novels. They also shape the novels where Nabokov appears to be working in his most aesthetically self-indulgent mode: *Glory* (*Podvig*, 1932), *The Gift* (*Dar*, 1952), *Lolita* (1955), *Pale Fire* (1962), and *Ada* (1969).

Nabokov frequently complained that pre-revolutionary and émigré Russian history was largely unknown to Western historians and intellectuals.[4] His family's frustration with this profound misunderstanding of Russian history asserted itself as soon as the Nabokovs arrived in England after their escape from Russia. Nabokov documents, for example, his family's dismay at H. G. Wells's enthusiastic support of the October Revolution. An acquaintance of his father and a former guest of the Nabokovs in their St. Petersburg home, Wells "proved impossible to convince that Bolshevism was but an especially brutal and thorough form of barbaric oppression—in itself as old as the desert sands—and not at all the attractively new revolutionary experiment that so many foreign observers took it to be" (*SM* 579).[5]

At Trinity College, the scene of his debating fiasco, Nabokov frequently argued about politics, especially with one "Nesbit," a pseudonym for a Cambridge acquaintance whose naïveté about Lenin's regime proved invulnerable to strenuous counter-argument (*SM* 583–85; see also *VNRY* 168). Decades later in the United States, the *New Yorker*'s renowned editor Katharine White caused offense when she asked Nabokov to make changes to an autobiographical story he had submitted to the magazine. Urging him to tone down what she regarded as a biased denunciation of Lenin's suppression of civil liberties, White received a withering response from Nabokov: "I am terribly sorry, but what you suggest is quite impossible. It is really not my fault that Americans know so little about former Russia."[6] The story would later become a chapter in *Speak, Memory*, the British title of its American predecessor, *Conclusive Evidence* (1951).

Nabokov's most extended battles on this front were waged in his correspondence with Edmund Wilson. He deplored Wilson's Marxist-Leninist sympathies, arguing that they rested primarily on myths fostered by Soviet propaganda. In a letter from 1949, Nabokov was moved to refute Wilson's badly informed contention that no important Russian poetry had been written during the first two decades of the twentieth century. Given his tendency to insist on the uniqueness of his own genius, Nabokov's retort assumed a surprising form: "The 'decline' of Russian literature in 1905–1917 is a Soviet invention. Blok, Bely, Bunin and others wrote their best stuff in those days. And never was poetry so popular—not even in Pushkin's days. I am a product of that period, I was bred in that atmosphere."[7]

NABOKOV AND THE RUSSIAN SILVER AGE

This book studies Nabokov's Russian and English novels against the backdrop of that "period" and its "atmosphere." It does so, first, by establishing Nabokov's profound debt to the discourses and preoccupations of prerevolutionary Russian liberalism, especially as they were articulated by his father and other intellectuals of his father's immediate acquaintance and milieu. Second, it establishes how these Russian contexts shape the terms in which Nabokov's art responds to political issues and crises pressed upon him during his years in emigration and in America, and then again during his final years on the banks of Lake Geneva in Switzerland. This project may seem counterintuitive given that Nabokov is certainly better known for heaping scorn on political art than for the sophistication of his engagement with political and ideological concerns in his fiction. But his art is in many crucial respects shaped by thoughtful explorations of political and ideological questions, and this book's chief goal is to accomplish something that Nabokov himself seems to have despaired of ever accomplishing on his own—namely, granting his English-speaking readers some sort of intellectual purchase on the extraordinary richness, and tragically unfulfilled promise, of the cultural and political traditions that Soviet rule had managed, as it were, to strike from the record.

In interviews, letters, and prefaces Nabokov could frequently give the impression that he regarded art as a domain into which history ought not to intrude, but a close attunement to historical particularities structured the goals he established for himself when translating and annotating the poem he considered the crowning achievement of Russian poetry, Pushkin's *Eugene Onegin.* In his essay "Problems of Translation: *Onegin* in English," Nabokov warns that

> one of the main troubles with would-be translators is their ignorance. Only by sheer unacquaintance with Russian life in the 'twenties of the last century

> can one explain, for instance, their persistently translating *derevnya* by "village" instead of "countryseat," and *skakat'* by "to gallop" instead of "to drive." Anyone who wishes to attempt a translation of *Onegin* should acquire exact information in regard to a number of relevant subjects, such as the Fables of Krïlov, Byron's works, French poets of the eighteenth century, Rousseau's *La Nouvelle Héloïse,* Pushkin's biography, banking games, Russian songs related to divination, Russian military ranks of the time as compared to western European and American ones, the difference between cranberry and lingenberry, the rules of the English pistol duel as used in Russia, and the Russian language.[8]

My own forays into Russian intellectual and political history aim to uncover what Nabokov refers to in the same essay as "not only the essential pattern of the text but also the borrowings with which that pattern is interwoven." Nabokov ends his essay on translation by calling for "such sense and such notes for all the poetry in other tongues."[9] The following chapters contend that the precise political and ideological stakes of Nabokov's thinking on matters ranging from art to Darwin, from law to metaphysics, remain locked in the foreign tongue of pre- and post-revolutionary Russian liberalism.

Nabokov argued time and again that the West's lack of familiarity with this tradition was a powerful obstacle to a full understanding of the betrayals and miseries of Bolshevism. This book argues, in turn, that the failure to gauge adequately Nabokov's manifold debt to the discourses of pre- and post-revolutionary Russian liberalism has obscured the complex political and ideological dimensions of his art. Like the protagonist of *The Gift,* who inspects the past for signs of the "fatal flaw" that has made Russia "so crabbed and gray," "so befooled and befuddled,"[10] Nabokov repeatedly looked back into Russia's political and intellectual history in an effort to understand the failure of his homeland's liberal experiment and his own position as an inheritor of that stillborn legacy. This book charts Nabokov's investments in that experiment, and studies his art in relation to the intellectual and activist contexts that sustained it.

Vital work has been done on Russian liberal thought since Nabokov's death, and the field of principles and preoccupations that convene under that name can no longer be said to be as uncharted as they seemed to Nabokov. Intellectual and legal historians such as Frances Nethercott, Richard Pipes, Randall Poole, Christopher Read, and Andrzej Walicki have mapped the period's debates and key figures in ways that illuminate Nabokov's position as their thoughtful inheritor. But in spite of Nabokov's best efforts to assert his intellectual and artistic debts to these men and their commitments, literary scholars have yet to read his work in relation to the political and ideological controversies that preceded and followed the upheavals of the Silver Age. This book aims both to rectify that omission and to reframe the predominantly Americanist terms in which Nabokov's politics have been examined. When Nabokov views, for example, the events of the McCarthyist period, he does so by channeling his glance back through early twentieth-century Russian debates about the nature of law and the legitimate boundaries of political power. In addition to these goals, this book argues that Nabokov understands his own politics as an inheritance from his father, and that the political instincts that supply his novels with their particular form and texture cast matters of ethics, justice, and art as meditations upon the life, work, defeats, and death of his father.

V. D. (Vladimir Dmitrievich) Nabokov (1870–1922), the man whose words Nabokov memorized and delivered in the debate at Trinity College, was one of the most eminent leaders of the liberal opposition against tsarist autocracy in pre-Soviet times.[11] He might have been expected to follow a radically different career trajectory. His father, Dmitri Nikolaevich Nabokov (1826–1904), served as minister of justice under Alexander II and Alexander III, and the family had been long distinguished for military and civil service to the state (*VNRY* 20–21).[12] V. D. Nabokov studied law at the University of St. Petersburg, taught criminal law at the Imperial School of Jurisprudence, and became one of the most highly respected criminalists of his time. In the face of strenuous family opposition, he renounced a career in court circles for the sake of joining the struggle against tsarist autocracy. A leading member of the Constitutional Democratic (Kadet) Party,[13] he served on its Central Committee and was a member of the State Duma, Russia's first elected national legislative assembly. For two months during the short interim between the 1917 February Revolution and Lenin's seizure of power on October 25 of the same year, V. D. Nabokov occupied the important post of head of the Chancellery of the Provisional Government. The Bolshevik coup drove the family first to the Crimea and then to western Europe; Nabokov's father continued his political work in Berlin, at that time the largest center of Russia's émigré community.

Though a born aristocrat, V. D. Nabokov's political principles and activities aligned him with Russia's "intelligentsia," a small but very significant body of educated men and women who opposed Russia's tsarist autocracy and social inequality. Christopher Read identifies four essential criteria that characterized this segment of Russia's population: a profound concern for the social question and a sense of identification with Russia's poor and oppressed; a critical and often hostile attitude toward the government, which it viewed as unjust and indefensible; a reflective turn of mind capable of articulating this hostility; and a self-ascribed responsibility to give voice to the needs of the downtrodden.[14] As Nabokov explained to Wilson in a letter from 1948, the main features of Russia's intelligentsia included "the spirit of self-sacrifice, intense participation in political causes or political thought, intense sympathy for the underdog of any nationality, fanatical integrity, tragic inability to sink to compromise, true spirit of international responsibility."[15] In *Speak, Memory,* he notes that the Russian word *intelligenty* "had more socially idealistic and less highbrow connotations than 'intellectuals' as used in America" (*SM* 595).

The period of V. D. Nabokov's most energetic political activism as one of Russia's prominent *intelligenty* was also the period in which, as his son put it in his letter to Wilson, "Blok, Bely, Bunin and others wrote their best stuff." It is commonly known as the Russian Silver Age, but Nabokov's friend, the literary scholar Gleb Struve (also the son of a prominent Kadet), preferred to call it the Russian Cultural Renaissance. In his account of this first decade and a half of the twentieth century, Struve notes that the period saw exciting developments in "all the areas of cultural and spiritual life—arts, letters, philosophy, religious, social, and political thought."[16] Marked by a broad revolt against the traditional values of the radical intelligentsia as they had crystallized in the 1860s and 1870s, Russia's Cultural Renaissance rejected the view of leading nineteenth-century nihilists such as Nikolai Chernyshevski and Dmitri Pisarev that positivism, materialism, and utilitarianism were the natural allies of progressive thought and social reform. The representatives of Russia's Cultural Renaissance challenged these theoretical outlooks under the banner of individualism, aestheticism, and religious and philosophical idealism (CR 183).

Struve is eager to point out that this cultural renascence was not an exclusively artistic phenomenon; he emphasizes that "great and heated controversies" in the sociopolitical sphere played a leading role in the period's artistic excitement and experimentation. He also depicts the period as one in which some of Russia's most prominent intellectuals moved from positivism to idealism (CR 183–85). The leader of these former "legal Marxists" who famously remade themselves into Kantian neo-idealists was Struve's own father Peter (Piotr) Struve (1870–1944), a public intellectual and political activist whom some consider "the most luminous intellect of his generation in Russia."[17] Other famous converts from Marxism to idealism included Nicholas (Nikolai) Berdiaev (1874–1948), Sergey Bulgakov (1871–1944), and Simon (Semion) Frank (1877–1950). Together with Peter Struve, these men would play a critical role in two landmark documents of the Russian Silver Age: *Problemy idealizma* (*Problems of Idealism,* 1902) and its sequel *Vekhi* (*Landmarks* or *Signposts,* 1909).

Gleb Struve's insistence that the anti-positivist and anti-materialist impulse of the Russian Silver Age energized both the artistic and political domains is also stressed by Christopher Read. Although Read admits that the differences between Russia's symbolist artists and the idealist thinkers who contributed to *Problems of Idealism* were substantial, he also notes that these groups were united in their commitment to philosophical idealism and political individualism (*RRRI* 13–14). He observes:

> All were resolutely opposed to the dominant positivist, scientific and materialist world outlook of the intelligentsia and what their collective achievement showed beyond all doubt was that this positivist outlook was undergoing perhaps the most severe attack it had faced in Russia. The result of the activities of these people was the creation of a thorough-going, non-positivist body of thought, not confined to aristocratic or academic circles but stretching down into all sections of educated Russian society and including many of the country's major creative talents. (*RRRI* 38)

Read also challenges the "mistaken belief that the symbolists were apart from, or above, politics and lived in a separate world devoted to art for art's sake." Though this may have been true in the 1890s, Russia's first revolutionary period "penetrated deeply into the formerly aloof creative intelligentsia and they, to a greater or lesser degree, were affected by the politicisation and polarisation brought about by the events of 1905" (*RRRI* 121).

The idealist revolt against positivism in the artistic domain manifested itself most conspicuously in its rejection of Chernyshevski's and Pisarev's epistemological realism (the view that reality is independent of perception) and their subordination of art to social utility (CR 185, 187–88). Whereas symbolists such as Valerii Briusov and Konstantin Balmont preoccupied themselves with "formal, technical, prosodic innovations," the younger symbolists mentioned by Nabokov in his letter to Wilson—Blok and Bely—were centrally concerned with religion and metaphysics (CR 190–91). Struve notes further that the richness and vitality of the period's poetry were celebrated in a variety of uniquely Russian "fat," or "thick," monthly reviews—*tolstye zhurnaly*. Struve's observation that art and politics commingled in these monthlies reveals an important aspect of the ideological context in which Nabokov developed as an artist.

Each of these journals, Struve explains further, had a well-defined political orientation, even if that political orientation frequently provided a surprising fit with the aesthetic tastes of their editors. His father's liberal (and after 1910, liberal-conservative) monthly, *Russkaia mysl'* (*Russian Thought*), consistently published the most innovative poets of the period, whereas the orthodox liberal *Vestnik Evropy* (*The Herald of Europe*) and the Populist *Russkoe bogatstvo* (*The Russian Wealth*) were both "stodgily conservative in artistic matters" (CR 197–98). As Nabokov's biographer, Brian Boyd, notes,

Nabokov's first major poetic breakthroughs came at sixteen and eighteen years of age when *Vestnik Evropy* and *Russkaia mysl'* each accepted one of his poems for publication (*VNRY* 118, 129).

Read has noted further that even the journals of the period devoted to artistic matters showed a lively preoccupation with the intellectual and political discussions of the day. *Vesy* (*The Scales*), for instance, published reviews of *Problems of Idealism* and *Vekhi,* and *Zolotoe runo* (*The Golden Fleece*) proclaimed its support of the liberation movement in its opening manifesto (*RRRI* 33–35). Read concludes: "Far from showing lack of interest in social and philosophical questions on the part of the symbolists, the journals indicate that the full meaning of their movement can only be comprehended when considered in relation to the intellectual environment" (*RRRI* 34).

Echoing Nabokov's words to Wilson, Gleb Struve bemoans the fact that this rich and varied cultural efflorescence has been either studiously distorted or wiped out from the annals of Russian history by Soviet officials (CR 200). And like Nabokov, too, Struve had a uniquely personal stake in this particular period of Russian history. When the Harvard historian Richard Pipes set out to write what was to become the influential, two-volume biography of his father, Struve energetically supported the project.[18] The biography was the most notable achievement in Pipes's wider effort to memorialize the forgotten voices of pre-revolutionary Russian liberalism. He also contributed, for example, to the English-language publication of V. D. Nabokov's political memoir *The Provisional Government* (*Vremennoe pravitel'stvo*). This project delighted Nabokov, who saw in it a welcome exception to Western ignorance of Russia's liberal traditions. After reading Pipes's introduction to his father's memoir, Nabokov expressed his pleasure and gratitude in a letter sent from his home in Montreux, Switzerland, on May 11, 1971: "I wish to tell you how infinitely gratifying it is to me to find in it this particular approach to Russian history at the revolutionary period. Few, indeed, are the foreign scholars who understand so penetratingly the terrible betrayal of the cause of liberty in the deepest sense of the word engendered on principle by the *earliest* Bolshevists."[19]

RUSSIAN LIBERALISM AND *LICHNOST'*

The "cause of liberty," resurrected in Pipes's introduction to *The Provisional Government* and invoked in such plangent tones in Nabokov's letter, was the central animating principle of the Russian liberal tradition to which V. D. Nabokov had dedicated his life. It was grounded in a foundational liberal respect for *lichnost',* a Russian term that can mean personality, person, individual, individuality, or selfhood. For V. D. Nabokov and some of his closest liberal allies, the term was used to designate the individual as a bearer of absolute value, dignity, and autonomy. This conception of personhood found its political expression in a commitment to constitutionalism, civil liberties, and a rule of law. Theoretically, it drew its sustenance from a broad philosophical tradition that encompassed ethics, legal theory, philosophy of science, epistemology, and metaphysics.

A passionate commitment to this particular conception of *lichnost'* constitutes Nabokov's greatest debt to his father and his father's political associates. Respect for the inviolable uniqueness and autonomy of the individual subject rests at the core of Nabokov's intellectual and artistic universe. It fueled his fierce opposition to all schools of thought that undermined human agency and refused to acknowledge personhood as a self-determining end: positivism, materialism, scientism, and utilitarianism (whether inspired by Darwin, Marx, or Freud). As the following chapters set out to show, Nabokov's efforts to refute these schools of thought borrowed key arguments from his father and some of his father's closest friends and political associates, but he also reflected critically upon these arguments, modulating, complicating, and sometimes altering them in his own way. Like many of his émigré friends, men whose fathers had also played central roles in the history of Russian liberalism, Nabokov understood himself partly through the lens of his genealogical attachment to a great generation of Russian liberal thinkers and activists. This view helps account for the urgent, personal dimension of the political and ideological inquiries that run through his art.

Pipes's introduction to V. D. Nabokov's *The Provisional Government* reaffirms this link when he stitches the history of Russia's liberation movement into the fabric of the Nabokovs' family life, casting great political developments as domestic affairs. Pipes singles out for attention the great national zemstvo congress held in St. Petersburg between November 6 and 19, 1904; it had been authorized by the minister of the interior on the condition that it take place in private homes.[20] Calling it "the most important public assembly held in imperial Russia up to that time," Pipes observes that the congress stirred high hopes across the nation:

> The country's population instinctively sensed its historic significance. Delegates departing for the congress were accompanied to railway stations by crowds of well-wishers. On their arrival in St. Petersburg they found that even though the meetings were held in private residences that had not been publicly advertised and shifted their locale from day to day, the cab drivers unerringly knew where to take them; and if they did not, friendly policemen in uniform or plain clothes offered them directions. Each day, a flood of congratulatory telegrams poured in. Addressed simply "Zemstvo Congress,

> St. Petersburg," they were delivered by the postal authorities to the correct destination. These telegrams exhorted the delegates to speak on behalf of the entire nation, not just the zemstva, and openly to advocate a constitution.[21]

The final sessions of the congress took place in V. D. Nabokov's home at 47 Bol'shaia Morskaia. It was here, presumably in the Nabokovs' large music room on the second floor, that the deputies "formally affixed their signatures to a document calling for the establishment in Russia of a constitutional regime with a parliament granted genuine legislative rights." "When the ceremony was completed," Pipes reports, "one of the deputies exclaimed that future generations would commemorate the great event to which they had been witness by a plaque at the entrance to Nabokov's house."[22]

The dreams engendered by these events were shattered thirteen years later when Russia fell into the hands of a party that scorned civil rights and the rule of law, and the Nabokovs, like most Russian liberals, sought refuge in the West. Although a plaque does now adorn the house at 47 Bol'shaia Morskaia, it makes no mention of the auspicious historical events described by Pipes. Instead, the plaque announces the Vladimir Nabokov Museum, an institution that celebrates the achievements of one of the twentieth century's most beloved writers of fiction. Nabokov's self-declared indifference to sociopolitical matters may sit oddly with his family home's historical pedigree, but this is not an insoluble paradox. As the following chapters attempt to show, Nabokov disavowed an interest in sociopolitical matters precisely because he was so profoundly committed to the liberal principles he inherited from his father. The plaque at 47 Bol'shaia Morskaia is mute on the subject of V. D. Nabokov's political career, but his son's Russian and English novels reverberate with concerns that were vital to the discourses of pre- and post-revolutionary Russian liberalism, and with thought experiments of the kind that pay tribute to the brave and optimistic political activists who had once milled in the family's music room.

FATHERS AND UNCLES

An episode in *Pnin* (1957) provides a potent case study of the novelist's ineliminable connection to these men. This short novel, wedged in between *Lolita* and *Pale Fire,* is Nabokov's most explicit fictional tribute to Russia's liberal tradition. It seems also to hint that he recognized that his own interests and commitments could seem unintelligible or even ludicrous to observers unfamiliar with the discourses and contexts of Russian liberalism. It certainly shows that he viewed those discourses and contexts as providing a safe harbor in which a specific kind of Russian could blossom into his best self.

Pnin's clownish mannerisms, unruly English, and general clumsiness make him a figure of fun in his role as professor at Waindell University. Even his most sympathetic American friends admit that his "mispronunciations are mythopeic" and that his "slips of the tongue are oracular."[23] Soviet émigrés are less generous. Pnin's young compatriot Oleg Komarov—"for whom an ideal Russia consisted of the Red Army, an anointed monarch, collective farms, anthroposophy, the Russian Church and the Hydro-Electric Dam"—contemptuously dismisses Pnin for his *"antikvarnïy liberalizm* [antiquarian liberalism]" (*Pnin* 347–48).

At The Pines, however, the country house of a Russian friend who plays host "every even-year summer" to a group of "liberals and intellectuals who had left Russia around 1920" (*Pnin* 381), Pnin undergoes a radical transformation. Among these "firm-principled exiles," conversation is conducted in a coded tongue incomprehensible to the uninitiated: with "a few rapid passwords—allusions, intonations impossible to render in a foreign language," they traverse "the course of recent Russian history, thirty-five years of hopeless injustice following a century of struggling justice and glimmering hope" (*Pnin* 387). Finally restored to his natural habitus, Pnin encounters perfect sympathy and understanding, and is endowed with a charm and grace that his Waindell colleagues fail to notice. Among these like-minded compatriots, a simple game of croquet occasions a metamorphosis in Pnin:

> As soon as the pegs were driven in and the game started, the man was transfigured. From his habitual, slow, ponderous, rather rigid self, he changed into a terrifically mobile, scampering, mute, sly-visaged hunchback. It seemed to be always his turn to play. . . . Pnin foreshadowed every stroke with nimble aim-taking oscillations of the mallet head, then gave the ball an accurate tap, and forthwith, still hunched, and with the ball still rolling, walked rapidly to the spot where he had planned for it to stop. With geometrical gusto, he ran it through hoops, evoking cries of admiration from the onlookers. (*Pnin* 391)

This charmed space grants Pnin a startling elegance, but the space and its "few rapid passwords" remain inaccessible, even incomprehensible, to his American colleagues. In the version of events communicated to the novel's narrator by Jack Cockerell, Waindell's most dedicated Pnin impersonator, this idyllic refuge for old Russian émigrés is contemptuously dismissed as "the chicken farm of some Privy Counselor of the Tsar" (*Pnin* 433).

Pnin rediscovers his voice and dignity in the midst of a community that is at once little known in the West and scorned by younger Russian colleagues such as Komarov. As Nabokov reminded his friends and readers, this important segment of the Russian emigration—a segment to which both he and his father belonged—had been erased from the annals of history by the distortions of Soviet propaganda and by the English-speaking world's general ignorance of Russia's pre-revolutionary past. In a letter to the editor of the London *Sunday Times* published on January 1, 1967, Nabokov insisted that Russia's

> liberal intelligentsia . . . was the backbone and marrow of émigré culture, a fact deliberately played down by Soviet historians; and no wonder: it was that liberal cultural core, and certainly not the crude and ambiguous activities of extreme rightists, that formed a genuine anti-Bolshevist opposition (still working today), and it was people like my father who pronounced the first and final verdict on the Soviet police state. (*SO* 214–15)

Pnin pays homage to this uprooted and forgotten community of Russian exiles whose legacy is as critical for understanding Nabokov as it is for appreciating Pnin. Nabokov's repeated claims that he was indifferent to political matters have made it seem difficult or unprofitable to reconstruct the ideologies and convictions that defined the community in which he was most at home. The failure to do so, however, has obscured the well-defined and deeply felt political project at the heart of Nabokov's poetics. Like Pnin, Nabokov finds his truest voice among these misunderstood and neglected "elderly Russians," these "fathers or uncles" (*Pnin* 381), who provide Pnin with a temporary home and a shared history in the midst of a life shaped by loneliness and exile.

The goal of this book is to reconstruct, parse, and interpret the "few rapid passwords—allusions, intonations" that connect Nabokov's world to the discourses of Russian liberalism. If Pnin's life is a loving recovery of the cultural heritage which Nabokov claimed as his own, his unusual name and his "*antikvarnïy liberalizm*" describe the uniquely personal bond that tied Nabokov to this forgotten community. Scholars concur that the most important single model for Pnin is Marc Szeftel, a Russian historian and Nabokov's colleague at Cornell University. As Nabokov's representative of Russian liberalism in exile, it is appropriate that Szeftel was the author of an influential essay describing the status of "personal-inviolability" rights in Russia after Alexander II's 1864 judiciary reforms.

In *Pniniad: Vladimir Nabokov and Marc Szeftel*, Galya Diment shows that Nabokov also endowed Pnin with extensive material culled from his own personal biography.[24] This leads her to assert that "it is quite obvious that the character and his maker had important traits and tastes in common" (*P* 48). Writing himself into Pnin enables Nabokov to lay claim to his own political and ideological commitments; the move also directs readers to the larger issue of bonds that connect sons to fathers. Scholars agree that Pnin owes his name to the late eighteenth-century Russian publicist and minor poet Ivan Petrovich Pnin (1773–1805), an illegitimate son of Prince P. N. Repnin. The common practice of endowing illegitimate children with only a part of their fathers' family names accounts for Pnin's truncated surname.[25] (This truncation intensifies the emphasis on paternity that is already built into Russian naming practices.) By casting his Pnin as an imaginary heir of Ivan Petrovich Pnin, Nabokov grants his creature a paternal legacy that resembles his own. In *Legal Philosophies of Russian Liberalism,* Walicki singles out Ivan Petrovich Pnin as one whose efforts to champion legally protected civil freedoms at the expense of autocratic privilege guarantee him a well-defined position in the history of Russia's pre-revolutionary liberal heritage.[26]

Nabokov inherited a similarly rich liberal legacy from his own paternal ancestors. Living in the aftermath of Russia's dashed hopes for a liberal rule-of-law state, Nabokov refused to forget the lost, auspicious moment in his homeland's history in which his father played a major role. Cut off from that history and his fatherland, he also felt the sting of dispossession embedded in Pnin's truncated name. He liked to contemplate the paths his life might have taken under a friendlier historical dispensation,[27] and he determinedly sought to educate his European and American acquaintances about Russia's forgotten liberal past and the savage brutality with which Lenin's regime put an end to the aspirations of his father and his father's liberal colleagues (*SO* 206, 214).

When asked to characterize his politics, Nabokov asserted that he adhered to the politics of his father, whom he described as "an old-fashioned liberal" (*SO* 96; see also *SO* 113). The phrase clearly eulogizes the politics that Komarov holds in such high contempt. Like Pnin's "*antikvarnïy liberalizm,*" V. D. Nabokov's "old-fashioned" liberalism can sound hopelessly vague and anachronistic when severed from the immediate context of the "fathers and uncles" whose intellectual convictions and political aspirations help make the phrase intelligible and historically specific. These men played leading roles in Russia's liberation movement, and their writings on moral philosophy, legal theory, epistemology, and the philosophy of science sought to provide theoretical support for their political struggles. Men like Peter Struve, Paul (Pavel) Novgorodtsev, Vladimir Vernadskii, Leon (Lev) Petrazhitskii, and Vladimir M. Hessen were among V. D. Nabokov's closest collaborators during and after Russia's revolutionary turmoils, and their various contributions to their respective areas of expertise have left visible traces on Nabokov's worldview. Moreover, the political and intellectual associations connecting these "fathers and uncles" often shaped the friendships made by their sons and nephews. As an émigré in Europe and America, Nabokov was friends with Peter Struve's son Gleb, Vernadskii's son George, and Sergey and George Hessen, the sons of V. M. Hessen's cousin, Joseph (Iosif) Hessen. These second-generation friendships flourished against the backdrop of bonds forged years earlier, in journals, clandestine societies, political congresses, and parliamentary sessions organized and fretted over by their fathers in pre-revolutionary Russia.

THE RUSSIAN REVOLUTION OF 1905–1906 AND THE KADET PARTY

The zemstvo congress of 1904 whose final sessions took place in the Nabokovs' St. Petersburg home is commonly regarded as having launched the 1905 Revolution (*SLL* 329, 366, 369). It was organized by the Union of Liberation, a clandestine liberal organization that was the Kadet Party's precursor and counted V. D. Nabokov among its members. V. D. Nabokov also contributed to the illegal and highly influential constitutionalist journal *Osvobozhdenie* (*Liberation*), the Union's precursor published abroad by Peter Struve.

Osvobozhdenie's domestic counterpart was *Pravo* (*Law,* or *Right*), the prominent St. Petersburg juridical weekly founded in 1898 and edited by Joseph Hessen, his cousin V. M. Hessen, Petrazhitskii, Avgust Kaminka, and V. D. Nabokov. Nabokov oversaw the journal's criminal-law section, and his work on its editorial board was the conduit for his involvement in politics.[28] In an obituary written on the occasion of V. D. Nabokov's death, Peter Struve explained that *Osvobozhdenie* and *Pravo* were equally dedicated to championing justice and rights. By adding further that while he himself contributed essays to *Pravo,* V. D. Nabokov wrote for *Osvobozhdenie,* Struve highlights the tight interconnection between the two journals' ambitions and concerns.[29]

The Union of Liberation's many successes were engineered by its leading theorists, Struve (a political economist) and Paul (Pavel) Miliukov (one of Russia's most eminent historians) (*RL* 161). Under their leadership, Russia's "liberationists" worked to unify the widest range of civil society in the struggle against autocracy by building a coalition between the socialist-oriented "democratic intelligentsia" on the left and the zemstvo constitutionalists on the right.[30] Nabokov would later refer with pride to the civic protest movement (*obshchestvennoe dvizhenie*) that the liberationists' united-front strategy helped bring into being, patiently explaining the finer points of pre-revolutionary Russian history to Wilson by insisting that "Bolshevik or Cadet, Narodovoltsy or Anarchist," these men lived lives "marked by a sense of duty, self-sacrifice, kindness, heroism" (*DBDV* 37). These virtues informed Nabokov's own friendships in Western Europe and the moral textures of his novels;[31] the wreckage of the Russian liberationists' ambitions, in turn, helped shape his understanding of the urgency of those values.

The revolution engineered by the Union of Liberation moved into its acute phase as general protests erupted in cities and the countryside. On January 9, 1905, a day popularly known as "Bloody Sunday," troops opened fire on peaceful protesters who had gathered to petition the tsar to implement sweeping reforms. These events left their mark on the young Nabokov. In *Speak, Memory,* he recalls being driven to school past Maria Square, whose trees had once "seen children shot down at random from the branches into which they had climbed in a vain attempt to escape the mounted gendarmes who were quelling the First Revolution" (*SM* 517). Three days after the bloodshed, his father denounced the government's brutality at a session of the St. Petersburg City Council on which he served as a deputy, and called for 25,000 rubles to be paid to the victims' families (*VNRY* 57).[32]

In spite of such bloody reprisals, the revolutionary wave forced the tsar to make concessions. Humiliated by Russia's defeat in its war with Japan, uncertain of the loyalty of his armed forces, and presiding over a country crippled by a general strike and peasant rebellions, Nicholas II issued on October 17, 1905, an imperial manifesto promising constitutional reforms. These included a national elected parliament with legislative authority (the Duma), the introduction of civil and political liberties, and open political-party activities.

The October Manifesto remade the map of Russian politics. The largest party to emerge from it was the Constitutional Democratic Party or the People's Freedom Party (a second title adopted at the party's second congress for the sake of greater mass appeal) (*FPP* 57). At the first party congress, V. D. Nabokov was elected to its Central Committee, the party's highest governing body. A member of the party's top leadership from the very beginning, he also provided much of the party's financial support during these years (BRR 23, note 56). The party's uncontested leader was Miliukov. Though many described him as tactless, arrogant, and authoritarian, few challenged his political abilities and erudition.[33] During the Russian period of Kadet activism, V. D. Nabokov was one of Miliukov's closest associates (*FPP* 379; *LRR* 21). They also coedited the party's unofficial daily newspaper, *Rech'* (*Speech*).

V. D. Nabokov's social rank and wealth made him stand out among his Kadet peers, but his status as a professor of criminal law made him representative of the Central Committee's composition. As historians frequently note, university professors (or ex-professors who had been dismissed from their posts for political reasons) were so prominent among the Kadet Party's leaders that the Constitutional Democrats became known as "a professors' party." Alexander (Aleksandr) Kerensky, the minister-president of the 1917 Provisional Government, would later recall that he thought of the Kadet leaders as a "faculty of politicians" (qtd. in *LRR* 20). Legal professionals (chiefly attorneys and professors of law) were the other dominant group (*LRR* 20; see also *LPRL* 295).

This feature of the Kadet leadership's social makeup highlights some important distinctions between Russian liberalism and its Western counterparts. George Fischer, for example, has emphasized that Russian liberalism did not reflect the outlook and aspirations of the bourgeoisie. The representatives of Russia's business middle class—its merchants and industrialists—were much more dependent on the state than their Western counterparts, a fact which made them, to quote Fischer, "timid, accommodating, often uncultured and politically passive."[34] The prime movers of Russia's liberal movement were, initially, members of the lower nobility (the gentry)[35] and, later, members of the professions (the intelligentsia).

These crucial differences explain why Russian liberalism did not develop a consistent defense of property rights and the free market. In the Russian context, the inalienable rights of classical liberalism applied to religious confession, press, assembly, association, and free speech.[36] These distinctions also account for arguments such as those of Pipes, who states that Russian liberalism after Alexander II's reforms was inspired not by economic self-interest but by "thwarted individualism and frustrated patriotism." Its supporters, he emphasizes, "stood nothing to gain and much to lose from the principles of political democracy and social (especially agrarian) reform" they espoused (*SLL* 285). V. D. Nabokov's family was keenly aware of this. As Nabokov recounts in *Speak, Memory,* his paternal grandmother bitterly complained that "dark forces" had

> seduced her gifted son into scorning the kind of "brilliant" career in the Tsar's service his forefathers had pursued. What she found especially hard to understand was that my father, who, she knew, thoroughly appreciated all the pleasures of great wealth, could jeopardize its enjoyment by becoming a Liberal, thus helping to bring on a revolution that would, in the long run, as she correctly foresaw, leave him a pauper. (*SM* 491–92)

V. D. Nabokov's political mission was at odds with his refined tastes and material self-interest, but he was no socialist revolutionary. Historians describe him as occupying a "fairly conservative" corner of the Kadet leadership's "moderate" or "centrist" constituency (BRR 23, note 56, 140). Robert Browder, for instance, describes him as "a constitutional monarchist," "a nationalist," "a libertarian but not an equalitarian," and, above all, "a jurist, greatly concerned with legitimacy and legality at a time when both were hard to discern and out of fashion."[37] V. D. Nabokov's conservatism is visible in *The Provisional Government,* his personal chronicle of the tumultuous revolutionary months that preceded the Bolshevik seizure of power. Like most Kadet conservatives, he describes Russia's masses as having no "political instinct" and no "healthy understanding of their own interests."[38] The faces of revolutionary soldiers strike him as "dull, vacant, brutal" and, on another occasion, as "senseless, vacant, and malevolent" (*PG* 146, 160). He greets the 1917 Spelling Reform as a "disgrace" (*PG* 100), and, in spite of his contempt for the old order, laments its fall in terms that echo Edmund Burke's reflections on the transformations wrought by the French Revolution. He recalls with wistful regret the "velvet carpets, gilded furniture, and heavy draperies" adorning the former Mariinskii Palace. He also recalls the "agitated solemnity," the "subdued conversations," and the "atmosphere of inaccessibility" that formerly characterized this "sanctuary of the higher bureaucracy." All these, he observes, were swept away by the revolutionary hunger for

> radical "plain living." Its splendid halls were invaded by crowds of disheveled and carelessly dressed people in jackets and blouses of the most proletarian kind. The splendid footmen exchanged their liveries for grey, double-breasted jackets, and lost all their dignity. The grand and solemn ceremonial of days passed was replaced by a vociferous bustle. (*PG* 137–38)

But in spite of his general conservatism, V. D. Nabokov was a "centrist" when it came to party policy. He was in favor of working with the parties on the left in the First State Duma and again, years later, during Russia's second revolutionary period (BRR 23, note 56; *LRR* 102–3, 115, 247–49). The party's "center" was dominated by Miliukov, who emphasized tactical expediency, party unity, and a commitment to the party's general program. William Rosenberg, a dedicated chronicler and frequent critic of the Kadet Party, notes that in spite of significant differences dividing the party's right and left factions, all Kadets subscribed to the principles outlined in the party program and shared a common system of values. The first among these was the party's *nadklassnost'* (non-class character) and *nadpartiinost'* (nonpartisanship), a broad nationalist commitment to the welfare of Russian society as a whole rather than to the advancement of any particular social class or socioeconomic interest. The party's commitment to remain "above classes" and "above politics" was tied to an equally firm commitment to legality and the supremacy of law, or "rule of law." Unlike "rule of man" arrangements, where governance and rules of conduct are discretionary preserves of an individual or group, "rule-of-law" governance subjects all citizens and governments to known, impartially enforced laws. By embracing *nadklassnost'*, *nadpartiinost'*, and a rule of law, the Kadets sought to prevent one social group from dominating others and to protect the individual from arbitrary power (*LRR* 13–15, 35, 469).

In contrast to parties on its left, the Kadet Party emphasized political rather than social reform, focusing its efforts on securing fundamental civil liberties for all Russians as individual citizens and putting an end to restrictions based on class, nationality, and religion (*LRR* 15). On the subject of social reform, the party program's non-class, nonpartisan, national character was most evident in its efforts to protect the equity rights of all groups. Rosenberg explains: "Worker and peasant interests could not be advanced at the expense of the gentry and bourgeoisie, while Russia's upper classes could not exploit her workers and peasants." On the highly contentious issue of agrarian reform, the party required that members support a substantial increase in the amount of land held by working peasants. This was to have been accomplished by expropriating land from large landowners with fair compensation (*LRR* 17).

In spite of adhering to the general principles outlined in the party program, the Kadets "rarely if ever presented a united front" (*LRR* 8). A party leader reviewing his colleagues in 1921 acknowledged that it had become almost proverbial that "wherever there are two Kadets, there is a right-wing Kadet and a left-wing Kadet" (qtd. in *LRR* 8). Different attitudes to rule of law and state power distinguished members of the party's right wing from their centrist and left-wing colleagues. Conservative Kadets such as Peter Struve, Novgorodtsev, Petrazhitskii, V. M. Hessen, and Vasilii Maklakov believed that "the essence of social order was authority, legally structured and administered" (*LRR* 34).[39] Consequently, they regarded the October Manifesto as the culmination rather than the beginning of the liberals' political struggle. Calling for cooperation with the government, they condemned the oppositional tactics masterminded by Miliukov and carried out by the Kadet deputies in the First State Duma.

Walicki speculates that Petrazhitskii's and Maklakov's conservatism was a function of their juridical training. As professional jurists, he notes, they were "deeply committed to the ideal of the rule of law, while Miliukov, as a political leader, was concerned above all with political power, political influence and, not least, his own political reputation in the eyes both of his followers and of the left-wing allies of his party." He adds that Miliukov was "more politically than legally minded" and often confused the cause of rule of law with the cause of parliamentary government (*LPRL* 398).

Unlike their right-wing colleagues, who argued that full democracy was premature and that constitutional monarchy was the most appropriate political system for current conditions in Russia, left-leaning Kadets had faith in the political maturity of the Russian people. Fearing revolution and anarchy less than the continuation of autocratic paternalism, they called for a rapprochement with mass movements and parties on the left (*LRR* 32–35). Their viewpoint dominated party strategy at its first two congresses and in the first State Duma.

THE FIRST STATE DUMA AND THE VYBORG MANIFESTO

The major achievement of the 1905–06 Russian Revolution was the establishment of the country's first broadly based legislative assembly. In spite of a relatively small popular base, the Kadets emerged as the largest party in the First State Duma (*FPP* 21). V. D. Nabokov was elected to the First State Duma as a deputy from St. Petersburg, and Zimmerman identifies him as one of the Duma's five "real leaders"—the men entrusted with making the major speeches, piloting bills through the legislative process, and serving on many parliamentary committees (BRR 199). The liberationists' alliance with the left continued to guide Kadet Party policy in the First State Duma as Kadet deputies adopted a confrontational attitude toward the government, lobbying aggressively for civil liberties and social reform. But the tsarist regime had no intention of liberalizing the country's institutions and responding to the Kadets' call (as formulated by Novgorodtsev in *Pravo*) to transform Russia into a state "founded on the respect for personhood, on the strict guarantee of personal rights [*osnovannomu na uvazhenii k lichnosti, na strogoi obezpechennosti lichnykh prav*]."[40] The Duma's legislative ambitions were cut short when the body was dissolved less than three months after it was summoned. Unable to assemble in St. Petersburg, roughly one third of parliamentary deputies were accompanied by non-Duma Kadets to Finland, where they held a series of meetings in the small town of Vyborg. Long and bitter deliberations produced the famous Vyborg Manifesto, which urged the Russian people to protest the Duma's dissolution by withholding taxes and refusing military service.

The measure was at once illegal and ill-conceived. Michael (Mikhail) Karpovich, the prototype of Pnin's host at The Pines and Nabokov's friend and Harvard colleague, characterizes the manifesto as "essentially a revolutionary measure."[41] Walicki calls it "a romantic gesture, indefensible from a legal point of view and devoid of real political significance" (*LPRL* 398). For Walicki, the proceedings at Vyborg highlight the deep schism between the party's legal-minded conservative faction and the centrist tacticians who prioritized political ends over legal considerations (*LPRL* 295–96). Though almost all of the Kadet deputies signed the document from a sense of duty and solidarity, many signatories were bitterly opposed.[42] Petrazhitskii, V. D. Nabokov's colleague on the editorial board of *Pravo* and one of the Kadet Party's most distinguished legal theorists, argued that the manifesto was unconstitutional and therefore in conflict with the party's core principles. Struve agreed with Petrazhitskii, but Miliukov urged acceptance (BRR 279, 281). Zimmerman's speculation that conservative Kadets such as V. D. Nabokov and Novgorodtsev agreed with the manifesto's critics is justified in Nabokov's case.[43] In *The Provisional Government,* he confesses to having opposed the appeal and considered it a mistake, but also to having felt "powerless to impede it" in the absence of an alternate plan of action (*PG* 82).

This revolutionary measure was deeply at odds with the Kadet Party's commitment to legality and peaceful reform. Repercussions were severe for the deputies who signed it and for the party as a whole. V. D. Nabokov and two thirds of the Kadet parliamentary group—a number that included almost all of the party's leaders—were stripped of their political rights and disbarred from participating in future elections. V. D. Nabokov was one of many Kadets to serve three-month jail terms in addition to these punishments (BRR 293–94). The Vyborg Manifesto, moreover, failed to elicit any significant response from the population at large, and the Kadets' strength and confidence were considerably diminished (*FPP* 364–65). In the wake of these events and defeats, the next three State Dumas became increasingly helpless and docile (BRR 304, 387).

In *Speak, Memory,* Nabokov recalls a photograph taken at the Finland Station in which his father, preparing to travel "to Vyborg for an illegal session," is seen carrying "his railway ticket tucked under the band of his hat" (*SM* 510). He also recalls secret letters from prison in which his father inquired about his eldest son's butterfly captures, and emphasizes that his father continued his publicistic work after his release. Nabokov explains that in spite of being barred from participating in public elections, his father was able to continue to write for "the bitterly liberal *Rech,* a task to which he devoted up to nine hours a day" (*SM* 510). Journalistic, political, and juridical activities preoccupied V. D. Nabokov until the outbreak of the First World War; these activities made him "one of the leading public men in the prewar period."[44] His essays on legal matters continued to appear in *Pravo* and elsewhere, and, from 1905 to 1915, he was president of the Russian branch of the International Criminology Association. In 1913 he won lasting acclaim for his outspoken coverage of the sensational trial of Mendel Beiliss for ritual murder.

With the outbreak of war, V. D. Nabokov was called into military service; he served at the front before being transferred to Staff Headquarters in St. Petersburg (*PG* 5). As he explains in *The Provisional Government,* he suspended his political and journalistic activities from July 1914 to March

1917 because he believed that military obligations and oppositional politics were ethically incompatible (*PG* 37–38). After the overthrow of the tsarist regime during the February Revolution, he served for two months as the administrator of the First Provisional Government. His political memoir is a detailed, candid, and respected account of the short-lived regimes that sought to bring order and stability to Russia during its second revolutionary period.

THE REVOLUTION OF 1917 AND THE FIRST PROVISIONAL GOVERNMENT

The First Provisional Government came into being on March 2, 1917, the day Nicholas II abdicated. The new body derived its tenuous authority from the Grand Duke Michael (Mikhail Aleksandrovich), who declined the powers transferred to him by his older brother. The grand duke's act of abdication was drawn up by V. D. Nabokov and another eminent lawyer, Baron B. E. Nol'de. Leonard Schapiro describes the act as "a valiant attempt to endow the new government with legitimacy, and therefore with authority, by stressing its continuity with both the Duma and the Emperor." But as Schapiro notes further, the act's claim that the Provisional Government had been formed at the initiative of the State Duma and had been endowed with full powers until such a time as a democratically elected Constituent Assembly could be convened, was no more than a lawyerly "ingenious formula." In point of fact, neither the Duma nor Nicholas II nor Grand Duke Michael disposed of full powers under Russian constitutional law.[45] Moreover, by the time the February Revolution erupted, the Duma's authority had been severely compromised not only by an exceedingly limited franchise but also by a number of internal and external organizations that exercised significant political influence.[46]

Although the First Provisional Government was not the Kadet Party's exclusive preserve, it was dominated by Miliukov and his closest Kadet associates (*LRR* 58). In spite of the growing anarchy at home and at the front, the Kadet ministers "pursued the politics of state rather than popular consciousness," privileging the interests of the nation as a whole over the long-standing grievances of peasants and workers (*LRR* 135). Their insistence on prosecuting the war to final victory and their unwillingness to undertake far-reaching economic reforms before the war's conclusion were vigorously opposed by soldiers at the front and by parties on the left committed to representing Russia's embittered masses (*LRR* 94–95).

Successful liberal democracies frequently manage to solve (or at least to occlude) the tensions between liberal and democratic values that proved insoluble to the Kadets in 1917. As liberals committed to the principles of legitimacy and legality, the Kadets were keenly aware of the fragility of their position as the country's new rulers. Their formal commitment to rapidly convening a democratically elected Constituent Assembly was born of a sincere and principled desire to secure the nation's confidence. Nonetheless, fears of social disintegration and mob rule, anxiety over election irregularities in a context of war, and escalating domestic instability led them to postpone elections. They worried that elections would deepen interclass conflict and social polarization, and that these, in turn, would set the stage for civil war (*LRR* 70–74, 159). Delaying elections also allowed them to ignore the growing mass opposition toward Miliukov's desire to prosecute the war to final victory and to annex Constantinople and the Dardanelles Straits as worked out in the so-called "Secret Treaties" between Russia and its allies (*LRR* 74–88, 106–11). Unlike the Kadets, the parties representing Russia's masses insisted that sweeping domestic reforms were more urgent than the country's international interests.

Rosenberg has persuasively argued that the Kadets' commitment to the liberal principle of *nadklassnost'* remained throughout the party's history "a convenient, although illusory, screen for the more subtle problem of the party's own narrow electoral base . . . since as national, nonpartisan liberals, rather than defenders of sectarian interests, party leaders could argue they 'deserved' power even if they lacked massive popular support." According to Rosenberg, the Kadets' continued insistence that traditional liberal values such as the rule of law, civil liberties, and national security were necessary preconditions for sweeping social reform severely undermined efforts to transform Russia into a participatory democracy at this critical time of war and revolution (*LRR* 90–91).

Calling for a rapprochement (*sblizhenie*) with parties to the left, V. D. Nabokov and other "conciliationist" Kadet leaders criticized Miliukov's imperialist attitudes toward the war. Even so, Miliukov continued to shape party policy, and at the ninth Kadet congress the Kadets formally aligned themselves with conservative groups (*LRR* 103–4, 174–75, 200–205, 252). During Miliukov's absence from Petrograd in September 1917, party control was assumed by V. D. Nabokov and other "conciliationists" who strove to reverse the party's drift to the right by embracing a forthright socialist program. They actively sought to endorse peasant representatives for local Kadet slates and to form electoral blocs with socialist moderates. These efforts failed. As Rosenberg writes, any hope of establishing a firm provisional authority had long vanished by then, and the only political question that remained was when the Bolsheviks would make their move and whether or not that move would succeed (*LRR* 236, 244–46, 249; *PG* 149–51).

In his chronicle of these events, V. D. Nabokov provides a detailed account of the provisional regime's overthrow by the Bolsheviks on the eve of the scheduled elections for a Constituent Assembly. As the chairman of the All-Russian Electoral Commission, V. D. Nabokov had been entrusted with drawing up the laws that would govern the upcoming electoral campaign. Refusing to recognize the Bolshevik government and confident that the revolutionary regime would not last, the Electoral Commission continued its work. On November 23, 1917, the Bolsheviks disbanded the commission and imprisoned its members. V. D. Nabokov was released after spending five days in the Smolnyi Institute (formerly a school for women that had been converted by the Bolsheviks into their revolutionary headquarters) (*PG* 169–75). Two days after the electoral commissioners' release, the Bolsheviks outlawed the Kadet Party and ordered the arrest of the party's leaders (*PG* 177). Unlike many of his colleagues, V. D. Nabokov evaded arrest by fleeing to the Crimea. During the civil war, he served as minister of justice in the Crimean Regional Government, a short-lived regime whose ministers were drawn from Kadet, Menshevik, Socialist Revolutionary, and Tatar ranks. After the Red Army overwhelmed White defenses and began its advance into the Crimea, the ministers of the Crimean Regional Government and their families were evacuated on a ship named *Nadezhda* (*Hope*) bound for Constantinople (*LRR* 378; *VNRY* 159). The Nabokovs never saw Russia again.

KADETS IN THE EMIGRATION

In *Speak, Memory,* Nabokov recalls playing chess with his father "under wild machine-gun fire from the shore" as Russia receded into the distance (*SM* 573). After a brief interlude in Greece, they boarded another ship for England. During the time he spent in London, V. D. Nabokov arranged for his two eldest sons, Vladimir and Sergey, to matriculate at Cambridge and Oxford, respectively. In Berlin, where he eventually settled with his wife and three younger children, he became the acknowledged leader of Russian émigré organizations.[47]

Tactical and ideological conflicts continued to undermine Kadet cohesion in the emigration, and V. D. Nabokov found himself once again at their center. As Pipes writes, the experiences of the 1917 Revolution pushed a large number of Russia's liberal intelligentsia to the right. Led by Peter Struve, this "patriotic" majority supported active struggle against the Soviet regime by renewing the civil war (with or without foreign intervention) and initiating terrorist subversion. Its representatives dreamed of a liberated Russia whose institutions rested on legality, property, and a firm (but democratically elected) state authority. Though they favored constitutional monarchy, they insisted that the ultimate decision would rest with the liberated Russian people. The "democratic" liberal-socialist minority formed the second group, and it was led (surprisingly, given his staunch conservatism in 1917) by Miliukov. Its adherents believed that in spite of its many terrible consequences, the 1917 Revolution was a progressive and constructive historical event that had been temporarily derailed by the Bolsheviks. They argued that active struggle against the regime was not only bound to fail but would sabotage the efforts of those groups struggling against Bolshevism inside Russia's borders. Once the revolution spent itself, they argued, Russia would become a socialist, democratic republic (*SLR* 327–29).

In spite of (or, more likely, because of) his participation in the left-aligned Crimean Regional Government, V. D. Nabokov's position in the emigration was decidedly conservative. Nabokov's abortive attempt at Cambridge to rally support for Allied intervention in Russia by memorizing his father's words shows that V. D. Nabokov was endorsing Struve's "patriotic" position as early as 1919. By December 1920, after Miliukov's "New Tactic" was rejected by Struve and the Kadet conservative majority, V. D. Nabokov became the leader of the party's conservative wing. Conceived in the immediate aftermath of the White Army's defeat, Miliukov's proposal had called for the Kadet Party to sever its ties to the White movement and form a coalition with the Socialist Revolutionaries who still enjoyed semi-legal status in the Soviet Union and continued to be popular among Russia's peasantry.

Miliukov met with little support. For the Kadet majority, the Socialist Revolutionaries had hopelessly discredited themselves during Russia's revolutionary periods, and Miliukov's call to break off ties with the White Army was considered to be indefensible on moral and patriotic grounds. As Pipes tells the story, most Kadets were unwilling to "turn their backs on homeless veterans who for years, under conditions of extreme hardship, had fought for their country, first against the Germans and Austrians and then against the Bolsheviks—years which Miliukov and his SR friends had spent polemicizing or drafting memoirs." In spite of having no strategy of its own, the Kadet majority felt that the one advanced by Miliukov was at once futile and dishonorable. Led by V. D. Nabokov, the party's right wing voted overwhelmingly against the New Tactic. As its leader, V. D. Nabokov became in effect the head of the Kadet Party and its supraparty organization, the National Union. But while V. D. Nabokov provided political leadership, Struve often supplied ideological direction (*SLR* 331–35, 341–42).[48] Miliukov, Maxim Vinaver, and a small group of Kadet dissidents joined the Socialist Revolutionaries and other splinter socialists to form the "Democratic Group of the Party of People's Freedom" (*LRR* 461).

For Rosenberg, the split spelled the death of the Kadet Party. Pipes, however, locates the party's final disintegration in an event that occurred less than a year later (I xiii–xiv). Like the national zemstvo congress of 1904, whose final sessions took place in the Nabokovs' home and launched the 1905 Russian Revolution, this event was intimately—and this time, most painfully—bound up with the Nabokovs' family life. In an effort to heal the schism, V. D. Nabokov invited Miliukov to share the impressions he had gathered during a recent visit to America (*VNRY* 190). On the morning of March 28, 1922, V. D. Nabokov made overtures for reconciliation which Miliukov declined (*Gi* 134). That night, assassins from an extreme reactionary Russian émigré organization had infiltrated Berlin's Philharmonia Hall with the intention to kill Miliukov. In Joseph Hessen's account of the events that followed, one of the assassins opened fire during a break in Miliukov's lecture. While Miliukov was being taken to safety, V. D. Nabokov and Avgust Kaminka threw themselves on the gunman. In the tussle that followed, another gunman came to his partner's rescue and fatally wounded V. D. Nabokov (*Gi* 134–35).[49] The assassins were apprehended, jailed, and finally set free by the Nazis (I xiv). Nabokov would bitterly observe in his autobiography that Hitler promoted the man who killed his father to the post of administrator of Russian émigré affairs (*SM* 511).

NABOKOV'S POLITICAL ART

I have lingered over this political narrative in order to establish a context for the book's contention that Nabokov's fiction is an echo chamber in which the politics of his Russian past resound, and a series of meditations upon V. D. Nabokov's interventions in the political and ideological conflicts that would come to preoccupy his son. The fact that these conflicts really did preoccupy the novelist has been acknowledged more effectively in recent years than it was during Nabokov's own lifetime. Jean-Paul Sartre, for example, observed in his 1939 review of a French translation of *Despair* that Nabokov wrote "on subjects of no significance."[50] This view, shared since by many readers of Nabokov's work, was nurtured by Nabokov himself. His fiction and discursive writings haughtily (and frequently) announce his utter lack of interest in sociopolitical matters. "Nothing bores me more than political novels and the literature of social intent" (*SO* 3), he observes with typical aplomb in an interview from 1962. His unapologetic disdain for writing energized by "social comment, humanistic messages, political allegories, overconcern with class or race" (*SO* 101), and his cool confession that he does not "give a damn for the group, the community, the masses, and so forth" (*SO* 33) seem calculated to fuel the outrage of politically engaged writers such as Sartre.

Nabokovians no longer take these pronouncements at face value, preferring instead to dwell on his prediction "that one day a reappraiser will come and declare that, far from having been a frivolous firebird, I was a rigid moralist kicking sin, cuffing stupidity, ridiculing the vulgar and cruel—and assigning sovereign power to tenderness, talent, and pride" (*SO* 193). "Reappraisers" of the kind imagined by Nabokov—Brian Boyd, Leland de la Durantaye, Zoran Kuzmanovich, Ellen Pifer, David Rampton, Leona Toker, Michael Wood, and others—have focused on the powerful moral vision of Nabokov's fiction. They remind us that Nabokov's stated disdain for didactic literature coexists with other sensitive renderings of the relationship between literature and the world in which it circulates. In a letter to George Noyes, for instance, Nabokov qualified some of the uncompromisingly aloof statements for which he has become famous: "I never meant to deny the moral impact of art which is certainly inherent in every genuine work of art. What I do deny and am prepared to fight to the last drop of my ink is the deliberate moralizing which to me kills every vestige of art in a work however skillfully written" (*SL* 56).[51]

Simon Karlinsky's introduction to Nabokov's correspondence with Wilson provides a useful gloss on the kind of distinction Nabokov had in mind: "The issue for Nabokov, as it had been for Chekhov and the Russian Symbolists, was not ignoring or suppressing the economic or social factors, but . . . of incorporating them organically into a literary work in ways that do not reduce the work to a sociological sermon or lesson and do not pander to quotidian topical preoccupations." Another remark by Karlinsky is in some ways even more revealing:

> Readers of Nabokov's numerous interviews in which he was wont to proclaim his "supreme indifference" to social purpose or moral message or general ideas are usually not aware that he was reacting to a powerful Russian tradition which twice within a century had enslaved literature and other arts in the name of the same social purpose, moral message and general ideas. The first time was in the nineteenth century, when Tolstoy and Chekhov were systematically attacked and some good lesser writers expelled from literature for not having the right kind of social awareness. The second time came in the Soviet period, when a number of writers whom Nabokov in various ways admired, such as Zoshchenko, Olesha, Zabolotsky and Mandelstam, were persecuted and in some cases destroyed by a government that began enforcing the Belinskian-Chernyshevskian demand for social relevance with labor camps and death sentences. The very vehemence of Nabokov's disclaimers stems from the fact that he was the only major Russian writer in history who had an effective forum for such a denunciation.[52]

Karlinsky's understanding of these issues hinges on two claims: first, that moral, social, and political concerns are seamlessly interwoven in the texture of Nabokov's fiction, and second, that Nabokov's resistance to explicitly political writing is a staunch defense of intellectual freedom.

In what is arguably the most moving chapter of *Speak, Memory,* Nabokov recalls with pride his father's eloquent opposition to capital punishment, his resolute campaign against despotism, and "his great gifts of statesmanship" (*SM* 509–10). Even his father's eloquence can seem, against all odds, to contrast with the talents of one of the twentieth century's greatest prose stylists: "he was also an admirable speaker," writes Nabokov, "an 'English style' cool orator, who eschewed the meat-chopping gesture and rhetorical bark of the demagogue, and here, too, the ridiculous cacologist I am, when not having a typed sheet before me, has inherited nothing" (*SM* 512).

This is not false modesty. Unlike his father, Nabokov possessed no talent (and in any case, no inclination) for political activism. As Morris Bishop, Nabokov's friend and colleague at Cornell, recalls, "he had small interest in politics, none in society's economic concerns. He cared nothing for problems of low-cost housing, school consolidation, bond issues for sewage-treatment plants."[53] Nonetheless, Nabokov's concerns were topical in a different way. Boyd is perhaps right to observe that "throughout Nabokov's life only one political issue ever excited him: the attitude those outside the country should take toward the Soviet Union" (*VNAY* 84). This "one political issue," however, is an elephant in the room of his art, and its presence there shapes his novels in frequently unexpected ways.

Richard Rorty perceptively notes that Nabokov's overarching preoccupation with cruelty allies him with a politically engaged writer like Orwell. Rorty errs, however, in dissociating Nabokov from writers (Dickens, Mill, Dewey, Habermas, and Rawls) whose efforts were directed at "serving human liberty." Instead, he aligns Nabokov with writers like Plato, Heidegger, and Proust who invested themselves wholeheartedly in "the pursuit of private perfection."[54] This stark dichotomy is misleading. When properly situated in the context of turn-of-the-century Russian intellectual and political history, Nabokov's "pursuit of private perfection" must be understood as a form assumed by his particular commitment to "serving human liberty." That commitment hangs suspended like a watermark in his fiction; his views on art, ethics, science, law, epistemology, and metaphysics are distributed around its organizing presence.

Nabokov's art is in some ways the natural place for work of this kind to be conducted. Russia's *intelligenty* frequently turned to literature in their struggle against autocracy and their efforts to promote progressive cultural values. Nethercott singles out V. D. Nabokov's writings on the death penalty as representative of this tradition: "he willingly conceded that by far the most powerful denunciations of the death penalty did not belong to the professional jurist's pen at all; rather, they were to be found in literary accounts, where the focus and common denominator of concern was the person in the noose or before the firing squad, victim of a state in flagrant breach of its own legally and morally sanctioned authority" (*RLC* 128). In his contribution to M. N. Gernet's collection of essays on the subject of capital punishment, V. D. Nabokov emphasized the persuasive powers of literature with particular force:

> In our Russian literature—not juridical, but artistic—this particular aspect of capital punishment is expressed with tremendous force and vividness. A few pages of Turgenev ("Tropman's Execution"), Tolstoy (Kryltsov's tale in "Resurrection"), Dostoevsky (the tale of Count Myshkin in *The Idiot*) are by far more convincing and irrefutable than the thousands of scholarly studies and columns of statistics. They do not *prove, they show,* and in this resides their power. One cannot argue with them—one can only block one's ears and shut one's eyes.[55]

This argument was a common feature of V. D. Nabokov's juridical and publicistic writings. Nabokov must surely have been acquainted, for instance, with an article his father wrote for the Manchester *Daily Dispatch* on the eve of his murder. Though the article was one of many V. D. Nabokov wrote in opposition to the death penalty, it would have been more memorable than the others due to what Boyd calls "a peculiarly 'Nabokovian' coincidence": the newspaper received V. D. Nabokov's contribution the very day that it reported his death (*VNRY* 34).[56] Once again, instead of appealing to conventional strategies of political persuasion (such as, for instance, statistical evidence showing the inefficacy of capital punishment as a crime deterrent), V. D. Nabokov was guided by literature: "This ethical evaluation of capital punishment," he wrote, "is the same one which is represented so irresistibly in the literary works of the great analysts of the human heart," such as Victor Hugo, Dickens, Turgenev, and Dostoevsky.[57] In a crucial sense, then, Nabokov is following his father's lead when he tackles the subject in his antitotalitarian novel *Invitation to a Beheading*. When asked in 1960 to support the California Committee Against Capital Punishment, Nabokov responded that in spite of agreeing wholeheartedly with its members' position, writing an article on their behalf would be useless since he had already done all he could "by writing a whole book on the subject" (qtd. in *VNRY* 35).

The following chapters are organized around relationships between Nabokov's novels and particular configurations of the disciplines of science and epistemology (chapter 1), law and politics (chapter 2), art and ethics (chapter 3), and metaphysics (chapter 4). Together, these chapters work out the book's contention that Nabokov's identification with his father's liberalism was not simply a general attitude of mind, but a coherent and historically specific view about the legitimate boundaries of human knowledge, the proper functions of government, and the unconditional value of the right to self-determination.

Chapter 1 addresses the vexed relationship between Nabokov's significant contributions to science and his strenuous opposition to Darwin's account of evolution by natural selection as an exhaustive, final theory. By drawing on the writings of liberal intellectuals closely associated with Nabokov's father, I argue that Nabokov's reluctance to endorse fully the claims of Darwinism is a form of political protest bent on challenging the legitimacy of the Soviet state on philosophical grounds. Like the small but influential group of Kadets who staked their political aspirations in an anti-positivist, Kantian-inspired ontological idealism, Nabokov's *The Gift* seeks to trump Chernyshevski's positivist legacy with a philosophical framework that accommodates both science and metaphysics.

Chapter 2 explores the visible traces of V. D. Nabokov's political activities and writings on criminal jurisprudence in his son's most famous and controversial novel. Locating *Lolita* in the context of the criminal prosecutions of American Communists at the height of the Cold War, I argue that the novel tests the promises and shortcomings of the principles that structured V. D. Nabokov's and Nabokov's own liberalism.

Chapter 3 extends my discussion of *Lolita* by showing that the Kantian orientation of V. D. Nabokov's jurisprudence and Russia's liberal neo-idealist philosophers also informs *Ada*'s complex argument about the relationship between art and ethics. The ethical framework generated by this reading sees Nabokov drawing meaningful moral distinctions between controversial sexual activities such as pedophilia, homosexuality, and incest—the three topics treated in succession by *Lolita, Pale Fire,* and *Ada.*

Chapter 4 returns to the intellectual history invoked in the first chapter's discussion of Fyodor's biography of Chernyshevski. In this reexamination of *Ada,* I argue that Nabokov mobilizes George Berkeley's idealist metaphysics to refute the materialist underpinnings of Marxist-Leninism, and to advance an argument about the ontological connection between art and life. This connection, I contend, underwrites Nabokov's tendency to project his sociopolitical interests and commitments onto the screen of fantasy. His invented worlds—*Glory*'s Zoorland, *Pale Fire*'s Zembla, *Ada*'s Antiterra—are testaments to Nabokov's unwillingness to forget history and its victims.

Chapter One

Homo Ludens, Homo Faber: Nabokov's Inexhaustible Gift

> I was not quite six, but that year abroad, a year of difficult decisions and liberal hopes, had exposed a small Russian boy to grown-up conversations. He could not help being affected in some way of his own by a mother's nostalgia and a father's patriotism.
> —Vladimir Nabokov

> Logically, the investigation of Marx begins precisely where the investigation of Darwin ends. . . . The spirit of their research is absolutely the same in both thinkers. That is why one can say that Marxism is Darwinism in its application to social science.
> —George Plekhanov

THE GIFT (*DAR*, 1952) is Nabokov's last, longest, and most ambitious Russian novel. It is also, in a sense, inexhaustible. Nabokov returned to it again and again as to a rich storehouse of plots and preoccupations. As Boyd notes, "Nabokov's imagination did not want to leave *The Gift* alone"; this last of his completed Russian novels "set up powerful reverberations in his mind that lasted for decades" (*VNRY* 505, 520). The short story "The Circle" ("Krug," 1934) was the first of many "satellites" (as Nabokov called them) to orbit the novel. Another supplement, to which Nabokov gave only the descriptive title "Second Addendum to *The Gift*," was recently published in Russian under the title Nabokov had provisionally assigned it, "Vtoroe dobavlenie k *Daru*," and in English as "Father's Butterflies." At the Library of Congress, a folder marked "*The Gift*, Part II" preserves several sketched chapters for a sequel (*VNRY* 516–17). Though the projected sequel was abandoned, Nabokov reworked its principal themes and motifs in the unfinished Russian novel he intended to call "Solus Rex" and in the two

English-language novels that make up the core of his literary reputation, *Lolita* (1955) and *Pale Fire* (1962).[1]

As Boyd perceptively observes, "almost all of Nabokov's major artistic projects for thirty years can trace their origins back to *The Gift*" (*VNRY* 520). Nabokov's repeated returns to *The Gift* are perhaps unsurprising given the novel's frankly autobiographical nature; he seems to have viewed it as no less subject to extension than his own life. According to Boyd, Nabokov put "his whole self in the book": "his love for Véra, his reverence for his father's memory, his passion for Russian literature and for lepidoptera, his blissful Russian past and his mottled émigré present" (*VNRY* 397). The extent to which this "whole self" was shaped by his father is revealed in *Speak, Memory,* the autobiography published several years after *The Gift*. There, he tells his readers that his passions for Russian poetry and lepidoptera were special inheritances from his father. "My father's library," he recounts, "taught me to appreciate authentic poetry," and it was his father who "passed on to me the *morbus et passio aureliani*" (*SM* 455, 508; see also *SO* 46). Nabokov's love for Véra was uniquely his own, and yet his unapologetic readiness to marry a Jewish woman can also be understood in the larger context of his father's fearless public denunciation of Russia's officially sanctioned anti-Semitism.[2]

V. D. Nabokov casts a shadow across his son's work that extends far beyond the pages explicitly dedicated to him in *Speak, Memory*.[3] Even so, the memoir establishes Nabokov's most startling image of his father's role as the presiding spirit over his own life.[4] Nabokov recalls summer afternoons spent with his family at Vyra, the family's country estate, when his father would be summoned away from luncheon by local villagers. After settling a dispute or granting a request, he would be subjected to a traditional rite of gratitude which involved being tossed high into the air and caught in the arms of the men below. Nabokov weaves these moments of childhood plenitude into the grief that followed his father's murder:

> From my place at table I would suddenly see through one of the west windows a marvelous case of levitation. There, for an instant, the figure of my father in his wind-rippled white summer suit would be displayed, gloriously sprawling in midair, his limbs in a curiously casual attitude, his handsome, imperturbable features turned to the sky. Thrice, to the mighty heave-ho of his invisible tossers, he would fly up in this fashion, and the second time he would go higher than the first and then there he would be, on his last and loftiest flight, reclining, as if for good, against the cobalt blue of the summer noon, like one of those paradisiac personages who comfortably soar, with such a wealth of folds in their garments, on the vaulted ceiling of a church while below, one by one, the wax tapers in mortal hands light up to make a swarm of minute flames in the mist of incense, and the priest chants of eter-

> nal repose, and funeral lilies conceal the face of whoever lies there, among the swimming lights, in the open coffin. (*SM* 379)

Nabokov's love and respect for his father, highlighted here by the passage's elegiac, reverential language, provide one explanation for his long-standing quarrel with Freud's narratives of filial hostility and aggression.

V. D. Nabokov hovers over most of his son's fiction, but he executes his loftiest act of levitation in *The Gift.* The novel's protagonist, Fyodor Godunov-Cherdyntsev, is consumed by the same passions as his creator. Foremost among these passions is Fyodor's desire to capture the unique essence of his father's life. Though his attempt to write his father's biography seems to end in failure, he nonetheless succeeds in painting a detailed portrait of a man who resembles in crucial ways Nabokov's own father. In the figure of Fyodor's father, Konstantin Godunov-Cherdyntsev, an aristocrat of unimpeachable integrity and a naturalist of international distinction, Nabokov translates his own father's political achievements into the language of science. This substitution enables Nabokov to work within the boundaries of a familiar discipline while simultaneously imposing some distance between his father and his father's fictional double. "Father's Butterflies" extends this aspect of Nabokov's project beyond the boundaries of *The Gift.* In it, Fyodor pieces together an account of a revolutionary, anti-Darwinian theory of evolution composed by Godunov on the eve of his ill-fated last expedition. Though Fyodor confesses that he might not be able to "correctly convey the author's reasoning," he undertakes this project "because of the abstruse kinship, that poetic bond that, independent of the scientific essence of the subject, connects me to the author."[5] Like Fyodor, Nabokov considered himself ill-equipped to evaluate his father's professional achievements, but a similar sensitivity to "abstruse kinship," a similar "poetic bond," enabled him to transform his paternal legacy into a unique personal poetics. In *The Gift,* key aspects of V. D. Nabokov's personal and professional biography give rise to literary, scientific, and metaphysical plots that enact their author's continuous effort to think through and lay claim to the inexhaustible gift bequeathed to him by his father.

NABOKOV, LEPIDOPTERIST

Fyodor's father shared none of V. D. Nabokov's political interests, and he did not participate in the pre-revolutionary struggles against tsarist autocracy. His scientific views and commitments, however, firmly locate him in the same Russian liberal tradition that molded his creator's worldview. His opposition to Darwin's evolutionary theory, in particular, enables readers to observe in a new light some of the anxieties that shaped Nabokov's own attitudes toward Darwin and fueled his tendency to subordinate science to philosophy.

Nabokov's own scientific achievements were more modest than those of Konstantin Godunov-Cherdyntsev. While acting as the curator of lepidoptera at Harvard's Museum of Comparative Zoology (MCZ) in the 1940s, Nabokov became an expert on a group of butterflies known as the "blues" (the tribe Polyommatini). In his "Notes on Neotropical Plebejinae," published in *Psyche* in 1945, he laid out a radical new classificatory arrangement for most of the groups of blues in tropical America. As Kurt Johnson has observed, the substantial "blues" fauna "helps science answer some of the most perplexing biological questions about evolution in the New World tropics."[6] Nabokov's contributions to taxonomy and systematics (the science that deals with questions of biological classification) was only fully recognized after lepidopterists Zsolt Bàlint, Dubi Benyamini, and Kurt Johnson carried out the fieldwork necessary to test the validity of Nabokov's proposed new genera.

The recognition of the significance of Nabokov's scientific work has revived debates concerning the uneasy relationship between Nabokov's science and his attraction toward what Boyd has referred to as a "top-down, mind-first explanation" of life's origins. Nabokov fully accepted evolution, considered Darwin a scientist of genius, and took great pleasure in reconstructing the phylogenetic links wrought by the evolutionary process among the blues.[7] At the same time, however, he strenuously resisted the notion that natural selection could operate as the only explanation for evolution, and he criticized the intellectual revolution inspired by Darwin's bottom-up rather than top-down principles.[8]

Nabokov's acceptance of the evolutionary process is incontestable. In "Notes on Neotropical Plebejinae," he writes that "while accepting evolution as a modal formula, I am not satisfied with any of the hypotheses advanced in regard to the way it works."[9] He agreed with the guiding Darwinian premise that species evolve over time in response to environmental pressures. He objected, however, to two interrelated aspects of Darwinism: its positivism (the belief that the world can be explained by observable phenomena alone)[10] and its utilitarianism (the belief that nature's extravagant beauty and variety are to be understood as by-products of wholly utilitarian processes). Nabokov encapsulates these objections in "The Art of Literature and Commonsense," where he criticizes the followers of "commonsense" for maintaining

> that life on earth, from the barnacle to the goose, and from the humblest worm to the loveliest woman, arose from a colloidal carbonaceous slime activated by ferments while the earth was obligingly cooling down. Blood may

> well be the Silurian sea in our veins, and we are all ready to accept evolution at least as a modal formula. Professor Pavlov's bell-hopping mice and Dr. Griffith's rotating rats may please the practical minds, and Rhumbler's artificial amoeba can make a very cute pet. But again it is one thing to try and find the links and steps of life, and it is quite another to try and understand what life and the phenomenon of inspiration really are. (*LL* 378)

Though Nabokov agrees with the basic facts of evolutionary change, he resists the reductive positivism of the empirical narratives inspired by Darwin. He intimates that "life," like "the phenomenon of inspiration," cannot be accounted for in exclusively positivist and utilitarian terms. Although "the Silurian sea" may well fill the veins of "the loveliest woman," and although loveliness may confer significant advantages in a competitive marketplace, Nabokov implies that this woman's unparalleled charm is the function of something other than her gradual evolution from "the humblest worm."

The phenomenon that sustained Nabokov's metaphysical convictions more than any other was mimicry. He believed that mimicry could not be explained exclusively in terms of natural selection.[11] According to Nabokov, nature's mimic forms display an artistry and sophistication that could not be accounted for by an organism's need to deceive predators:

> "Natural selection," in the Darwinian sense, could not explain the miraculous coincidence of imitative aspect and imitative behavior, nor could one appeal to the theory of "the struggle for life" when a protective device was carried to a point of mimetic subtlety, exuberance, and luxury far in excess of a predator's power of appreciation. I discovered in nature the nonutilitarian delights that I sought in art. Both were a form of magic, both were a game of intricate enchantment and deception. (*SM* 465; see also *SO* 153)[12]

Scattered throughout Nabokov's literary oeuvre, statements of this kind point to an extremely complex relationship between his science and metaphysics. Several scholars have attempted to explain this relationship by locating Nabokov's scientific writings in the context of debates in evolutionary biology before and after his years at Harvard's MCZ.

Kurt Johnson and Steve Coates regard Nabokov's reservations about the comprehensiveness of Darwin's theory of natural selection as a matter of timing. They note that his scientific work was conducted at a time when the neo-Darwinian synthesis (which integrates Darwin's theory of natural selection with principles drawn from the field of population genetics) was still in its infancy. Had he worked later, they suggest, he would have abandoned his skeptical views about natural selection. The scientific discoveries that refute beyond any reasonable doubt the grounds upon which Nabokov resisted natural selection gained currency during and after his hectic years of research at Harvard.[13] As Stephen Jay Gould has written, Nabokov's skepticism toward Darwin's theory was shared by many of his contemporary professional biologists. Before the advent of the neo-Darwinian synthesis, they, too, had felt that Darwinian evolutionary models lacked full explanatory power: "when Nabokov wrote his technical papers in the 1940s, the modern Darwinian orthodoxy had not yet congealed, and a Nabokovian style of doubt remained quite common among evolutionary biologists, particularly among taxonomists immersed in the study of anatomical detail and geographic variation."[14]

In support of their argument that Nabokov's anti-Darwinism was principally an issue of timing, Johnson and Coates refer to a public dispute between Nabokov and a fellow colleague. In a 1950 letter to the *Lepidopterists' News,* F. Martin Brown of the American Museum of Natural History took issue with the lists and tables Nabokov published in conjunction with his 1949 paper "Nearctic Members of the Genus *Lycaeides.*" Brown argued that these tables, which recorded taxonomic characteristics such as wing-scale counts, had not been submitted to proper statistical analysis and were therefore useless. Unfamiliar with the new discipline of biological statistics, Nabokov defended the methods that had preceded its advent and concluded with a non sequitur that could never have hoped to persuade Brown: "After all, natural science is responsible to philosophy—not to statistics."[15] As Johnson and Coates point out, the possibilities of statistical analysis for the study of biological phenomena were being recognized and realized at the very moment that Nabokov's scientific work was drawing to a close. "The basic principles of statistics are not difficult to learn," they write, "and had Nabokov continued his academic career and developed his innovative scale-counting methods, it is reasonable to suppose that he would have learned them" (*NB* 330).

Johnson and Coates further speculate that Nabokov would have been receptive to the "elegant explanations of biological phenomena" that recent advances in genetics have made possible (*NB* 328–29). Dieter E. Zimmer endorses this argument when he suggests that Nabokov would have revised his views about mimicry

> if he had seen the evidence coming in after he had quit his work as a research lepidopterist. His conception of evolutionary theory was still guided by nineteenth-century slogans like "struggle for life" and "survival of the fittest" which imply a creature single-mindedly fighting and sweating and toiling for subsistence without a minute to spare for non-utilitarian delights like art. Instead, evolution, far from being a deploy of "unskilled forces," has itself turned out to be refined and subtle and staggeringly complex.[16]

Situating Nabokov's scientific career within its historical context has enabled scholars to shorten the distance between Nabokov's views and those of his scientific peers. Illuminating as they are, however, these accounts tell us little about the instincts and reasons that impelled Nabokov to subscribe so vehemently to the views he expressed. Charles Lee Remington, the distinguished Yale lepidopterist who worked with Nabokov at Harvard's MCZ, agrees with Johnson and Coates that Nabokov's views might have been different had his scientific work taken place at a different time, but he also conjectures that "Nabokov had such a strong metaphysical investment in his challenge to natural selection that he might have rejected the evolutionary conclusions for his own satisfaction."[17] Boyd endorses this view when he speculates that Nabokov "was too emotionally attached to a top-down explanation for existence to have accepted Darwinism, although he would probably have accepted many of the local advances in Darwinian theory and especially the clarifications of the power of natural selection in mimicry."[18]

Remington's acknowledgment that more compelling scientific explanations might not have weakened Nabokov's mistrust of Darwinism is salutary. Nabokov's attraction to metaphysical conceptions of the universe informs the most intimate aspects of his biography. It is difficult to imagine that a few more months or years would have altered his apparently settled opinion that "natural science is responsible to philosophy—not to statistics." Remarks of this kind were a common element in Russian debates at the turn of the century. Seen in that context, Nabokov's commitment to a top-down explanation of life's origins and his deference to the special claims of philosophy begin to look like strategic refutations of an ideology whose victory had heralded the onset of a new period of tyranny and oppression in Russia. The full story of Nabokov's opposition to Darwinism is no discrete and self-contained chapter in the history of science; it is also deeply rooted in the intellectual and political history of his native land.

In his recent monograph on the intersections between Nabokov's art and science, Stephen Blackwell acknowledges how closely Nabokov's attitudes toward Darwin's theory of evolution were conditioned by these historical forces. He notes that "Nabokov emerged from his chrysalis at a time when his core identity was rejected and negated in his homeland, both practically and philosophically. His life and career, as artist and scientist, were set in a contest with the positivist materialist philosophy embodied by the Bolsheviks, and in many ways it was a life-or-death battle waged in ink." According to Blackwell, Nabokov sought to trump "the Bolsheviks' ideology of positivist certainty, teleology, mass conformity and control" with "an artistic and scientific program based on individuality, curiosity, beauty, and the unknown" (*QS* 6).

Though Blackwell argues that Nabokov's art and science "were fundamentally related and, by corollary, mutually illuminating," he also emphasizes that Nabokov maintained a strict separation between what he wrote "in his fictional or memoiristic works and what he wrote as a professional lepidopterist" (*QS* 53, 38). As Blackwell observes, the only document that might throw this conclusion into doubt is an essay on mimicry Nabokov began writing in 1941 while working at Harvard's MCZ. Nabokov describes the essay in its early stages as "a work on mimicry (with a furious refutation of 'natural selection' and the 'struggle for life')."[19] On several occasions between April 1942 and April 1943, he delivered a lecture titled "The Theory and Practice of Mimicry," and in May 1942 he gave a copy of the essay to Edmund Wilson in the hope that Wilson could find a publisher for it (*NB* 265, 269, 277–78; *VNAY* 44). In a letter dated May 6, 1942, Wilson reported having read and liked the piece, and recommended the *Yale Review*, the *Virginia Quarterly*, and the *Atlantic Monthly* as possible venues for publication (*DBDV* 66).[20] These venues (and indeed Wilson's role as assessor) strongly suggest that the essay's protest against Darwinism must have addressed a wider audience than a strictly scientific essay could have reached. Blackwell sums up his detailed reconstruction of the abortive progress of Nabokov's essay on mimicry by concluding that beyond the informal anti-Darwinian comments made in *Speak, Memory*, there is no record of what the essay contained or the exact nature of Nabokov's views on mimicry at that particular time in his life (*QS* 13–14, 38–39).

Johnson and Coates similarly draw attention to the strict separation Nabokov maintained between the literary and scientific domains: "Nabokov never tried to advance his own explanation for mimicry in any kind of formal or scientific setting that can be examined today." It was only in his art, they note further, that "he felt free to express his awe about mimicry in terms that had more to do with human feelings and natural wonder than with laboratory science" (*NB* 329). A year later, Johnson underscored this point when he observed that Nabokov guarded his private beliefs much more scrupulously than many practitioners of science who allow their metaphysical inclinations to influence their scientific work.[21]

These observations contain the key to understanding the relationship between Nabokov's science and metaphysics. By refusing to allow his metaphysical views to intrude upon his scientific work and vice versa, Nabokov was expressing his commitment to an understanding of disciplinary integrity that had played a vital role in Russia's pre-revolutionary intellectual history. As Alexander Vucinich has shown in his detailed history of Darwin's reception in Russia, Darwinism was a key point of reference in Russia's heated ideological contests. Even members of the scientific community, Vucinich notes, "viewed Darwinism not only as an ordered system of scientific thought but also as a unique expression of philosophical ideas and ideological statements."[22] Nabokov's anti-positivist and anti-utilitarian opposition to Darwinism allied him with an influential group of Russian neo-idealist philosophers who argued that positivist models of reality and utilitarian ethics failed to provide a philosophical basis for a liberal or progressive politics. The first extended philosophical document of Russia's liberal movement, the symposium *Problems of Idealism* (*Problemy idealizma*), takes this argument as its point of departure.

LIBERALISM, NEO-IDEALISM, AND *LICHNOST'*

In 1901, V. D. Nabokov's longtime political ally Peter Struve was exiled to Tver as punishment for having participated in a student demonstration in St. Petersburg. During his time in Tver, two projects absorbed Struve's attention: first, the launch of the illegal constitutional journal *Osvobozhdenie* and, second, work on *Problems of Idealism,* a symposium that was to provide a philosophical defense of liberalism.[23] Both projects made their debut in 1902.

Problems of Idealism has recently been edited and translated into English by Randall Poole, who writes that the symposium "was conceived as a theoretical statement of Russian liberalism in the first stages of the liberation movement" and that "it constitutes the theoretical counterpart" to the first issues of *Osvobozhdenie* (EI 5–6). The symposium was sponsored by the Moscow Psychological Society, a learned society established in 1885 which became the philosophical center of the revolt against positivism in the Russian Silver Age. Though the society's founding members tended toward positivism, idealism became the dominant philosophical orientation after Nicholas (Nikolai) Grot became its chairman in 1888 (EI 3). As Poole notes, the society's neo-idealist critiques of positivism vigorously defended free, disinterested philosophical argument against positivist efforts to put an end to "unscientific" philosophical speculation.

By the turn of the century, the Moscow Psychological Society had also become the theoretical center of Russian liberalism, and the society journal—*Voprosy filosofii i psikhologii* (*Questions of Philosophy and Psychology*)—regularly published essays and studies in liberal political philosophy, including what have come to be considered classic texts of Russian liberalism (EI 5). For the society's leading philosophers, neo-idealism provided not only the most persuasive theoretical defense of the autonomy of philosophy against reductive positivism, but also of constitutionalism and rule-of-law liberalism (EI 1). Poole notes that six of the society's most prominent philosophers were main theorists of Russian liberalism: Boris Chicherin (1828–1904), Vladimir Soloviev (1853–1900), the brothers

Sergey (1862–1905) and Evgenii Trubetskoi (1863–1920), Paul Novgorodtsev (1866–1924), and Sergey Kotliarevskii (1873–1939/41) (EI 5).

In the March 2, 1903, issue of *Osvobozhdenie,* Struve explicitly established the connection between *Problems of Idealism* and the liberation movement by enjoining his readers to attend to the symposium's profound political significance. The terms in which he casts his argument set a precedent for a political reading of Nabokov's deceptively apolitical fiction: "Though this abstract book does not openly state its views on the burning political and social questions of the day, it thinks of them nonetheless; it is animated by them and it grieves over them." For Struve, the symposium represented "the strengthening and broadening of the union between philosophical idealism and practical-political idealism first championed in the brilliant publicistic writings of Vladimir Soloviev." Such a union "is as necessary for philosophical thought as it is for the work of liberation." Russia's liberationists, he continued, must stake their efforts on the "high and irrefutable" idealist principles whose rejection "opens the door to bestiality."[24]

By publicizing the connection between neo-idealism and liberalism that the society had advanced for fifteen years, *Problems of Idealism* became the Moscow Psychological Society's main institutional contribution to the campaign for constitutional reform (EI 5). The symposium's efforts to supply a theoretical foundation for political practice has moved Christopher Read to describe *Problems of Idealism* as a species of "philosophical liberalism" (*RRRI* 15–24). Eight of the symposium's twelve contributors would play active roles in the founding of the Union of Liberation (Struve, Novgorodtsev, Sergey Bulgakov, Evgenii Trubetskoi, Nicholas Berdiaev, Simon Frank, Bogdan Kistiakovskii, and Dmitri Zhukovskii), while six had been involved in the setting up and publication of *Osvobozhdenie* (Struve, Bulgakov, Frank, Kistiakovskii, Sergey Oldenburg, and Zhukovskii).[25] Four would become Kadets: Novgorodtsev was a leading Kadet from the time of the party's inception; Struve was elected to the Kadet Central Committee after his return to Russia in the fall of 1905;[26] Evgenii Trubetskoi was a party member from October 1905 to February 1906 and again after 1917; Oldenburg was elected to the Kadet Central Committee in 1917 (EI 451–54; BRR 57).

Novgorodtsev and Struve, the symposium's organizers, would serve as Kadet deputies in the First and Second State Dumas (Novgorodtsev in the first, Struve in the second). Although Bulgakov would never formally join the Kadet Party, he would be elected to the Second State Duma as a nonparty member (he considered himself a Christian socialist), and would distinguish himself as one of the Kadets' most influential allies (*RRRI* 62; BRR 330–31). Three symposium contributors later went on to serve in the Provisional Government: Struve worked briefly in the Foreign Ministry; Oldenburg served as minister of education from July to August 1917; and, like

V. D. Nabokov, Alexander (Aleksandr) Lappo-Danilevskii was appointed to the committee charged with preparing the electoral law for the Constituent Assembly (EI 451–53; *LRR* 192; *PG* 92).

Struve's and Novgorodtsev's political activities brought them into close proximity to V. D. Nabokov. As members of the Kadet Central Committee, they belonged to a small inner circle of party leaders. The first Central Committee, elected in 1905, was composed of twenty-six members; the second, elected in 1907, was expanded to forty (*LRR* 20). As Terence Emmons writes, genuine "status and power" within the party were directly linked to membership on the Central Committee; furthermore, members of the Kadet leadership "had been in mutual contact socially, in the zemstvos and in more expressly political settings, over a period of many years preceding the founding of the party. In many cases these contacts date from the late 1880s and early 1890s, and in a fair number they extend back to the university years and even beyond that to childhood" (*FPP* 63, 64). This was certainly true of Struve and V. D. Nabokov, who met in high school (both attended the Third Gymnasium in St. Petersburg) long before V. D. Nabokov began submitting contributions to Struve's *Osvobozhdenie* and Struve began submitting contributions to *Pravo.*[27] Struve and Nabokov also met regularly at the "evenings" hosted by K. K. Arsenev in the late 1880s which were attended by a number of future leaders of the Kadet Party (*FPP* 65). Struve mentions in the obituary he wrote on the occasion of V. D. Nabokov's death that he and Nabokov were especially close after 1919.[28]

Like Struve, Novgorodtsev moved in the same political circles as V. D. Nabokov. A professor at Moscow University, Novgorodtsev was one of Russia's most distinguished social philosophers. Like V. D. Nabokov, he served on the Kadet Party's Central Committee and was elected to the First State Duma. Shortly after the Duma's convocation, the Kadet deputies elected a committee of twenty-one members; this committee imposed structure and discipline on the Kadet parliamentary group and their nonparty adherents. Both V. D. Nabokov and Novgorodtsev served on this committee, and their names come up together in the annals of the First State Duma, the 1917 Provisional Government, and in the emigration.[29] As signatories of the Vyborg Manifesto, Novgorodtsev and V. D. Nabokov lost their political rights but resumed active political struggle during the second revolutionary period. As in the case of his relationship with Struve, V. D. Nabokov's association with Novgorodtsev became particularly close in the emigration at the time when they both served as editors of the Kadet newspaper *Rul'* (*The Rudder*) (*LRR* 449–50). In a front-page tribute published in *Rul'* directly below a large picture of V. D. Nabokov lying in an open coffin, Novgorodtsev noted that he had known the departed for nearly twenty years. Writing from Prague, Novgorodtsev also recalled the last letter V. D. Nabokov wrote him before his murder. Received on the eve of his death, the letter mourned the wreckage of their shared political aspirations and sought Novgorodtsev's counsel in an effort to redefine the political obligations of Russian liberals in exile.[30]

The participation of so many symposium contributors in liberal politics should not obscure the fact that the majority of Kadet leaders subscribed to what might be termed as a "soft" positivism. Some contributors to *Problems of Idealism* (Bulgakov and Berdiaev, for example) even complained that the party's atheism prevented it from becoming the true voice of Russia's people (*RRRI* 64, 73). Contemporaries and intellectual historians frequently describe Miliukov's positivism as a shaping force in his scholarship and political thinking.[31] Read notes that although most Kadet leaders confined their attention to day-to-day political activity and did not preoccupy themselves with philosophical questions, prominent Kadet intellectuals such as Miliukov and Alexander (Aleksandr) Kizevetter (both close friends and political associates of V. D. Nabokov) can be described as "liberal materialists" (*RRRI* 21). The same is true of the distinguished legal scholar Sergey Muromtsev (1850–1910), a founding father of the Kadet Party and the chairman of the First State Duma. Like these men, V. D. Nabokov focused his energies on political activism rather than philosophical deliberation, but unlike them, he was no positivist.

Intellectual historians such as R. V. Ivanov-Razumnik, Leszek Kolakowski, and Randall Poole emphasize the symposium's significant position in Russian intellectual history (Poole calls it "a philosophical watershed").[32] Walicki characterizes the symposium as "a challenging, self-confident manifesto of the neo-idealist revival in Russian thought" (*LPRL* 352). For cultural historians such as Gleb Struve, Bernice Glatzer Rosenthal, and Martha Bohachevsky-Chomiak, *Problems of Idealism* was a landmark document in the general revolt against positivism during the Russian Silver Age.[33]

Within the vocabulary of pre-revolutionary Russian intellectual history, "positivism" functioned as a catchall term for a variety of materialist, utilitarian, scientist, and dogmatic rationalist positions.[34] Poole's elaboration upon this terminological shorthand is instructive:

> In ethics, epistemology, ontology, and social philosophy, neo-idealism emerged as a response to the dominant positivist background, the main characteristics of which were *reductionism,* which dismisses as a meaningless proposition (i.e., neither analytic nor empirical) the possibility of being beyond the positively given data of sense experience; *scientism,* the claim, consistent with the positivist reduction of being to natural phenomena, that the natural sciences cover everything; and *utopianism,* or faith in human perfectibility through (in this case) application of natural scientific methods to man and society. (EI 4)

Russia's neo-idealist philosophers argued that speculative philosophy constituted a free and autonomous discipline that was incompatible with a positivist outlook. But while they defended philosophy from the colonizing forces of positivism, they also paid tribute to Russia's intellectual history by insisting that particular philosophical outlooks generate specific political principles. The positivist foundations of Marxism and its political offshoot, the Russian Social-Democratic (SD) Party, fueled their deepest revulsion. As Read observes, "the idealists were at their most united when criticizing the Marxist world view" (*RRRI* 15).

The principal contribution of Russia's neo-idealist philosophers to liberal political theory was an ontologically based conception of *lichnost'*. Inspired by Kant, Russia's neo-idealists argued that human subjectivity is irreducible to naturalistic explanations and that people bear an absolute value and dignity by virtue of being ends-in-themselves. Accepting Kant's conclusion that the rational agent can rise above material necessity, they viewed this ability as proof that the self is metaphysically grounded. Their effort to combine Kantian idealism with the personalistic traditions of Orthodox theology (in which the human being's likeness to God constitutes selfhood) generated a liberal political theory that stood on a very different foundation than the positivist conceptions of liberal doctrine associated with John Stuart Mill in England and Miliukov in Russia (EI 4–5).

As in Kant, their argument concerning the self's irreducibility to naturalistic explanations drew sustenance from an ethical idealism that dominated the currents of thought represented in the symposium. Contributors to the symposium argued that positivism's strict reliance upon empirically derived knowledge discounted the uniquely human capacity for moral deliberation. Drawing on Hume's and Kant's propositions that what *ought to be* cannot be reduced to what *is*,[35] they argued that the empirical world reflected only positive facts and had nothing to say about moral standards and ideals. In their eyes, positivist conceptions of reality failed to acknowledge the fact of moral obligations and could not explain the individual's capacity to rise above impulse, inclination, and desire in the name of satisfying those obligations. Moral ideals, they insisted, could not be evaluated empirically, and the capacity to adhere to these ideals proved that human beings enjoyed a certain level of autonomy relative to their natural and social environments (EI 13–14). Finally, they argued that positivism's refusal to acknowledge the "ideal" as a legitimate philosophical category made it impossible for positivist thinkers to provide a theoretical foundation for social and political reform. As Novgorodtsev wrote in the preface to the symposium, the idealist movement's principal aim was to restore to respectability "the categorical imperative of morality, which gives primary importance to the principle of the absolute significance of personhood [*lichnost'*]." Russia's future social and political structures, he elaborated, should disregard "the simple demand of expediency" and be guided instead by "the progressive principles of moral consciousness."[36]

Liberalism was seen as the natural defender of the special dignity conferred upon human beings by their autonomy. The right to self-determination—the cornerstone of liberal theory both in Russia and elsewhere—became for Russia's neo-idealists a spur to social and political reform. In his contribution to the symposium, Novgorodtsev wrote: "The self-determining person is that point, that focus, in which social goals and demands are refracted and acquire their moral character" (EIPL 305). Two years later, in 1904, Novgorodtsev once again emphasized this core commitment to liberal values when he stated that Russia's idealist philosophers were united in prioritizing "the principle of the person, its absolute dignity, its natural and inalienable rights."[37]

Contributors to the symposium interpreted the neo-idealist focus on individual autonomy and moral ideals as a protest against the political apathy they associated with deterministic models of social progress such as Marxism. "Idealism," Caryl Emerson writes in her foreword to *Problems of Idealism,* "is completely alien to those sorts of naïveté that counsel us to await a change in environment that will then bring about (for the most part automatically) a change in the self. . . . In contrast, living by ideals is supremely realistic, since coherence or justice is at no point expected from the outside world or imposed upon it."[38] Evgenii Trubetskoi's contribution to the symposium closes with a version of that point: "The human mind, whether it makes a scientific discovery or falls into error, is in any event one of the prime movers in history, an independent factor irreducible to economic or other causes."[39]

Trubetskoi's criticism of Marxist determinism anticipates Nabokov's own attacks on Marx and Freud. In Nabokov's early novel *The Eye* (*Sogliadatai,* 1930), for example, Smurov laments the fate of "the private individuum, with his two poor 'u's, hallooing hopelessly amid the dense growth of economic causes." Marx, in turn, is derided as "that crabbed bourgeois in Victorian checkered trousers" whose magnum opus is nothing more than "the fruit of insomnia and migraine." *Das Kapital*'s guiding thesis—that "the whole course of humanity can be explained . . . as the struggle between an empty and a stuffed belly"—is likened by Smurov to an astrologist's mad claim.[40] In *Speak, Memory,* by contrast, Nabokov celebrates "the essentially human urge to reshape the earth, to act upon a friable environment (unless he is a born Marxist or a corpse and meekly waits for the environment to fashion him)" (*SM* 621).

Arguing that idealism provided a more powerful theoretical foundation for progressive reform than positivism, Russia's neo-idealists committed themselves to political action by what would have been, at the time, an unexpected route; turn-of-the-century Russian culture, after all, frequently associated positivism with progressive political ideals and idealist philosophy with reactionary conservatism (EI 26). Emerson's description of the period's guiding assumptions is especially lucid:

> In this polarization, certain prejudices—or perhaps merely reflexes of the mind—had formed around certain terms. Positivism was associated with progress, with empirical science, with Realism in psychology and literature, and thus with the courage to see the world concretely, "as it really exists." Idealism, on the other hand, was felt to be pie-in-the-sky, dreamy, abstract, passive, a mystical realm, and therefore reactionary.[41]

These assumptions enjoyed an august genealogy. In the context of Russian intellectual history, the tight bond between positivism and social progress had been established by the "men of the sixties" and their most distinguished representative, the radical publicist Nicholas (Nikolai) Chernyshevski (1828–89). Chernyshevski's materialism, positivism, and utilitarianism shaped the terms in which he waged his struggles against tsarist autocracy.

Nabokov lets his own hostility toward these philosophical positions shape *The Gift,* where a biography of Chernyshevski, penned by the novel's protagonist, serves as the novel's fourth chapter. Reading Chernyshevski's biography in conjunction with *Problems of Idealism* and other seminal documents of pre-revolutionary Russian intellectual history provides an essential context for Nabokov's quarrel with positivism, and by extension, his quarrel with Darwinism.

NABOKOV AND IULII AIKHENVALD

Nabokov's most direct connection to Russia's neo-idealist philosophers can be traced to his friend Iulii Aikhenvald (1872–1928), one of the most distinguished literary critics and theorists in pre-revolutionary Russia and the emigration.[42] A Kadet Party member and author of a weekly literary column in *Rech'* and *Rul',* Aikhenvald served as the Moscow Psychological Society's secretary and as editor on the board of the society's journal (*VNRY* 256; EI 76, note 220).[43] After moving to Berlin and becoming acquainted with Nabokov's work (at a time when Nabokov was writing under the pen name Sirin),[44] Aikhenvald became his first prominent public supporter (*VNRY* 200). The two men cultivated a warm friendship and a close professional association until Aikhenvald's death in 1928 (*VNRY* 256).

Boyd asserts that the informal literary circle founded by Aikhenvald and Raisa Tatarinov "involved Vladimir Sirin more than any other in which he ever took part." The group's members "gathered in apartments or small cafés for brief talks on literary, philosophic, political, and scientific themes or readings of new works by poets and writers, followed by tea and discussion." Nabokov's contributions included readings from his own poetry and fiction, as well as talks on topics such as Pushkin, Gogol, Blok, Conrad, Freud, and "the horrors of Soviet literature" (*VNRY* 256–57). Aikhenvald died two days after attending a party hosted by Véra and Vladimir Nabokov in their home at 12 Passauer Strasse. After leaving the party, Aikhenvald was struck down by a tram he had failed to see as a result of his poor eyesight (*VNRY* 287–88). Nabokov's moving tribute to Aikhenvald appeared in the December 23, 1928, edition of *Rul'*.[45] Aikhenvald's death also prompted Nabokov to compose a poem titled "Pereshel ty v novoe zhilishche" ("You Have Moved to a New Home") published in *Nashe nasledie.*

As Stephen Blackwell argues in his monograph on *The Gift,* Aikhenvald exerted "the most clearly identifiable formative influence" on Nabokov during the mid-1920s. Blackwell believes that Nabokov and Aikhenvald "were kindred spirits in a deep sense," and that their mutual admiration was grounded in "a remarkably similar outlook on literature."[46] Blackwell dwells in particular on their shared mistrust of deterministic accounts of literary creation. In his best-known work of literary criticism, *Siluety russkikh pisatelei* (*Silhouettes of Russian Writers,* 1909), Aikhenvald wrote:

> The most real and certain thing that one can encounter here is the writer (i.e., his writings). Only he is a fact. Everything else is doubtful. There are no movements; there are writers. That means that however many writers there are, there are that many movements, and each one in his own essence defines himself. There is no society; there are individuals. (10; qtd. in *ZP* 27)

This view strikingly resembles Nabokov's own remarks on the subject of literary movements. When an interviewer solicited his opinion about the French "anti-novel," Nabokov answered: "I am not interested in groups, movements, schools of writing and so forth. I am interested only in the individual artist" (*SO* 4; see also *SO* 173). "One of the functions of all my novels," he told Nicholas Garnham in an interview from 1968, "is to prove that the novel in general does not exist. The book I make is a subjective and specific affair" (*SO* 115).

This shared insistence on prioritizing individual originality over group affiliations is no simple literary affectation; rather, these priorities are rooted in a philosophically and politically motivated refusal to subject the self to positivist explanations. Though Blackwell concentrates on the aesthetic affinities between Nabokov and Aikhenvald, he draws attention to the political implications of the literary views they held in common: "This refusal to recognize artistic classifications is, for both authors, part of an agenda that focuses always upon the value of the individual, and one senses in their writing that any retreat from this extreme position would be to affirm the power of autocrats and tyrants, if not to play directly into their own hands" (*ZP* 27).

Nabokov must have also been attracted by the philosophical dimension of Aikhenvald's literary criticism. As Michael Wood has perceptively observed, Nabokov's "devious narratives . . . are not about philosophy . . . they are philosophy."[47] Blackwell notes that Aikhenvald's theoretical essays proceed from the conviction that "art, and especially literary art, is essentially philosophical in nature." For Aikhenvald, the meaning of an artwork can be discovered not by way of scientific, historical, or sociological analysis, but only "through a process that relates what is expressed . . . to other philosophical truths that have been probed or discovered over the course of human culture." One such truth is the principle that stood at the center of Russian neo-idealist philosophy: the irreducibility of the self to external explanations. "For Aikhenvald," Blackwell states, "the individual, unrepeatable personality of the author was the eternal and eternally mysterious component in artistic creation, and to ignore this personality—to claim that verbal art is a logical consequence of various social and psychological processes—was to destroy the very concept of art within human art."[48]

Aikhenvald's unwillingness to contaminate autonomous domains of intellectual activity (such as art and philosophy) by bringing them into contact with arguments and theories generated in the sociopolitical sphere also influenced his response to *Problems of Idealism.* In a detailed review of the volume, he argued that the symposium's attempts to root liberalism in philosophical idealism were insufficiently philosophical. Finding much to praise in the volume, he nevertheless criticized its contributors for betraying their responsibilities by mixing philosophical questions with ideas drawn from Russian sociology and Russia's publicistic traditions.[49] Aikhenvald's general disdain for utilitarian morality and sociology, articulated with elegant understatement in the review's concluding remarks, explains why Nabokov would have found the older man's views so congenial:

> *Problems of Idealism* victoriously struggles with utilitarian ethics and gains the upper hand over the "subjective method" of Russian sociology. But this ethical system and this fantastical philosophical method are not very strong; victory over them is easy. *Problems of Idealism* shows well that service to progressive civic ideals and a spiritualist worldview are fully compatible. But no one familiar with the history of philosophy ever doubted it.[50]

Aikhenvald's formal training in philosophy and his idealist commitments help account for his readiness to view liberalism and idealism as natural allies.[51] But his complaint that the symposium was insufficiently philosophical must have been especially cutting to those contributors who had explicitly sought to defend philosophy as an autonomous discipline.

V. D. NABOKOV, NEO-IDEALISM, AND THE "CONTRABAND" CRITIQUE

Nabokov's efforts to refute Chernyshevski's philosophy in the fourth chapter of *The Gift* replicate the "contraband" critique adumbrated in Aikhenvald's review of *Problems of Idealism* and mobilized by those symposium contributors who argued for the autonomy of distinct spheres of human consciousness and experience. As Poole explains, "Russian neo-idealists used the term (or, when not the term, the concept) 'contraband' to describe the intellectual distortion and muddling that result when elements from one area of thought (ethical or metaphysical) are smuggled into another (empirical or natural scientific)." Distortions of this kind could only be prevented by delimiting separate domains of human experience and consciousness (EI 35).

The "contraband" critique had a distinguished genealogy in Russian intellectual history, and its influence extended well beyond the pages of *Problems of Idealism.* One of its earliest formulations occurs in the work of the idealist legal philosopher Boris Chicherin, Russia's most eminent nineteenth-century theorist of Russian liberalism. Chicherin invokes a version of the "contraband" critique in his book *Nauka i religiia* (*Science and Religion,* 1879). Paul Valliere underscores the conceptual kinship between the "contraband" critique and political liberalism when he observes that Chicherin's insistence on disciplinary autonomy is an outflow of his liberal commitment to freedom of conscience. "Conscience in this context," Valliere elaborates, "means the responsibility that a philosopher, artist or moralist feels toward his discipline. Freedom of conscience is the right to exercise this responsibility openly and without interference."[52]

Among the contributors to *Problems of Idealism,* the "contraband" critique is most elaborately articulated by Bulgakov, but it is also featured in the essays submitted by Struve, Novgorodtsev, and Kistiakovskii. It was also frequently invoked in Novgorodtsev's and Struve's writings throughout this period, and it played a key role in the symposium's sequels, *Vekhi* and *Iz glubiny* (*Out of the Depths*) (EI 38–40). The critique's appearance in an essay by Vladimir Vernadskii, which was published as a companion piece to *Problems of Idealism,* is particularly relevant to the troubling aspects of Nabokov's own understanding of the relationship between science and metaphysics.

Like Novgorodtsev, Vernadskii (1863–1945) was one of Moscow's outstanding "public men" at the turn of the century. A professor of mineralogy at Moscow University and a distinguished earth scientist, he belonged to the Moscow Psychological Society and was one of Russia's most prominent liberal intellectuals (EI 10). He was a founding member of the Union of Liberation and, like V. D. Nabokov, was elected to the Kadet Party's Central Committee at its first congress (BRR 19, note 38). Vernadskii's biographer, Kendall Bailes, describes him as "a national political figure who stood among the inner circle of those who forced major concessions from the autocracy in the fall of 1905 and then watched angrily and for the most part helplessly as the tsarist government attempted to limit those concessions in the years after 1906." Within this inner circle, Vernadskii and V. D. Nabokov were both known for their passionate and vocal campaigns against capital punishment.[53]

Vernadskii's status as one of Russia's most eminent scientists (he made significant contributions to the fields of geology, mineralogy, crystallography, and geochemistry) made him an especially valuable contributor to the neo-idealist platform. According to Novgorodtsev, Vernadskii's essay was motivated by a general sympathy for the symposium's guiding principles, but instead of contributing to *Problems of Idealism,* he chose to publish his essay in the Moscow Psychological Society journal (EI 10). The essay was based on a series of influential lectures he had delivered at Moscow University on the subject of the history and philosophy of science. After the essay was published in *Voprosy filosofii i psikhologii,* it was published, under the same title, as a book.[54]

In the essay (and, indeed, throughout his career generally), Vernadskii rejected the common assumption that positivism and scientific inquiry were natural partners (EI 10). Like the contributors to the symposium, he worked to establish the importance of disciplinary autonomy by arguing that scientific knowledge was inescapably provisional and should not be allowed to encroach on other areas of human consciousness and experience. This formulation of the "contraband" critique became the cornerstone of his philosophy of science and also of what his biographer calls his "scientific liberalism." According to Bailes, Vernadskii's involvement in liberal politics was the direct outcome of his scientific worldview.[55]

Nabokov could have become acquainted with the "contraband" critique by way of several routes. As a major document of Russian intellectual history, *Problems of Idealism* appeared under the rubric "Religion, philosophy, psychology, ethics" in the list of holdings cataloguing V. D. Nabokov's home library. (Its highly controversial sequel, *Vekhi,* is listed in the catalogue's supplement.)[56] Although Nabokov was as intimately familiar with his father's well-stocked library as Van and Ada were to become with the library at Ardis Hall, it is unlikely that he read *Problems of Idealism* when it sat on his father's bookshelf. Indeed, it seems more likely that he knew about it from Aikhenvald, who reviewed the volume in 1903. It is also likely that he read the volume during the extensive research into Russian intellectual history he undertook while writing Chernyshevski's biography for *The Gift.* As Fyodor reflects (in the third person) upon his scholarly labors, "he read a great deal—more than he had ever read" (*Gift* 202).

Nabokov could also have come to know *Problems of Idealism* through his friendship with Struve's son Gleb. As Alexander Dolinin has written in his introductory remarks to Nabokov's letters to Gleb Struve, Struve and Nabokov met for the first time in England. (Boyd notes further that Struve advised Nabokov on a choice of university [*VNRY* 165–66].) In Berlin they became intimate friends. According to Dolinin, they met frequently, published in the same journals, belonged to the same literary circles, and shared their poetry with each other. After Struve moved to Paris in the spring of 1924, their friendship continued uninterrupted: Nabokov sent Struve his new work for publication in the Parisian newspapers edited by Gleb's father Peter, sought his advice in literary matters, and thought of him as his most dedicated supporter and best critic. In his turn, Struve referred to himself as Nabokov's personal "propagandist." During the first decade of Nabokov's literary career, Struve energetically promoted his work by glowingly reviewing all of Nabokov's major output and introducing his work to French and English audiences. And though their friendship cooled after 1932, the two men preserved a warm feeling toward each other to the very end of their lives.[57]

Vernadskii's scientific reputation and his political associations with V. D. Nabokov could easily have introduced Nabokov to his philosophy of science; it is also possible that Nabokov became acquainted with it through his friendship with Vernadskii's son George (1887–1973). Like the Nabokovs, the Vernadskiis sought refuge in the Crimea and help from the British to emigrate during the civil war. During the Crimea's evacuation, however, Vladimir Vernadskii and his wife and daughter decided to remain behind.[58] George Vernadskii and his wife Nina went into exile, and George Vernadskii went on to become a distinguished professor of Russian history at Yale. Nabokov socialized with George Vernadskii in Paris and appealed to him on several occasions when seeking employment in the United States (*VNRY* 437, 485; *VNAY* 14, 17).

Nabokov's most direct contact with the "contraband" critique would have come through his father's work. Though V. D. Nabokov was not in the habit of explicitly establishing a *zhizneponimanie,* or theoretical outlook, for his work, his legal writings and his private life indicate that he shared many affinities with Russia's neo-idealist philosophers. In a commemorative essay written on the occasion of V. D. Nabokov's death, Alexander (Aleksandr) Makletsov aligns V. D. Nabokov with the "classical school" of Russian jurisprudence that opposed the dissolution of criminal law within the nascent field of criminal sociology.[59] He notes further that V. D. Nabokov's legal philosophy was most explicitly anatomized in his inaugural lecture at the Imperial School of Jurisprudence on September 9, 1896.[60] In this lecture, titled "Soderzhanie i metod nauki ugolovnago prava" ("The Science of Criminal Law: Contents and Method"), V. D. Nabokov advances a version of the "contraband" critique that had also been used to protect the discipline of criminal law from positivist encroachments by his teacher and mentor, the patriarch of classical criminal law Nikolai Tagantsev (1843–1923).[61] As Tagantsev's student at St. Petersburg University, V. D. Nabokov would have been familiar with a version of the "contraband" critique Tagantsev elaborated in his published lectures.[62] Like his mentor, V. D. Nabokov opposed positivist approaches to crime on the grounds that they deny the existence of free will and, by extension, the concept of responsibility (*ideia otvetstvennosti*), which V. D. Nabokov calls the "alpha and omega of all constructions of criminal law."[63] By his own account, these commitments ally him with the "classical" school of criminal law.

In her *Russian Legal Culture Before and After Communism* (2007), Frances Nethercott provides a detailed account of the ways in which Russia's "classical" school of legal thought was being challenged during this period (as elsewhere in the West) by a younger generation of legal theorists who, under the influence of positivism, viewed the individual as a socially determined being. Guided by the findings of sociologists and anthropologists, this new generation of legal scholars resisted foundational classical premises (free will and moral responsibility, crime as a breach of norms) by focusing on what Nethercott calls "the idea of the criminal as flesh and blood reality in the dock." They argued that crime should be viewed through the lens of socioeconomic relations and that criminality was a direct function of poverty, social alienation, or disease (*RLC* 3).

V. D. Nabokov adopts two strategies in defending the classical school of criminal law against criminal sociology and anthropology. These strategies anticipate both the guiding methodology of *Problems of Idealism* and Fyodor's biography of Chernyshevski. The first, a procedural challenge, echoes the "contraband" critique of Russia's neo-idealist philosophers. V. D. Nabokov argues that the positivist conflation of law and criminal sociology fails because it ignores critical disciplinary boundaries: whereas criminal law is a legal discipline, criminal sociology is a social discipline; whereas a sociologist defines crime as a disruption of a community's normal conditions, a jurist defines crime as a breach of legal norms (Sm 4). He argues that "the true domain of influence for a jurist" must remain "criminal law itself, that is, the totality of legal norms that are used to regulate crime and punishment as legal relationships" (Sm 8). "For the Russian jurist, in particular," he repeats later, "it would be inexcusable to reject the autonomy of the discipline of criminal law" (Sm 10).

V. D. Nabokov's frustration with criminal sociologists whose "*pium desiderium* is the abolition of the entire system of legal concepts that have been derived from the study of criminal legislation" parallels the frustration of Russia's neo-idealist philosophers with the colonizing tendencies of sociology (Sm 6). His remarks about sociology's illegitimate incursions into the legal domain anticipate with striking precision Novgorodtsev's response in *Problems of Idealism* to the charge that his own legal philosophy is insufficiently sociological: "to insist on sociologism here," writes Novgorodtsev, "is as little appropriate as in mathematics, for example. It is necessary to abandon once and for all this thought that sociology is some kind of science of sciences, without which it is impossible to take a step: it is simply one possible research method, with a strictly defined sphere of application" (EIPL 299–300).

While V. D. Nabokov's insistence on the importance of disciplinary boundaries allies him with Russia's neo-idealists, he also anticipates their rejection of disciplinary isolationism. In particular, he praises the empirical sciences when they do not seek to annex other disciplines to themselves. "In pointing to the destructive tendencies of the representatives of the new school standing in opposition to the work of classical jurists," he states, "we do not mean to deny their contributions . . . to our discipline." By quoting Tagantsev, he notes that sociological research has provided criminal law with useful strategies for fighting recidivism, and that anthropological findings have helped it determine the importance of criminal classification (Sm 7–8).

He could acknowledge, then, that "the results of sociological and anthropological research can have and often did have great significance for jurists," but he also insisted that this kind of research should not become a juridical goal (Sm 9). Criminal law, he contends, cannot flourish under the spell of empiricism because it needs "proper guidance from theory" (Sm 11). V. D. Nabokov's insistence that legal theory should set juridical goals, and that the empirical sciences should play a decisively auxiliary role in the process, sets an important precedent for his son's assertion that natural science is ultimately responsible to philosophy rather than statistics.

THE GIFT AND RUSSIA'S "FATAL FLAW"

V. D. Nabokov's fictional stand-in, Konstantin Godunov-Cherdyntsev, is an eminent scientist rather than a distinguished jurist or prominent political reformer. And like his creator—that is, unlike his creator's father—he has little interest in political affairs (even though, suggestively, political affairs often interfere with his scientific endeavors). These differences notwithstanding, Godunov's scientific pursuits are organized around a set of conspicuously idealist principles that collide with the philosophical views of

Russian Marxism's most revered and influential Russian forebear. By having Fyodor launch his career with a biography of Chernyshevski, Nabokov targets the same enemy as the one chosen by the contributors to *Problems of Idealism:* the radical intelligentsia whose all-encompassing positivism and utilitarianism came to be regarded by many as having laid the groundwork for the Soviet tyranny.

Significantly, Fyodor's *Life of Chernyshevski* is not exhaustively critical. Fyodor reserves sincere praise for Chernyshevski's courage and spirit of self-sacrifice in his opposition to tsarist autocracy. He observes, for instance, "that such uncompromising radicals as Chernyshevski . . . were, no matter how you looked at it, real heroes in their struggle with the governmental order of things" (*Gift* 202–3). Fyodor thereby pays tribute not only to Chernyshevski, but also to a long line of Russian liberationists whose ranks would come to include V. D. Nabokov. Alexander Yakovlevich, one of Fyodor's closest acquaintances in Berlin, establishes this genealogy when he reminds a gathering of fellow émigrés that "the best principles of the Russian liberation movement" had their origins in the "basic features" of Chernyshevski's political struggle: "reverence for the whole human race, the cult of freedom, ideas of equality—equality of rights" (*Gift* 197).[64]

Although Fyodor admires Chernyshevski's courage and the political ideals attributed to him by Alexander Yakovlevich, he strenuously objects to their philosophical foundations. Indeed, a preoccupation with foundations moves Fyodor to undertake the biography, which can be viewed as the unexpected consequence of Fyodor's need to come to terms with the totalitarian dullness he encounters in a Soviet chess magazine:

> The conscientious student exercises of the young Soviet composers [of chess problems] were not so much "problems" as "tasks": cumbrously they treated of this or that mechanical theme . . . without a hint of poetry; these were chess comic strips, nothing more, and the shoving and jostling pieces did their clumsy work with proletarian seriousness, reconciling themselves to the presence of double solutions in the flat variants and to the agglomeration of police pawns. (*Gift* 174)

Fyodor finds himself struggling to reconstruct the intellectual pedigree of these Soviet chess problems:

> Suddenly he felt a bitter pang—why had everything in Russia become so shoddy, so crabbed and gray, how could she have been so befooled and befuddled? Or had the old urge "toward the light" concealed a fatal flaw, which in the course of progress toward the objective had grown more and more evident, until it was revealed that this "light" was burning in the window of a

> prison overseer, and that was all? When had this strange dependence sprung up between the sharpening of thirst and the muddying of the source? In the forties? in the sixties? and "what to do" now? (*Gift* 175)

The final question marks the dawning of an answer: "*chto delat'?* [what is to be done?]"[65] recalls Chernyshevski's famous novel *What Is to Be Done?* (1863) and its no less influential offspring: Lenin's pamphlet from 1902 named after Chernyshevski's novel. During his research for Chernyshevski's biography, Fyodor comes to identify this "fatal flaw" with the positivistic materialism that guided Chernyshevski and other Nihilists in their opposition to autocracy. Decades later, their positivistic materialism was used by Lenin to justify the Bolsheviks' violent overthrow of the Provisional Government. According to Fyodor, the utilitarian dreariness of these Soviet chess problems, and, indeed, Soviet totalitarianism itself, are direct products of a philosophical assault on human agency in which history is viewed as a predetermined march toward a materialist utopia.

Russian adaptations of Darwinism played an important role in the transformations lamented by Fyodor. Nihilists and their ideological allies made Darwin's theory of evolution a cornerstone in their opposition to autocracy. They saw in Darwin's emphasis on biological change and adaptation an irrefutable challenge to the official ideology's insistence on the timelessness of the established political order. Vucinich observes: "In the Russia of the 1860's Darwinism was widely accepted as an idea giving unity to all the sciences of life, a new philosophical orientation, and a call to social action."[66]

Nihilists and their successors (chiefly Populists, Anarchists, and Marxists) viewed Darwinism as an enormous victory for the spirit of science and sought to integrate Darwinian evolutionary theory into their positivist outlook. At the same time, ideological considerations promoted in these Russian radicals a deep skepticism toward Darwin's emphasis on the struggle for existence and natural selection as prime movers of evolution. Leading members of the radical intelligentsia worked to reconcile Darwinism with social theories that regarded cooperation, rather than conflict and competition, as the chief mechanism of social progress. As Vucinich observes, Social Darwinism found no home in Russia (*DRT* 30–31, 384–85).[67]

Like Chernyshevski and other spokesmen for Russia's radical groups, Nabokov was repelled by what many considered to be the ethical implications of Darwin's theory of evolution. His repulsion, however, was generated by different ideological reasons. Kinbote's frequently quoted "anti-Darwinian aphorism"—"The one who kills is *always* his victim's inferior"[68]—is adumbrated in Nabokov's early story "The Dragon" and elaborated once again in *King, Queen, Knave* (*VNRY* 280–81). In *Speak, Memory,* Nabokov anticipates Kinbote's adage with a witty inversion of the Marxist call for a proletarian revolution: "'Struggle for life' indeed! The curse of battle and toil leads man back to the boar, to the grunting beast's crazy obsession with the search for food. . . . Toilers of the world, disband! Old books are wrong. The world was made on a Sunday" (*SM* 617).

The Soviet chess problems that move Fyodor to write Chernyshevski's biography are hopelessly colored by the plodding utilitarianism that Nabokov associates with both Soviet rule and evolution driven exclusively by natural selection. Chernyshevski's demand that artists subject their work to social usefulness was no less repugnant to Nabokov. Like Chernyshevski's philosophy and Darwinian evolutionary theory, the chess problems composed under the Soviet dispensation are, in Nabokov's eyes, crude products of an ideology that sees the human being as nothing more than a laboring animal. In preparing his biography of Chernyshevski, Fyodor is convinced that he must "extend his field of activity two decades in either direction" (*Gift* 200). This scrupulously wide view of Chernyshevski's life and work would have exposed Fyodor (and, of course, Nabokov) to several significant and explicit connections between Russian Marxism and Darwinian evolutionary theory.

Kolakowski notes that the philosophical features of Russian Marxism were largely derived from Engels; his philosophical contributions "were upheld by later Marxists and regarded especially by the Russians (Plekhanov, Lenin) as the Marxist philosophy *par excellence.*" Though many Marxists believed that Engels's dialectic of nature clashed with Marx's philosophical principles, it was nevertheless congenial to the ontological preoccupations of Russia's radical philosophers. As Kolakowski observes, Engels formulated his argument that nature behaved dialectically

> under the influence of Darwin's discoveries and in the intellectual atmosphere of Darwinism. The main trend of opinion, shared by Engels, was to interpret life, knowledge, and social phenomena from the point of view of naturalism, which treats human history as a prolongation and a special case of natural history, and assumes that the general laws of nature apply, in specific forms, to the destiny of mankind.[69]

In the eyes of Lenin and George (Georgii) Plekhanov, the fathers of Russian Marxism, the naturalistic orientation of Engels's philosophy affirmed the intellectual bond between Russian radicalism (as exemplified by Chernyshevski) and its Western counterparts.

Plekhanov, the official philosopher of Russia's Social Democrats, especially agreed with Engels's insistence that Marxism is simply Darwinism applied to the study of human society (*DRT* 356–57, 384). (Engels offered this remark in a eulogy at Marx's graveside.) As Plekhanov wrote in *The De-*

velopment of the Monist View of History, Marx's singular achievement was a grand extension of Darwin's system:

> Darwin succeeded in solving the problem of how there originate vegetable and animal species in the struggle for existence. Marx succeeded in solving the problem of how there arise different types of social organization in the struggle of men for their existence. Logically, the investigation of Marx begins precisely where the investigation of Darwin ends. . . . The spirit of their research is absolutely the same in both thinkers. That is why one can say that Marxism is Darwinism in its application to social science.[70]

By the 1930s, when Nabokov was writing *The Gift,* the positivist-materialist-utilitarian tradition which had conscripted Darwinism into its struggle against autocracy had become a central component of the Soviet regime's ideological program. For those who, like Nabokov, surveyed Russian history from the vantage point of stinging disappointment, the heroic tradition associated with Chernyshevski and his fellow liberationists seemed to conceal a "fatal flaw." By contrast, the neo-idealist philosophers who had tried to root the struggle for freedom in idealist (rather than positivist) principles were retrospectively perceived as "prophetic and tragically accurate."[71]

CONTRABAND: FYODOR'S PROCEDURAL CRITIQUE

The Gift is Nabokov's most explicit and sustained attack on positivistic and utilitarian efforts to displace philosophy from what Nabokov regarded as its rightfully privileged position in human culture. He pursues this agenda by having Fyodor critique Chernyshevski's philosophical assumptions on two fronts. The first—procedural—attack replicates the "contraband" critique used by V. D. Nabokov, Vladimir Vernadskii, and the authors of *Problems of Idealism.*

Bulgakov's formulation of the concept of "contraband" became "one of the most important principles in the neo-idealist development of Russian liberalism" (EI 36). It also offers a particularly useful framework for understanding both Nabokov's decision to write Chernyshevski's biography and his lifelong unwillingness to accept the full contours of Darwin's system. Bulgakov observes that although scientific knowledge plays a vital role in establishing the laws governing physical phenomena, it cannot yield a final theory because positive science "studies only fragments of a reality that widens constantly beyond the eyes of the scientist." This perpetually receding horizon-line prevents science from answering pressing metaphysical and ethical questions. Bulgakov concludes that metaphysics alone can answer questions that lie beyond the ken of science.[72] Six decades later, Nabokov was still expressing a strikingly similar view.

When asked in a 1964 interview with Alvin Toffler about the place of the irrational "in an age when the exact knowledge of science has begun to plumb the most profound mysteries of existence," Nabokov immediately dismissed Toffler's premise. Calling this supposed victory "a journalistic illusion," he insisted that

> the greater one's science, the deeper the sense of mystery. Moreover, I don't believe that any science today has pierced any mystery. We, as newspaper readers, are inclined to call "science" the cleverness of an electrician or a psychiatrist's mumbo jumbo. This, at best, is applied science, and one of the characteristics of applied science is that yesterday's neutron or today's truth dies tomorrow. But even in a better sense of "science"—as the study of visible and palpable nature, or the poetry of pure mathematics and pure philosophy—the situation remains as hopeless as ever. We shall never know the origin of life, or the meaning of life, or the nature of space and time, or the nature of nature, or the nature of thought. (*SO* 44–45)

The elusive nature of human knowledge is also, in part, determined by what Nabokov viewed as the inescapably subjective character of human cognition. In an interview two years earlier, Nabokov had explained:

> Reality is a very subjective affair. I can only define it as a kind of gradual accumulation of information; and as specialization. If we take a lily, for instance, or any other kind of natural object, a lily is more real to a naturalist than it is to an ordinary person. But it is still more real to a botanist. And yet another stage of reality is reached with that botanist who is a specialist in lilies. You can get nearer and nearer, so to speak, to reality; but you never get near enough because reality is an infinite succession of steps, levels of perception, false bottoms, and hence unquenchable, unattainable. You can know more and more about one thing but you can never know everything about one thing: it's hopeless. (*SO* 10–11)

Nabokov's simultaneous faith in and skepticism about science has an important precedent in Vernadskii's companion piece to *Problems of Idealism.* In "O nauchnom mirovozzrenii" ("On the Scientific Worldview"), Vernadskii supported the symposium's neo-idealist program by arguing that the scientific worldview is subject to the same limitations as art, religion, and philosophy. "The historian of science," he observes, "must always keep in mind that the picture he is providing is incomplete and limited . . . since he is dealing with the unfinished and, perhaps, infinite process of the development or discovery of the human intellect."[73] As Bailes notes, Vernadskii's sensitivity to the epistemological limitations of science led him to insist that scientific inquiry requires a tolerant environment in which scientific views can be openly debated, altered, and refuted.[74]

Vernadskii insisted further that the scientific worldview does not provide an objective account of reality but rather "a complex and idiosyncratic expression of social psychology [*slozhnym i svoeobraznym vyrazheniem obshchestvennoi psikhologii*]" (Onm 1461–62). Though unchanging scientific truths have been discovered, these form a small part of the scientific worldview. The latter, in turn, is inescapably contaminated by the biases of human cognition and social contingency:

> Only a few, still very small, areas of the scientific worldview which have been proven irrefutably correspond to formal reality and are scientific truths. Its strictly and precisely observed individual parts and aggregations of facts may be indubitable and fully correspond with reality, but their explanation, significance, and connection with other natural phenomena are perceived by us differently during different time periods. Undoubtedly, during any time period, the true and accurate is always closely mixed and interconnected with the schemes and constructions of our intellect. . . . The scientific worldview is not a depiction of the cosmos revealing its eternal and stable features to an autonomous human intellect. [*Nauchnoe mirovozzreniie ne est' kartina Kosmosa, kotoraia raskryvaetsia v svoikh vechnykh i nezyblemykh chertakh pered izuchaiushchim ee, nezavisimym ot Kosmosa, chelovecheskim razumom*]. (Onm 1417)

Vernadskii's strict differentiation between scientific facts and scientific worldviews establishes a precedent for Nabokov's willingness to acknowledge the truth of evolution "as a modal formula" while resisting the view that evolutionary "links and steps of life" can provide an understanding of life itself. Echoing Vernadskii's skepticism about scientific worldviews erected upon flimsy factual foundations, Nabokov objects to positivistic-materialist-utilitarian conceptions of reality derived from Darwin's theory of evolution.[75]

According to Vernadskii, scientism is incompatible with the true spirit of scientific inquiry because it fails to acknowledge that science derives its authority from philosophy. His rejection of the view that science will one day supplant philosophy offers a way to interpret Nabokov's curious response to F. Martin Brown. Vernadskii asserts that the view that philosophy will be made redundant by science

> can hardly pass the test of science itself. Throughout human history we have never observed the existence of science without philosophy, and, when we study the history of scientific thought, we see that philosophical concepts

> and philosophical ideas have always entered into science as necessary, all-penetrating factors. Only in abstract form and in the imagination (which do not correspond to reality) can science and the scientific worldview have sufficient weight of their own, developing without the influence of ideas and concepts developed in a spiritual sphere by other means. (Onm 1432)

Science must draw its legitimacy from philosophy, but philosophy cannot disregard scientific facts: "The growth of science inevitably calls forth, in its turn, an extraordinary expansion of the boundaries of the human spirit's philosophical and religious consciousness; religion and philosophy, having grasped the facts discovered by the scientific worldview, expand further and further the secret recesses of the human mind" (Onm 1437). The relationship between science and philosophy is not, however, egalitarian. Science depends upon philosophy in a way that outstrips philosophy's responsibility to science:[76]

> The system that guides scientific thinking is crude and imperfect; it is mainly improved through the philosophical work of the human intellect. . . . For philosophy and religion are closely connected to those forces of the human spirit that run deeper than logic and whose influence has a powerful impact on how logical inferences are perceived and understood. (Onm 1454–55)

Vernadskii refined *Problems of Idealism*'s "contraband" critique by insisting that the necessary cross-fertilization between science and other spheres of human activity cannot be allowed to compromise disciplinary autonomy. All disciplines develop interdependently (Onm 1431), but they overreach their authority when they seek to bring other disciplines under their command. Much as Christianity sought unsuccessfully to suppress the advancement of science, science cannot but fail in its efforts to abolish religion:

> It is possible that the same result will be achieved by the trends that are currently observed in science, when science is beginning to assume the same position relative to religions as Christianity has occupied for a long time relative to science. Just as Christianity was not capable of defeating science in its *domain,* but was able in the course of this struggle to better define its own essence, similarly science will not be capable of overcoming Christianity or any other religion, but will more closely determine and clarify the boundaries of its own authority. (Onm 1433–34; emphasis in original)

According to Vernadskii's version of the "contraband" critique, disciplinary symbiosis must strike a balance with disciplinary autonomy: "all these sides of human spiritual life, while powerfully affecting one another, are completely distinct in the fields they occupy" (Onm 1434). This principle leads Vernadskii to reject the possibility that a final, all-encompassing theory is within reach (Onm 1444).

The harmonious coexistence of disciplinary symbiosis and autonomy postulated by Vernadskii provides a useful interpretive framework for Nabokov's various expressions about the bonds of kinship connecting art and science. "There is no science without fancy, and no art without facts," he told Alfred Appel, Jr., in an interview from 1966 (*SO* 79). His concluding remarks in the "Translator's Introduction" to *Eugene Onegin* state that "in art as in science there is no delight without the detail." When he expressed similar views on other occasions, he implied that the crossover between these different spheres of human endeavor is a function of their dependence upon humanity's higher faculties, or, to quote Vernadskii, they are all "sides of human spiritual life" (Onm 1434). Nabokov insisted to his students: "A book, no matter what it is—a work of fiction or a work of science (the boundary line between the two is not as clear as is generally believed)—a book of fiction appeals first of all to the mind" (*LL* 3–4).[77]

Vernadskii never abandoned his early skepticism toward the capacity of science to provide a comprehensive account of reality. In his final work, published a year after Nabokov denied that "science has begun to plumb the most profound mysteries of existence," Vernadskii wrote that a scientist "cannot forget, as Newton clearly expressed at the end of his life, that compared with the masses of questions which we can pose and attempt to answer about the awesome phenomena of reality, he was like a little boy constructing sand castles on a beach."[78]

Like Vernadskii, the contributors to *Problems of Idealism* challenged scientism by insisting that no sphere of inquiry can rightfully encroach upon the territory of another. At the same time (like Vernadskii again), they repeatedly assigned philosophy a privileged place within these delimited spheres of inquiry. Bulgakov notes: "Precise knowledge, metaphysics, and religion must exist in a certain harmonious relation, the establishment of which always constitutes the task of philosophy" (BP 89).

As the symposium's most elaborate account of the "contraband" critique, Bulgakov's opening essay lays the methodological foundation for Fyodor's engagement with Chernyshevski's philosophical materialism. According to Bulgakov, a mechanistic worldview cannot sustain a theory of progress because it cannot identify goals worth pursuing. Political and economic democracy, and the free development and perfectibility of the person, are ideals derived from ethics and metaphysics (BP 105). A theory of progress such as Marx and Engels's scientific socialism is a theodicy and is thus incompatible with a strict positivistic dispensation (BP 91). The conviction that positive science can provide humanity with such goals "arises from the same source generally as all religious truths, or what is religiously taken for truth. Its source is *religious faith,* but a faith that has crept in clandestinely, as contraband, without regal grandeur, but that has nonetheless secured regal dominion where it was assumed only science was called to rule" (BP 96).

Fyodor employs a version of the "contraband" critique in his attempt to discredit Chernyshevski's materialism, gleefully calling attention to the confusions scattered across Chernyshevski's philosophical writings. Among such "fatal inner contradictions" is "the dualism of the monist Chernyshevski's aesthetics—where 'form' and 'content' are distinct, with 'content' preeminent—or, more exactly, with 'form' playing the role of the soul and 'content' the role of the body; and the muddle is augmented by the fact that this 'soul' consists of mechanical components" (*Gift* 239; see also 246, 256). Echoing Vernadskii and Russia's neo-idealist philosophers, Fyodor ridicules the notion that materialism can provide a complete account of human existence: "Such methods of knowledge as dialectical materialism curiously resemble the unscrupulous advertisements for patent medicines, which cure all illnesses at once." This assessment is not meant to suggest that materialism is entirely without value as a narrower philosophical category: "Still," Fyodor concedes, "such an expedient can occasionally help with a cold" (*Gift* 249). Intellectual integrity, he implies, echoing his father, is founded upon a scrupulous respect for disciplinary boundaries.

Fyodor challenges Plekhanov's contention that greater philosophical rigor could have averted the contradictions that undermine Chernyshevski's reputation as a materialist philosopher. He does this first by calling attention to Plekhanov's observation that Chernyshevski occasionally lapses into ontological dualism when explaining historical events as products of conscious calculation rather than blind economic forces. In Plekhanov's view such self-interested calculations qualify as opinions, and opinions can only be accommodated by philosophical idealism.[79] Fyodor, however, applies Plekhanov's critique of Chernyshevski to Plekhanov himself, suggesting that the very existence of human thought refutes materialist doctrine: "Anything which comes into the focus of human thinking is spiritualized. Thus the 'calculation' of the materialists was ennobled; thus, for those in the know, matter turns into an incorporeal play of mysterious forces" (*Gift* 282). Fyodor's argument recalls Bulgakov's assertion that "all philosophers are metaphysicians by the very nature of human thought" (BP 87).

PLAY: FYODOR'S FIRST METAPHYSICAL CRITIQUE

Fyodor replicates the two-pronged methodology of *Problems of Idealism* and his father's inaugural lecture when he supplements his procedural refutation of Chernyshevski's materialism with a metaphysical critique.[80] In a manner that is consonant with Nabokov's own later arguments in *Speak, Memory,* Fyodor contends that nature's inherent playfulness belies both Darwinism and Chernyshevski's utilitarian materialism. Fyodor learns from his father that the sophistication of mimetic disguise "was not explainable by the struggle for existence" but "seemed to have been invented by some waggish artist precisely for the intelligent eyes of man" (*Gift* 110). This elevation of play to the status of philosophical first principle informs Fyodor's approach to his surroundings in Berlin. A casual glimpse of two postal workers amusing themselves spurs Fyodor's metaphysical meditations:

> Beyond the bridge, near the small public garden, two elderly postal workers, having completed their check of a stamp machine and grown suddenly playful, were stealing up from behind the jasmine, one behind the other, one imitating the other's gestures, toward a third—who with eyes closed was humbly and briefly relaxing on a bench before his working day—in order to tickle his nose with a flower. Where shall I put all these gifts with which the summer morning rewards me—and only me? Save them up for future books? Use them immediately for a practical handbook: *How to Be Happy*? Or getting deeper, to the bottom of things: understand what is concealed behind all this, behind the play, the sparkle, the thick, green grease-paint of the foliage? For there really is something, there is something! And one wants to offer thanks but there is no one to thank. The list of donations already made: 10,000 days—from Person Unknown. (*Gift* 328)

Thomas Karshan has provided an illuminating account of the aesthetic, philosophical, and ideological preoccupations that intersect in Nabokov's inclination to see the world as intrinsically playful. Karshan traces this interest in play to Nabokov's first contribution to the literary circle founded by Aikhenvald and Raisa Tatarinov. The same month, Nabokov's paper was published in the Latvian journal *Slovo* as a report on a heavyweight boxing match between Hans Breitensträter and Paolino Uzcudun.[81] The report's introductory remarks—written by Nabokov at the age of twenty-five—celebrate the playful nature of existence:

> Everything in the world is playing [*vse v mire igraet*]: the blood in the beloved's veins, the sun on the water, and the musician on the violin. Everything good in life—love, nature, the arts and family puns—is play. And when we are truly at play, whether we are destroying a tin battalion with a pea, or we meet over the rope barrier of a tennis net, we feel deeply in our muscles the true essence of that play which occupies that astonishing juggler who tosses from hand to hand, in an unbroken sparkling parabola, the planets of the universe.[82]

Nabokov's commitment to play as a foundational aesthetic and metaphysical principle is reaffirmed in *The Gift*'s efforts to refute the philosophical foundations of Russia's radical tradition. Though the novel's fourth chapter seeks specifically to discredit Chernyshevski's philosophical ideas, it also raises its sights on his successors. In a letter from July 14, 1938, to his American literary agent Altagracia de Jannelli, Nabokov wrote that Chernyshevski's biography "lifts my novel to a wider plane, lending it an epic note and, so to say, spreading my hero's individual butter over the bread of a whole epoch. In this work (Chernyshevski's life), the defeat of Marxism and materialism is not only made evident, but it is rounded out by my hero's artistic triumph" (*SL* 27).

If one of Nabokov's chief aims in writing Chernyshevski's biography was to refute "Marxism and materialism," his central opponents would have been Plekhanov and Lenin, the fathers of Russian Marxism. Together with Chernyshevski, Plekhanov is identified by James Scanlan as Russia's most distinguished and influential theoretician of philosophical materialism. Scanlan observes further that both Plekhanov and Lenin "name as their first philosophical master neither Marx nor Engels but the Russian radical publicist Nicholas Chernyshevski."[83] They are, above all, indebted to Chernyshevski's materialism, a fact to which Fyodor alludes when he quotes Lenin's assertion in *Materialism and Empirio-Criticism* (1909) that Chernyshevski was "the only truly great writer who managed to remain on a level of unbroken philosophical materialism from the fifties right up until 1888" (*Gift* 245).

Fyodor is quoting from the "Supplement to Chapter Four, Section I" (subtitled "From What Angle Did N. G. Chernyshevsky Criticise Kantianism?") of Lenin's philosophical magnum opus.[84] Here Lenin mobilizes Chernyshevski's philosophy to refute (and abuse) his adversaries in the Social-Democratic Party. Chernyshevski is described as "the great Russian Hegelian and materialist" who "regards as metaphysical nonsense *all* deviations from materialism, both in the direction of idealism and in the direction of agnosticism."[85] Lenin suggests in conclusion that Chernyshevski's theoretical contributions would have rivaled those of Marx and Engels had Russian life been less backward.

In his memoir *Encounters with Lenin* (*Vstrechi s Leninym*), Nikolai Volskii (better known under his pen name Nikolai Valentinov) reports that Lenin confessed to him and others that Chernyshevski introduced him to philosophical materialism and played the most decisive role in his political and intellectual development. Though Nabokov could not have read Volskii's book before writing *The Gift* (it was published for the first time in 1953 with an introduction by Nabokov's friend Michael Karpovich), he may have felt retrospective vindication had he read Volskii's redaction of Lenin's assertion that "Chernyshevski was my favorite author. . . . You can't find another

Russian revolutionary who understood and condemned the cowardly, base, and perfidious nature of every kind of liberalism with such thoroughness, acumen, and force as Chernyshevski did. . . . Only Chernyshevski had a real, overpowering influence on me before I got to know the works of Marx, Engels, and Plekhanov, and it started with *What Is to Be Done?*"[86]

By the time Nabokov wrote *The Gift,* Lenin and Chernyshevski were already tightly coupled in his mind. Fyodor quotes the words Lenin's lifelong partner, Nadezhda Krupskaia, addressed to Lunacharskii: "There was hardly anyone Vladimir Ilyich liked so much . . . I think he had a great deal in common with Chernyshevski." In the same paragraph, Fyodor refers to the assertion made by Chernyshevski's biographer, Yuri M. Steklov, that Chernyshevski's "The Anthropological Principle in Philosophy" was the "first philosophical manifesto of Russian communism" (*Gift* 246).

Another admirer and intellectual descendant of Chernyshevski was Plekhanov, Russia's leading Marxist theorist. He, too, publicly acknowledged a profound debt to Chernyshevski: "My own intellectual development occurred under the enormous influence of Chernyshevski; the analysis of his views was a major event in my literary life."[87] Plekhanov defended materialism on the ground that nothing falls outside the purview of utilitarian explanations. In his *N. G. Chernyshevsky,* Plekhanov turns his attention to *play,* an activity in which he sees a challenge to materialist doctrine. He begins his polemic by distancing himself from Chernyshevski's utilitarian prescriptions for artistic production. He argues that Chernyshevski was wrong to counter the Kantian notion that "art is play" with a polemical assertion that art must serve a utilitarian purpose. Plekhanov agrees with Kant's assertion that "art is play," but he departs from Kant in deriving from this maxim further evidence for a materialist conception of reality. Drawing on the work of Herbert Spencer and Wilhelm Wundt, Plekhanov argues that art is a materialist endeavor because play replicates activities that promote survival. Plekhanov's conclusion that "play is the child of labor" enables him to argue that art is biologically determined.[88]

This argument figured prominently in Plekhanov's lifelong polemic against philosophical idealism. In her introduction to the fifth volume of the Soviet edition of Plekhanov's philosophical works, V. Shcherbina writes: "The consistency and persistence with which he advanced the idea that art is socially conditioned is explained by the vital need to eliminate idealism and vulgar views of all kinds from the path of revolutionary thought."[89] Plekhanov includes a more detailed account of his views on the relationship between play and labor in his *Unaddressed Letters* (pub. serially 1899–1900), a historically materialist account of the origins and development of art. "Work is older than art," he asserts with emphasis, for "man first looked upon objects and phenomena from the utilitarian standpoint, and only later did he begin to regard them from the aesthetic standpoint."[90] He further admits that the entire materialist edifice would crumble if the reverse could be demonstrated:

> If play really were older than work, and art really older than the production of useful things, then the materialist explanation of history—at least in the form the author of *Capital* imparts to it—*would not stand up to the criticism of facts,* and my whole argument would have to be turned upside down: I would have to argue from the dependence of economic activity on art, not from the dependence of art on economic activity.[91]

Nabokov's familiarity with Plekhanov may well have been limited to the latter's writings on Chernyshevski, but those writings would have supplied him with ample evidence of Plekhanov's ideological subordination of play to labor. The prominence of this argument in Plekhanov's *N. G. Chernyshevsky* makes it possible to view Nabokov's insistence in *The Gift* that play is a foundational metaphysical category as part of his larger effort to refute Plekhanov's philosophical claims.

Karshan has persuasively argued that the most important influence on Nabokov's ideas about play was Aikhenvald's essay "Pokhvala prazdnosti" ("Praise of Idleness"), and that "Braitenshtreter-Paolino" extends the older man's tribute to play.[92] Aikhenvald anticipates Nabokov's elevation of play to the status of philosophical first principle by invoking Adam and Eve's prelapsarian life in the Garden of Eden. He writes that "industriousness is not an absolute virtue," but "the punishment brought upon us by God's hand . . . , a characteristic of servitude which has eaten away deeply into the distorted heart of humanity over centuries of forced labor."[93] Cultural and technological progress should seek to recover this lost state of fecund idleness in order to liberate humankind from its enslavement to labor. Aikhenvald speaks as a committed idealist for whom play is the most direct manifestation of humanity's spiritual essence:

> We must not leave our bodies and our spirits inactive, but develop them as integrated physical-spiritual organisms; such development is achieved not through labor but through creative *play,* in the broadest and philosophical, Schillerian meaning of this word. By "play" we mean pleasurable work, work without strain and effort, capable of causing excitement and arousing curiosity in such a way as to cease being experienced as work. By "play" we will understand a free and graceful movement of forces, an unconstrained and uncoerced artistic creativity. After all, the human being is an artist, a free artist, and the more leisure he has, the more wholeheartedly he can give himself to art both in an aesthetic sense, as well as in the sense of a more general and

all-encompassing artistic work that is part of the architectonic construction of the world in spiritual collaboration with the Creator.[94]

Fyodor is the fictional embodiment of the type of creature Aikhenvald envisions. His last-minute decision to skip an appointment with a student he is paid to tutor is characteristic of his life in Berlin:

> But suddenly the unpleasant feeling of lateness was replaced in Fyodor's soul by a distinct and somehow outrageously joyful decision not to appear at all for the lesson—to get off at the next stop and return home to his half-read book, to his unworldly cares, to the blissful mist in which his real life floated, to the complex, happy, devout work which had occupied him for about a year already. He knew that today he would receive payment for several lessons, knew that otherwise he would have to smoke and eat again on credit, but he was quite reconciled to this for the sake of that energetic idleness . . . , for the sake of the lofty truancy he was allowing himself. And he was allowing it not for the first time. Shy and exacting, living always uphill, spending all his strength in pursuit of the innumerable beings that flashed inside him, as if at dawn in a mythological grove, he could no longer force himself to mix with people either for money or for pleasure, and therefore he was poor and solitary. (*Gift* 83)

The artistic imperatives that prevent Fyodor from tending to his material needs seem eager to undermine Plekhanov's conceptualization of art as a mimic form of labor. Qualifying as neither work nor play, Fyodor's lifestyle leads him to embrace the kind of productive idleness that Aikhenvald posited as the highest achievement of human life.[95]

Fyodor understands his own scorn for aesthetic and ethical utilitarianism as a paternal inheritance. Godunov, too, disdained the utilitarian impulse of the social and applied sciences privileged by Chernyshevski and Plekhanov. Fyodor writes that his father "was entirely uninterested in ethnography, a fact that for some reason greatly irritated certain geographers, and his great friend, the Orientalist Krivtsov, almost wept when reproaching him: 'If only you had brought back one wedding song, Konstantin Kirillovich, had described one local dress!'" (*Gift* 113). In "Father's Butterflies," Fyodor draws attention to his father's refusal to put his scientific knowledge in the service of practical considerations:

> He detested applied entomology—and I cannot imagine how he could work in present-day Russia, where his beloved science is wholly reduced to anti-locust campaigns or class struggles against agricultural saboteurs. This horrid debasement of "sublime curiosity" and its hybridization with unnatural

> factors (social ones, for instance) explain (apart from the general numbing of Russia) the artificial oblivion that has befallen his work in his homeland. (FB 213)

Fyodor's reflections upon his father's scientific legacy establish the ideological foundations of Godunov's aristocratic contempt for applied science. Like non-utilitarian forms of artistic expression, pure science was viewed with hostility not only by the Nihilists and their allies but also by the Soviet state.

The Soviet emphasis on practical applications of scientific knowledge (especially as they related to the country's economy and national defense) tied funding for scientific research to usefulness.[96] Writing for an audience familiar with Russian history, Fyodor hardly needs to mention that the Soviet approach to scientific matters marked no real departure from the approach of the tsars. Nicholas II, for instance, was following in the footsteps of his reactionary father when he promoted specialized technical and commercial schools at the expense of the country's universities. This programmatic assault upon university education was inspired by a conviction that trade schools were less subversive than universities.[97] Godunov's—and by extension Nabokov's—quarrel with applied science is therefore only superficially elitist. Instead, their passionate defense of pure science can be seen as a form of resistance against tsarist and Soviet infringements upon intellectual freedom.[98]

FATE AND FREE WILL: FYODOR'S SECOND METAPHYSICAL CRITIQUE

V. D. Nabokov never constructed a systematic account of his philosophical views, but his juridical writings and documented beliefs suggest that he had much in common with Russia's neo-idealist philosophers. Most significantly, he shared their view that the human individual cannot be fully explained by empirical observation alone. He also replicated their argument that this irreducibility is bound up with the concept of self-determination:

> In all the phenomena that come into being by means of the creative power of the human mind, there is something that does not yield to ultimate, exhaustive analysis [*est' nechto, ne poddaiushcheesia konechnomu, ischerpyvaiushchemu analizu*]. In ignoring this factor, we are at risk of not understanding or understanding one-sidedly the phenomenon under discussion, since mind and will are capable of rising above the external circumstances of environment, time period, and so on [*razum i volia sposobny stat' vyshe vnesh-*

> *nikh uslovii sredy, epokhi i t.d.*]. As an example of such an error, we can refer to [Hippolyte] Taine's "History of English Literature." The book adheres to the view that literature is a natural product of race, environment, and time while, in principle, leaving no room at all for free individual activity in accordance with the notion that human vice and virtue are essentially the same kinds of by-products as sulphuric acid or sugar. As a result, the author cannot adhere firmly to his own method, since it becomes completely incomprehensible how, during the same time period and under the same conditions, such absolutely perfect antitheses as the works of Byron and the works of Keats could appear. (Sm 18)

The human being's innermost core, V. D. Nabokov concludes, "will remain forever mysterious, never fully expressed, never completely understood." "The operation of chemical reagents," he states further, can neither explain human consciousness nor predict the consequences of its actions (Sm 19).

Several other considerations suggest idealist sympathies. Boyd notes that V. D. Nabokov observed formal religious practices such as taking his younger children to church and reading the "Twelve Evangels" at Easter as required by Russian Orthodox custom (*VNRY* 153; see also 72). While serving time in prison, he read the Bible daily because, as he notes in his prison reflections published as *Tiuremnye dosugi,* he wanted to know it beyond the familiar Gospels.[99] In speaking about a nineteenth-century Russian philanthropist to the Russian chapter of the International Union of Criminalists, V. D. Nabokov stated, without the least trace of self-consciousness, that "the fragrant purity of his moral makeup was truly a gift from God" (and emphatically not, as he elaborated further, "the fruit of a conscientious effort to mortify the flesh or a rational aspiration for self-perfection").[100] Though his literary son did not share his father's religious conservatism,[101] the two did share an abiding interest in the workings of fate.

In the obituary printed in *Russkaia mysl'* on the occasion of V. D. Nabokov's death, Peter Struve suggested that V. D. Nabokov was convinced that his life was organized by fatidic patterns: "In the depths of every great individual there is always a vital idea, a defining metaphysical feeling [*opredeliaiushchee metafizicheskoe oshchushchenie*]. Calm, almost cold, and in any case always reserved and frequently skeptical, Nabokov carried in his soul this kind of profound feeling. This was the feeling of fate [*oshchushchenie roka*]."[102] Readers of *The Gift* will note the striking parallel between Struve's description of V. D. Nabokov's "defining metaphysical feeling" and Fyodor's description of the "most important" attribute of his father's personality:

> In and around my father, around this clear and direct strength, there was something difficult to convey in words, a haze, a mystery, an enigmatic re-

> serve which made itself felt sometimes more, sometimes less. . . . It sometimes seems to me nowadays that—who knows—he might go off on his journeys not so much to seek something as to flee something, and that on returning, he would realize that it was still with him, inside him, unriddable, inexhaustible. I cannot track down a name for his secret, but I only know that that was the source of that special—neither glad nor morose, having indeed no connection with the outward appearance of human emotions—solitude to which neither my mother nor all the entomologists of the world had any admittance. (*Gift* 114-15)

As Boyd notes, Nabokov's mother wrote to her son expressing her astonishment at the accuracy with which he had managed to capture in Godunov every nuance of her husband's personality (*VNRY* 398).

In his memoir *V dvukh vekakh* (*Two Centuries*), Joseph Hessen tells a story that bears out Peter Struve's reminiscences. Upon his release from the Smolnyi where he had been detained by the Bolsheviks, V. D. Nabokov hurried to the Mariinskii Theater to attend a benefit performance for the Literary Fund (he was the organization's president). In response to his friends' anxiety about his safety, he coolly replied that "the bullet meant for me has not yet been poured [*Eshche ne otlita pulia, kotoraia dlia menia prednaznachena*]" (*Vdv* 381–82). In the narrative trajectory he lends to his father's life in *Speak, Memory,* Nabokov pays tribute to the eerie fact that his father was finally slain by a bullet. As Boyd has noted about the autobiography, "again and again Nabokov foreshadows his father's death, reticently but ineluctably, as if he had no choice but to reconstitute the insidious designs of fate" (*VNRY* 9).

It is perhaps surprising that a man who dedicated himself so thoroughly to the struggle for political freedom should believe in fate. The same paradox structures the novels and autobiography of his son. The idea that life is ordered by fate was deeply appealing to Nabokov. Boyd has compellingly argued that he felt liberated rather than degraded by the thought that he could discern fatidic patterns in his life. Boyd further contends that John Shade's approach to this conundrum in *Pale Fire* also applies to his maker: "Yet far from being appalled at the way even his most creative acts and freest fancies disclose a deeper design somehow working through him, he seems to sense an infinite tenderness behind it all, prompting his imagination to the utmost, taking care of his present with an eye to what will come, in a way that not only permits but promotes his freedom."[103]

Nabokov's attempt to reconcile the competing claims of fate and free will is most elaborately described in *The Real Life of Sebastian Knight.* The novel's narrator explains that his half-brother's novel *Success* "deals mainly with the methods of human fate." These methods are never tyrannical because they are never foolproof. Though fate is eagerly intent upon bringing the novel's protagonists together ("touching up now this possibility now that one; . . . timing the least detail and leaving nothing to chance"), chance and human autonomy effortlessly derail its plans ("the shadow of a flaw, the stopped hole of an unwatched possibility, a caprice of free will . . . spoils the necessitarian's pleasure and the two lives are diverging again with increased rapidity"). When success is finally achieved, "it is reached by such delicate machinations that not the merest click is audible when at last the two are brought together."[104]

But Nabokov also acknowledged that "the contrapuntal genius of human fate" or the "tender ghosts humoring a lucky mortal," as he calls these agents in his autobiography, were not always benevolent (*SM* 479). Shade's faith in the "iambic" rhythm of "galaxies divine" is cruelly betrayed when he is shot and killed only moments after articulating his newfound metaphysical optimism (*PF* lines 975–76). These moments of doubt underscore Nabokov's reluctance to let his metaphysical yearnings congeal into dogma. He worried that fate was a construct of the human mind and he worried further that if fate did exist, it might be insensitive, ungenerous, and cruel. In the preface to *The Defense,* Nabokov casts himself as an evil demiurge who playfully and methodically destroys Luzhin:

> I greatly enjoyed taking advantage of this or that image and scene to introduce a fatal pattern into Luzhin's life and to endow the description of a garden, a journey, a sequence of humdrum events, with the semblance of a game of skill, and, especially in the final chapters, with that of a regular chess attack demolishing the innermost elements of the poor fellow's sanity. (*Def* 8)

But if Nabokov was skeptical about divine benevolence (and even about the existence of a deity), he seems to have felt no anxiety that personal autonomy was diminished by fate. He seems to have felt invigorated by his intuitions that an otherworldly force steered his life in competition with chance and free will; he certainly celebrated the possibility that it had done so in his love for Véra, and *The Gift* does the same for Fyodor and Zina. It may be that his willingness to live with the contradictions posed by his yearning to believe in the coexistence of fate and free will was, as so much else in his life, conditioned by his energetic hostility toward positivism and materialist determinism. The existence of fate may serve as a challenge to the possibility of full human freedom, but it would also unequivocally refute schools of thought that were deeply repugnant to Nabokov.

Like free will, then, fatidic patterns have the power to refute materialist determinism, and it is therefore fitting that they provide organizing principles for Fyodor's and Chernyshevski's lives. The arrangements that bring together Fyodor and Zina grant Fyodor the thrill of retrospective recognition (*Gift* 363–64). Fate also plays a conspicuous role in Fyodor's understanding of Chernyshevski's destiny. Quoting extensively from the work of an invented biographer, Fyodor depicts fate as Chernyshevski's nemesis:

> Such was the fate of Chernyshevski that everything turned against him: no matter what subject he touched there would come to light—insidiously, and with the most taunting inevitability—something that was completely opposed to his conception of it. . . . For everything he was returned "a negative hundredfold," in Strannolyubski's happy phrase, for everything he was back-kicked by his own dialectic, for everything the gods had their revenge on him. (*Gift* 217)[105]

Fate's cruelest revenge is to provide Chernyshevski with a son who would come to reject every aspect of his father's positivism:

> Created apparently out of everything that his father could not stand, Sasha, hardly out of his boyhood, developed a passion for everything that was weird, chimerical, and incomprehensible to his contemporaries—he lost himself in E.T.A. Hoffmann and Edgar Poe, was fascinated by pure mathematics, and a little later he was one of the first in Russia to appreciate the French "*poètes maudits.*" (*Gift* 296)

Chernyshevski's philosophical convictions rendered him incapable of dealing with his son's developing mental illness: "Chernyshevski drove Sasha to agonizing insomnia with his endless admonitions (as a 'materialist' he had the fanatic effrontery to suppose that the main cause of Sasha's disorder was his 'pitiful material condition'), and he himself suffered in a way that he had not done even in Siberia" (*Gift* 298).

Chernyshevski's troubled relationship with his son provides a sharp counterpoint to the relationship between Fyodor and his father, emphasizing the myriad differences between Chernyshevski and Godunov. Fyodor flirts with the possibility—if perhaps only metaphorically—that fate had sentenced Chernyshevski to a journey that resembled in so many ways the one to which passion drove Godunov. Chernyshevski's journey was yet another punishment, fate's insistence that the hardened materialist acknowledge the spiritualized nature of the universe:

> There lurks a secret retribution in the fact that he who had constructed his philosophy on a basis of knowing the world was now placed, naked and alone, amidst the bewitched, strangely luxuriant, and still incompletely described nature of northeast Siberia: an elemental, mythological punishment which had not been taken into account by his human judges. (*Gift* 244)

Callously indifferent to the vast disparity between the circumstances surrounding his father's and Chernyshevski's journeys to Siberia, Fyodor laments Chernyshevski's extreme boredom and longing for reading material as he traveled through the distant lands Godunov would explore so zestfully years later (*Gift* 284).

The most explicit contrast between Chernyshevski's and Godunov's philosophical commitments emerges in "Father's Butterflies." Written most likely in early 1939 and preserved at the Library of Congress since the 1950s, the 52-page manuscript describes Godunov's revolutionary "spherical" theory of natural classification (FB 198–99). Fyodor acknowledges that Godunov's contemporaries dismissed his theory as confused and delirious, but he reminds his readers that groundbreaking scientific discoveries often meet with derision (FB 215).[106]

According to Godunov's theory of natural classification, thought predates the evolutionary process:

> How is it conceivable, in fact, that amid the huge jumble containing the embryos of countless organs (of which up to forty-three are currently represented), the magnificent chaos of nature never included *thought*? One can doubt the ability of a genius to animate marble, but one cannot doubt that one afflicted by idiocy will never create a Galatea. Human intelligence, with all its limitations and rights, inasmuch as it is a gift of nature, and a perpetually repeated one, cannot fail to exist in the warehouse of the bestower. It may, in that dark storehouse, differ from its species seen in sunlight as a marble god is distinct from the convolutions of the sculptor's brain—but still it *exists*. (FB 219; emphasis in original)

Godunov's deductive logic echoes Novgorodtsev's contribution to *Problems of Idealism,* where Novgorodtsev challenges the view that morality is socially constructed. Novgorodtsev anticipates Godunov's argument when he states that the basic mistake of a "positivist-historical" conception of ethics

> has long been indicated by philosophers who remained free of positivist prejudices. It was long ago explained how it is scarcely possible, by the path of evolution, to account for the development of everything from nothing and to forget that the development of something becomes incomprehensible unless we admit the existence of "a substratum already containing elements, if only in potential, of what will later emerge." (EIPL 296)[107]

Like Novgorodtsev's metaphysically grounded understanding of conscience, Godunov's insistence that thought is irreducible to mechanistic evolutionary processes contrasts sharply with Chernyshevski's contention that the human intellect is fundamentally no different from that of non-human animals. "Thinking," Chernyshevski claims, "consists in choosing with the aid of memory from the different combinations of sensations and conceptions prepared by the imagination those that correspond to the needs of the thinking organism at the given moment." To illustrate his point, Chernyshevski dismisses any qualitative difference between "the process that takes place in Newton's nervous system in discovering the law of gravity and the process that takes place in the nervous system of the fowl that finds an oat grain in a dung heap."[108]

Godunov employs several terms to describe the entity he associates with the "gift" of thought. The "bestower" ("gift-giver" [*daritel'*] in the Russian original of "Father's Butterflies") is alternately referred to as "nature," "the spirit of nature," and "nature's mind."[109] Though the exact identity of this "gift-giver" remains unknown, Godunov's research into natural mimicry provides him with what he considers to be proof that this entity makes itself known by way of its peculiarly artistic sensibility. It articulates its "spiritual alliance" (FB 219) with human intelligence by planting in nature records of its own love of inutile beauty:

> Yet, long before the dawn of mankind, nature had already erected stage sets in expectation of future applause, the chrysalis of the Plum *Thecla* [*Strymonidia pruni,* the Black Hairstreak] was *already* made up to look like bird droppings, the whole play, performed nowadays with such subtle perfection, had been readied for production, only awaited the sitting down of the foreseen and inevitable spectator, our intelligence of today (for tomorrow's, a new show was in preparation). (FB 220; emphasis in original)

According to Godunov, contemporary mimetic patterns preserve the inherent "homogeneousness (*oneness*)" of "the prime compound" from which nature created its first life forms (FB 227). To illustrate his point, he refers to the caterpillar of the local Siberian owlet moth found exclusively on the chumara plant. The caterpillar closely resembles the yellow flowers of the shrub, but, curiously, it appears only at the end of the summer when the chumara plant is past its bloom. A mimetic conjunction of this kind, he argues, cannot promote survival: "against the dark green of the leaves, the caterpillar, uncircled by flowers, stands out in sharp contrast" (FB 222). Godunov interprets this as a refutation of the notion that mimicry is an *evolved* protective mechanism and as support for his conviction that "the incredible artistic wit of mimetic disguise . . . seemed to have been invented by some waggish artist precisely for the intelligent eyes of man" (*Gift* 110). As Fyodor observes, paraphrasing his father, "Let us leave in peace the famous 'struggle for survival': strugglers have no time for art. The happy impression of enchanting irrationality experienced by the observer at the sight of a disguised *tschumarae*—an imaginary flower, an impossible flower—that is what nature, our intelligent accomplice and witty mother wanted to achieve, and did" (FB 223).[110]

Blackwell notes that "Godunov-Cherdyntsev's speciation theory is uncompromisingly idealistic" (*QS* 40). The same idealist foundations underpin Fyodor's refutation of Chernyshevski's materialist philosophy. Fyodor's impatience with Chernyshevski's axiom that "the tangible object acts much more strongly than the abstract concept of it" (*Gift* 261) seems related to his father's distinctly idealist understanding of "species":

> By "species" he intends the original of a being, nonexistent in our reality but unique and definite in *concept*, that recurs ad infinitum in the mirror of nature, creating countless reflections; each one of them perceived by our intelligence, reflected in that selfsame glass and acquiring its reality solely within it, as a living individual of the given species. An aberration, or chance deviations are but the consequence of less "faithful" areas of the mirror, while the recurrent falling of a reflection on one and the same flaw may yield a stable local race, the *idea* of which tends toward the periphery of the circle, the center of which, in turn, is the *idea* of the species. (FB 216; emphasis added)[111]

This idealist formulation leads Godunov to conclude that "it was not species that evolved in nature, but the very concept of species" (FB 225). Fyodor embraces the metaphysical implications of his father's theory, telling his readers that "the species concept" has its origins "in nature's mind" (FB 220).

Godunov's and Fyodor's prioritization of intangible concepts over material phenomena is of a piece with Russia's neo-idealist philosophers' insistence on the primacy of ideas as movers of the historical process. Evgenii Trubetskoi, for example, rejects the Marxist principle that social change is a reflection of economic relations by means of an argument that resembles Godunov's idealist reformulation of Darwin:

> There is not the slightest semblance between the economic phenomena that, according to Marx and Engels, serve as the real basis of history, and the intellectual [*ideinyi*] reflection of these phenomena in the human mind or in the institutions created by people. How is this to be explained? Clearly, by the fact that the properties of any reflection depend not only on the characteristics of the reflected object, but also on those of the reflecting medium. In order to explain how economic relations are reflected in people's minds, it is necessary to take into account not only economic relations, but also the human mind, in general the whole human psyche, which reworks, in conformity with the laws of logic and psychology, all the diverse material of the

> impressions derived from the economic sphere. Here the economic explanation of history finds its limits: it is clear that by economic causes alone we will not explain any idea—religious, moral, or political—not even those ideas that justify or sanction economic interests. In order to understand anything about the origin and development of ideas, it is necessary to look closely at the characteristics of the human psyche, that is, to introduce into history a factor reducible to neither productive forces nor economic relations.[112]

Godunov's "idea"-based theory of natural classification and Trubetskoi's efforts to restore the human mind to a central place in assessments of historical development resonate with V. D. Nabokov's critique of criminal sociology. V. D. Nabokov's inaugural lecture sums up the disciplinary distinctions between criminal law and criminal sociology by noting that the former views crime and punishment as conceptions (*poniatiia*) whereas the latter views them as phenomena of social life (*iavleniia obshchestvennoi zhizni*). According to V. D. Nabokov, these views are irreconcilable, and a jurist must remain committed to the study of crime as a legal concept (*iuridicheskoe poniatie*). This involves the examination of "the entire intricate complex of legal norms that are used to regulate people's interpersonal relationships." "The events of real life that pass before his eyes," V. D. Nabokov continues, "have meaning for him and enter into his area of study only to the extent to which they relate to these norms. Consequently, jurists concern themselves with the perpetrator of the crime only insofar as, as N. S. Tagantsev has put it, he has contributed to the fact of the crime" (Sm 5). He firmly opposes the positivist school's efforts to abolish these "concepts derived from abstraction" and notes further that the discipline of criminal law cannot survive in the absence of such a conceptual system (Sm 5–6).

V. D. Nabokov's leanings toward philosophical idealism recall Godunov's muted endorsement of a transcendent order in the closing lines of "Father's Butterflies." In a scene that establishes a kind of dialogue with *Speak, Memory*'s account of V. D. Nabokov's acts of celebratory levitation, Fyodor recalls sitting on a veranda at the age of fourteen with a "difficult and strange" book, listening to his father cross the lawn in the company of an anonymous guest. As his father passes beneath an open window, Fyodor overhears him say: "Yes, of course it was in vain that I said 'by chance,' and by chance that I said 'in vain,' for here I agree with the clergy, especially since, for all the plants and animals I have had occasion to encounter, it is an unquestionable and authentic . . ." (FB 234).[113] Fyodor notes further: "The awaited final stress did not come. Laughing, the voice receded into the darkness—and now I have suddenly remembered the title of the book."

This cryptic exchange has generated much speculation and debate. As Boyd has noted, Godunov's comment to his nameless interlocutor echoes the opening words of Pushkin's famous lyric "Dar naprasnyi, dar sluchainyi, / Zhizn', zachem ty mne dana?" ("Vain gift, chance gift, / Life, why were you given to me?").[114] This intertextual moment confirms and amplifies Dolinin's thesis that Fyodor's *The Gift* (*Dar*), so steeped in the spirit of Pushkin's verse, responds dialogically to Pushkin's "Dar naprasnyi, dar sluchainyi."[115] "*Da . . . naprasno,*" the first words spoken by Godunov in the Russian original, call to mind the poem's opening words, and the Russian equivalents of "in vain" and "by chance"—"*naprasno*" and "*sluchaino*"—are uttered by Godunov in his conversation with his anonymous interlocutor.[116] As Jane Grayson has argued, the missing word in the closing ellipsis must be "*dar*"—the "gift"—that will become the title of Fyodor's novel.[117]

Pushkin's lyric formulates a metaphysical question about origins and ends:

> Vain gift, chance gift,
> Life, why were you given to me?
> And why by some secret fate
> Should you be condemned to death?
>
> Who with hostile power
> Brought me out of nothingness,
> Who has filled my soul with passion,
> Who has agitated my mind with doubt?
>
> No goal lies before me:
> My heart is empty, my mind is idle,
> And the monotonous noise of life
> Wearies me with melancholy.[118]

Godunov disagrees with Pushkin's notion that life is a gift bestowed "in vain" and "by chance." His extensive travels and research—"the plants and animals" he has had "occasion to encounter"—confirm his sense that life has meaning and purpose. This view puts him in agreement "with the clergy," a condensed allusion to a famous exchange between Pushkin and Metropolitan Philaret, at the time the most prominent hierarch of the Russian Orthodox Church.[119] Godunov's first words to his unnamed interlocutor channel the first lines of the metropolitan's riposte to Pushkin's poem:

Ne naprasno, ne sluchaino	Not in vain, not by chance
Zhizn' ot Boga mne dana,	Was life given me by God,
Ne bez voli Boga tainoi	And not without God's mysterious will
I na kazn' osuzhdena . . .	Is it condemned to death . . .[120]

A second lyric by Pushkin, "V chasy zabav il' prazdnoi skuki" ("In times of diversion or idle boredom"), accommodates the metropolitan's corrective by having its speaker iterate a more orthodox view.[121]

Boyd views this as the most vivid example of Godunov's tendency to speak, as it were, in Pushkin's voice, an occurrence Fyodor mentions—tellingly—in connection with his preparations to write his father's biography:

> He continued, however, to wait—the planned work was a wafture of bliss, and he was afraid to spoil that bliss by haste and moreover the complex responsibility of the work frightened him, he was not ready for it yet. Continuing his training program during the whole of spring, he fed on Pushkin, inhaled Pushkin (the reader of Pushkin has the capacity of his lungs enlarged) . . . . Pushkin entered his blood. With Pushkin's voice merged the voice of his father. (*Gift* 97, 98)

The Pushkin with whom Godunov's voice begins to merge is specifically the Pushkin of "V chasy zabav il' prazdnoi skuki," the poem in which he "agrees with the clergy" that life has meaning and purpose. This reading is bolstered by Gennady Barabtarlo's conviction that the first lines of Godunov's monologue refer not to himself but to Pushkin. Barabtarlo persuasively argues that instead of "yes, of course it was in vain that *I* said 'by chance,' and by chance that *I* said 'in vain,'" the English-language translation should read: "yes, of course it was in vain that *he* says 'by chance,' and by chance that *he* says 'in vain'" (emphasis added).[122] Instead of speaking about himself, Godunov is referring to Pushkin's change of heart and aligning himself with the metaphysical position Pushkin adopts in his response to Philaret.

Barabtarlo offers another compelling hypothesis with respect to the anonymous book Fyodor suddenly remembers reading that fragrant evening on his family's country estate. The book, he suggests, might be one of two works by Darwin that were part of V. D. Nabokov's St. Petersburg library—*L'expression des èmotions chez l'homme et les animaux* (cat. no. 2268) or *The Origin of Species* (cat. no. 2287).[123] As Barabtarlo points out, Darwin's silent presence in this scene would add another dimension to the addendum's anti-Darwinian spirit.

Barabtarlo's reconstruction of the scene is persuasive on several counts. Fyodor recollects the words his father had spoken twenty years earlier but cannot initially recall the name of the book he was reading that evening. His father's words lead him to expect the "final stress" to begin with the word "*dar*," the "gift" that is the subject of Pushkin's lyric.[124] Expected but unspoken, "*dar*" is a mnemonic trigger, and Fyodor suddenly remembers the serendipitous overlap between the unspoken word and the name of the anonymous book's author—*Dar*win. This characteristically Nabokovian coincidence is amplified twenty years later by the fact that Fyodor has already written or is contemplating writing a novel titled *Dar* (*The Gift*). Boyd notes the thematic significance of Barabtarlo's solution by observing that Godunov's words to his unnamed interlocutor function as a counter-argument to Darwin's claim that life is a product of evolutionary accident.[125]

The narrative threads that connect *The Gift* to its satellites call attention to the ideological implications of Nabokov's abiding interest in metaphysics. He broke off writing *The Gift* to write a short story inspired by the novel. In his prefatory remarks to "The Circle" ("Krug," 1936), he notes that "the story will produce upon readers who are familiar with [*The Gift*] a delightful effect of oblique recognition, of shifting shades enriched with new sense, owing to the world's being seen not through the eyes of Fyodor, but through those of an outsider less close to him than to old Russia's idealist radicals."[126] The story's protagonist, Innokentiy Ilyich Bychkov, is the son of the village schoolmaster at Leshino, the Godunovs' country estate. Growing up in the shadow of the Godunovs' wealth and privilege, he is keenly aware of his own social disadvantage. Their courtesy and generosity toward him only sharpen his resentment, and Fyodor's sister's confession of love for him comes too late to assuage it.

A chance encounter in Paris many years later brings Innokentiy face to face with Fyodor's aged mother, his sister Tanya, and Tanya's husband and young daughter. In their shabby apartment, Innokentiy is surprised by his spiteful reaction to his hosts' diminished circumstances:

> And now, listening to the melodious, beautifully idiomatic Russian in which the child replied to Tanya's questions, he caught himself thinking, malevolently and quite absurdly, "Aha, there is no longer the money to teach kids foreign languages!"—for it did not occur to him at that moment that in those émigré times, in the case of a Paris-born child going to a French school, this Russian language represented *the* idlest and best luxury. (emphasis in original)

As in *The Gift*, the good and the civilized are linked to the inutile, but this particular epiphany is temporarily withheld from Innokentiy and shared with the reader alone. The epiphany reserved for Innokentiy—that "nothing is lost, nothing whatever" and that "Tanya had remained as enchanting and as invulnerable as she had been in the past"—is another example of Nabokov's obsessive attempt to tame the violence of history and ideology by bringing it under the control of memory and art.[127]

In *Speak, Memory,* Nabokov asserts that he learned this special strategy from his mother:

> As if feeling that in a few years the tangible part of her world would perish, she cultivated an extraordinary consciousness of the various time marks distributed throughout our country place. She cherished her own past with the same retrospective fervor that I now do her image and my past. Thus, in a way, I inherited an exquisite simulacrum—the beauty of intangible property, unreal estate—and this proved a splendid training for the endurance of later losses. (*SM* 387)

In the same paragraph in which Nabokov laments the consequences of poverty and exile upon his relationship with his mother (he could only visit her infrequently; he was absent from her deathbed), he describes "the dim little photographs" that clustered around her "in crumbling frames." Nabokov insists that these treasured possessions were superfluous, for, as Innokentiy discovers in the Godunovs' apartment, "nothing had been lost. As a company of traveling players carry with them everywhere, while they still remember their lines, a windy heath, a misty castle, an enchanted island, so she had with her all that her soul had stored" (*SM* 395).

These images enliven and fortify, but Nabokov's deceptively innocent cluster of Shakespearean allusions offers something less than full consolation. Lear's windy heath, Hamlet's misty castle, Prospero's enchanted island are icons of excruciating loss. The plots they conjure up—of disinherited children, murdered fathers, and dukedoms lost and recovered only at great cost—remind readers that memory is at once kindly muse and ruthless tyrant. The images and lines carried everywhere by Nabokov's itinerant players traffic in both solace and pain.

Intimately acquainted with loss, Nabokov knew that its expression could carry him to the brink of sentimentality. This is something he works hard to resist in *Speak, Memory,* that long record of epitaphs. Only in the afterword to *Lolita* would he allow himself to find words for the personal nature of his suffering: "My private tragedy, which cannot, and indeed should not, be anybody's concern, is that I had to abandon my natural idiom, my untrammeled, rich, and infinitely docile Russian tongue for a second-rate brand of English."[128] This uncharacteristic lament tallies the cost of this tragedy for Nabokov's art, but it also serves as shorthand for a host of attendant personal losses.

Dolinin argues that Nabokov responded to the loss of his mother tongue by willfully disowning his former self. This forsaken Russian identity, Dolinin rightly claims, was shaped by its "vital ties with contemporary literary and historical contexts." More contentiously, Dolinin argues further that the Russian émigré writer who had committed himself to keeping alive Russia's literary traditions in European exile would later betray this commitment by adopting the image of "a born cosmopolitan genius who has never been attached to anything and anybody but his autonomous imagination and personal memory."[129]

Nabokov was, indeed, attached to the self-image described by Dolinin, but he emphatically did not interpret this attachment as a betrayal of the loyalties that tied him to his Russian past. This self-image was nourished precisely by the liberalism that Nabokov identified as his most treasured paternal inheritance and his passport to a new language and a new life. The ideological commitments and filial affections that molded Nabokov's Russian identity are neither forsaken nor forgotten. They accompany him to new lands and new cultural settings, and continue to shape his responses to new circumstances and challenges.

Like the Godunovs, the Nabokovs exchanged their aristocratic governess-and-tutor-taught English and French for their native tongue when the forces of history sent them into exile. But they permitted themselves this "idlest and best luxury" in the privacy of the home and in the company of other, similarly dispossessed, compatriots. Unable to earn a living by writing fiction for a dwindling Russian-speaking audience, Nabokov had to feed new stories and new lines to his company of itinerant players. And yet Nabokov's English-language novels, masquerading in their fantastic new robes, cannot conceal old household ghosts. The continued presence of these familiars must have brought solace to Nabokov, but they must also have served as painful reminders that no simulacrum, however richly imagined or vividly remembered, provided sufficient compensation for the loss of people and things he had loved best.

Chapter Two

Lolita and the Communists

> My father Vladimir Nabokov was a liberal statesman, member of the first Russian parliament, champion of justice and law in a difficult empire.
> —Vladimir Nabokov

> The name of Vladimir Dmitrievich Nabokov will be inscribed in gold letters in the history of the Russian science of criminal law and Russian legal consciousness.
> —Alexander Makletsov

> Attacks on liberalism, as such, have received their justification in states where personal freedom reached its peak and had shown its objectionable side.
> —Vasilii Maklakov

MINGLING AMBITION and regret, the lovelorn predator of Nabokov's *Lolita* (1955) articulates a startling and surrealistic fantasy. Humbert Humbert's uncontrollable appetite for the young girl he has abducted and systematically raped for many months suddenly transforms itself into a dream of total penetration. Humbert imagines this less as a bloody and psychotic crime against his victim, Dolores Haze, than as a wish to overcome an insuperable obstacle nature has erected against his all-consuming desires: "My only grudge against nature was that I could not turn my Lolita inside out and apply voracious lips to her young matrix, her unknown heart, her nacreous liver, the seagrapes of her lungs, her comely twin kidneys."[1] Unable (or, thankfully, unwilling) to satisfy this desire, Humbert nevertheless successfully submits his victim to other kinds of penetration—most explicitly by way of physical intercourse, but also by way of his unrelenting violation of her will and autonomy. Humbert is a perceptive observer of what his crimes do to Dolly, and he will later acknowledge that her indifference toward outcomes in everything from tennis to playacting is a function of his having broken something deep within her (*L* 196, 218).

It is usual to look for the earliest stirrings of *Lolita* in *The Gift* or the early novella *The Enchanter.* Humbert's fantasy, however, also establishes a vital connection between *Lolita* and *Invitation to a Beheading,* a novel whose first draft Nabokov rapidly pieced together during a short break from his work on *The Gift.* While drafting Fyodor's biography of Chernyshevski, Nabokov recalls interrupting his work to write the first draft of *Invitation to a Beheading* in "one fortnight of wonderful excitement and sustained inspiration" (*SO* 68).[2] Scholars have come to recognize that *Invitation to a Beheading* was somehow occasioned and inspired by Nabokov's work on the Chernyshevski chapter in *The Gift,* and Boyd and Dolinin have convincingly argued that the central plot of a prisoner awaiting execution in *Invitation to a Beheading* has its origins in Chernyshevski's unhappy history.[3] The thematic links that connect Fyodor's biography of Chernyshevski to Nabokov's first extended foray into political critique also tie *Invitation to a Beheading* to *Lolita.* The connection was adumbrated by Nabokov himself when he singled out the two novels in an interview from 1966, observing that *Invitation to a Beheading* was the novel he held in "the greatest esteem" and *Lolita* the novel for which he felt "the most affection" (*SO* 92).

The dream of total penetration that fills Humbert's mind in 1950s America is a version of a trope that first captured Nabokov's attention in 1930s Berlin while he was immersed in research that led him to write his first novel about the miseries and horrors of totalitarianism. Cincinnatus C., the hero of *Invitation to a Beheading,* is sentenced to death because he is literally opaque in a society whose individuals are fully transparent: "He was impervious to the rays of others, and therefore produced when off his guard a bizarre impression, as of a lone dark obstacle in this world of souls transparent to one another; he learned however to feign translucence, employing a complex system of optical illusions, . . . cunningly illuminated facets and angles at which he turned his soul."[4] As he matures, however, the authorities uncover his deception and put him on trial. The totalitarian regime in which he lives views his curious ontology as a capital offense and he is sent first to jail and then to the scaffold.

Invitation to a Beheading was published serially in the 1935–36 issues of the prestigious "thick" émigré monthly *Sovremennye zapiski* (*Contemporary Annals*). Like other such journals, *Sovremennye zapiski* combined literary texts with a wide variety of other political and intellectual writings. It included, for instance, the political memoirs of some of V. D. Nabokov's closest associates such as Fyodor Rodichev, Vasilii Maklakov, and Paul Miliukov. Ten years earlier, the journal had published a series of articles on "rule-of-law socialism" by the Kantian idealist philosopher of law Sergey Hessen

(1887–1950). The principal aim of the articles was to promote a socialist political framework capable of honoring liberalism's commitment to legality. Hessen argued that socialists must acknowledge the "impenetrability of an individual by another person, including the state [*nepronitsaemost' lichnosti dlia drugogo litsa, v tom chisle i gosudarstva*]." This, according to Hessen, was liberalism's "eternal idea" (*vechnaia ideia*). The concept was ultimately derived from the classical liberal principle of personal inviolability, and Hessen's essays were committed to making it work as a hedge against state activity and social pressures. The penultimate installment in Hessen's series argues that human subjectivity transcends sociological accounts of human identity: "the individual personality is not exhausted by its functions; it is at heart universal, containing in itself a nucleus that lies deeper than organized social collectives."[5]

It is reasonable to hear a version of Nabokov's voice in this assertion, and to guess that he may have known this specific installment of Hessen's work; the volume in which it was printed also included Nabokov's short story "Uzhas," published under his pen name Vladimir Sirin. Nabokov was a frequent contributor to the journal, which also published work by most of his favorite émigré writers. In turn, Sergey Hessen had a hand in editing the journal alongside some of Nabokov's closest friends in the emigration.[6] But Nabokov would not have needed to read this specific essay or to hear of it from his friends on the editorial board of *Sovremennye zapiski* in order to become familiar with one of Hessen's lifelong preoccupations.[7] Boyd refers to Sergey Hessen's younger brother George as "the companion of [Nabokov's] early manhood," and Nabokov's letters testify that they remained close friends in America (*DBDV* 111, 215, 254). Boyd further reports that Nabokov visited Sergey Hessen at his home in Prague in 1932, two years before he began writing *Invitation to a Beheading*.[8]

Connections between the families ran deep and crossed generations. Sergey and George Hessen's father Joseph had been one of V. D. Nabokov's closest friends and colleagues in Russia and the emigration, where they edited together the journals *Pravo*, *Rech'*, and *Rul'* (*VNRY* 206). In *Gody izgnaniia* (*The Years of Exile*), Joseph Hessen describes his twenty-year relationship with V. D. Nabokov as rooted in "joint and harmonious social activism" and "an ever-growing cloudless friendship" (*Gi* 118). In his own memoirs, Sergey Hessen describes his intellectual apprenticeship among *Pravo*'s editors. The paper's editorial board met regularly in his family's apartment, located next door to the offices of *Pravo*. Hessen fondly recalls helping his father proofread *Pravo* and listening in on conversations between his uncle V. M. Hessen, Lev Petrazhitskii, Avgust Kaminka, N. I. Lazarevskii, and V. D. Nabokov on political, juridical, and literary topics.[9] Joseph Hessen, finally, played a critical role in Nabokov's literary development. "In the years after V. D. Nabokov's death," Boyd writes, "none did more than Hessen to ensure that Sirin met his public" (*VNRY* 206). As head of the Berlin publishing house Slovo, he took enormous pride in the firm's role as "godfather" (*krestnym ottsom*) to Sirin's career (*Gi* 93). Nabokov paid homage to Hessen's unflagging interest and support in an obituary on the occasion of his death:

> He was my first reader. Long before my books began to come out with his publishing firm, he let me, with a fatherly connivance, feed *Rul'* my unripe rhymes. . . . [He] would bring the sheet of paper close to his face . . . and then he would look at me with half-sarcastic benevolence, lightly shaking the sheet but saying only "Mm-hmm," and would add it without haste to the pile of copy.[10]

In a speech delivered at Joseph Hessen's seventieth birthday celebration and reproduced in *Gody izgnaniia,* Nabokov poignantly recalls the times when Hessen "had not yet taken up an integral and permanent residence in my soul" (*kogda Vy ne byli dlia menia vot takim slitnym, pripisannym k naseleniiu moei dushi*), but was the "distant," "legendary Hessen" detested by his elderly aristocratic relatives for what seemed to them his ruinous influence on his father. But even as a child, Nabokov recalls, he somehow intuited that Hessen was allied with the powers of the good. As a grown man, Nabokov suggestively concludes, "I think with envy of that climatic zone of Russian history in which you flourished, and agonizingly try to figure out the many, very many, things that you recall with such ease" (*Gi* 95–96).

By whatever route he first encountered it, Nabokov's investment in Sergey Hessen's trope of impenetrability provides a crucial link between Nabokov's English-language fiction and that "climatic zone of Russian history" Nabokov acknowledged in such moving terms to have sought to understand. In *Invitation to a Beheading,* the trope operates as a thought experiment urged upon the novelist by his detailed study of the Russian radical tradition's crude materialist metaphysics and realist epistemology.[11] In *Lolita,* it grants Nabokov a means of exploring the promises and limitations of the "old-fashioned liberalism" he inherited from his father and his father's closest liberal colleagues. He mounts this exploration in a novel that methodically studies the extent to which liberal values are vulnerable to the conditions and dispensations that liberal states bring into being.

NABOKOV AND MCCARTHYISM

Nabokov's long-standing interest in the liberal principle outlined by Sergey Hessen is a reminder that his novels are permeated by considerations that his work on *The Gift* had trained him to regard as deeply political. It also shows that specifically Russian strains of liberal theory influenced his art long after his family's flight to western Europe and then America. This is obviously true of political dystopias such as *Invitation to a Beheading* and *Bend Sinister*, where liberal principles constitute a shadow standard against which dictatorships are measured and found wanting. *Lolita*, however, tests liberal values from the inside—that is, from within the world's first modern liberal state.

Lolita's account of the sexual passion of a middle-aged European man for a twelve-year-old American girl generated considerable controversy following its Paris debut.[12] Discussions of the novel's reception history, however, rarely focus on Nabokov's claim to have been more disturbed by the charge that the novel was "anti-American" than by the furor concerning its supposedly pornographic character: "This is something that pains me considerably more than the idiotic accusation of immorality," he states in "On a Book Entitled *Lolita*," the afterword he wrote for the novel's American debut.[13] He defended himself by saying that no nation has a monopoly on "philistine vulgarity," and that he had chosen "American motels instead of Swiss hotels or English inns" for the simple reason that he was "trying to be an American writer and claim only the same rights that other American writers enjoy." By contrast, he adds, "my creature Humbert is a foreigner and an anarchist, and there are many things, besides nymphets, in which I disagree with him" (OB 296).

Nabokov's description of Humbert as "a foreigner and an anarchist" makes it possible to reconstruct, in a particularly suggestive manner, the emotional and intellectual currents that animated Nabokov's life in 1950s America. These currents had a shaping force on *Lolita*. The phrase invites readers to recognize that *Lolita* studies two different, but ultimately related, political contexts. In the primary documents that chronicle the turbulent events surrounding Russia's second revolutionary period, the term "anarchy" was consistently applied to the chaos, violence, and lawlessness unleashed by the Bolsheviks. This is the case both in V. D. Nabokov's *The Provisional Government* and in the memoirs of V. D. Nabokov's closest friends and associates, such as Joseph Hessen, Vasilii Maklakov, Paul Miliukov, Daniel (Daniil) Pasmanik, Maxim Vinaver, and others (*PG* 43, 119). By the time Nabokov wrote his afterword to *Lolita*, anarchy had also become linked in his mind with Stalin's concentration camps and ruthless imperialism. Communism's rejection of law as an autonomous and binding mechanism of social order justifies these associations. A reader encountering Nabokov's afterword in 1957 and 1958 would have been well equipped to regard the conjunction of the words "foreigner" and "anarchist" as raising the specter of Communism.

The terms in which Nabokov emphasized his difference from Humbert are thus highly significant. Most immediately, they emphasize not just the extent to which he viewed himself as an American, but also the keenness with which he wanted to be viewed as an American by others. His anxiety that *Lolita* might be perceived as "anti-American" is rooted in his deep and enduring affection for his new homeland. In interviews from 1962 and 1964, when he and Véra were already living in Europe in order to be closer to their son, he continued to fashion for himself an American identity: "In America I'm happier than in any other country. . . . I feel intellectually at home in America. It is a second home in the true sense of the word" (*SO* 10). To Douglas Davis of the *National Observer* he was even more forceful about his total commitment to America's political and intellectual life: "America is my home now. It is my country. The intellectual life suits me better than any other country in the world. I have more friends there, more kindred souls than anywhere."[14] When asked in 1966 to translate Lincoln's Gettysburg Address into Russian by Roy Basler of the Library of Congress, Nabokov responded that the offer gave him "intense pleasure" and that the address was "a work of art I have always admired." After requesting that his name be mentioned alongside the translation and that the honorarium be passed on to a charity, Nabokov completed the translation within days of receiving Basler's letter.[15]

Placing the accent on Nabokov's full integration in America's national fabric reveals how troubling his dismissal of Humbert as a "foreigner" can be. Nabokov must have recognized that to use the term "foreigner" as a term of aspersion, and to establish a direct contrast between this insult and his own identity as "an American writer" who could lay claim to "the same rights that other American writers enjoy," ran counter to the liberal principles that nourished his love for America. Nabokov's use of the term "foreigner" in this context becomes even more vexatious when considered in light of the political atmosphere in which *Lolita* developed and made its debut.

This period was among the most dramatic in Cold War history. In the late 1940s and 1950s, the nation's political life was dominated by the anti-Communist purges and constitutional violations that became synonymous with McCarthyism. The House Un-American Activities Committee (HUAC) launched its infamous campaign against Hollywood's motion picture industry in 1947, the same year in which the projects that would become *Lolita* and *Speak, Memory* began to absorb Nabokov's creative energies.[16] By 1953, the year of *Lolita*'s completion, Czechoslovakia and China had fallen under Communist rule, the Soviet Union had exploded an atomic bomb, the United States and the U.S.S.R. had supported opposing sides in the Korean War, and a series of atomic spy rings had been uncovered in the United States. These last events led to the execution of two Jews named Ethel and Julius Rosenberg for conspiracy to commit espionage.

It should come as no surprise, then, that "foreigners" in the United

States felt at risk during this period. Three years before Nabokov wrote his afterword to *Lolita* and labeled Humbert a "foreigner," President Eisenhower's attorney general announced that "12,000 citizens were being investigated for denaturalization, and 12,000 aliens for deportation as 'subversives.'"[17] David Suchoff and Morton Horwitz have provided powerful accounts of the anti-Semitic undercurrent of the American crusade against Communism and of the fears experienced by the American Jewish community during the Rosenbergs' protracted legal battles and ultimate execution.[18] As a recently naturalized Russian-born refugee married to a Jewish woman, Nabokov was understandably reluctant to be labeled "anti-American" at a time when the government of his "second home" was regarding foreigners with suspicion.

If Nabokov trusted his family pedigree and his own passionate anti-Bolshevism to protect him from being targeted as a potential Communist sympathizer, he must have also relied on his fellow Americans to understand the intricacies of pre- and post-revolutionary Russian politics. But letters, prefaces, and interviews attest to Nabokov's lack of faith in his new compatriots' knowledge of Russian political history. *Pnin*'s narrator sounds a typical Nabokovian complaint when he laments the ignorance of "American intellectuals, for whom the notion of Russian emigration was made to mean by astute communist propaganda a vague and perfectly fictitious mass of so-called Trotskiites (whatever these are), ruined reactionaries, reformed or disguised Cheka men, titled ladies, professional priests, restaurant keepers, and White Russian military groups" (*Pnin* 430). To be suspected of Communist sympathies by professional anti-Communists who knew so little about Russia's émigré communities was unlikely to surprise him.

Nabokov also knew that political power could not be trusted to act rationally in times of crisis. In weighing the leverage afforded him by his impeccable anti-Communist credentials, he might have recalled a story told by Joseph Hessen in *Gody izgnaniia.* Though the memoir was published after Nabokov's death, he could have heard the story from Hessen himself or from Hessen's son George, a close friend of Nabokov's both in European and American emigrations. (In the same letter to Wilson in which he reported working on the projects that would become *Speak, Memory* and *Lolita,* Nabokov also reported a recent and "delightful" visit from "my friend George Hessen" [*DBDV* 215].) If he had not heard the story from either father or son, he certainly would have heard stories like it from others who had faced similar trials.

Joseph Hessen opens his memoir by describing his flight from Russia to Finland. Before his escape he had carefully selected Bolshevik newspapers that he hoped would communicate to outsiders the noxious character of the new regime. He camouflaged them as packing material in his luggage, but they were nonetheless seized at the border by representatives of the newly established Finnish counterintelligence office. Though the officials assured him that his activism in liberal politics was well known to them, they also told him that there was no guarantee that he would not use these newspapers to spread Bolshevik propaganda. The Bolshevik papers were confiscated and Hessen was placed in detention until his political trustworthiness could be ascertained (*Gi* 1–2). Stories such as these make it impossible to assume that Nabokov would have considered himself above suspicion at the height of the American crusade against domestic Communism. Certainly other Russians in America were not above Nabokov's own suspicions.

The afterword to *Lolita* shows Nabokov making an effort to establish his status as a patriotic American: first, he makes his status as an American writer a basic matter of possessing "the same rights that other American writers enjoy"; second, he distances himself from his novel's protagonist by identifying Humbert as "a foreigner and an anarchist" (OB 296). Mingling self-defense with denunciation, these assertions bring him uncomfortably close to the confessional discourses that shaped inquiries into domestic subversion during the Cold War. "On a Book Entitled *Lolita*" affirms the writer's loyalty to America at a time when congressional hearings, loyalty programs, FBI investigations, blacklists, and criminal prosecutions of the American left dominated the nation's political life.[19]

If Humbert's description as "a foreigner" is a trace of Nabokov's sense of vulnerability in 1950s America, it is also a trace of the way in which Nabokov's commitment to liberal values was starting to buckle under the weight of his hatred of Communism. In the eyes of a liberal who knew that Stalin had imprisoned millions of his own citizens in concentration camps, subjugated Eastern Europe, and had clear designs for further expansion by force and fraud, liberal rectitude may have begun to look like unconscious collusion with the enemy. Nabokov's experiences in the Crimea during the Russian Civil War, for example, had shown him firsthand how liberal values can become complicit in their own undoing.

Nabokov's recognition that unintended complicity between liberalism and its enemies was possible is articulated in a letter from 1952 addressed to the editor of the *Cornell Daily Sun*. In the letter, Véra Nabokov states that Senators McCarthy and McCarrau "are making a tragic mistake" by affixing the "Communist" label to "everybody left of Thomas Dewey." "Nothing," she adds, "pleases the Communists more" than to be given the "chance to hide behind the Democrats' backs." She adds further that "it would be an even more tragic mistake if the outraged intelligentsia accepted the silly challenge and girded its loins in indiscriminate quixotic defense of *all* the accused." The case of Alger Hiss, she argues, should remind the editors that "the unfortunate method of accusing indiscriminately the guilty and the innocent should not be used as a proof that whoever has been accused by them is innocent."[20] Véra Nabokov's letter supports Boyd's contention that the Nabokovs "disapproved of McCarthy's random accusations and unscrupulous cross-examinations of alleged Communists" even though they "believed many of his charges were correct, that there was serious Communist infiltration in high places in American officialdom" (*VNAY* 186).

Unlike most of his American compatriots, Nabokov was unwilling to overlook the threat posed by Soviet Communism when the U.S.S.R. was America's ally in the Second World War. After the war ended and the Cold War began, Nabokov's anti-Communism was no longer the voice of thoughtful, informed nonconformity, but the voice of sometimes rational, sometimes hysterical, majority opinion. Nabokov must have been gratified to see his adoptive country begin to take the Communist threat seriously again, but he also probably felt uncomfortable to hear his voice blend in with the chorus. Misgivings of this kind are registered in Véra Nabokov's letter to the *Cornell Daily Sun* and in other instances in which the Nabokovs felt compelled to distinguish between their own brand of anti-Communism and the anti-radical and anti-liberal attitudes commonly referred to as McCarthyism.

McCarthy's name stirred the family's passions in a variety of ways long after he and other professional anti-Communists had been discredited. In a 1964 interview for *Life* magazine, for instance, Nabokov decried "the attitude of foolish or dishonest people who ridiculously equate Stalin with McCarthy," and who confused "the ruthless imperialism of the USSR with the earnest and unselfish assistance extended by the USA to nations in distress" (*SO* 50). As late as 1971, in a letter sent from Switzerland to Oliver Caldecott of Penguin Books, Véra Nabokov reported that her husband was "extremely annoyed" by a blurb on the back cover of *Pnin* that mentioned "such Nabokovian enemies as McCarthyism." She went on to explain that "VN has never criticized or attacked McCarthy for the simple reason that he found anti-McCarthyists much more repulsive than McCarthy himself" (*SL* 495–96).

Another letter written in the same year, this time to the Jesuit publication *America,* shows that Nabokov's anti-Communism could lead him to assume uncharacteristic positions for a man who preferred to avoid the messy world of political advocacy and debate. In the letter, Véra Nabokov noted that her husband "very much regrets" the magazine's "neutral a-political character. What is needed, he thinks, is vigorous political propaganda" (*SL* 494–95). Twenty-one years earlier Nabokov had considered contributing himself to this project when he proposed an article on the subject of Soviet-American relations. Having come upon a Soviet journal while conducting research for his course in European fiction, he wrote Katharine White of the *New Yorker:*

> I have found some extraordinary things, plays and articles, in the Soviet periodical "Zvezda" for 1949 that cast a brilliant and terrible light on Soviet-American relations. Would you like me to write a piece of 4000–5000 words on the subject? It would contain samples of the Soviet notion of the American way of life culled from some plays and a remarkable warning, in August 1949!—of their Korean policy. (*SL* 106)

The article was never written, but Nabokov's excited language and zeal to expose the duplicity of Soviet foreign policy bring him awkwardly close to what Richard Hofstadter has famously identified as the period's "paranoid style."[21]

Nabokov's professed indifference to political matters is also difficult to square with a number of later incidents in which he cast a livid political light on what seem like politically neutral issues. During his time at Cornell University, for example, Nabokov was frustrated by the fact that Douglas Fairbanks, one of his colleagues in the Russian Department, could not speak Russian. He submitted a formal complaint to the university administration not on the grounds that Fairbanks was violating a principle of academic integrity, but because the man's linguistic approach to teaching Russian compromised national security: "At a time when the country desperately needs Russian-language experts, it is distressing to think what havoc Mr. Fairbanks' MA's and PhD's are bringing into the work of the State Department and of other agencies which require not phonemes, but able translators, and who engage Cornell alumni on the false assumption that a Cornell diploma is still a guarantee of scholarship" (*SL* 264). As Charles Lock has observed in relation to this letter, "the massive critical attention directed toward Nabokov has a collective way of overlooking such nasty political 'realities' as this letter enshrines."[22] Though the letter's implications are not as menacing as Lock implies, it does demand that readers be prepared to recognize how Nabokov could force seemingly apolitical issues into political contexts. Nabokov's apparent insistence that pedophilia is somehow to be understood as the calling card of a foreign anarchist achieves the same effect.

Nabokov's 1958 complaint regarding Fairbanks was no isolated incident. It had already been preceded, in 1957, by a dispute with fellow Russian Roman Jakobson. Having learned that the latter did not support his candidacy for a job at Harvard, Nabokov abandoned a collaborative project that he, Jakobson, and Marc Szeftel had agreed to launch together, all the while refusing to acknowledge that he was motivated by a sense of personal injury. Instead, he accused Jakobson of being a Communist sympathizer: "After a careful examination of my conscience, I have come to the conclusion that I cannot collaborate with you in the proposed English-language edition of the SLOVO. Frankly, I am unable to stomach your little trips to totalitarian countries, even if these trips are prompted merely by scientific considerations" (*SL* 216).[23]

Nabokov's letter to Jakobson clashes with sentiments he expressed in *The Gift*. Godunov inspires his son's admiration when he sets aside political differences in the name of scientific considerations. At the height of Russia's war with Germany, Fyodor recounts, his father "traveled to Geneva to meet a fat, bald, extraordinarily jovial German professor . . . for a scientific consultation." After discussing "a work of many volumes, stubbornly continuing publication in Stuttgart with longstanding cooperation of foreign specialists on separate groups of butterflies," Godunov and Russia's formal enemy "peaceably parted—each in his own direction" (*Gift* 129). The fictional naturalist of international repute who "looked upon the war as a tiresome obstacle," and who, by his own example, gave his son license "not to notice the war" (*Gift* 127), sits awkwardly with a story reported by Andrew Field and Brian Boyd. The same year he broke off relations with Jakobson, Nabokov befriended the FBI agent charged with ferreting out Communists at Cornell, going so far as to tell him that he would be proud to have his son join the FBI in that role.[24]

The gulf that separates World War I (waged for competing economic and imperialist interests) from the Cold War (fought between two clearly demarcated sides, one totalitarian, one liberal-democratic) also separates the man who wrote *The Gift* from the man who thought that an FBI career in domestic anti-Communism on America's university campuses might be a meaningful career for his much-loved and only son. These vastly different contexts explain why Nabokov could ill-afford to adopt Godunov's indifference to political conflict. Yet, in spite of feeling the urgency of Soviet totalitarianism and expansionism, Nabokov must have also worried that the Cold War and his own anti-Communism were driving him into positions that were repugnant to him not only by virtue of his instinctive individualism and apolitical temperament, but also by virtue of his liberal political convictions. Godunov's haughty disinterest in the First World War clearly provided no useful model for Fyodor's future encounter with Soviet and Nazi totalitarianism. More poignantly still, it seems that the heroism and sacrifices that characterized the political career of Nabokov's own father also left a son unprepared to cope with the challenges Communism posed to liberal values.

Revisiting the high points of his father's political career as he penned *Speak, Memory*, Nabokov must have been keenly reminded of what it meant to be a political liberal. In his autobiography, Nabokov describes with pride his father's fearless public criticism of government-sponsored anti-Semitism during the Kishinev pogrom of 1903 and the trial of Mendel Beiliss for ritual murder in 1913 (*SM* 509, 510). Joseph Hessen recalls that V. D. Nabokov alone suffered the consequences of the government's displeasure over his daring condemnation of the Kishinev pogrom. To everyone's surprise, *Pravo,* the weekly in which the article appeared, escaped punishment, but V. D. Nabokov was deprived of his court title and his teaching post at the Imperial School of Jurisprudence (*Vdv* 171). In his monograph on the Beiliss affair, Maurice Samuel describes V. D. Nabokov's efforts to expose the Russian government's violation of Russia's judicial procedures as one of "the most violent attacks" carried out by the Russian liberal press. V. D. Nabokov's spirited accounts of the proceedings led Samuel to group him among the attorneys who—bravely and free of charge—made up Beiliss's defense team.[25] What did this liberal legacy mean to Nabokov as he watched McCarthy and McCarrau indiscriminately denounce "everybody left of Thomas Dewey" as Communist?

In his assessment of V. D. Nabokov's scholarly career, Makletsov provides an earlier image of the stakes of this legacy in a quotation culled from a paper V. D. Nabokov presented to the International Congress of Criminalists in 1910. The quoted words warn against the temptation to violate civil rights for the sake of security:

> The principles according to which criminal punishment can be inflicted only upon the guilty, that the criminal may only be punished in proportion with his guilt, that the punitive authority of the state is limited by the statutes of the criminal code, that the acts of the unsound of mind carry a different legal meaning than the acts of the sound of mind, that the task of the judge consists of bringing an individual case under the standard of the law, these are not only abstract jurisprudential theses, but also the fruits of a prolonged political battle for the guarantee of personal liberty from authority in general, however this may be called. . . . To sacrifice these principles for the sake of social security would mean shaking the very foundations which prop up the sanctity and inviolability of individual rights. Whatever practical gain could be derived from this, it is not worth the sacrifice.

"These words constitute the leitmotif of [V. D.] Nabokov's creed as a scholar," wrote Makletsov. He noted further that V. D. Nabokov strenuously objected against the transformation of criminal law into an organ of the secret police, and prophetically foresaw how "the idea of security risk [*ideia opasnago sostoianiia*]" was used in Soviet jurisprudence to erect a Jacobin-style "regime of suspicion [*rezhim 'podozritel'nykh'*]."[26]

Nabokov's work on the memoir which eulogizes his father's life and political ideals overlapped with his work on the novel that would become *Lolita.*[27] As the novel that marked Nabokov's most concerted effort to become an American writer (OB 296), *Lolita* is a candid, sustained, and ultimately courageous meditation upon the Russian liberal principles and political realities that had shaped his understanding of the political order of his "second home." Admiring, embracing, and submitting that political order to penetrating critique, Nabokov constructs the novel's plots and structures in spaces connecting the crushed promise of Russian liberalism to the challenges facing 1950s America.

RUSSIAN LIBERALISM AND THE REVIVAL OF NATURAL LAW

Nabokov's novel about a foreigner's sexual exploitation of a young American girl inquires into the promises and limitations of liberal principles. This inquiry was conducted at a moment when Nabokov's anti-Communism had brought him into a vexed relation to his own intellectual heritage. Founded upon liberal principles, the United States was the first modern nation to programmatically safeguard the individual against interference by state and society. But in spite of his heartfelt approval of America's way of life and its political structures, Nabokov was alert to the costs of America's "easygoing, good-natured atmosphere" (*SO* 27). Those costs include the fate of Dolores Haze, a young girl who is robbed of her childhood by "a foreigner and an anarchist" whose crimes go undetected in a nation that takes pride in prioritizing law over politics, and personal freedoms over the public good.

In a lecture titled "Readers, Writers, and Censors in Russia" (Boyd calls it a "standby lecture for public occasions since 1941"), Nabokov drew attention to the tensions between liberty and political power (*VNAY* 359). The lecture ends with a short poem by Pushkin excerpted here:

> To give account to none, to be one's own
> vassal and lord, to please oneself alone,
> to bend neither one's neck, nor inner schemes,
> nor conscience to obtain some thing that seems
> power but is a flunkey's coat.[28]

Like Pushkin, Nabokov yearned to live in a world in which personal liberties would never be subjected to political concerns. But also like Pushkin, Nabokov understood that such a life could only flourish within the framework of a dependable legal order.

The critical importance of a legal order capable of protecting citizens from various forms of coercion must have become especially vivid for Nabokov as loyalty programs, congressional hearings, blacklists, and indiscriminate criminal prosecutions began to characterize life in America in the late 1940s and early 1950s. During *Lolita*'s gestation, national security concerns demanded that individuals endure precisely the kinds of indignities resisted by Pushkin. As Americans were asked to give account of themselves and expose their own and their friends' political convictions for the sake of national security, Nabokov was being forced to revisit debates that dominated Russian intellectual life at the height of his father's legal and political careers. These debates focused on the complex relationship between law and politics adumbrated in Pushkin's poem.

Pushkin had belonged to a small group of Russian "liberal conservatives" who distinguished themselves from their peers by their recognition that only stable legal institutions could protect individual liberty and sustain effective political structures. Peter Struve was part of that group. His philosophical affinity to Pushkin has been emphasized by Leonard Schapiro in a review of Pipes's biography of Struve.[29] Nabokov's thinking on political matters is in several ways strikingly similar to that of Struve. In particular, Nabokov seems to have fully absorbed Russian liberalism's central premise that political and economic reforms are to be regarded as secondary to a foundational commitment to maximizing human freedom and constraining political authority. In an interview from 1963, Nabokov defined his "political creed" in the following terms: "Freedom of speech, freedom of thought, freedom of art. The social or economic structure of the ideal state is of little concern to me. My desires are modest. Portraits of the head of the government should not exceed a postage stamp in size. No torture and no executions. No music, except coming through earphones, or played in theatres" (*SO* 34–35). He affirms these values again seven years later in an interview with Nurit Beretzky for *Ma'ariv:* "I am ready to accept any regime—Socialistic, Royalistic, Janitorial—provided mind and body are free" (qtd. in *VNRY* 62). If these principles are, as Nabokov suggests, "classical to the point of triteness" (*SO* 34), they are so for the same reason that Pnin's liberalism can seem like an antiquarian's unfashionable bauble: they articulate values that have lost their shiny novelty because liberals consider them to be essential and timeless. They also echo the classical formulation of liberal values articulated in a frequently cited article by Struve in a 1905 issue of *Osvobozhdenie:* "I want to subordinate myself to no authority, to no police station, regardless of how it is decorated: with the double-headed eagle or the Phrygian cap, whether its 'mirror of justice' descends from Peter the Great or from Karl Marx."[30]

Considered in isolation from the Russian liberal traditions that shaped his worldview, Nabokov's political assertions can sound either whimsically facetious or hopelessly vague. But Nabokov is articulating deeply held and sharply defined intellectual convictions. His expression of these convictions in terms that echo the language of Struve's memorable call for legally protected freedoms speaks to the thoroughness of his immersion in the liberal creed of his father and his own closest friends in the emigration. Vladimir Tatarinov, a journalist at *Rul'* and a friend of Nabokov in Berlin,[31] wrote that all of V. D. Nabokov's public activities were driven by his overarching commitment to the struggle for law and the abolition of coercion ("*Bor'ba za pravo i protiv nasiliia—vot kakov byl lozung vsei zhizni Nabokova*"). Tatarinov's characterization of V. D. Nabokov once again recalls Struve's formulation: "He could not reconcile himself with coercion regardless of its monarchist, republican, socialist or Bolshevik origins."[32] Joseph Hessen describes Iulii Aikhenvald, another Kadet closely connected to Nabokov, as "an instinctive opponent of all forms of coercion [*organicheskim protivnikom vsiakogo nasiliia*]" (*Gi* 164). Hessen recalls Aikhenvald's reaction to the gift of a book authored by his son, a professor of political economy working for the Bolsheviks in the Soviet Union. Though the book was enjoying a sensational success in the Soviet Union, and though Aikhenvald's son was at the height of his fame, Hessen was shocked that Aikhenvald, "a touchingly solicitous, loving family man," could speak of his son as of a stranger when showing him his son's gift. Hessen sums up the rupture between father and son with a poignant conclusion: "The ties of blood kinship evaporated without a trace in the crucible of hatred toward a supporter of coercion [*uzy krovnogo rodstva bessledno isparilis' v gornile nenavisti k storonniku nasiliia*]" (*Gi* 165).

When Nabokov claims that he is "ready to accept any regime—Socialistic, Royalistic, Janitorial—provided mind and body are free," he is aligning himself with men like his father, Aikhenvald, Peter Struve, and Joseph Hessen who dreamed of turning Russia into a liberal rule-of-law state. Nabokov implies that legally protected freedoms are pre-political and must be honored by all legitimate configurations of power. Read in conjunction with *Lolita,* Nabokov's remarks on his "unfashionable" political views establish the depth of his interest in the legal discourses of Russian liberalism.

In the essay in which Struve declared his refusal to submit to any form of legally unrestrained political authority, he also described Lenin's party in terms that provide a context for my contention that Humbert's "anarchism" ought to be understood as a brand of Communism:

> The tactics of Social Democracy, of course, are determined by its character as a narrow body of intellectuals which aspires to represent the working class. But this is only one source of its tactics. The other lies in the very world outlook of Social Democracy, which lacks any *idea of law.* Social Democracy wishes to overcome the reactionary violence of autocracy with the revolutionary power of the people. It has in common with its enemy the cult of power: it merely desires a different carrier of power and assigns it different tasks. In its world outlook, law is not the idea of the just but the command of the *strong.*[33]

For Schapiro, such early assessments of Social Democracy had prophetic force. Within weeks of taking power, the Bolsheviks swept away the entire edifice of Russian law. And though a new legal system of courts, codes, and procedures was gradually reestablished, there was never any doubt that the new judiciary was a mere appendage to party power.[34] Schapiro notes further that the legal system abolished by the Bolsheviks had (in principle, at least, if rarely in practice) recognized the validity of rule-of-law principles: "After 1864 Russia had created and developed a Bench and a Bar of the highest standards, and a modern legal system in no way inferior to that of any country of the European continent." The tragedy lay in the fact that "this legal system was only too frequently set aside or circumvented by martial law, by executive powers and the like."[35] Nabokov drew attention to this critical distinction between tsarist and Communist attitudes toward the law in a 1948 letter to Wilson:

> Under the Tsars (despite the inept and barbarous character of their rule) a freedom-loving Russian had incomparably more possibility and means of expressing himself than at any time during Lenin's and Stalin's regime. He was protected by law. There were fearless and independent judges in Russia. The Russian *sud* [legal system] after the Alexander reforms was a magnificent institution, not only on paper. . . . Under the Soviets, from the very start, the only protection a dissenter could hope for was dependent on governmental whims, not laws. No parties except the one in power could exist. (*DBDV* 222–23)

This passage, written eleven months after Nabokov informed Wilson of his intention to write a short novel that would become *Lolita,* is part of a long letter dedicated to correcting Wilson's idealized understanding of Soviet Russia. Nabokov felt that the things he wanted to convey to his American friend were so important that he concluded the letter with the promise to try to publish it (*DBDV* 223). Most importantly, the letter shows once again that during *Lolita*'s gestation, Nabokov was reflecting upon the relations between law and politics in the context of pre-revolutionary and post-revolutionary Russian structural reforms.

It is significant, then, that Nabokov's twenty-year residence in the United States immersed him in a system that embodied the ideal—championed by his father and cherished by the son—of rule of power submitting to rule of law. It is significant, too, that Nabokov had earlier seen that ideal come apart at the seams in the months preceding and following the Bolshevik coup. In the aftermath of the 1917 Revolution, Russian liberals were haunted by the knowledge that their own commitment to the law had, by a grim irony, given the Bolsheviks room to flourish. Nabokov's sensitivity to these historical ironies and self-recriminations organizes his entire outlook on law and politics in America. His sympathy for some key aspects of the anti-Communist campaigns that had become associated with McCarthyism must be understood in relation to the effort of Russian liberals, V. D. Nabokov among them, to come to terms with their own culpability in the Bolsheviks' seizure of power and its ultimate entrenchment. Russian history had made Nabokov aware not only of the cruel specter of tyranny, but also of the dreadful costs of legally protected civil freedoms.

RECHTSSTAAT AND NATURAL LAW

The Kadets distinguished themselves from other pre-revolutionary Russian political groups through their effort to transform their country into a liberal rule-of-law state. Their conception of *pravovoe gosudarstvo* derived from the continental European legal concept of *Rechtsstaat,* a term rooted in German jurisprudence that can be translated as "state of law," "state of justice," or "state of rights" (*LRR* 134; TT 133). Inspired by Kant and related to the Anglo-American concept of the rule of law, *Rechtsstaat* refers to a "constitutional state" in which political authority is circumscribed by the law for the sake of protecting its citizens from the arbitrary exercise of governmental power. The citizens of a *Rechtsstaat* share legally defined civil liberties which can be defended in the courts. A *Rechtsstaat*'s judiciary must, therefore, be independent from political authority and impartial in applying the law.

The Kadets' core objective to turn Russia into a state based on law was difficult to realize in a country in which the law was viewed with suspicion. As Walicki explains at length, their efforts to subject political power to the rule of law were vigorously opposed on both sides of the political divide. Leftist Populists, Anarchists, and Marxist-Leninists viewed legalized rights as an obstacle to social progress. Right-wing Slavophiles rejected juridical rationalism as a Western import that would undermine their commitment to social policies based on agreement on core values. Monarchists argued that only an all-powerful central government could guarantee national security, and that unlimited autocracy was superior to a constitutional monarchy or to a parliamentary republic.[36]

Walicki identifies Novgorodtsev and Petrazhitskii as the Kadet Party's principal legal theorists (*LPRL* 6). Like Chicherin and Soloviev (Russia's most influential nineteenth-century liberal legal philosophers), and together with other Kadets such as Peter Struve, Vladimir M. Hessen, Bogdan Kistiakovskii, and Sergey Kotliarevskii, Novgorodtsev and Petrazhitskii lent theoretical support to the Kadets' struggle to institute a rule-of-law state by arguing for the existence of a "right law"—that is, a legal model that was more than a compendium of arbitrary statutes imposed by the sovereign or the state. Legal positivism, the doctrine that law derives from the essentially arbitrary will of legislators, was their chief target. Seeing in legal positivism an equation of might with right, they accused positivists of putting political authority (whether that authority was vested in a monarch or a simple democratic majority) above the law, and of creating conditions in which tyranny could flourish.[37]

Against this, Novgorodtsev and Petrazhitskii argued that law is prepolitical, and that civil rights (freedom from political control) were more important than political rights (freedom as political participation). They supported this position by arguing that civil rights and the rule of law were conceivable without full political freedom, but that the reverse was not true. Within the rule-bound society they advocated, law would set rules for politics and not vice versa (*LPRL* 5).

To counter what they saw as the relativism of positivist jurisprudence, the Kadet Party's most prominent legal philosophers sought to rehabilitate the legal normativity associated with natural law. "Discovered" rather than "made," natural law is generally conceived as a system of justice common to all humankind, independent of sociopolitical contingencies, and derived from reason or nature. While acknowledging the validity of the historicist critique of natural law, legal scholars such as Novgorodtsev, Petrazhitskii, Kotliarevskii, and V. M. Hessen stressed the Kantian distinction between "what is" and "what ought to be," arguing that empirical, historically relative law must always be measured against a normative, trans-empirical, "just" law.[38] For these philosophers, law's chief responsibility was to protect the absolute significance of human dignity. Sergey Hessen articulates this core liberal principle in terms that are clearly indebted to Kant:

> The sphere of individual rights is understood not in its specific, always historically determined content, but in its essence, as the *impenetrability of the person for another person* (including the state), as that absolute nucleus of personhood that will not allow an individual to become a mere instrument used to satisfy the needs of others.[39]

Hessen's injunction against turning an individual into an instrument for the satisfaction of another's needs is inspired by Kant's second formulation of the categorical imperative: "So act that you use humanity, whether in your own person or in the person of any other, always at the same time as an end, never merely as a means."[40] Readers of *King, Queen, Knave, Laughter in the Dark, Despair, The Defense, Bend Sinister, Lolita, Pale Fire,* and *Ada* will note that Kant's "Formula of Humanity" shapes Nabokov's moral universe (see chapter 3).

For neo-idealist liberal philosophers such as Struve and Novgorodtsev, natural law provided a vital connection between ethical idealism and Russian liberalism (EI 16). In a seminal essay published at the height of his preparations for *Osvobozhdenie* and *Problems of Idealism,* Struve made explicit the logic connecting ethical idealism, liberalism, and natural-law theory. "Natural law," he wrote, "constitutes the essential and eternal content of liberalism" because its "roots repose in the ethical concept of the individual and his self-realization."[41]

The defense of natural-law principles was also a defining feature of Novgorodtsev's philosophical career. In 1901 Novgorodtsev published his book *Kant i Gegel' v ikh ucheniiakh o prave i gosudarstve* (*Kant and Hegel in Their Theories of Law and the State*). A philosophical justification of natural law, the book argued that Kantian neo-idealism provided the best defense of the autonomy of natural law against positivist reductionism. A year later, in his contribution to *Problems of Idealism,* Novgorodtsev stressed the connection between natural-law doctrine, ethical idealism, and liberal political theory. Modern theories of natural law, he wrote, provide

> the first formulations of the idea of the inalienable rights of the person. Seen from this point of view, natural law is the expression of the autonomous, absolute significance of the person, a significance that must belong to it in any political system. In this respect natural law is more than a demand for better legislation: it represents the protest of the person against state absolutism, reminding us of the unconditional moral basis that is the only proper foundation of society and the state. (EIPL 313)

During the planning stages of *Problems of Idealism,* one of the first men Struve considered as a potential contributor was V. M. Hessen, Joseph Hessen's cousin and V. D. Nabokov's colleague on *Pravo*'s editorial board (EI 19; *LPRL* 220). Though V. M. Hessen was not among the final contributors, his theory of "evolutionary natural law" explains why Struve immediately thought of Hessen as an appropriate choice. In his own contribution to the symposium, Novgorodtsev happily observes that Russian legal theory had recently experienced a groundswell of interest in natural-law doctrine. He also identifies Hessen's contribution to this phenomenon as an effective response to the challenge posed by "the indisputable fact of the variability of legal ideals," and calls attention to Hessen's "brilliant article" titled "Vozrozhdenie estestvennago prava" ("The Revival of Natural Law") and published in *Pravo* the same year as *Problems of Idealism* (EIPL 285–86, 281).

In this influential two-part essay, V. M. Hessen argues that the positivist definition of law as an instrument of power negates the possibility of ideological critique, without which the campaign for reform becomes theoretically meaningless:

> In order to demonstrate that natural law is impossible, the positivist school argues the following: called to serve material interests, the law is always and necessarily a reflection of *material force;* as a result, an ideological critique of the law is meaningless and pointless.
>
> Of course, if, from all existing theories of law, the only true conception of the law is the ancient theory of the Gaelic barbarian—"My law is the edge of my sword" and "Woe to the vanquished"—then natural law is impossible.
>
> But if, together with the ancient Romans . . . , we are convinced that the true meaning of the law does not lie in the "protection of interests" but in the "fulfilment of justice," . . . we cannot but reject the theory which identifies the law with the rule of power, the conqueror's weapon of domination over the vanquished.
>
> Positivist legal theory denies the possibility of an ideological evaluation and critique of the laws currently in operation.[42]

V. M. Hessen further observes that the world's most significant liberal reforms—the abolition of slavery and serfdom, for example, and the freedoms associated with movement and conscience—were generated under the ideological aegis of natural-law theory.[43] A revival of natural law, he predicts, would enable Russia's reformers to confront critical issues surrounding freedom and justice in a country whose institutions lagged far behind the liberal institutions of the West.

According to Hessen, legal positivism's principled insistence on "the incommensurability of the moral and legal domains" renders it incapable of advancing the aims of Russia's reform movement. By contrast, natural law's conception of law and ethics as "different aspects of the same order" enable it to support reform efforts ("*Pravo i etika, pravo i pravoubezhdenie—razlichnyia iavleniia odnogo i togo zhe poriadka*"). Quoting from Petrazhitskii's influential *Vvedenie v nauku politiki prava* (*Introduction to the Science of Legal Policy*), Hessen insists that moral ideals must guide Russian reformers in their struggle against autocracy: "The theory of natural law was not alone responsible for its demise; it was sold for so many silver coins and crucified, so that today it might with greater force rise from the dead and illuminate the path of humankind with the light of the ideal."[44]

As members of *Pravo*'s editorial board, V. M. Hessen and Petrazhitskii had regular contact with V. D. Nabokov. Walicki notes that *Pravo*'s editors met every Thursday and its members "became a closely-knit group of friends holding the same, or very similar, political views."[45] He notes further that the journal's title, *Pravo,* advertised its sympathy for natural-law theory. Quoting from Roscoe Pound's *The Ideal Element in Law,* Walicki observes that the Russian word *pravo* "stands for both *iustum* and *dextrum*": that is, "it means both the objective 'law' and the subjective 'right,' both what is 'legal' and what is 'just'" (*LPRL* 220). Unlike the word *zakon* (existing legal statute), the word *pravo* assumes a natural kinship between law and justice. As Joseph Hessen, the weekly's editor in chief, would later recall, this "name entered and became part of the soul" ("*nazvanie eto voshlo i stalo chast'iu dushi nashei*") of all editors of *Pravo* (*Vdv* 152).[46]

In the same memoir, Joseph Hessen further recalls the apprehensions with which *Pravo*'s founders invited V. D. Nabokov to join their ranks: "In general we all came from one class, one social level. But Nabokov, the son of a Minister, a gentleman of the tsar's chamber, married to the millionairess E. I. Rukavishnikov, living in a mansion on the Morskaia, arriving at meetings of the editorial board in a coach, seemed to us someone from another planet" (*Vdv* 154; qtd., in part, in *VNRY* 33). These apprehensions turned out to be unfounded, and Hessen stresses how quickly and thoroughly V. D. Nabokov disproved their assumptions:

> Vladimir Dmitrievich revealed himself to us as an excellent comrade, an extraordinarily conscientious worker, a man of a well-rounded education with an "elegant" publicistic style. Spiritually even-tempered, with a delicate inner tactfulness and benevolent disposition, he not only did not sow discord, but helped bring the team closer together and assumed responsibility for the journal's most important and dangerous articles.

Hessen underscores the opprobrium and enmity V. D. Nabokov incurred by his decision to join the militant *Pravo*. Relatives and acquaintances treated him with "malicious hostility" and the tsar's inner circle never forgave his defection to the opposition camp (*Vdv* 154–55).

The two *Pravo* editors who, together with Novgorodtsev, were credited with reviving natural-law theory in Russia in the first decade of the twentieth century had further ties to V. D. Nabokov by virtue of their political work. Both Petrazhitskii and V. M. Hessen belonged to the Kadet Central Committee. During the legislative activity begun before the opening of the First State Duma, Petrazhitskii worked with V. D. Nabokov and Joseph Hessen to produce a draft bill on the subject of amnesty and government abuses. At the same time, V. D. Nabokov and V. M. Hessen (again together with Joseph Hessen and three other Kadets) worked on a draft bill to abolish capital punishment and extraordinary laws (BRR 199, note 31). After Petrazhitskii, V. D. Nabokov, and other Kadet deputies to the First State Duma lost their right to participate in elections after the Vyborg appeal, V. M. Hessen was one of the Kadet leaders who replaced them in the Second State Duma (BRR 23, notes 54, 55). In *The Provisional Government,* V. D. Nabokov recalls how V. M. Hessen voluntarily placed himself under arrest in order to join him and his fellow electoral commissioners during their brief incarceration in the Smolnyi. Hessen's brave gesture of solidarity was cut short when he was "sent away almost by force" twenty-four hours after his arrival (*PG* 174).

Unlike Novgorodtsev, Petrazhitskii, and V. M. Hessen, V. D. Nabokov did not explicitly align himself with the school of natural law. Even so, his words on the subject of law, free will, and justice suggest that his inclinations were significantly tilted in this direction. He concluded his inaugural lecture at the Imperial School of Jurisprudence, for instance, by admonishing his audience to remember the difference between *de lege lata* and *de lege ferenda* (the law as it exists and the law as it ought to be), and to approach the efforts to reform Russia's outdated criminal code with this distinction in mind (Sm 22). His foundational belief in the existence of free will led him to subscribe to a Kantian-inspired ethical idealism in which the will's capacity for self-determination is inseparable from its capacity to respond to universally binding moral principles. Quoting with approval from A. D. Gradovskii's essay "Znachenie ideala v obshchestvennoi zhizni" ("The Significance of the Ideal in Social Life"), he aligns himself with Petrazhitskii's celebration of "the light of the ideal" when he insists that "living in society demands not only the study of the laws by which a society develops, but also the norms by which the will of the individual—a rational and moral creature—must act" (Sm 19).

Anticipating V. M. Hessen's argument that legal positivism is theoretically incompatible with social critique, he criticizes the historicist school for logical inconsistency. If the law is intrinsically arbitrary, he states, it is incoherent to wish "to repeal it with the stroke of a pen, replacing it with a different, improved one." He also opposes positivism's "complete absorption of the principle of justice by the narrow practical criterion of expediency" (Sm 7). "The formation and development of law is impossible without a prior conception of the known ideal of justice [*ideala spravedlivosti*]," he explains later, "which the law strives to achieve. The idea of justice lies at the foundation of all basic legal statutes. The realization and protection of interests is achieved by other means" (Sm 14). His argument that "law differs from other possible means of protecting one's interests because in its fulfillment human conscience finds peace and is able to reconcile itself with its demands" (Sm 14–15) anticipates V. M. Hessen's contention that "the true meaning of the law does not lie in the 'protection of interests' but rather in the 'fulfilment of justice.'"

Although the term "justice" (*spravedlivost'*) was common currency among liberationists of both positivist and idealist inclination, V. D. Nabokov explicitly aligns it with natural-law doctrine. (This is theoretically appropriate. As W. Friedmann notes, the concept presupposes a "universal audience" sharing common values and, therefore, "must base itself on a natural law philosophy.")[47] The thesis that law must be true to the "idea of justice," V. D. Nabokov states, "tempts one to subscribe to the views that helped found natural-law theory." Its various modern incarnations take as their point of departure the view that "the idea of law is given to the human being by nature, and must serve as the only source from which, through the intervention of reason, one can obtain and develop the foundations that shape social relationships [*ideia prava dana cheloveku ot prirody i dolzhna sluzhit' edinstvennym istochnikom, iz kotorago pri posredstve razuma mogut byt' pocherpnuty i razvity nachala, opredeliaiushchiia obshchestvennyia otnosheniia*]" (Sm 15).

In spite of these intellectual affinities, however, V. D. Nabokov did not explicitly align himself with the proponents of natural-law doctrine. There are several reasons why he might not have wished to do so. First, there is the matter of timing. When V. D. Nabokov delivered his inaugural lecture in 1896, idealist orientations in legal philosophy tended to be associated with arguments supporting autocratic rule. It was only in 1896, to quote Novgorodtsev, that "the first pronouncements were made in Russian legal studies about the necessity of the revival of natural law." Novgorodtsev notes further that these first stirrings, originating in his own work and that of Petrazhitskii, "were met with mistrust and doubt. It seemed strange and unlikely that an idea, so firmly condemned by the whole movement of thought in the nineteenth century, would ever again be resurrected as a legitimate and necessary concept in the philosophy of law" (EIPL 274). Only six years later, in 1902, was Novogorodtsev able to speak with confidence of a "surprising growth of interest in the idea of natural law" (EIPL 281).

It is therefore possible to speculate that V. D. Nabokov did not explicitly ally himself with the school of natural law because its "revival" was still in its infancy when he began his teaching career. Another reason is alluded to in Makletsov's appraisal of his scholarly career. As Makletsov writes, V. D. Nabokov's jurisprudence was most profoundly influenced by Tagantsev, professor of criminal law at St. Petersburg University and one of the most distinguished theorists of criminal law during the second half of the nineteenth century and the first decades of the twentieth.[48] V. D. Nabokov had studied under Tagantsev and took up his position at the Imperial School of Jurisprudence at Tagantsev's invitation.[49] As Boyd observes, Tagantsev "considered Nabokov his natural successor as a teacher and scholar" (*VNRY* 27–28). In *The Provisional Government,* Nabokov describes Tagantsev as a friend of twenty years' standing.[50]

Tagantsev, in turn, had been the pupil of the influential criminal lawyer Vladimir Spasovich (1829–1907), who resigned from his university post under duress in the aftermath of the publication of his "ideologically suspect" book on criminal law (*RLC* 7, 8, 160, note 2). As key representatives of the "classical" school of criminal law, Spasovich and Tagantsev insisted that free will and moral responsibility were foundational juridical concepts. Nethercott notes further that they favored a metaphysical grounding of crime and punishment that contrasted sharply with the positivist view that the individual was a socially determined being (*RLC* 3). Spasovich articulates his opposition to criminal anthropology in terms that are analogous to Nabokov's rejection of "statistics" in favor of "philosophy" in his response to F. Martin Brown.[51] The study of criminal law through the lens of anthropological statistics, Spasovich argues, transforms the autonomous field of criminal law into a satellite of sociology, political science, and politics. It also leads, Spasovich observes further, to the "effacement of the human individual."[52] Tagantsev locates the source of criminal anthropology in the new discipline of "moral statistics" ("*Moral'naia statistika porodila ugolovnuiu antropologiiu*") and is sharply critical of the positivists' efforts to absorb the science of criminal law into criminal sociology and anthropology: "Attempts to establish the natural-historical symptoms of the criminal person, . . . attempts to grasp the common biological characteristics among individuals, . . . present themselves not only as pointless, but also as harmful, both in theory and in practice, leading . . . to the erroneous formulation of the principles that guide the state's punitive activities."[53]

Though "classical" theorists of criminal law like Spasovich and Tagantsev vigorously resisted the reductive nature of positivist accounts of human subjectivity, they were nevertheless deeply attracted to what Spasovich called positivism's "humanizing ethos" in regard to punishment (*RLC* 45). Nethercott observes that "the odd cocktail of theoretical positions" endorsed by Tagantsev was the consequence of, on the one hand, his commitment to "classical" jurisprudential principles and, on the other, his recognition that criminal sociology and anthropology held out the promise of establishing a more humane penal system. This "oscillation between classical 'absolutist' and relativist positions" explains why Tagantsev was intensely criticized for his logical inconsistencies.[54]

V. D. Nabokov's unwillingness to identify himself openly with natural-law doctrine and his frequent (though always carefully qualified) praise of the contributions made by criminal sociologists and anthropologists to criminal law can be explained as a similar appreciation of the practical benefits of positivist accounts of crime. His commitment to penal reform and the restoration of the criminal to public life moderated the anti-positivist orientation of his jurisprudence. This is seen most explicitly in *Tiuremnye dosugi* (*Prison Reflections*), a series of articles he wrote while serving time in prison for signing the Vyborg appeal. The series was published in *Pravo* shortly after his release (*VNRY* 76).

Though he was no supporter of social and biological determinism, V. D. Nabokov does accept some of the key premises of criminal anthropology and sociology. He argues that one should neither "completely disregard the role of the individual mind" nor "view human actions generally and criminal acts in particular as inescapable products of external forces and conditions."

Nonetheless, he also acknowledges that "the enormous significance of these forces and conditions, and their influence on the development of one personality type or another, cannot be contested." Like Nabokov in "The Art of Literature and Commonsense," he rejected the famous criminal typologies of the eminent anthropologist Cesare Lombroso by referring to Lombroso's "*uomo delinquente*" as "a fantastical entity [*fantasticheskaia velichina*]."[55] But unlike his son, he conceded that "psychophysical defects . . . undoubtedly predispose one towards crime, weakening the capacity for resistance, blunting the force of moral consciousness." Social circumstances are equally important: "If we add to this unfavorable social conditions, such as poverty, an absence of moral education, a poor social environment, the presence of bad examples, premature sexual intercourse, alcoholism, etc., then the seed has fallen into fertile ground" (*Td* 1872).

The conception of human subjectivity that emerges from the pages of *Tiuremnye dosugi* makes significant concessions to sociological and anthropological determinism. V. D. Nabokov suggests that the will is not only a metaphysical given but also a product of social and psychological factors. The state's efforts to reform criminals through incarceration and highly regulated prison activities are doomed to failure, he contends, because imprisonment "reinforces and intensifies those conditions of personal and social existence that have a positive effect on the growth of crime" (*Td* 1877–78). Prison life is not conducive to reforming criminals because it does not train them to resist temptations and exercise critical judgment:

> The development and strengthening of one's will is possible only in the real and unceasing intercourse of free life, in the struggle of conflicting interests. The prison regime's leveling of unequal individualities, its demand, above all else, of strict obedience, its depersonalization of the inmate, sets in place an environment in which the inmate is never called upon to "exercise his will [*uprazhniat' svoiu voliu*]." (*Td* 1875)

Punishment must be individualized, V. D. Nabokov insists, if it is to serve a remedial function. The sentencing judge must take into account the criminal's psychological makeup, financial situation, personality, and motives (*Td* 1876–77, 1924–25).

These arguments are indebted to the pioneering work of Ivan Foinitskii (1847–1913), a professor of penology at St. Petersburg University who made the principle of individualized punishment the cornerstone of his theory of crime and punishment (*RLC* 55, 57). It was fitting that V. D. Nabokov should be guided by Foinitskii in his reflections on Russia's penal system while incarcerated in the famous St. Petersburg prison Kresty (The Crosses). *Tiuremnye dosugi* opens with a recollection of an educational field trip to Kresty twenty years earlier, when V. D. Nabokov was a second-year university student. The field trip was supervised by Foinitskii (*Td* 1812). It is possible to view *Tiuremnye dosugi* as a tribute to that day and to the university professor who influenced V. D. Nabokov on the subject of penal law.

Foinitskii's moderate sociological and anthropological approach to the task of reforming Russia's penal system inspired a number of younger criminalists, but it was also criticized by his contemporaries for abandoning classical juridical norms (*RLC* 54, 59). Tagantsev, for instance, raised the typical objection leveled by classicists against positivists: by attaching punishment to the criminal personality rather than to the criminal act itself, Foinitskii was undermining the fundamental juridical principle *nulla poena sine lege* (no penalty without a law) (*RLC* 51, 59). This principle was pioneered by the leading figure of the classical school of criminal jurisprudence, Paul Johann Anselm von Feuerbach (1775–1833). Feuerbach was responsible for developing the foundational principles that guided jurists like Spasovich and Tagantsev in their efforts to modernize Russian criminal justice (*RLC* 43).

It is to "the great [*genial'nyi*] Feuerbach" that V. D. Nabokov turns in *Tiuremnye dosugi* when cutting short his flirtation with positivism (*Td* 1922). Though he predicts that political and social reforms will lead to the extinction of entire categories of crimes, he ultimately rejects the attendant positivist argument that legal penalties should be replaced by methods of social improvement (*Td* 1921). The fundamental purpose of punishment, he writes, has been formulated "with exhaustive completeness and brilliant clarity" by Feuerbach, who showed that social life cannot exist in the absence of a system of normative directives and prohibitions. These "norms" become meaningful in the eyes of citizens only if the legislator sanctions them with the threat of punishment (*Td* 1922–23).

V. D. Nabokov's defense of Feuerbach's principle *nulla poena sine lege* against criminal sociology and anthropology is most explicit in his inaugural lecture. He chastises positivist penologists for seeking to replace punishment as a legal consequence of crime with the kinds of "penal substitutes" popularized by the father of criminal sociology, Enrico Ferri (1856–1929).[56] V. D. Nabokov argues that criminal lawyers cannot support such a project without dissolving the entire modern discipline of criminal law. The commitment of positivist penologists to a sociopolitical approach to crime is incompatible with the principle *nulla poena sine lege,* and sociologists who seek to preserve Feuerbach's principle within a positivist conception of crime are merely sabotaging their own laudable efforts to improve society (Sm 6).

Feuerbach consistently serves as a fixed and reliable point of reference in V. D. Nabokov's jurisprudential writings, and he is also most likely responsible for the Kantian orientation of V. D. Nabokov's legal thinking (*RLC* 43).

In evaluating the proposed reforms to the 1845 Code of Punishments,[57] for example, V. D. Nabokov praised Feuerbach (once again celebrated as "the German criminalist of genius") for being the first European to decriminalize consensual sodomy between adults.[58] V. D. Nabokov quotes Feuerbach's explicitly Kantian justification for decriminalizing consensual sodomy in the explanatory notes from 1813 to the Bavarian codex of 1810 (the same document that contains Feuerbach's famous maxim *nulla poena sine lege*):

> The present codex does not contain any resolutions against the individual whose actions, though immoral in their violation of internal duties towards oneself, do not infringe upon the rights of others: onanism, sodomy, bestiality, fornication—these are serious violations of moral commands, but in the sphere of external legislation they belong not as sins but only insofar as they infringe upon the rights of other people [*ne v kachestve grekhov, a lish' naskol'ko imi narusheny prava drugikh lits*]. (qtd. in Pp 154)

Feuerbach and V. D. Nabokov both endorse this critical distinction between private morality and public justice.

The distinction was pioneered by Kant. According to Kant, law and morality draw their sustenance from a common moral law (the categorical imperative); this argument makes Kant one of the most influential modern proponents of natural-law doctrine. At the same time, however, Kant also draws a sharp distinction between law and morality: whereas morality is a matter of an individual's internal motives, legality concerns itself with actions punishable by an external standard of law.[59] This distinction leads Kant to insist that the aim of public law is "not to teach virtue but only to set forth what is *right*" (*MM* 388; emphasis in original). Kant defines "the principle of right" as "the sum of the conditions under which the choice of one can be united with the choice of another in accordance with a universal law of freedom." The first of the principle's three conditions stipulates that public justice must concern itself "only with the external and indeed practical relation of one person to another, insofar as their actions, as deeds, can have (direct or indirect) influence on each other" (*MM* 387). As Frederick Rauscher notes, this explicitly excludes duties to the self.[60]

V. D. Nabokov endorses this Kantian distinction between public justice and private morality on other occasions. He rejects, for instance, the argument that legalizing consensual sodomy is tantamount to sanctioning vice because "the domain of criminal law and the domain of morality do not overlap"; as such, "the abolition or creation of laws in one area does not touch the other" (Pp 168). Later in the document V. D. Nabokov reiterates this point when he states that "the moral education of the nation" does not constitute "the goal of criminal legislation" (Pp 170–71). His claim that consensual adult sodomy may be punishable only in cases when it "offends public morality"—but, significantly, not when practiced in private—echoes Kant's insistence that the reach of public justice be limited to actions that have a bearing on others (Pp 162).

Kant's separation of law and morality originates in his liberal skepticism concerning shared values: "since people differ in their thinking about happiness and how each would have it constituted," he writes, a state cannot legitimately impose any specific conception of happiness upon its subjects. "A government established on the principle of benevolence toward the people like that of a *father* toward his children," he continues, "in which the subjects, like minor children who cannot distinguish between what is truly useful or harmful to them . . . is the greatest *despotism* thinkable (a constitution that abrogates all the freedom of the subjects, who in that case have no rights at all)."[61] V. D. Nabokov follows Kant in prioritizing freedom over shared values not only in his choice of political affiliation, but also in his jurisprudence. The "common good [*obschee blago*]," he argues, is too slippery a value for lawmaking. The logic that would allow the state to punish homosexuals for harming their physical and psychological health would, logically, also have to see smokers and drug addicts punished. Indeed, he adds mischievously, the "common good" would require that all insalubrious professions (such as mining and typesetting) be criminalized, and that punishment be meted out to all those whose actions fail to advance the interests of society and state (such as "convinced and confirmed bachelors") (Pp 162).

As a defense of the right to self-determination, Kant's Formula of Humanity constitutes the keystone of his theory of justice and deontological ethics. It draws its energy from the unconditional value of humanity and stipulates that people never be treated instrumentally, but always as ends in themselves (*GMM* 80). A similar rejection of utilitarian calculations underwrites V. D. Nabokov's protest against laws seeking to regulate prostitution at the expense of the rights and dignity of its practitioners. The legally enforced treatment and prevention of sexually transmitted disease, he insists, cannot be allowed to infringe upon "the inviolable rights of personhood [*nerushimye prava chelovecheskoi lichnosti*]" (Pp 181).

V. D. Nabokov's own efforts to introduce a more humane system of punishment into the Russian penal system accounts for his abiding appreciation of positivist contributions to criminal law. It also probably played a significant part in his unwillingness to subscribe openly to natural-law doctrine even as he consistently invoked its guiding premises. Interestingly, his son seems to have willfully disowned the positivist elements of his paternal legacy and reinterpreted his father's interest in positivist models of human behavior in a decidedly idealist light. This move is best illustrated in Nabokov's approach to Marx and Freud. His dismissal of Freud on ethical and legal grounds in an interview from 1968 is a caricature of his father's closely calibrated synthesis of positivist and idealist principles: "I also suggest that the Freudian faith leads to dangerous ethical consequences, such as when a filthy murderer with the brain of a tapeworm is given a lighter sentence because his mother spanked him too much or too little" (*SO* 116).

V. D. Nabokov's condemnation of the Russian penal system's "leveling" approach to punishment underwent a neat ideological inversion before reappearing as one of his son's frequent arguments against Marxism. Repeated in *Despair, Invitation to a Beheading,* and *Pale Fire,* the version cited here appears in *Bend Sinister,* a political dystopia modeled upon the crude materialism of an invented authority named Fradrick Skotoma:

> At every given level of world-time there was, he said, a certain computable amount of human consciousness distributed throughout the population of the world. This distribution was uneven, and herein lay the root of all our woes. Human beings, he said, were so many vessels containing unequal portions of this essentially uniform consciousness. It was however quite possible, he maintained, to regulate the capacity of the human vessels. If, for instance, a given amount of water were contained in a given number of heterogeneous bottles . . . the distribution of the liquid would be uneven and unjust, but could be made even and just either by grading the contents or by eliminating the fancy vessels and adopting a standard size. He introduced the idea of balance as a basis for universal bliss and called his theory "Ekwilism." This he claimed was quite new. True, socialism had advocated uniformity on an economic plane, and religion had grimly promised the same in spiritual terms as an inevitable status beyond the grave. But the economist had not seen that no leveling of wealth could be successfully accomplished . . . so long as there existed some individuals with more brains or guts than others.[62]

Viewing Russian history from the perspective of stinging disappointment, Nabokov transforms his father's sociologically inspired injunction against "leveling" into an idealist critique of Marxist materialism. Here, that injunction guides Nabokov's condemnation of the sociological theories mobilized by the Bolsheviks to sanction their consistent violations of human rights and dignity.

LOLITA AND THE PERILS OF LEGAL POSITIVISM

The natural-law strain of Nabokov's own political thinking emerges in his contribution to a panel discussion arranged by the Emergency Service Committee at Wellesley College in 1941. He invokes principles borrowed from natural-law doctrine in the course of arguing that democracy is a prepolitical ideal that resides in humankind's moral intuitions: "Democracy is not really a political phenomenon . . . it is the natural condition of every man ever since the human mind became conscious not only of the world but of itself." Echoing V. M. Hessen's observation that the law should be more than "the conqueror's weapon of domination over the vanquished," Nabokov adds: "Morally, democracy is invincible. Physically, that side will win which has the better guns."[63]

V. D. Nabokov would have been quick to point out that his son's paean to democracy is, in fact, a paean to *liberal* democracy. Democracy's status as the only "*normal state* of affairs," Nabokov explains in his contribution to the Wellesley panel, turns on "the splendid paradox . . . that while stress is laid on the rule of all and equality of common rights, it is the individual that derives from it his special and uncommon benefit. Ethically, the members of a democracy are equals; spiritually, each has the right to be as different from his neighbors as he pleases."[64] It is unlikely that Nabokov's omission of the qualifier "liberal" is an index of his lack of familiarity with the specialized nomenclature of political discourse. In a letter to Wilson from 1948, for instance, he draws attention to what he calls "the gap existing between fundamentally different systems of thought (totalitarianism and liberalism)" (*DBDV* 221). Had Nabokov been untutored in the subtleties of political discourse, he would have persisted in equating liberalism with democracy.[65] Though Nabokov may not have been as alert as his father to subtle political distinctions, he was keenly aware of the dangers posed by unlimited democracies. His oft-cited essay "The Art of Literature and Commonsense" sounds a typical liberal warning against the potential tyranny of unrestrained democratic majorities:

> It is instructive to think that there is not a single person in this room, or for that matter in any room in the world, who, at some nicely chosen point in historical space-time would not be put to death there and then, here and now, by a commonsensical majority in righteous rage. The color of one's creed, neckties, eyes, thoughts, manners, speech, is sure to meet somewhere in time or space with a fatal objection from a mob that hates that particular tone. (*LL* 372)

It is likely, therefore, that he knew that a simple democracy did *not* guarantee each individual's "right to be as different from his neighbors as he pleases." Nabokov must have recalled this distinction when he referred to himself as a "liberal" rather than a "democrat" (*SO* 96, 113).

If the two words Nabokov uses to denounce Humbert are read in conjunction with each other rather than separately, Nabokov's identification of

Humbert as "a foreigner and an anarchist" emerges from his sophisticated understanding of the kind of legal culture that liberal political structures require. The classical liberal conception of freedom, in Hayek's paraphrase of Kant's famous prescription for the perfect state, is "necessarily one of freedom under a law which limit[s] the freedom of each so as to secure the same freedom for all."[66] In sharp distinction to anarchism, Hayek adds, liberalism "recognizes that if all are to be as free as possible, coercion cannot be entirely eliminated, but only reduced to that minimum which is necessary to prevent individuals or groups from arbitrarily coercing others."[67]

Humbert's anarchism lies in his refusal to be constrained by law. It is interesting, then, that this refusal asserts itself for the first time in the United States, when Dolly's unexpected invitation to sexual intercourse gives him "the odd sense of living in a brand new, mad new dream world, where everything was permissible" (*L* 125). (In Europe, by contrast, Humbert tells us that he was "a law-abiding poltroon" [*L* 15].) Furthermore, Humbert's positivist conception of the law is diametrically opposed to the legal principles that underwrite American national identity. This positivist and antiliberal attitude toward the law (rather than his European background) allows Nabokov to suggest that Humbert's crimes are "un-American" and to dismiss him as a "foreigner" without lapsing into xenophobia.

As Charles Haines has noted, the genesis of American statehood is an important chapter in the history of natural-law philosophy. The leaders of the American Revolution consistently invoked principles derived from natural-rights doctrine to sanction the right to rebellion against the arbitrary exercise of governmental powers, and the Declaration of Independence enshrined these principles into law when it pronounced that men are "endowed by their Creator with certain unalienable rights, that among these are Life, Liberty, and the pursuit of Happiness." These principles structured one of V. D. Nabokov's most memorable and frequently cited political pronouncements. At the zemstvo congress of July 1905, he urged the opponents of tsarist autocracy "to defend the natural rights" (as these had been formulated in the resolutions of the November congress of 1904) "by all peaceful means, not excluding disobedience of the orders of the authorities which violate these rights."[68] The prioritization of citizens' rights over governmental authority in America's founding documents empowered the courts to claim the prerogative to review and overturn legislative acts by measuring them against constitutional standards. Like the opponents of Russian liberalism, critics of the American system insist that the principle of judicial review or judicial supremacy is anti-democratic and opposed to the common good.[69]

One of Humbert's key strategies for justifying his crimes against Dolly is to refute natural-law principles and tacitly endorse legal positivism by implying that the cultural relativity of legal norms authorizes their violation. Echoing opponents of natural-law theory, he denies that his relationship with Dolly is subject to any "higher law," arguing instead that the law is always an arbitrary function of power. His tortured confession is the work of a mind determined to vindicate actions it knows to be wrong by turning to various positivist configurations of reality. The social sciences provide him with numerous arguments in support of his efforts to believe that there is nothing immoral in a grown man's sexual relationship with an underaged girl. Sexologists, for instance, assure him that he has "all the characteristics which . . . start the responses stirring in a little girl: clean-cut jaw, muscular hand, deep sonorous voice, broad shoulder" (*L* 39); sociologists inform him that "among Sicilians sexual relations between a father and his daughter are accepted as a matter of course" (*L* 140); legal historians teach him that the law is contingent upon cultural norms, that "little slave flowers" could be "casually plucked between business and bath . . . in the days of the Romans," and that "tiny entertainers" could be used "fore and aft between the mutton and the rose sherbet" by "dignified Orientals" in what Humbert longingly calls "luxurious times" (*L* 116).

The sensuous, appreciative tones in which Humbert invokes these examples are symptoms of his self-indulgence, but their proliferation shows him to be struggling against his own dim awareness that his arguments are sophistic. Though he insists that only in recent times has "the old link between the adult world and the child world" been severed "by new customs and new laws" (*L* 116), he recognizes that his crime is indefensible regardless of historical circumstances. As he admits on several occasions, beneath the sociologist's mask he has donned lurks a "despicable and brutal" monster whose "sterile and selfish vice" has led him to disregard "all laws of humanity" (*L* 268, 261, 288).[70]

Humbert's story anatomizes the dangers implicit in the moral relativism encouraged by positivist conceptions of the law. *Lolita* suggests that even people as vicious and depraved as Humbert are morally self-aware in ways that challenge the legal-positivist claim that there is no connection between law and ethics, and that both are socially constructed. Note, for example, that he castigates himself for having violated "all laws of humanity" in spite of reveling in the historical precedents for his crime. American jurors inclined to approach Humbert's relationship with Dolly from a legal-positivist perspective would have to find him guilty of statutory rape, but, depending on their moral outlooks, might agree with him that his misfortune is to be a nympholept in twentieth-century Europe and America. To argue that Humbert's sexual relations with Dolly violate laws that are not merely arbitrary is to insist, instead, upon a universally binding set of legal ideals, or—what is the same—to reject the claims of legal positivism in favor of natural law.

But if *Lolita* stakes its legal commitments in natural law, it also acknowledges an ineliminable rift between innate ideas about justice and existing legal statutes. Though Humbert's implicit critique of natural law is opportunistic, he is right to note that the law cannot escape a certain degree of arbitrariness. "I found myself maturing amid a civilization which allows a man of twenty-five to court a girl of sixteen but not a girl of twelve" (*L* 15), he complains about age-of-consent laws. Designed to distinguish between those considered competent to consent to sexual intercourse and those who are not, age-of-consent laws are forced to make the uneasy decision as to when an individual can be reasonably expected to reach sexual autonomy. The difficulty of correlating age with sexual autonomy accounts for the inconsistency in such laws: they vary from period to period, state to state, country to country, and sex to sex.[71] These inconsistencies, however, need not invalidate the claim made by proponents of natural law that the law ought to reflect principles that reasonable people can agree to be valid.

Walicki notes that Russia's pre-revolutionary liberal philosophers expended time and effort responding to historicist critiques of natural law (*LPRL* 137–38, 211, 265). Novgorodtsev seems almost to be offering a proleptic gloss on Humbert's attempt to dissolve the claims of natural law in historical relativism when he writes in his contribution to *Problems of Idealism:* "The only argument the historical mode of thought brings against the autonomy of the moral problem is the empirical observation about the historical changeability of moral concepts. The conclusion is that all morality is the product of history, wholly dependent on temporary and local conditions" (EIPL 287). Novgorodtsev's response to the historicist challenge was guided by Kant's view that absolute moral and legal standards are "regulative ideas":

> As the law of unconditional "ought," the categorical imperative is the form of and call to searching. This form must be fulfilled, and the call must lead to a definite result. But this absolute form can never be filled by an adequate content, and the moral call can never be satisfied by an achieved result. . . . In accordance with the purely formal character of the supreme moral criterion, Kant had to reject the possibility of an absolute moral content that could pretend to eternal recognition. (EIPL 309; see also *LPRL* 304–5)

His further assertion that "the formal principle of morality equally eliminates both ethical conservatism and the ethical utopia of earthly perfection" exposes the sophistry behind Humbert's self-justification when he implies that historical relativism authorizes him to imitate the ancients or that the inconsistency of current laws gives him license to violate them.

Dolly's sexual precocity abets Humbert's attempt to justify his crimes by underscoring the arbitrariness of America's age-of-consent legislation. It is with roguish self-satisfaction that he informs the "frigid gentlewomen of the jury" that Dolly first seduced him (*L* 124). Humbert interprets Dolly's proposition as a form of consent, but Nabokov refutes this notion by crafting various scenarios that reveal Dolly's lack of autonomy and capacity for consent. Her proposition is largely fueled by her unreflective obsession with Hollywood glamour magazines and by her mistaken assumption that sexual intercourse with Humbert will be no different from intercourse with Charlie Holmes, her thirteen-year-old summer-camp paramour (*L* 44). When Dolly "seduces" Humbert, she does so from a position of naïveté and ignorance, something which he sees but refuses to acknowledge:

> She saw the stark act merely as part of a youngster's furtive world, unknown to adults. What adults did for purposes of procreation was no business of hers. My life was handled by little Lo in an energetic, matter-of-fact manner as if it were an insensate gadget unconnected with me. While eager to impress me with the world of tough kids, she was not quite prepared for certain discrepancies between a kid's life and mine. Pride alone prevented her from giving up. (*L* 125)

Humbert also downplays the physical pain this sexual act inflicts upon Dolly (*L* 131–32). Passages like these reveal that Humbert has raped Dolly, something he admits in the final pages of his chronicle when he sentences himself to "at least thirty-five years for rape" while dismissing the rest of the charges (*L* 290).

Dolly's relationship with Quilty extends *Lolita*'s exploration of the nature of sexual autonomy. When Dolly runs off with Quilty she is two years older than she was when she "seduced" Humbert at the Enchanted Hunters. This second affair demonstrates that her capacity to determine her own actions increases as she gets older. Though her choices remain limited, Dolly's evolving maturity enables her to avoid the worst forms of exploitation. Humbert is pained to hear seventeen-year-old Dolly tell him that she had loved Quilty when she decided to abscond with him at the age of fourteen (*L* 260). But in spite of her increased maturity and emotional attachment to the famous playwright, Dolly's energetic participation in Quilty's plans to abduct her is played out against a backdrop of complete helplessness (*L* 266–67). Her lack of opportunities when she agrees to run off with him, and the false promises with which he lures her away from Humbert, make informed consent impossible (*L* 259–60).

Nabokov's decision to make Dolly seventeen when Humbert confronts her at Coalmont may have been influenced by his father's assessment of the proposed reforms to the 1845 Russian Code of Punishments. Though Nabokov reports having read his father's "Plotskie prestupleniia" ("Carnal

Crimes") for the first time only after Andrew Field found V. D. Nabokov's *Sbornik statei po ugolovnomu pravu* (*A Collection of Articles on Criminal Law*) at a secondhand bookstore in 1961, it is highly unlikely that he was unacquainted with it before this late date (*SM* 512). In a tribute to V. D. Nabokov's scholarly career published on the front page of *Rul'* several days after his death, Makletsov singled out the *Sbornik* as the crowning achievement of V. D. Nabokov's early jurisprudence, and "Plotskie prestupleniia" as the very best legal study of sexual crime in its field.[72] Ten years later, Makletsov repeated these claims about the essay's prominence in a longer tribute commemorating the tenth anniversary of V. D. Nabokov's death.[73] (More recently, Laura Engelstein tacitly endorsed this assessment by treating V. D. Nabokov's "Plotskie prestupleniia" as a key document in the debates surrounding gender and the juridical subject in late imperial Russia.)[74] Even if Nabokov remained unfamiliar with Makletsov's evaluation of his father's scholarly contributions (an unlikely scenario), it is difficult to imagine that he was still ignorant of his father's esteemed writings on sexual crime as late as 1961.

In "Plotskie prestupleniia," V. D. Nabokov dwells at length on age-of-consent legislation and agrees on seventeen as the appropriate age of sexual majority (Pp 144). But he also argues further—as if in response to Quilty's abduction of Dolly—that the seduction of a girl under the age of twenty-one through the use of false promises should constitute a crime punishable by law (Pp 171). In adding this important qualification, V. D. Nabokov may be drawing on Kant's argument about the connection between deception and coercion. In *Groundwork of The Metaphysics of Morals,* Kant explains why deception precludes the possibility of consent: "He who has it in mind to make a false promise to others sees at once that he wants to make use of another human being *merely as a means,* without the other at the same time containing in himself the end. For, he whom I want to use for my purposes by such a promise cannot possibly agree to my way of behaving toward him, and so himself contain the end of this action" (*GMM* 80).

Lolita highlights the problems that plague the attempt to translate ethical principles into legal statutes, but it also affirms that certain ethical principles must remain integral to the shaping and interpretation of the law. The debate over what constitutes an appropriate sexual age of consent highlights liberalism's difficult task of finding that minimum degree of coercion "necessary to prevent individuals or groups from arbitrarily coercing others."[75] Though the notion of consent predates modern liberal doctrine, it remains a key liberal value tied to the liberal principle of human inviolability. It is significant, then, that Humbert invokes Sergey Hessen's metaphor for the "eternal truth" of liberalism as a measure of his offense against Dolly. His surrealistic fantasy of total penetration vividly expresses his desire to possess and objectify her.

Humbert cannot plead ignorance in the matter of Dolly's pain because he, too, has felt the penetrating sting of objectification. Upon learning that his wife Valeria has been conducting an affair with another man and plans to leave him, he claims to have suffered the kind of helplessness he will later associate with Dolly: "Valeria, after applying a wet napkin to her knee, went on talking—*into* me rather than to me" (*L* 25; emphasis in original). This feeling is replicated when Quilty mocks Humbert's efforts to track him down by identifying himself by droll names in hotel registries: "the most penetrating bodkin," Humbert notes, "was the anagramtailed entry in the register of Chestnut Lodge 'Ted Hunter, Cane, NH'" (*L* 236). Dolly's betrayal of Humbert's sentimental attachment to their sojourn at The Enchanted Hunters replays in a minor key the infractions against the sanctity of selfhood that Humbert perpetrated against her.

In *Invitation to a Beheading*, Cincinnatus's unique ontology makes him immune to external penetration even as it sends him to the scaffold. Dolly, too, possesses that kernel of inviolable personhood that remains inaccessible even to the worst kinds of violence inflicted upon her. Her remark to her friend Eva Rosen about the loneliness of death sparks an epiphany in Humbert: "It struck me . . . that I simply did not know a thing about my darling's mind and that quite possibly, behind the awful juvenile clichés, there was in her a garden and a twilight, and a palace gate—dim and adorable regions which happened to be lucidly and absolutely forbidden to me, in my polluted rags and miserable convulsions" (*L* 267). But if Dolly's mind, like that of Cincinnatus, successfully deflects Humbert's penetrative gaze, her body is exposed, vulnerable, and violated.

LAW AND REVOLUTION

Liberalism's emphasis on law explains why legal professionals dominated the Kadet Party's highest ranks. But although lawyers and professors of law were the most widely represented professional group on the Kadet Central Committee, the extent to which they influenced party policy remains a matter of debate. The party's shortcomings have been acutely observed (in somewhat contradictory forms) by historians on both the right and left. Critics such as Shapiro, Pipes, and Walicki suggest that the Kadet leadership compromised its chances to bring order and stability to Russia by prioritizing political expedience over legality (*zakonnost'*). For critics such as Rosenberg and Karpovich, the Kadets failed precisely because their commitment to legality crippled their ability to react effectively to revolutionary and counterrevolutionary crises.

This debate was especially bitter with respect to Kadet tactics in the First State Duma. The question of whether the party had been right to prioritize political goals over legal principles during the critical months of the First State Duma was obsessively revisited in the emigration. Though his father was the most likely direct source of Nabokov's familiarity with this controversy, Nabokov was also no doubt familiar with it from his close ties to *Sovremennye zapiski* and his many years' residence among Russia's émigré communities in Berlin and Paris. In America, he probably encountered it again in the social milieu associated with Karpovich, the Harvard historian who was instrumental in securing the Nabokovs' entry into the United States, and who remained a dedicated supporter of Nabokov's interests in America. Karpovich is generally considered to be the prototype of Al Cook (born Kukolnikov), the hospitable Americanized Russian émigré whose country home provides an oasis for Pnin and his kindred Russian intellectuals (*VNRY* 378; *VNAY* 14–15).

In an influential article from 1955 titled "Two Types of Russian Liberalism: Maklakov and Miliukov," Karpovich revisits the argument that revolutionary tactics fatally compromised Kadet policy in the First State Duma.[76] The argument was initially made famous by Vasilii Maklakov when *Sovremennye zapiski* began in 1928 to publish his memoirs in serial form. Other books followed, and Maklakov's argument was promoted and extended by those who, like him, believed that the Kadets had forfeited the gains of the 1905 October Manifesto by intransigently opposing the tsarist regime and by refusing to press for reforms within the constitutional framework set up by the manifesto.[77] They argued further that the Kadet Party's indifference to the claims of legality set a dangerous precedent that was gleefully imitated by the Bolsheviks.[78]

Prominent Kadet conservatives such as Peter Struve, Novgorodtsev, Petrazhitskii, and V. M. Hessen shared Maklakov's prioritization of law over politics. A Kadet leader throughout the party's career, Maklakov was the Kadets' most valued orator in the Duma and one of the country's most talented lawyers (BRR 127). With Kadet lawyers Nikolai Teslenko and Osip Pergament, he was responsible for the legal defense of the Kadets tried for signing the Vyborg appeal (BRR 293). Six years later, he gained an international reputation for his work as a defense lawyer in the famous Beiliss trial whose proceedings V. D. Nabokov reported for *Pravo* (*LRR* 21). Maklakov and V. D. Nabokov were both nominated as potential ministers of justice in a cabinet that their political allies in the Fourth Duma hoped to form on the day that Nicholas II acceded to their pressure for constitutional reform.[79] In Paris, Maklakov became the official representative of Russian émigrés in

France, a position which made Nabokov confident that Maklakov could obtain a French visa for him and his family (*VNRY* 394). Boyd reports further that after moving his family to Paris, Nabokov socialized with Maklakov and other former political colleagues of his father (*VNRY* 437).

Karpovich's claim that Maklakov and Miliukov represented "the two main components of the Kadet Party" (TT 130) is useful for understanding V. D. Nabokov's predicament as a professional jurist and political activist during Russia's revolutionary periods. It also helps expose the intellectual dilemmas inherited by Nabokov from his father and the traces these dilemmas have left on his most controversial novel. Like Walicki, Karpovich ascribes Maklakov's overarching commitment to legality to his legal training (TT 132). As a principled opponent of legal arbitrariness, Maklakov blamed the Miliukov-led Kadets for assuming an uncompromisingly hostile attitude toward the regime after the promulgation of the October Manifesto. The "historical state power," he argued, had the advantage of inspiring obedience and thus offered the only bulwark against anarchy. By aligning themselves with the country's radical elements, the Kadets missed their chance to contribute to Russia's peaceful evolution toward a liberal rule-of-law state (TT 135–36).

Karpovich emphasizes the contrast between Maklakov's preoccupation with legality and Miliukov's political pragmatism. This pragmatism, Karpovich contends, was inspired by Miliukov's youthful discovery of positivism (TT 133). In a similar vein, Karpovich argues that Miliukov's positivism accounts for his "characteristically empirical" defense against Maklakov: the party, Miliukov reminded Maklakov, was not being guided by "abstractions and armchair [*kabinetnye*] deliberations," but by practical considerations (qtd. in TT 137). Miliukov accused Maklakov of prioritizing means over ends, and argued that under certain conditions even a liberal might legitimately become a revolutionary (TT 138).

Historians tend to be skeptical toward Maklakov's optimism about Russia's chances of peaceful evolution after the passage of the October Manifesto, pointing out that his critique was distilled in the purifying glow of retrospective analysis (TT 135). For these historians, Miliukov's claim that the government had no intention to liberalize the country's institutions rings true (BRR 274; *FPP* 17). Unlike Miliukov and Maklakov, V. D. Nabokov left no body of retrospective reflections upon his life in politics and the errors of the past. Judging from the writings that do survive, he was in full agreement with Miliukov and Miliukov's closest advisors. His focus on the tsarist regime's murderous hypocrisy in the wake of the October Manifesto is deeply at odds with Maklakov's retrospective rendition of these events in *The First State Duma.* In an article from February 3, 1906, published in Peter Struve's weekly *Poliarnaia zvezda* (*The Polar Star*), V. D. Nabokov denounces the government's "internal war" against political opposition in the immediate aftermath of the manifesto's promulgation, and concludes that "the historical mission of the First State Duma is the total abolition of the autocratic bureaucracy and the heralding of a new governmental order."[80] In his detailed postmortem analysis of the First State Duma, he defends the Kadets against the charge that different tactics might have prevented the Duma's dissolution. Such a charge, he argues, can only be leveled by someone whose life has been isolated from the facts of recent Russian history: isolated, that is, from the stubbornness with which the government continued to refuse "to embark on the path of constitutionalism." He notes, bitterly, that "Russia's rulers never renounced the principles of autocracy," preferring rather "to remain the unaccountable masters of the destinies of Russia's people and merely tolerate the Duma as a necessary evil, and then not any Duma, but only the trivial kind that will agree to dance to the government's tune."[81]

But although V. D. Nabokov belonged to Miliukov's inner circle and supported the Kadets' tactics in the First State Duma, he was also a professional jurist. Like Maklakov, Petrazhitskii, V. M. Hessen, and other jurists on the Kadet Party's right flank, he was keenly sensitive to the difficulties of combining political struggle with a defense of law. Walicki suggests that Miliukov's prioritization of political over legal ends successfully dominated Kadet Party policy because "the overwhelming majority of the Kadets were not only overpoliticized," but also lacked "a strong legal consciousness" (*LPRL* 398). In spite of being one of Miliukov's closest political allies, V. D. Nabokov emphatically did not belong to this Kadet majority.

V. D. Nabokov's commitment to legality is everywhere manifest in his writings and political activities. Makletsov aptly notes that he "fought for the idea of law his entire life."[82] When the tsarist regime unleashed a new wave of political repressions during the 1905–06 Revolution, he repeatedly denounced the government's unscrupulous violations of the law. The terms in which he frames his indignation anticipate Humbert Humbert's confession that his most severe moral delinquencies against Dolly began the moment he felt himself to be living in a world in which "everything was permissible" (*L* 125). They also anticipate Véra Nabokov's fears that the indiscriminate allegations against "everybody left of Thomas Dewey" might transform the United States from a state of law into a state of power. V. D. Nabokov's outrage is directed at the government's refusal to honor legal limitations upon its power and its legally positivistic equation of might with right:

> In these conditions the question of legality, of rights, is not posed; these terms are overthrown. Physical force takes over. A fist is raised over each one of us, and all arguments and reasoning capitulate before the real eloquence of this gesture. . . . Everything is permitted, nothing will have to be accounted for

> [*vse pozvoleno, ni za chto otvechat' ne pridetsia*], as long as there is the outward cause of the struggle against revolution.[83]

He also criticizes the country's judiciary for making no effort to curb such violations. The magistracy, he observes, "has accepted in dead silence" the governor general's expulsion of the district court members of Tomsk. "The entire judicial establishment," he continues, "should have protested against this obvious unlawful action, which transforms the last remnants of judicial independence into an empty sound." He speculates bitterly that "perhaps we will live to see the day when the minister of justice will thank in his official records the legal officials subordinated to him for their zealous service during the present difficult time."[84]

In *The Provisional Government,* V. D. Nabokov's detailed analysis of the legal difficulties posed by Grand Duke Michael's abdication can seem over-fastidious and painfully detached from the revolutionary upheavals that were tearing the country apart (*PG* 49–54). But to V. D. Nabokov, the unlawfulness of Nicholas II's transfer of power to his brother was "more than a matter of juridical quibbling" even though, as he admits, the monarchy had no hope of survival under prevailing political conditions (*PG* 50–52). In his role as head of the Chancellery to the first Provisional Government, he agonized over the fact that he was unable to obtain from the provisional regime a record of the critical first sessions that might establish "the fundamental principles of its power." Appeals to Miliukov to reconstruct the proceedings from memory, he complains, went unanswered (*PG* 59). In the same document, he opposes the Provisional Government's arrest of Nicholas II on the grounds that it was "contrary to the axioms of state law" (*PG* 71).

V. D. Nabokov's deep-seated commitment to legality is best exemplified by his actions during the civil war. At the Kadet conference held in October 15 (October 28, New Style), 1918, in Ekaterinodar, V. D. Nabokov opposed the party's support of a White military dictatorship. Together with Maxim Vinaver and other Kadets who had sought refuge in the Crimea, he insisted that the Kadets' support of General Denikin's anti-Bolshevik Volunteer Army be conditional upon its adoption of a liberal administrative program (*LRR* 330, 334). Overruled by the Kadet majority, V. D. Nabokov and Vinaver rejected the party's endorsement of a "military solution" and committed themselves to a liberal-socialist compact that they believed to be the only effective challenge to Bolshevism.[85] Upon their return to the Crimea, they established a provisional regional government that sought to combine the best of the Kadet Party's liberal traditions with a commitment to social reform (*LRR* 331, 335–36, 357).

The Crimean Regional Government began its work on November 15, 1918, and though it dissolved five months later, its short history is important for understanding the way in which Nabokov's experience of Russia's civil war colored his experience of Cold War America. Though formally a coalition regime composed of Kadets, Mensheviks, Socialist Revolutionaries, and Tatars, it was generally considered a Kadet administration. Its power rested in the hands of a Kadet quadrumvirate: Solomon Krym (prime minister), Maxim Vinaver (minister of foreign affairs), Nicholas (Nikolai) Bogdanov (minister of internal affairs), and V. D. Nabokov (minister of justice). In V. D. Nabokov's retrospective account, the government's mission was to establish local order, rule-of-law governance, and democratic foundations. These goals, he implies, were critical to the government's parallel mission of ensuring that the Crimea would remain part of Russia after the end of the civil war.[86] Guided by a spirit of conciliation with the left and moved to abandon the Kadets' traditional statist orientation, the regime combined a commitment to liberal principles with a sensitivity to local needs (*Rg* 176; *LRR* 362, 366). In the words of the Crimean Kadet leader and publicist Daniel (Daniil) Pasmanik, "the Crimea was to serve for all Russia as an example of cultured, democratic government, satisfying all just demands of the population, avoiding all mistakes of socialist passion, and fighting with Bolshevik demagogy. In a word, a model laboratory experiment" (*Rg* 113; qtd. in *LRR* 357).

The liberal experiment in the Crimea constitutes a significant and complicated chapter in V. D. Nabokov's political career; its lessons shaped not only Nabokov's response to the Communist threat in America but also the fabric of what he thought of as his most "American" novel. Shortly after coming to power, the Kadet ministry repealed all former decrees restricting the press, assembly, and worship. They also abrogated pre-revolutionary laws restricting libraries, reopened the local university, and granted complete freedom to private educational institutions (*NpKv* 180–81; *Rg* 176, 180; *LRR* 372). As the head of the commission charged with the writing and publication of the new laws, V. D. Nabokov played a pivotal role in the government's efforts to establish a liberal rule-of-law regime and uphold civil liberties. Vinaver recalls: "Anyone familiar with Nabokov's exceptional stylistic and editorial talents will be able to imagine the stringent and irreproachable style in which our laws were written, and will regret—as I do—that this work, overseen by Nabokov, was not preserved" (*NpKv* 180).[87]

In his role as minister of justice, V. D. Nabokov revitalized the local judiciary. Personally drafting a comprehensive program for reconstructing judicial institutions, he set up new courts at every level and dispatched a series of memoranda to the region's administrative authorities warning them not to interfere in judicial matters (*LRR* 372; *Rg* 180). In *Speak, Memory,* Nabokov refers to his father's staunch efforts to curb the abuses by White Army soldiers and officers when he recalls that his father was "in constant friction with trigger-happy elements in Denikin's army" (*SM* 511). V. D. Nabokov's remarkable commitment to judicial correctness in time of war is best illustrated by an event described by Pasmanik. When twenty well-known Bolsheviks (many of whom had personally killed White Army officers and innocent citizens) were arrested, V. D. Nabokov insisted that their cases be entrusted to the local judicial investigator. Knowing that the convicted would not be put to death under a regime that had revoked the death penalty and anticipating future reprisals when the Bolsheviks returned to power, witnesses refused to testify. White Army officers demanded a speedy trial and the application of capital punishment. Pasmanik recalls that V. D. Nabokov remained faithful to the idea of legality, arguing repeatedly that he could not change the laws when dealing with the enemy. After an agreement was reached to move the proceedings to the distant, more peaceful Kerch, the accused were shot and killed en route by the Volunteers responsible for their conveyance.[88] In his attempt to come to terms with the collision of values posed by these events, Pasmanik cites the view of a popular local social activist: "Nabokov was right to refuse to reverse the law, but the officers were also right to mete out punishment to the murderers" (*Rg* 145–46).

Keenly sensitive to the provisional nature of their administration, the Crimean Kadets avoided radical social reforms that might have national consequences. Nonetheless, they passed a series of laws that aimed to redress Russia's traditional social injustices. A law that regulated Crimean mortgages and leases led to substantial increases in the region's harvests, and social insurance and labor-exchange legislation was passed in an effort to convince workers of the benefits of liberal democracy (*Rg* 178; *NpKv* 188–89; *LRR* 372–73). Such measures, coupled with the Kadets' commitment to civil freedoms, did not go unrewarded: in the elections for the region's new city dumas, the Kadets secured almost a third of all the votes cast (*Rg* 175; *LRR* 374).

The key role played by V. D. Nabokov in these events demonstrates his deep-seated commitment to rule-of-law principles when such principles were at their most vulnerable. Yet this luminous episode in his political career provides a most painful example of the tension between legal principle and political expedience. In his admiring portrait of V. D. Nabokov, Pasmanik describes him as an "ardent defender of the idea of legality," but notes further that such a position is "not always appropriate in revolutionary times." He recalls that during his frequent arguments with V. D. Nabokov, the latter always insisted that "lawlessness ruined Russia," a verdict that is suggestively echoed in his son's ascription of anarchism to his most famous literary creation. According to Pasmanik, V. D. Nabokov's strenuous efforts to submit the activities of the Volunteers to the rule of law were guided by his conviction that lawlessness would lead to the complete disintegration of the White Army.[89] Though they often disagreed, Pasmanik concedes that on this subject V. D. Nabokov turned out to be prophetic (*Rg* 122).

After the Bolsheviks recaptured the peninsula and the Crimean Regional Government collapsed, V. D. Nabokov came to rue his involvement in the Kadets' liberal experiment in the Crimea. In letters and conversations with friends he confessed that he regretted his participation in an enterprise he had come to regard as a grave political error.[90] By condemning his activities in the Crimea, V. D. Nabokov was realigning himself with Kadet conservatives such as Novgorodtsev, Maklakov, and many others for whom the Crimean experiment in liberal-socialist politics fatally undermined the anti-Bolshevik movement and bolstered Tatar separatism. By refusing to accept martial law, these critics argued, the Crimean Kadets placed their personal political ambitions above the most immediate need to defeat Lenin's armies (*Rg* 166–67; *LRR* 362, 367, 374–75, 408–10; NP 15, 16, 23). They argued further that Crimean liberalism played into Bolshevik hands. Those "trigger-happy" White "elements" with whom V. D. Nabokov was in "constant friction" were, arguably, protecting the foodstuffs and materiel that were being diverted from the Whites to the Reds (*LRR* 368). Thinking back upon his time in the Crimea, V. D. Nabokov must have agreed with those critics who had argued that the peninsula's lack of press restrictions encouraged its Tatar separatists and leftist agitators to wage a bitter campaign against the government and the White Army (*Rg* 142; *LRR* 372, 373). Retrospective analysis must have led him to agree with White Army commanders who complained that the peninsula's freedoms of press, assembly, and movement allowed the Bolsheviks to consolidate their forces and prepare unimpeded for their next offensive (*Rg* 126–29; NP 16).

V. D. Nabokov's doubts about the political wisdom of civilian rule in the Crimea must have preyed upon him even before the regime disintegrated. Among the documents collected in his personal folder and preserved at the Hoover Institution is a telegram received in Sevastopol on February 13, 1919, and sent to him by his younger brother Konstantin, at the time chargé d'affaires at the Russian embassy in London. Explicitly not an official directive but a personal communication from one brother to another, the telegram counsels V. D. Nabokov to "accept every compromise [*idti na vse kompromissy*] for the sake of attaining the unification of Russia's anti-Bolshevist forces." Only by rallying around a single political and military authority, Konstantin Nabokov concludes, "will we be able to save Russia from anarchy and terror [*ot anarkhii i terrora*]."[91] His brother's words must have haunted V. D. Nabokov after anarchy and terror overwhelmed the Crimean peninsula and, later, the whole of Russia.

During the last weeks of the government's existence, V. D. Nabokov lobbied for, drafted, and oversaw the implementation of a number of "administrative-repressive" laws that made allowances for extrajudicial arrests and censorship of the press. In response to criticism of these measures from the left, he argued at the last meeting of the Crimean zemstvo conference that he considered these measures "indispensable" (*neobkhodimy*) in light of recent Bolshevik victories in the Crimea's northern districts and the enormous death toll sustained by the Volunteer Army in the Crimea's defense (*Rg* 142–43, 173, 177; *NpKv* 204–5; *LRR* 377).[92] It is likely that V. D. Nabokov, like Pasmanik, sailed away from Russia's shores convinced that these "exceptional" laws should have been introduced from the very first and that war was no time for liberal niceties (*Rg* 177–78).

For left-leaning historians such as Rosenberg, the Crimean Kadets' valiant struggle to combine liberal principles with social reform constitutes the most laudable chapter in the party's history:

> Their program was liberal in the best sense of the word, in that the Crimean people were their primary concern, rather than the abstract interests of the Russian state. And despite the sharp opposition of Tatars and radicals, the Crimean ministers never yielded to the temptation to crush their opponents by force. Their ultimate weapon remained persuasion; and in this they contrasted sharply with their colleagues in Kiev, Ekaterinodar, Odessa, and other parts of Russia, who now abandoned any sense of compromise for strict military rule in a vague hope of eventually realizing liberal ideals. (*LRR* 380; see also *NpKv* 187–88)

It is unlikely that such a summing up would have consoled a man whose commitment to liberal values in the Crimea was seen by many as having played a role in the victory of a regime that openly scorned such values and systematically enveloped the country in an iron mantle of despotism and terror. It is far more likely that V. D. Nabokov departed from the Crimea having learned the lesson articulated by Pasmanik, another Kadet whose loyalties to the White Army collided with loyalties to Solomon Krym's administration. The Crimean Regional Government, Pasmanik concludes bitterly, "did not want to reconcile itself to the idea that it existed and worked in a revolutionary period that could not prosper by the laws of a calm and peaceful time. It also forgot that it was fighting against a party that paid no heed to universally recognized norms, freedom of speech, press, assembly, and so forth" (*Rg* 142). V. D. Nabokov's eldest son carried this lesson to America, and *Lolita* is one of its products.

As Raymond Pearson has observed, it is less surprising that V. D. Nabokov repudiated his involvement in the Crimean Regional Government than it is that, as a conservative Kadet, he participated in it at all (NP

18).[93] His relations with Vinaver were already strained before he assumed the justice portfolio in the Kadets' Crimean regime. Moreover, he had already witnessed firsthand the self-undermining nature of liberal values in times of war. In *The Provisional Government,* written mere weeks before he joined Solomon Krym's Kadet administration, he recalled with agonizing clarity how shrewdly Lenin had exploited the Provisional Government's fidelity to the country's recently legislated liberal provisions. When, during a break in the Provisional Government's March sessions, Miliukov asked his colleagues whether they were "really going to allow" Lenin and his friends unrestrained passage into Russia under German protection, V. D. Nabokov reports that "he got a fairly unanimous reply to the effect that there were no formal grounds for refusing Lenin entry; on the contrary, Lenin had a right to return, inasmuch as he had been granted amnesty, and inasmuch as the means to which he was resorting in order to make the journey were not formally criminal." "Bound by its own proclamations about freedom," V. D. Nabokov observes, "the Provisional Government was surprisingly passive in the face of [Lenin's] destructive activity" in the press and elsewhere (*PG* 143–44; see also *PG* 118–19). These judgments sit poignantly with the civil liberties legislation he dutifully drafted and sought so ardently to uphold during his tenure as minister of justice in the Crimea.

Nabokov refers to these events in *Speak, Memory,* suggesting only that they had little impact on his life during his sixteen-month sojourn on Russia's Riviera. Kept busy by a youthful romance, poetry, and butterflies, he toyed with the idea of joining Denikin's army only because he thought it might bring him closer to his first love, "Tamara" (*SM* 573). Though he does not pause in his memoir to deliberate on the complicated facets of his father's activities in the Crimea, he gives them full play in *Lolita,* the novel in which he confronts the dilemmas he was facing as a Russian writer living in America at a time when his adoptive country was caught up in its own war with Bolshevism. Unlike the memoir, *Lolita* demonstrates that Nabokov had fully absorbed the lessons taught by his father's messy and painful entanglement in the conflict between law and politics. He must have viewed his father's Crimean experiences, and the self-recriminations that followed them, as a forceful reminder of the awkward bargains demanded by national survival during times of war.

LIBERAL RIGHTS AND THE PUBLIC GOOD

Ellen Pifer shows that *Lolita* is rooted in American political history when she notes that Humbert's crime is a direct violation of the rights articulated in America's Declaration of Independence:

> By depriving the child of her autonomy, of her right to life, liberty, and the pursuit of happiness, Humbert knows he committed not only a sexual crime but a political one. Having enslaved another human being to his passionate will, he is guilty of all the timeworn devices of tyranny. . . . Not surprisingly, Lolita seizes the first opportunity to escape her oppressor. Her liberation occurs, appropriately enough, on the Fourth of July—America's annual "Independence Day" celebration.[94]

Indeed, this suggestive concurrence speaks to Nabokov's respect and admiration for America's commitment to personal freedoms. But *Lolita* also confronts the limitations of such a commitment. Pifer's celebratory account notwithstanding, fourteen-year-old Dolly is not a right-bearer under the U.S. Constitution, and her Fourth of July liberation substitutes one form of tyranny for another. America's constitutional provisions not only abet the very circumstances from which Dolly must escape, but fail to provide her with the resources necessary for a meaningful liberation. Humbert's and Quilty's exploitation of Dolly show what Nabokov had learned secondhand from his father's experiences in the Crimea—namely, that liberal policies are incapable of providing security or containing social friction.

As an American citizen under the age of majority, Dolly has no constitutionally specified rights. Not only is the American Constitution silent on the subject of rights for juveniles, but, as Barbara Bennett Woodhouse has argued, the jurisprudence covering children's constitutional rights was severely crippled in the 1920s when the Supreme Court defined the child as a form of parental private property. American children, she notes, have enjoyed "few independent rights outside the context of criminal or administrative proceedings, because children's rights (generally called 'interests') are conceptualized as subsumed within the rights of parents. Children's interests are defined by parents, who exercise their constitutionally protected rights to physical custody and control of children's upbringing."[95]

Unlike the extension of rights to historically disenfranchised groups such as women and people of color, the extension of rights to children is fraught with difficulties. Hayek's remarks about the modern formulation of liberal freedom underscore the interconnectedness between rights and responsibilities: "This freedom could also be assured only to those capable of obeying the rules intended to secure it. Only the adult and sane, presumed to be fully responsible for their actions, were regarded as fully entitled to that freedom, while various degrees of tutelage were regarded as appropriate in the case of children and persons not in full possession of their mental faculties."[96]

But even if children were deemed capable of assuming the responsibilities associated with freedom, their economic dependency would require a form of social interventionism that is difficult to reconcile with a strict liberal dispensation. As Michael S. Wald has observed, a lack of financial resources and marketable skills make the full emancipation of children extremely difficult: such schemes "would only be feasible if the state were willing to assume care of children or the state compelled parents to pay for their children to live elsewhere." The socioeconomic infrastructures necessary to serve children in any meaningful way would have to include programs protecting them from abuse and exploitation, as well as programs ensuring easy access to education, nutrition, medical care, shelter, and financial aid.[97] In short, if children's needs are to be taken seriously, the liberal nation must cede substantial ground to the welfare state.

Narrative is the chief conspirator in Dolly's sexual exploitation by Humbert and Quilty. Nabokov loads the dice against Dolly by selecting personal circumstances that expose her to the unscrupulous machinations of two pedophiles. But Dolly's tragedy is also a function of her socioeconomic surroundings. Nabokov chose those surroundings with great care as he shaped for her a life capable of shedding light on America's callous indifference toward its weakest and most vulnerable individuals. Tossed aside by Quilty, Dolly spends two years "doing some restaurant work in small places" (*L* 260). The man she marries is "hard of hearing" as a result of having participated in "a remote war" (as Humbert puts it with careless hauteur) (*L* 257), and hopes to escape the poverty and squalor of his current life by seeking employment in Alaska. Dolly herself—pregnant, debt-ridden, and "hopelessly worn at seventeen"—is reduced to appealing for money to a man whom she still fears and would rather forget (*L* 250, 261).

Humbert is most directly responsible for the tragic patterns that dominate Dolly's life. ("*You* merely broke my life" is the unspoken accusation he hears Dolly level against him during their last meeting [*L* 262; emphasis in original].) But America's prioritization of civil freedoms over the common good seems to share this blame as the novel carefully establishes that a lack of communal bonds and social networks had a hand in Dolly's fate. Nabokov was no Marxist, but he was not insensitive to the plight of the world's most vulnerable members. In "Russian Writers, Censors, and Readers," he notes that "in the days of Pushkin or Gogol a large majority of the Russian nation was left out in the cold in a veil of slow snow beyond the amber-bright windows, and this was a tragic result of the fact that a most refined European culture had arrived too fast in a country famous for its misfortunes, famous for the misery of its numberless humble lives."[98] His anti-Communism was generated, in part, by his knowledge that the Bolsheviks not only continued but exacerbated this suffering. In his response to a longtime friend's publication of a collection of "letters from home" obtained from prisoners taken in the Russo-Finnish War and titled *Meeting with Russia: Life in the*

Soviet Union: Letters to the Red Army, 1939–1941, Nabokov wrote to Vladimir Zenzinov on February 28, 1945: "As you quite rightly remark, nothing, nothing has changed—the same soldiers going mad from the same hunger and grief as five hundred years ago, and the same oppression and the same bare-bellied children in the mud, in the dark" (qtd. in *VNAY* 84).

In "Russian Writers, Censors, and Readers," Nabokov defines "the deep pathos that pertains to all authentic art" as "the breach between its eternal values and the sufferings of a muddled world," and even concedes that "this world, indeed, can hardly be blamed for regarding literature as a luxury or a toy unless it can be used as an up-to-date guidebook."[99] If Nabokov's frequent denunciations of Marxism seem superficial, *Lolita*'s engagement with some of its guiding principles is decidedly not so. In his most controversial novel, Nabokov examines the heartbreaking costs of living in a society that subordinates social ends to liberal ideals. The exhilarating freedom that nurtured his own stately, unencumbered drives across America in search of butterflies also feeds Humbert's vices and Dolly's isolation.

There is thus dramatic irony in Dolly's reminder to Charlotte that "this is a free country" (*L* 42). America's citizens and law enforcers are never seen to violate the constitutional provisions that protect the private sphere. During his first cross-country journey with Dolly, Humbert happily discovers that a speeding offense fails to elicit questions about his domestic relations (*L* 160). His fears that "some busybody, some Humane Society" might put an end to his affair with Dolly are never realized (*L* 161). Similar fears lead him to assume that the Aztec Red convertible pursing him and Dolly "was operated by a detective whom some busybody had hired to see what exactly Humbert Humbert was doing with that minor stepdaughter of his" (*L* 203). A second mordant irony of the novel is that Dolly's mysterious protector is another sexual predator stalking his prey.

Indeed, Humbert exploits the inadequacy of America's welfare provisions to further entrap Dolly. He recalls with shame "the reformatory threat" by which he "terroriz[ed] Lo" into silence and submission (*L* 139, 141). As "the ward of the Department of Public Welfare," he tells Dolly, "you, happy neglected child, will be given a choice of various dwelling places, all more or less the same, the correctional school, the reformatory, the juvenile detention home, or one of those admirable girls' protectories where you knit things, and sing hymns, and have rancid pancakes on Sundays" (*L* 140).[100]

Nabokov's haughty liberalism—"freedom of speech, freedom of thought, freedom of art. The social and economic structure of the ideal state is of little concern to me" (*SO* 34–35)—seems hopelessly ill-equipped to guard against Dolly's fate. But the Nabokov who wrote *Lolita* seems to agree with critics of liberalism who tell us, as Ronald Beiner does, that "the liberal good . . . is not good enough, and that liberal community defeats the possibility of a sense of meaningful collective purpose."[101] *Lolita*'s ambivalence toward liberal values is generated by a communitarian sensitivity to the ways in which a commitment to personal freedoms undermines the state's capacity to protect not only itself but also its most vulnerable members. The liberal state betrays these individuals not only because it fails to provide them with the goods necessary for human flourishing, but also because it turns a blind eye to the exploitation and violence that America's commitment to personal privacy can occlude.

Key moments in *Lolita* indicate that the state's capacity to protect Dolly against the likes of Humbert is significantly circumscribed by the legal provisions designed to protect individuals from state interference. For instance, the social service monograph Humbert discovers during his covert legal inquiries states that "there is no principle that every minor must have a guardian; the court is passive and enters the fray only when the child's situation becomes conspicuously perilous" (*L* 161). This passivity inhibits the state's capacity to intercede effectively on Dolly's behalf, and Humbert draws comfort from the knowledge that even a modicum of discretion will enable him to act with impunity.

Humbert's resentment against his colleague and fellow pedophile Gaston Godin both recognizes the opportunities afforded by a formal commitment to privacy and exposes the crimes that such a commitment might help conceal:[102]

> There he was, devoid of any talent whatsoever, a mediocre teacher, a worthless scholar, a glum repulsive fat old invert, highly contemptuous of the American way of life, triumphantly ignorant of the English language—there he was in priggish New England, crooned over by the old and caressed by the young—oh, having a grand time and fooling everybody; and here was I. (*L* 171)

The ease with which Godin becomes integrated into the fabric of his adoptive country is a moving tribute to American openness and tolerance.[103] Godin escapes detection because he deceives his neighbors and because his neighbors do not automatically assume the worst of foreigners. His ignorance of the English language and his refusal to give up his European habits are in themselves no reason for suspicion. Like Humbert and Quilty, Godin successfully conceals his crimes because he lives in a country that protects privacy and assumes innocence. But if Humbert's description of Godin speaks to the virtues of American tolerance, it also doubles as a critique of a society made vulnerable by such virtues. Significantly, Godin's crimes are exposed not in the United States but in Naples, where his involvement in "a *sale histoire*" prevents him from returning to America (*L* 171).

LOLITA AND THE SMITH ACT

Nabokov's second emigration brought him to a country that took pride in its commitment to the principles that structured his father's liberalism. Though he delighted in America's openness, Nabokov was not indifferent to the most serious challenge to his father's and his own political ideals. In the late 1940s and early '50s, when the Communist issue dominated domestic politics in the United States, Nabokov was once again confronted by the paradox that bedevils all liberal societies: a commitment to personal freedoms leaves the state vulnerable to those who wish to destroy it.

This irony drives a story that is at once a tribute to American liberalism and a clear-sighted recognition of the enormous costs exacted by a commitment to liberal principles. Humbert is able to abuse and exploit a minor because his private life is protected from arbitrary public interference. Though these crimes and Communism's legal nihilism are very different things, Nabokov invites us to consider them as analogous when he identifies Humbert as "a foreigner and an anarchist." To see them as comparable threats is not to allegorize the novel. Nabokov's personal history and passionate anti-Communism make the following analogy an apt one: the freedom-loving, tolerant Americans who do not interfere in Humbert and Dolly's domestic relations, or in Godin's erotic transactions with young boys, recall the principled ministers of the Provisional Government who allowed Lenin free passage into Russia because they had no formally legitimate grounds for keeping him out, and the ministers of the Crimean Regional Government whose commitment to civil freedoms allowed the Bolsheviks to flourish in their midst. In *Lolita,* Nabokov distills the lessons learned by his father into a narrative that highlights the ways in which liberal freedoms can nurture their own demise. Though *Lolita* is no coded account of the political trials that coincided with its composition, the novel reflects Nabokov's interest in the intellectual predicaments made visible by the Communist prosecutions at the height of the Cold War. The trials and the novel are shot through with the competing claims of individual rights and the social good, legal principle and political pressure.

Humbert's attempt to justify his violations of American law by highlighting the cultural and historical relativism of legal and moral standards signals the dangers that arise when law is conceived in a strictly positivist light. It also warns against the danger that would attend the adoption of legal positivism as a nation's guiding legal philosophy. If Humbert's contempt for the law is an iteration of Communism's claim that the law is simply an extension of power, his legal-positivist attempt at self-vindication allies him with the Cold War justices whose deference to political expedience made possible the constitutional violations that became synonymous with McCarthyism.

One of the most famous and far-reaching of these constitutional violations took place under the auspices of the 1940 Alien Registration Act (popularly called the Smith Act after its congressional sponsor). Initiated by a number of anti-Communists who sought to mobilize the legal order against the Communist Party of the United States (CPUSA), it was passed by Congress in response to the strong anti-foreign sentiment that gripped the country on the eve of the Second World War. The Smith Act made it illegal to advocate the overthrow of the government by force or violence, or to organize a group dedicated to that end. Michael Belknap's assessment of the legislation is instructive: "Bent on protecting the United States from foreign dangers, Congress passed a law proscribing the speech of domestic radicals. In an attempt to preserve democracy, it enacted a statute which was itself a major threat to democratic values."[104] Described as "a foreigner and an anarchist" by his creator, Humbert took shape in Nabokov's mind at a time when America's constitutional provisions were being severely eroded in the interests of national security.

In July 1948, sixteen months after Nabokov informed Wilson that he was working on a short novel about a man who liked little girls and five years before he completed *Lolita,*[105] President Truman's attorney general secured an indictment charging the leaders of the CPUSA with violation of the Smith Act.[106] This "most important of the anti-Communist cases"[107]—a three-year, headline-grabbing legal saga—would culminate in a Supreme-Court ruling that subordinated freedom of expression to national security. The trial and the subsequent appeals of the Eleven (as the Communist leaders charged under the Smith Act came to be known in the press) stand as an egregious example of what Belknap calls "political justice."[108]

Nabokov's identification of Humbert as "a foreigner and an anarchist" is a challenge to see his crimes in a political light. To refuse to rise to the challenge is to overlook the political sophistication and courage of *Lolita*'s confrontation of the moral, legal, and political dilemmas posed by America's efforts to uncover Communist subversion. *Lolita* suggests that Nabokov was deeply troubled by the high price his adoptive country seemed willing to pay for its security even as he worried that a slackening in the domestic war against Communism made it vulnerable. The most self-consciously "American" of Nabokov's novels flows out of a context in which all the promises and all the blind spots of his father's liberalism were being put to the test. The Communist prosecutions and the judiciary's endorsement of the Smith Act called into question America's status as a rule-of-law state in which the law set the rules for politics rather than vice versa.

An escalation in Cold War tensions played a pivotal role in the criminalization of the CPUSA, but it is unlikely that these political pressures would have been able to encroach upon civil liberties so thoroughly in the absence of a concurrent shift in the nation's legal thinking. The appellate courts upheld the convictions of the Eleven because a number of key justices were devoted to the principle of judicial restraint. Rejecting "higher law" ideals, the principle of judicial restraint shares the legal-positivist identification of the law with the will of the legislators. The judiciary's increased deference to the nation's elected officials was a direct response to the perceived excesses carried out by previous courts in the name of natural law.

During the second half of the nineteenth century, the principle of judicial review was consolidated and expanded to encompass judicial oversight of socioeconomic legislation. American courts, guided by natural-law principles, struck down vital legislation relating to matters of public health, housing, insurance, minimum wage, and labor hours. By the time of the Great Depression, the principle of judicial review had become the bane of American political life. President Roosevelt's efforts to end the courts' stranglehold on legislative matters initiated a sweeping change in the ideological commitments of the judiciary and its hierarchy of values.[109] The courts' shift from a commitment to judicial review to a commitment to judicial restraint involved a greater recognition of the limitations of the non-elected organ of the Constitution, and a matching deference to elected legislatures in matters of social and economic legislation.[110] By surrendering the socioeconomic domain to the legislators (except in cases of conspicuous violations of constitutional provisions) and by turning its attention to issues relating to civil liberties, the judiciary's new humility was complemented by a continued commitment to "higher law" principles.[111]

The uneasy truce struck between the principles of judicial review (derived from natural-law doctrine) and judicial restraint (allied with legal positivism) was severely challenged at the height of the Cold War when the restriction of civil liberties was widely accepted as the necessary price of national security.[112] The House Un-American Activities Committee's unscrupulous methods of investigation were validated when the Supreme Court denied by a vote of 6–2 the request made on behalf of the Hollywood Ten to review their 1948 convictions for contempt of Congress. As Schrecker writes, "the Court based its reluctance to challenge what it perceived to be the will of the people—or at least of the Congress—on the doctrine of judicial restraint."[113]

The appellate court justices who upheld the convictions of the Eleven for violating the Smith Act similarly defended their decisions by invoking the principle of judicial restraint. Chief judge Learned Hand, the Second Circuit's most distinguished jurist and a staunch proponent of judicial restraint, ruled against the CPUSA because, he argued, legislators were responsible for striking compromises among conflicting interests, and because courts had no authority to disrupt these compromises.[114] The Supreme Court announced its decision on June 4, 1951, ruling against the defendants by a vote of 6–2.[115] Chief Justice Fred Vinson, the Court's most deeply committed member to the principle of judicial restraint, stated in the official opinion that the special circumstances of the Cold War made the CPUSA a danger to national security.[116] Justice Felix Frankfurter, also a firm advocate of judicial restraint, concluded in his concurring opinion: "Free-speech cases are not an exception to the principle that we are not legislators, that direct policymaking is not our province. How best to reconcile competing interests is the business of the legislatures, and the balance they strike is a judgment not to be displaced by ours."[117]

Justices Hugo Black and William Douglas were ideologically opposed to Vinson and Frankfurter in matters of civil liberties. Though committed to non-interference in legislative measures when these sought to regulate the socioeconomic sphere, Black and Douglas consistently gave a radical interpretation to the freedoms enshrined in the First Amendment. For Black and Douglas, constitutional guarantees such as freedom of speech enjoyed a preferred position in American law which placed them beyond the regulatory purview of the legislator.[118] Drawing a strict separation between conspiracy itself and advocating conspiracy to overthrow the government, Black used his dissenting opinion to rebuke his colleagues for weakening the First Amendment and for allowing political pressures to distort the law:

> So long as this Court exercises the power of judicial review of legislation, I cannot agree that the First Amendment permits us to sustain laws suppressing freedom of speech and press on the basis of Congress' or our own notions of mere "reasonableness." Such a doctrine waters down the First Amendment so that it amounts to little more than an admonition to Congress. The Amendment as so construed is not likely to protect any but those "safe" or orthodox views which rarely need its protection. . . . Public opinion being what it now is, few will protest the conviction of these Communist petitioners. There is hope, however, that in calmer times, when present pressures, passions and fears subside, this or some later Court will restore the First Amendment liberties to the high preferred place where they belong in a free society.[119]

Had Nabokov heard or read about Black's principled refusal to subordinate the law to political pressure, it may have reminded him of his father's unwillingness "to reverse the law" for the sake of punishing Crimea's Bolshevik murderers.

Though hostile toward Communism, Douglas also dissented from the majority opinion by arguing that the prosecution had not produced sufficient evidence to convict the defendants for either committing or advocating conspiracy. Pointing out that the evidence rested largely on Marxist-Leninist literature that was both legal and readily available, Douglas criticized his colleagues for making freedom of speech dependent not on the nature of the utterance, but on the identity of the speaker, and argued further that anti-conspiracy legislation cannot be used to turn speech into seditious conduct. "The political censor has no place in our public debates," he wrote. "Unless and until extreme and necessitous circumstances are shown, our aim should be to keep speech unfettered and to allow the processes of law to be invoked only when the provocateurs among us move from speech to action." In his concluding exhortation, Douglas correlates the Soviet disregard for liberal freedoms with America's willingness to abandon its commitment to civil liberties in the interest of national security:

> Vishinsky wrote in 1938 in *The Law of the Soviet State,* "In our state, naturally, there is and can be no place for freedom of speech, press, and so on for the foes of socialism."
>
> Our concern should be that we accept no such standard for the United States. Our faith should be that our people will never give support to these advocates of revolution, so long as we remain loyal to the purposes for which our Nation was founded.[120]

Douglas and Black's words resonate in richly suggestive ways with V. D. Nabokov's publicistic and political career. Their subordination of political expedience to freedom of expression is certainly of a piece with his position in "The Internal War," an article from 1906 in which he considers the very questions at the center of *Dennis v. United States.* Here he condemns a new censorship law passed by the tsarist regime prohibiting "the public disclosure or dissemination of deliberately false or distorted information about the activity of government institutions or officials, with the goal of arousing people's hostility toward them." By quoting Jules Simon, V. D. Nabokov frames his objection in terms that recall Black's cautionary words about the fragility of civil rights during times of political turmoil: "Anyone can understand, said J. Simon, how easy it will be, in certain cases, *for a government unscrupulous in its means,* to connect the most negligible disturbance that takes place at an uncertain time in any place to a piece of news reported (perhaps even in a merely speculative manner) by a newspaper whose leanings do not appeal to the government."[121] Years later, however, this unequivocal condemnation of censorship gave way to a more politically pragmatic approach. In *The Provisional Government,* V. D. Nabokov lamented the fact that the provisional regime "did not consider it possible to counteract even the most extreme and destructive propaganda that was beginning to [be] spread orally and in the press" by the Bolsheviks (*PG* 144). By March 1919, when it became clear that Lenin's armies would likely recapture the Crimea, V. D. Nabokov took up his pen and drafted the Crimean Regional Government's "wartime censorship" legislation (*NpKv* 186–87; *Rg* 177).

THE RIGHT VS. THE GOOD

Lolita is a durable record of Nabokov's anxiety that his adoptive country's founding commitment to liberal values collided with its national interests. The novel's engagement with American values is much more complex than the accusation of anti-Americanism would suggest. Its satirical representations of American hypocrisy in regard to sex, race, religion, and parenting do not extend to America's commitment to the rights and freedoms spelled out in its founding documents. *Lolita* depicts a nation that takes rights seriously, or—less generously—a nation in which the respect for rights is a by-product of a generalized complacency about national security and a callous indifference to the welfare of others.

The media coverage of the government's assault on the CPUSA underscored the impossibility of guarding against individuals such as Humbert, Quilty, or Godin without dismantling the nation's commitment to privacy rights. The government's extensive reliance on undercover informants in the Communist prosecutions has its own analogy in *Lolita*'s foreword, penned by the fictional "John Ray, Jr., Ph.D." Only a comprehensive machinery of surveillance, Ray suggests, could protect victims such as Dolly:

> The wayward child, the egotistic mother, the panting maniac—these are not only vivid characters in a unique story: they warn us of dangerous trends; they point out potent evils. "Lolita" should make all of us—parents, social workers, educators—apply ourselves with still greater vigilance and vision to the task of bringing up a better generation in a safer world. (*L* 5)

The "general lesson" John Ray, Jr., extracts from Humbert's narrative conjures up visions of a society willing to condone the invasion of the private sphere in the name of public profit. As the stock characters of psychology—"the wayward child, the egotistic mother, the panting maniac"—individuals become the targets of a civic-minded citizenry determined to privilege security over personal freedoms.[122]

To the extent that Ray's appeal to invasive methods of surveillance provides a refracted image of the totalitarian regimes depicted in *Invitation to a Beheading* and *Bend Sinister*, *Lolita* offers the unsettling reminder that without such mechanisms the state cannot protect itself or its weakest members. Though child abuse is certainly not limited to liberal societies, Humbert is protected from the kind of interference that Nabokov's earlier fiction explicitly associates with tyranny. In *Bend Sinister,* for example, Paduk's regime sends spies disguised as nannies into people's homes (*BS* 325–26). Significantly, no such spying interferes with Humbert's sexual enslavement of Dolly. Though he often feels that he and Dolly "lived in a lighted house of glass, and that any moment some thin-lipped parchment face would peer through a carelessly unshaded window" (*L* 169), his anxiety springs from paranoia rather than from a nosy neighbor's intrusion into his personal life. Charlotte's replication of the invasive techniques associated with police states when she breaks into Humbert's desk and reads his diary is difficult to condone, but it is important to remember what she uncovers. The swiftness of her subsequent demise feeds our sense of poetic justice and sets the stage for the tragedy to come, but it also diverts attention from a lesson that Nabokov found deeply repugnant: being a snoop can have positive consequences. As fruitless (and naive) as it is to speculate about fictional paths not taken, it is nonetheless possible to imagine that Humbert would not have been able to sexually enslave Dolly had Charlotte lived.[123]

If Nabokov registered the clash between civil freedoms and security during his sojourn in the Crimea, he witnessed it again in Cold War America. *Lolita* is rooted in Nabokov's new ambivalence toward the promises, pieties, and impossibilities of his father's and his own political ideals. It depicts a modern liberal nation whose commitment to protecting civil liberties helps conceal a naive, self-satisfied, atomistic society. But if blindness and vulnerability are the consequences of a commitment to civil liberties, the effects of doing away with such a commitment are harrowing. In *Pnin,* the novel Nabokov began writing while still completing *Lolita,* Pnin recalls a Holocaust victim with the same poignancy that runs through Humbert's epiphanies regarding his violence against Dolly:

> In order to exist rationally, Pnin had taught himself, during the last ten years, never to remember Mira Belochkin—not because, in itself, the evocation of a youthful love affair, banal and brief, threatened his peace of mind . . . , but because, if one were quite sincere with oneself, no conscience, and hence no consciousness, could be expected to subsist in a world where such things as Mira's death were possible. One had to forget—because one could not live with the thought that this graceful, fragile, tender young woman with those eyes, that smile, those gardens and snows in the background, had been brought in a cattle car to an extermination camp and killed by an injection of phenol into the heart, into the gentle heart one had heard beating under one's lips in the dusk of the past. (*Pnin* 394)

Mira and Dolly are both victims of colossal moral delinquencies, but Mira's tragedy is more difficult to contemplate because it was the explicit aim of institutional policy, or—to quote from Nabokov's foreword to *The Waltz*

Invention—"only an administrative detail."[124] If Dolly's fate is facilitated by the state's non-interference in the private sphere, Mira's fate is a direct consequence of a state's decision to dismantle the private sphere in the name of public profit, that most slippery of moral goods.

In an essay published at the height of the anti-Communist hysteria, Hannah Arendt condemned the political repression of alleged Communists as a form of totalitarianism. Like Nabokov, Arendt had escaped to the United States from Nazi Germany by way of France. Unlike him, she publicly denounced her adoptive country's betrayal of liberal values in its war against domestic subversion. Ends never justify means, she argued in Kantian fashion, for ends are not only unpredictable but morally untrustworthy. Lenin's classless society and Hitler's race society, she reminded her readers, served as such ends in the recent past. "The breach of the law (or for that matter, the risking of civil liberties in order to trap a bad man)," she contends, "is necessarily the beginning of the end of civil liberties for all."[125]

Arendt's words are echoed by those whose lives were destroyed by the Soviet subordination of legal principles to social ideals. "I am encouraged to believe that all we have been through will have served to turn people against the idea, so tempting at first sight, that the end justifies the means and 'everything is permitted,'" writes Nadezhda Mandelstam in her chronicle of the Soviet purges that sent her husband, the poet Osip Mandelstam, and countless others to their deaths.[126] Humbert's relations with Dolly, nurtured in the self-serving delusion "of living in a brand new, mad new dream world, where everything was permissible" (*L* 125), underscore the kinship between anarchy and tyranny.

If *Lolita*'s allegiance to personal freedoms is ultimately stronger than its allegiance to the public good it is perhaps because, to use a phrase borrowed from Kuzmanovich, Dolly is "acceptable collateral damage" in a utilitarian calculation that would sacrifice her for the good of others.[127] But in light of Nabokov's zealous anti-utilitarianism and keen understanding of the nullity of *all* calculations for a parent's beating heart (to paraphrase him in his preface to *Bend Sinister*), it is much more likely that he privileges liberty in *Lolita* for the same reasons Isaiah Berlin, the most famous descendant of Russia's liberal tradition, prioritizes liberty over all other goods. In Berlin's tragically configured universe, only liberalism can accommodate the irreconcilable nature of human values:

> If, as I believe, the ends of men are many, and not all of them are in principle compatible with each other, then the possibility of conflict—and of tragedy—can never wholly be eliminated from human life, either personal or social. The necessity of choosing between absolute claims is then an inescapable characteristic of the human condition. This gives its value to freedom as

> Acton conceived of it—as an end in itself, and not as a temporary need, arising out of our confused notions and irrational and disordered lives, a predicament which a panacea could one day put right.[128]

The fate of Dolly, like the story of America's Cold War persecution of real and alleged Communists, is a personal and political tragedy precipitated by clashing claims and values. It is also a tragedy born of Nabokov's unwillingness to obscure, for the sake of a happy ending, the ineluctable tension between liberal principles and security. Dolly dies at the age of seventeen and Humbert is apprehended for a crime that is a mere postscript to the long line of offenses that punctuate his American sojourn. These distressing outcomes challenge us to acknowledge the force of Arendt's assertion that "it is dangerous and risky to live in freedom."[129]

The essence of V. D. Nabokov's personality, writes Novgorodtsev in his front-page obituary for *Rul'*, was fully revealed when he rose "without hesitation and without a thought to himself to defend the life of the one he referred to as his friend-enemy [*Takim iavil on sebia i v tot rokovoi moment, kogda, ne koleblias' i ne dumaia o sebe, vstal na zashchitu togo, kogo nazyval svoim drugom-protivnikom*]."[130] The tragic irony of these events could not have been lost upon a grieving son. That his father should die in the act of protecting the life of a former friend, now turned political opponent, must have served Nabokov as a permanent reminder of his father's capacity to live up to the moral convictions that sustained his political activism, his jurisprudence, and his relations with the local villagers whose rites of gratitude he remembered so vividly. In a letter to Wilson from December 15, 1940, Nabokov recalled this aspect of his father's character when he told the following story:

> I know of a case when a famous Cadet taking part in a secret meeting of different groups for a conference that had to be hastily dissolved because it was learnt that the Cheka had got wind of it, risked his life staying behind in order to warn an obscure Menshevik (whom he hardly knew and of whose party he disapproved) who, it was apprehended, might come later and be trapped. (*DBDV* 37–38)

It is perhaps less important that the story's unnamed Kadet was Nabokov's father (as asserted by Véra Nabokov) than that Nabokov clearly held such conduct in the highest esteem (*DBDV* 39, note 14). As the next chapter will show, he revisits the story's lesson in *Ada* when he elicits from Lucette, on the eve of her death, the same prioritization of duty over self-interest showcased so movingly by his father on the night of his own.

Ever since he became a student at the Tenishev School in St. Petersburg, Nabokov was made to feel that he was betraying the high standards set by his father. His composition of *Lolita* marks an effort to take up the burden of that revered and complicated paternal legacy. Just as his father imperiled many things he cherished by his political activism, Nabokov stood much to lose by writing and publishing a novel about a man's obsessive love for little girls. Friends and editors warned him on multiple occasions that such a scandalous novel might be prosecuted for obscenity, destroy his reputation, and lead to his dismissal from Cornell (*VNAY* 255, 263, 270).[131] For a middle-aged immigrant with limited employment possibilities such a turn of events would have been financially disastrous.

But Nabokov's greatest act of courage lies in *Lolita*'s unsentimental engagement with the promises and limitations of liberalism. Like his father, who rose up to defend the life of a political adversary at the cost of his own, Nabokov bestows life upon a character who endangers his most prized political principles. Humbert Humbert's heinous acts tempt us to rethink our prioritization of freedom over security. It also lures us into thinking that our opponents, unlike our friends, are unworthy of protection.

If Nabokov was as quick to admit to Humbert's moral depravity as he was to insist that his novel has "no moral in tow" (OB 296), it may be because he knew that the right to free speech he was laying claim to as an American could be contested with particular ease in a political climate that subordinated liberal rights to the public good. Russian history had taught Nabokov about the deep connection between moral and political censorship long before the French Ministry of the Interior banned *Lolita* by invoking a law proscribing subversive political publications (*VNAY* 301). In "Russian Writers, Censors, and Readers," Nabokov draws attention to this connection. Though the tsarist autocrats sought to censor political subversion, he states, upright Russian radicals "were as great a nuisance in regard to art as was the government." "The radical critics fought despotism," he notes sadly, "but they evolved a despotism of their own." For Nabokov, censorship is a violation of civil freedoms regardless of its sources and intentions:

> What [the radicals] demanded of an author was a social message and no nonsense, and from their point of view a book was good only insofar as it was of practical use to the welfare of the people. There was a disastrous flaw in their fervor. Sincerely and boldly they advocated freedom and equality but they contradicted their own creed by wishing to subjugate the arts to current politics.

Nabokov's assertion that "readers are born free and ought to remain free" serves as a reminder that *Lolita* tests liberal values both at the level of theme and marketplace.[132] If readers are to exercise their freedom, as Nabokov insists, the question of whether or not *Lolita* teaches the right lessons must play no part in determining whether or not it should be available on a liberal nation's bookshelves.

Lolita is a long, long way from V. D. Nabokov's spontaneous and heroic defense of Miliukov, but it is less vulnerable to the vicissitudes of cultural forgetting. V. D. Nabokov rose up to save the life of the man he referred to as his "friend-enemy," but his son endowed the character who posed the greatest threat to his convictions and aspirations with the gift of immortality. The "aurochs and angels, the secret of durable pigments, prophetic sonnets, the refuge of art" that should make Dolly "live in the minds of later generations" (*L* 291) also guarantee that Humbert Humbert will continue to cast a dark shadow across what Lionel Trilling, writing three years before *Lolita*'s completion, referred to as "the liberal imagination."

Chapter Three

Kant's Eye: *Ada,* Art, Ethics

> A careful examination of the motives that prompt people's actions shows that all deeds, good and bad, noble and base, heroic and craven, are prompted by one cause: a man acts in the way that gives him most pleasure. He is guided by self-interest, which causes him to abstain from a smaller gain, or a lesser pleasure, in order to obtain a larger gain or a greater pleasure.
> —Nicholas Chernyshevski

> There can be no sharper antithesis than that between Marx and Kant and idealist philosophy in general.
> —Peter Struve

> The person is the border between the kingdom of necessity and the kingdom of freedom, and it is in the moral calling of personhood that man first discovers his infinite tasks and his participation in the world of freedom.
> —Paul Novgorodtsev

VAN VEEN, THE FIRST-PERSON narrator of *Ada or Ardor: A Family Chronicle* (1969), turns to autobiography after a life spent as a playboy, acrobat, philosopher, psychologist, and writer of science fiction. His family memoir is a collaboration with Ada Veen, his sister and lover. As a result of a complicated affair between their parents—Demon and Marina—Van and Ada are raised as first cousins, a domestic ruse that fails to deceive them. They fall in love during their first idyllic summer together at the family estate at Ardis, and for the remainder of their lives they strive to overcome the obstacles that keep them apart. The novel, an unapologetic celebration of their mutual love and genius, takes the form of an unfinished manuscript penned by Van and glossed by Ada at the end of their long lives.

As critics have noted, their manuscript is, among other things, an elaborate attempt to assuage their sense that they are complicit in the suicide of their half-sister Lucette.[1]

Among Van's recollections of Lucette is a visit she pays him at Kingston University to deliver a letter from Ada. During this visit, Lucette reminds Van of the schemes he and Ada devised to enable them to snatch a few moments of sexual pleasure away from her ubiquitous presence. Whether tying her to a tree in imitation of a fairy tale plot or locking her in a bath or closet, the strategies Van and Ada viewed as innocent remain, from Lucette's perspective, cruel acts of deception. She recalls, in particular, a closet in which she claims to have been locked up "at least ten times." Van's response is revealing: "*Nu uzh i desiat'* (exaggeration). Once—and *never* more. It had a keyless hole as big as Kant's eye. Kant was famous for his cucumicolor iris."[2] This exchange looks back to a moment in Van and Ada's childhood at Ardis, when they "could no longer restrain their amorous excitement, and under the absurd pretext of a hide-and-seek game they locked up Lucette in a closet . . . , and frantically made love, while the child knocked and called and kicked until the key fell out and the keyhole turned an angry green" (*A* 170).

Van's offhand reference to Kant and his "cucumicolor iris" is characteristic of the chronicle's dense allusiveness and dazzling, sensual diction. It also provides an incisive clue about the ethical dimension of Nabokov's work, and the extent to which ethics, aesthetics, and politics are always intertwined in his fiction. That Lucette's green eye should conjure up Kant's cucumber-colored iris in Van's guilt-stricken conscience is not surprising given Van's formal training as a philosopher and Kant's fame for his uncompromising prohibition against all forms of deception. Whatever Van might say, Kant was more famous for his rigor in ethical matters than he was for the color of his eyes.

ART, DECEPTION, *POSHLOST'*

The argument that Kant's moral philosophy suffuses Nabokov's fiction seems counterintuitive.[3] Nabokov, after all, is a writer for whom art *is* deception: "art at its greatest is fantastically deceitful and complex" (*SO* 33). In his introductory lecture to his course on European fiction (published under the title "Good Readers and Good Writers"), Nabokov offers a parable to illustrate art's dependence on deception: "Literature was born not the day when a boy crying wolf, wolf came running out of the Neanderthal valley with a big gray wolf at his heels: literature was born on the day when a boy came crying wolf, wolf and there was no wolf behind him" (*LL* 5). Art derives its powers of deception from nature: "Every great writer is a great deceiver, but so is that arch-cheat Nature. Nature always deceives" (*LL* 5). Deception is presented as a kind of natural first principle in Nabokov's remarks on art and nature: "all nature is magic and deception"; "all reality is a mask"; and "deception is practiced even more beautifully by that other V.N., Visible Nature."[4] But although Nabokov insists that deception must play an integral role in the production of art, he also locates deception at the heart of art's degraded double—*poshlost'*. In his monograph on Gogol, Nabokov struggled to establish an adequate definition of this Russian word, insisting that its closest English equivalents—"cheap, sham, common, smutty, pink-and-blue, high falutin', in bad taste"—fail to capture the word's nuances.[5] Nabokov regards *poshlost'* as an unsettling combination of the base and the elevated, the vulgar and the sensitive, the material and the spiritual. As he explains, the commercial artist who tries to depict "a nice little boy" by gracing him with freckles trades in *poshlost'* because he obtains the idea of innocence at the cost of "a faintly racial" stereotype. In another example, compassion is infected by *poshlost'* when it is combined with lasciviousness: "Kind people send our lonely soldiers silk hosed dummy legs modeled on those of Hollywood lovelies and stuffed with candies and safety razor blades." This hybrid quality of *poshlost'* breeds deception, an essential component of its ontology. Frank vulgarity does not qualify: "Obvious trash, curiously enough, contains sometimes a wholesome ingredient, readily appreciated by children and simple souls." By contrast, *poshlost'* "is especially vigorous and vicious when the sham is *not* obvious and when the values it mimics are considered, rightly or wrongly, to belong to the very highest level of art, thought or emotion."[6]

In an essay titled "Philistines and Philistinism," Nabokov underscores once again the kinship between *poshlost'* and deception: "*Poshlism* is not only the obviously trashy but mainly the falsely important, the falsely beautiful, the falsely clever, the falsely attractive. To apply the deadly label of *poshlism* to something is not only an esthetic judgment but also a moral indictment. The genuine, the guileless, the good is never *poshlust.*"[7] The ethical dimension of Nabokov's denunciation of *poshlost'* hints at the risks he is taking in aligning art with deception. If honesty inoculates "the genuine, the guileless, the good" against the contagion of *poshlost'*, the artist's deceptions might be expected to divorce art from those "other states of being" where "curiosity, tenderness, kindness" are "the norm" (OB 296). To safeguard his cherished belief that art is at once morally good and inherently deceptive, Nabokov must engage in the kind of work familiar to him as a lepidopterist. In *Ada,* he establishes a taxonomy of deception by uncovering fine distinctions within a concept that is, by nature, protean and duplicitous.

Like Nabokov's writings about play, his writings on *poshlost'* recall an essay by his friend and Kadet Party member Iulii Aikhenvald titled "Bessmertnaia poshlost'" ("Immortal *Poshlost'*").[8] Aikhenvald argues that *poshlost'* is a product of our dual ontology as creatures of matter and spirit. Openly invoking the language of Kant and Russia's neo-idealist philosophers, Aikhenvald explains that this "ancient cosmic *poshlost'*" is born of "our simultaneous belonging to two kingdoms—the kingdom of freedom and the kingdom of necessity."[9] Kant's influence upon this formulation is made explicit two pages later: "I am 'the first stroke of God,' the beginning without end, a pale contour—the first stitch in God's chasuble. And here I am, 'my body decaying into dust, my mind commanding the thunder,' I am 'a reasoning reed,' I am a humble object of nature and also its independent subject, in the Kantian sense [*v kantovskom smysle*]—I am the legislator of nature, the master, or, at least, the harbinger of its thunders."[10]

Though *poshlost'* is an ineliminable aspect of the human condition according to Aikhenvald,[11] it can be overcome on a personal level through moral actions. Continuing to echo Kant and Russia's neo-idealist philosophers, Aikhenvald associates the moral with the non-material:

> Within the boundaries of self-awareness and personal conduct, each individual is always granted the possibility to triumph over one's dualism. This is accomplished through love and heroism, through beauty and goodwill, through the triumph of the idealistic state of mind. For instance, when for the sake of a right purpose the line of greatest resistance is chosen and the instinct for self-preservation is suppressed, the self-loving voice of the flesh is silenced and the surge of the spiritual wave is high—it is there that the sticky web of *poshlost'* falls apart, that the self breaks the yoke of dualism, and ascends, if not to the very peak, at least towards the summit of the Great. The One, the self-sufficient Godhead.[12]

Aikhenvald's pithy conclusion—"The one who is kind is not *poshl* [*Kto dobr, tot ne poshl*]"—anticipates Nabokov's claim that "the genuine, the guileless, the good is never *poshlust*."[13] Both statements could serve as a gloss on *Ada*'s moral and artistic preoccupations and, more broadly, to Nabokov's tendency to bind ethics to aesthetics. His oft-cited prediction that "one day a reappraiser will come and declare that, far from having been a frivolous firebird, I was a rigid moralist kicking sin, cuffing stupidity, ridiculing the vulgar and cruel" (*SO* 193) reminds readers that in Nabokov's moral universe vulgarity and cruelty are versions of the same class of moral delinquency.

NABOKOV, KANT, AND RUSSIAN LIBERAL PHILOSOPHY

E. A. C. Wasianski, Kant's friend, amanuensis, executor, and the last of his three "official" biographers, tells a story that offers a useful point of entry into the ethical preoccupations that shape *Ada*. Wasianski's recollection has been repeated by Kant's subsequent biographers, but Erwin Panofsky's rendering of the event is particularly moving:

> Nine days before his death Immanuel Kant was visited by his physician. Old, ill and nearly blind, he rose from his chair and stood trembling with weakness and muttering unintelligible words. Finally his faithful companion realized that he would not sit down again until the visitor had taken a seat. This he did, and Kant then permitted himself to be helped to his chair and, after having regained some of his strength, said, "Das Gefühl für Humanität hat mich noch nicht verlassen"—"The sense of humanity has not yet left me." The two men were moved almost to tears. For, though the word *Humanität* had come, in the eighteenth century, to mean little more than politeness or civility, it had, for Kant, a much deeper significance, which the circumstances of the moment served to emphasize: man's proud and tragic consciousness of self-approved and self-imposed principles, contrasting with his utter subjection to illness, decay and all that is implied in the word "mortality."[14]

As a parable of human autonomy, this seemingly gratuitous act captures the dual ontology Aikhenvald sees at the heart of human identity. Kant's insistence on the necessity of observing "self-approved and self-imposed principles" even in the midst of excruciating physical debility signals the individual's simultaneous subjection to and autonomy from the laws of nature. Aikhenvald played a prominent role in the Moscow Psychological Society, and his remarks on *poshlost'* reflect the society's Kantian orientation (see chapter 1). As Poole has persuasively argued, the men responsible for the remarkable edifice of Russian liberal theory were all members of the Moscow Psychological Society and all deeply indebted to Kant. Chicherin, the patriarch of Russian liberal philosophy, Soloviev, Evgenii Trubetskoi, Kotliarevskii, and Novgorodtsev were particularly influenced by Kant's definition of personhood, his understanding of right, and his theory of justice and natural law.[15] As chapter 2 has shown, the view that liberalism and ethical idealism were mutually reinforcing moved Russia's liberal philosophers to embrace natural-law doctrine. Like Kant, they regarded moral consciousness as the keystone to all legal, political, and ethical considerations. Also like Kant, they viewed utilitarian approaches to ethics as incompatible with liberalism's core commitment to protecting human dignity and the right to self-determination. They echoed Kant in arguing, first, that the capacity to act as one ought (that is, in opposition to impulse, desire, or utilitarian calculation) endows the human individual with a special dignity, and second, that defending that dignity is liberalism's principal goal (EI 29). Novgorodtsev wrote in a 1904 issue of *Novyi put'*: "Contemporary idealist philosophy can well indicate that in its practical ideals it continuously emphasizes and advances the principle of the person, its absolute dignity, its natural and inalienable rights. For all the various shades dividing even idealists themselves, it is that point in relation to which they are in full agreement."[16]

Nabokov's first documented encounter with Kant can be traced to that "roll call of names" he comes across during his extensive research into Russian intellectual history for Chernyshevski's biography. As an exasperated Fyodor observes about the intellectual discourses of the 1860s, "some extravagantly praised Kant, others *Kont* (Comte), others again Hegel or Schlegel" (*Gift* 202). As a professor of literature in the United States, Nabokov exasperated his own students by insisting that they familiarize themselves with the source of every allusion in a given literary work. Such meticulousness makes it reasonable to guess that he held himself to the same standard when confronting what Fyodor calls "the mishmash of philosophical ideas" that dominated Chernyshevski's time (*G* 202). (This is certainly how he guided himself in his work on Pushkin's *Eugene Onegin.*)

Nabokov's interest in Kant may also have derived from his friendship with the Hessens.[17] Sergey Hessen was a committed Kantian. In his short autobiography he poignantly describes the long, peripatetic history of his much-valued and much-labored-on book on Kant's philosophy. Begun early in his philosophical career but never completed, the manuscript followed him into exile and served as the source for many lectures and articles on "Kant's ethical rigorism" and other Kantian-related topics before burning up in the 1944 Warsaw Uprising.[18] An important essay drawing deeply on Kant's moral philosophy appeared in *Sovremennye zapiski* in 1931 under the title "Bor'ba utopii i avtonomii dobra v mirovozzrenii F. Dostoevskogo i Vl. Solov'eva" ("The Struggle Between Utopia and the Autonomy of the Good in the Worldview of F. Dostoevsky and Vl. Soloviev").

But like his love of poetry, butterflies, and liberal values, Nabokov's familiarity with Kant can also be traced back to his father. Russian translations of Kant's *Critique of Practical Reason* and *Critique of Pure Reason* appear as items 2198 and 2199 in the section titled "Religion, Philosophy, Psychology, Ethics" of V. D. Nabokov's library catalogue.[19] And as chapter 2 has shown, V. D. Nabokov's jurisprudence was profoundly influenced by Kantian legal philosophy as it had been distilled in the work of Russia's "classical" school of criminal law. If perchance Nabokov was unaware of Kant's guiding force in his father's jurisprudence, he certainly knew that his father had read a book on the subject of Kant's philosophy during his three-month imprisonment. Twice during his clandestine correspondence with his wife, V. D. Nabokov mentions that Kuno Fischer's book on Kant's *Critique of Pure Reason* (borrowed from the prison library) was part of his daily reading regimen (alongside books by D'Annunzio, Nietzsche, Mikhailovskii, the Bible, a history of the French Revolution, and a book on criminal law).[20] Nabokov published his father's letters from prison in a 1965 issue of *Vozdushnye puti* (*Aerial Ways*) one year before beginning to write *Ada* at a rapid pace. Having certainly reread the letters before publishing them, Nabokov may have been curious about Fischer's book on Kant and decided to do some reading of his own. What is certain is that by the time *Ada* was completed, Nabokov could allude to Kant in a way that was contextually appropriate and thematically resonant. *Ada*'s engagement with Kant's moral philosophy sheds light not only on Nabokov's own personal ethics but also on his idiosyncratic views about art and deception.

LUCETTE AND *HUMANITÄT*

In the *Critique of Pure Reason,* Kant identifies freedom as the cornerstone of his political and moral philosophy. Though he concedes that the perfect state may never come into being, he also insists that

> the idea of this maximum is nevertheless wholly correct when it is set forth as an archetype, in order to bring the legislative constitution of human beings ever nearer to a possible greatest perfection. For whatever might be the highest degree of perfection at which humanity must stop, and however great a gulf must remain between the idea and its execution, no one can or should try to determine this, just because it is freedom that can go beyond every proposed boundary.[21]

For Poole, these words lie at the core of Kant's influence upon the development of Russian neo-idealism and liberal philosophy of progress.[22] They also provide a way into Nabokov's thinking about the interconnectedness of law, politics, and ethics. His examination of liberal political arrangements in *Lolita* is followed in *Ada* by an equally penetrating exploration of the core ethical premises that structured Russia's liberal neo-idealist traditions and his father's political activism and jurisprudence. Van's reference to Kant's "cucumicolor iris" is a still point around which the novel's ethical preoccupations revolve, and the novel itself explores the moral objections Russia's neo-idealist liberal philosophers leveled against the utilitarianism of the radical left.

Nabokov's antipathy toward deterministic models of reality is well documented, but *Ada* is far more subtle than Nabokov's characteristic polemic against Marxist and Freudian determinism because it acknowledges that individual freedom is frequently (and perhaps always) compromised by external pressures. Boyd's argument that Van and Ada's premature initiation of Lucette into their erotic games sets off a chain of events that culminates in Lucette's suicide is both persuasive and morally attractive. But to read Lucette's tragedy as a direct consequence of Van and Ada's sexual manipulation casts Lucette's fate in a deterministic scheme that can just as easily exonerate Van and Ada from charges of moral misconduct. In a world without choice, Van and Ada cannot be held accountable for actions that are predetermined. Nabokov does not forgive Van and Ada for their abuse of their half-sister's innocence and affection, but he also suggests that Lucette is a free agent and that suicide need not be the outcome of a causally determined sequence of events.

Lucette's autonomy—her "humanity," or *Humanität,* in the Kantian sense—is most explicitly demonstrated by her selfless courtesy to Robert and Rachel Robinson—"old bores of the family" (*A* 380)—on the night of her death. For Boyd, this is the novel's consummate moral action, and it establishes a standard against which all others must be weighed.[23] Van and Lucette, bound for America on a luxurious ocean liner, attend a film screening on board the ship. Van is on the verge of succumbing to Lucette's persistent sexual advances when Ada, now an actress, appears on screen in the film they are watching. Van leaves the theater, and Lucette is about to pursue him in an attempt to reverse the damage that has occurred. Her pursuit, however, is blocked by the Robinsons, who take advantage of Van's departure to seat themselves next to Lucette. Replicating Kant's legendary civility toward his physician, Lucette's response at this moment emblematizes the potential to rise above the self-interest that deterministic models see at the heart of human conduct. Knowing that her own happiness hangs in the balance, Lucette still manages to bestow upon the Robinsons "her last, last, last free gift of staunch courtesy that was stronger than failure and death. They were craning already across her, with radiant wrinkles and twittery fingers toward Van when he pounced upon their intrusion to murmur a humorous bad-sailor excuse and leave the cinema hall to its dark lurching" (*A* 392). Lucette's courtesy has unexpected, and tragic, consequences. Van is able to escape from her and masturbate in her absence, thus releasing himself from the desire that had tempted him to succumb to her advances. Rejected once again, Lucette commits suicide by drowning.

Lucette's sublime courtesy to the Robinsons during a moment of extreme emotional crisis stands in sharp contrast to the sexual turmoil that engulfs Van's potential for self-control. Van seems to recognize that he could have overcome his physical desires. He buries that acknowledgment, however, by figuring Lucette's death as an unavoidable consequence of life on Antiterra. "In other more deeply moral worlds than this pellet of muck," he writes in his letter to Ada in the wake of Lucette's suicide, "there might exist restraints, principles, transcendental consolations, and even a certain pride in making happy someone one does not really love; but on *this* planet Lucettes are doomed" (*A* 398; emphasis in original). This is a specious self-defense. Lucette's courtesy to the Robinsons (occurring five pages before Van's letter to Ada) preemptively refutes his claim that only a different world order or the promise of "transcendental consolations" can inspire moral action on Antiterra. By choosing not to pursue Van, Lucette rises above self-interest and follows instead the Kantian injunction that one ought to and therefore can be courteous even to those one does not love.

Van's feelings of culpability further undermine his denial that absolute moral values exist on Antiterra. Having penned a defense of his actions in his letter to Ada, Van immediately offers readers a glimpse of the remorse that frequently punctuates his family chronicle: "Some poor little things belonging to [Lucette]—a cigarette case, a tulle evening frock, a book dog's-eared at a French picnic—have had to be destroyed, because they stared at me" (*A* 398). That Van should experience such guilt is further evidence that he implicitly acknowledges the existence (and even, perhaps, the value) of an ethical standard from which he strives to extricate himself. And here again, as in his recollection of Lucette's cucumicolor iris, the spasm of guilt springs from a sense that he is being observed.

Kant regards the capacity to rise above fear, inclination, and other empirical conditions in order to follow unconditional, universally binding maxims of conduct as proof of our autonomy. His argument that human ontology is both free and determined emerges from his conviction that we are at once part of phenomenal nature and members of a noumenal dimension. Every event in nature is bound inescapably by the law of causality, and as such, human action is always constrained by external necessity.[24] Yet we simultaneously know ourselves to be the authors of our own actions, from which Kant infers that we are at once empirical beings, bound up by the laws of nature, and transcendent beings, bound by the laws of duty. According to this model, autonomy manifests itself most fully through the choice of disinterested moral action. Moral agents disregard the context-based, interest-driven utilitarian calculation as they commit themselves to actions that square with reason alone.[25] To see Lucette's "last, last, last free gift of staunch courtesy" as a Kantian moral standard against which the novel's actions are measured is to argue for the importance of moral obligations in a novel whose dominant characters are always denying the existence of such obligations. Van's narrative is, among other things, an elaborate exercise in attenuating their force. Recurring cross-generational patterns would seem to commit the novel's cast of characters to a relentless determinism that minimizes free choice. The family tree which precedes the opening chapter reveals that Princess Sofia Temnosiniy's marriage to Prince Vseslav Zemski (at the ages of 15 and 71 respectively) establishes a family pattern of aging men marrying young girls (Peter Zemski's to Mary O'Reilly at 52 and 18; Ivan Durmanov's to Dolly Zemski at 39 and 15; Dedalus Veen to Countess Irina Garin at 38 and 17). Marina draws attention to this pattern when she tells Van that "the Zemskis were terrible rakes (*razvratniki*), one of them loved small girls" (*A* 185), not yet knowing that both Demon and Van will follow this trend with an intensity all their own.

Genetic determinism also threatens to reveal that Van and Ada are full siblings and that Ada and Lucette are not. Whereas Ada's coloring identifies her as the daughter of her putative "Uncle" Demon, Lucette's freckles and red hair identify her as Dan Veen's only true daughter. In addition to these marital and genetic patterns, uncanny parallels shape the lives of parents and children.[26] Demon and Marina's manipulation of Aqua (Marina's twin sister and Van's alleged mother) prefigures Van and Ada's cruelty toward Lucette. The fact that Aqua commits suicide at an "astorium in St. Taurus," and Lucette commits suicide shortly after a vacation on "Minataor," seems to bind them to almost preternaturally explicit patterns (*A* 27, 381).[27] The workings of fate and heredity suggest a deterministic order that undermines the claim that we are autonomous creatures capable of following the dictates of disinterested moral duty.

Van invokes these patterns, in part, to exonerate himself and Ada from any blame regarding the death of Lucette.[28] This is made explicit when Van suggests that physical suffering impedes ethical thinking: "Rather humiliating that physical pain makes one supremely indifferent to such moral issues as Lucette's fate." (Van would love to be "supremely indifferent" to her fate, but his sense of humiliation suggests that he cannot get beyond the "moral issues" raised by her death.) He concludes by tacitly acknowledging that his search for such exculpatory physical impediments is hollow and opportunistic: "and rather amusing, if that is the right word, to constate that one bothers about problems of style even at those atrocious moments" (*A* 466).

Van's attempt to ignore his complicity in Lucette's destiny by making an appeal to physical pain contrasts sharply with Kant's pain-defying civility in the presence of his physician and Lucette's courtesy ("stronger than failure and death") to the Robinsons (*A* 392). And yet Van's capacity to worry about "problems of style" during moments of acute physical suffering is a cheeky assertion of autonomy in the face of external pressures. Van hopes to diminish the implications of this confession by implying that "problems of style" are trivial next to genuinely significant "moral issues such as Lucette's fate." But as his detailed reconstruction of the events that preceded his half-sister's suicide intimates, "problems of style" and "moral issues"—or art and ethics—are inexorably connected.

ART AND ETHICS

Richard Rorty describes Nabokov's insistence on a kinship between art and ethics as an example of the artist's attraction to problems and conditions (for example, suffering) that others ignore. However, as Rorty rightly points out, being curious about one's own artistic obsessions often prevents one from being sensitive to the obsessions or suffering of others. Together with Van, Humbert Humbert and Charles Kinbote exemplify this form of egotism. According to Rorty, Nabokov yearned to see artistic gifts map effortlessly onto moral virtue, but he was honest enough to recognize that there is no necessary connection between the selective curiosity of the artist and the kind of moral concern that pits itself against cruelty and suffering.[29] Rorty is right to argue that Nabokov did not always trust his pronouncements about the congruence of art and ethics. He does not, however, explain why Nabokov felt justified in asserting their validity. *Ada*'s moral vision suggests that his reasons amounted to more than mere wishful thinking.

Art and ethics converge when Lucette reminds Van about the library closet in which he and Ada locked her up at Ardis. Van attempts to correct what he claims is Lucette's misleading exaggeration regarding the frequency of such events by drawing attention to her angry green eye spying through the closet's keyhole. For Van, this recollection calls to mind Kant's "cucumicolor iris," an association that he has either retrospectively fabricated or still remembers decades later when he composes his family chronicle.[30] It is unclear whether Van is aware of the irony that suffuses his offhand reference to Kant. Though he ostensibly invokes Kant's exacting vision in response to what he sees as Lucette's overstatement, his own feelings of culpability offer a better rationale for the quip: Van seems to imagine himself held to a Kantian standard. Yet the most revealing aspect of this remark is its sensuously clinical diction. Van's invocation of Kant's green eye, his "cucumicolor iris," turns to the resources of art to deflect attention from a gross moral delinquency.[31] Van's and Ada's aesthetic engagement with the world repeatedly identifies them as creatures capable of reveling in natural beauty. What they fail to see, or perhaps pretend not to see, is that within the Kantian framework to which Van subjects himself in his remark about Lucette's accusing eye, their capacity to experience aesthetic pleasure is also a sign of their moral obligation toward others.

In *Critique of the Power of Judgment,* Kant argues that "the beautiful is the symbol of the morally good" because the faculty that enables us to derive universally binding moral laws also enables us to make aesthetic judgments that we can suppose to be valid for all humankind.[32] The connection originates in a process of abstraction that insulates the mind from private concerns such as inclination, desire, and ambition: "*Taste* is the faculty for judging an object or a kind of representation through a satisfaction or dissatisfaction *without any interest.* The object of such a satisfaction is called *beautiful.*"[33] Kant's insistence that detachment is at once a moral and aesthetic condition sets a convincing precedent for Nabokov's insistence that good reading must combine "an artist's passion" with "a scientist's patience." Nabokov's argument also turns on the idea of detachment: "The enthusiastic artist alone is apt to be too subjective in his attitude towards a book, and so a scientific coolness of judgment will temper the intuitive heat" (*LL* 5). For both Kant and Nabokov, aesthetic impartiality derives from a moral commitment to that which is other.[34] Roger Scruton glosses this central premise of Kant's aesthetics in terms that are equally suited to Nabokov: "Disinterested contemplation is a recognition that the object matters—matters so much that our interests have no bearing on our judgment."[35]

After Van tells Lucette that the closet's keyless hole was "as big as Kant's eye," he seems unsure that this analogy will have any meaning for her. His follow-up explanation—"Kant was famous for his cucumicolor iris" (*A* 298)—can be read as a philosopher's attempt to speak about Kant in the language most familiar to Lucette, a student of art history at Queenston College. But his assumption that Lucette will appreciate his sensuous description of Kant's iris echoes Kant's conclusion that one's capacity to make an appeal to aesthetic judgment confirms the autonomy of others endowed with a similar capacity. It also underscores Van's past and future failures to grant Lucette the autonomy and respect she deserves as someone who shares his love of beauty.

LUCETTE AND *ACHTUNG*

Before jumping overboard Lucette makes one final effort to seduce Van. She calls him on the telephone and asks him if she can join him in his suite, as he had promised. Having masturbated twice in her absence, Van finds it easy to withstand the temptation and, to avoid another encounter, tells her that he is not alone:

> No doubt he was morally right in using the first pretext at hand to keep her away from his bed; but he also knew, as a gentleman and an artist, that the lump of words he brought up was trite and cruel, and it was only because she could not accept him as being either, that she believed him. (*A* 393–94)

Van seems confident that his deception was "morally right," but his certitude is undercut by his recognition—"as a gentleman and an artist"—that he has betrayed his half-sister. This is fitting given that Van's credentials as gentleman and artist are more trustworthy than his credentials as moral philosopher. After all, the physical pain that can make him "indifferent to moral issues such as Lucette's fate" seems hopelessly ineffectual when confronted by his artistic concern with "problems of style."

Van's moral compass is unreliable because he refuses to apply the rules of art and social decorum to the sphere of ethics. Lucette's courtesy toward the Robinsons is a consummate lesson in "style," but Van's effort to preserve his self-professed innocence requires that he turn a blind eye to the connection between style and moral virtue. He justifies his deception on the telephone with Lucette by claiming that his lie was motivated by a desire to protect her from what would have certainly become a heartbreaking affair. But this rationale is only superficially compelling: "as a gentleman and an artist" Van knows that his deception is as morally unworthy as his two "disgusting but necessary" acts of masturbation prior to Lucette's phone call (*A* 393). The lie—"the lump of words" generated by fatigue and sexual satiety—marks his humiliating surrender to his physical nature.

Van is repelled by his deception because it is "trite and cruel," useful adjectives for diagnosing his moral failures. The deception is "trite"—a near-synonym for *poshlost':* stale, tired, commonplace—not only because it is conjured up from "the first pretext at hand," but also because deception is, in itself, an instrument of degradation. Van knows that turning to "the first pretext at hand" bespeaks a carelessness and thoughtlessness unworthy of both gentlemen and artists. But no lie, however elaborate or thoughtful, would have prevented such degradation, and Van surely knows that the three words with which he deceives Lucette on the telephone—"*Ya ne odin* (I'm not alone)" (*A* 394)—are morally neither better nor worse than the complex deceptions he and Ada devised for her as children. All lies, as Kant has famously argued, are cruel because they undermine the rational being's capacity to set up his or her own ends. Van's deception of Lucette is morally wrong because it makes her thing-like.

Lucette's refusal to accept Van as either trite or cruel is a gesture of respect commensurate with her courtesy toward the Robinsons. For Kant, respect is basic to ethics because, to quote Kantian scholar Allen Wood, "it is our fundamental experience of *objective value.* Respect is directed at something whose worth we recognize by reason from within ourselves, and we recognize that worth as essentially greater than the worth of any object of inclination (whether of desire or aversion)."[36] The respect that characterizes Lucette's conduct toward Van and the Robinsons is inexplicable in terms of contingent motivating feelings and has no motivating factor other than itself. As Kuno Fischer succinctly observes, only this ground of determination can make Lucette's action "virtuous" from a Kantian perspective.[37] Neither her aversion toward the tiresome Robinsons nor her infatuation with Van can bring Lucette to diminish their human dignity by acting discourteously toward the Robinsons or by thinking that Van could be trite or cruel.

The plangent tones of Van's description of Lucette's act of courtesy on the eve of her death (he calls it "her last, last, last free gift of staunch courtesy that was stronger than failure and death") suggest that the moral force of her conduct is not lost upon him even though he refuses to acknowledge its implications. Like Lucette's Kantian iris, which Van imagines holding him to account for his youthful transgressions, Lucette's Kantian action is a reproach to Van for his moral failures as an adult. In its disinterestedness, this act belies Van's denial that higher moral principles are relevant on his "pellet of muck," and summons up the awe and wonderment at the heart of Kant's conception of "*Achtung.*" Kant uses the term *Achtung* (usually translated as "respect" and sometimes as "reverence") to refer to the feeling experienced by finite rational beings when confronted by the force of self-legislated moral law. Recognizing the secondary importance of inclinations in the face of unconditional moral commands gives rise to a feeling of reverential respect.[38] "The moral law strikes down self-conceit," writes Kant in the *Critique of Practical Reason,* and

> what in our own judgment infringes upon our self-conceit humiliates. Hence the moral law unavoidably humiliates every human being when he compares with it the sensible propensity of his nature. If something represented *as a determining ground of our will* humiliates us in our self-consciousness, it awakens *respect* for itself insofar as it is positive and a determining ground.[39]

Kant's description of the humiliation produced by the moral law anticipates—in reverse—Van's confession, late in life, that he is "rather humiliat[ed]" by the power of "physical pain" to make him "supremely indifferent to such moral issues as Lucette's fate" (*A* 466). His cavalier allusion to Lucette's tragic end, offered on the second-to-last page of his family chronicle, should recall a series of antecedent humiliations. As a nonagenarian, Van is humiliated by the implacable authority of physical pain, but his humiliation can only be sharpened by the recollection that neither severe emotional distress nor heartbreaking disappointment prevented Lucette from being respectful and compassionate. Lucette's ability to honor unconditional moral commands even when they conflicted with her personal desires is a source of shame for Van and must elicit in him the feeling of reverential respect that Kant ascribes not only to the moral law but also to those who submit to it.

Obedience to the moral law, according to Kant, inspires the same feeling of *Achtung* as the moral law itself:

> A humble common man in whom I perceive uprightness of character in a higher degree than I am aware of in myself . . . holds before me a law that strikes down my self-conceit when I compare it with my conduct, and I see observance of that law and hence its *practicability* proved before me in

> fact. . . . *Respect* is a *tribute* that we cannot refuse to pay to merit, whether we want to or not; we may indeed withhold it outwardly but we still cannot help feeling it inwardly. (*CPR* 202; emphasis in original)

Kant is a shrewd psychologist when he notes that this feeling of *Achtung* causes us pain. Our instinct, he observes, is to recoil from its implications:

> *So little* is respect a feeling of *pleasure* that we give way to it only reluctantly with regard to a human being. We try to discover something that could lighten the burden of it for us, some fault in him to compensate us for the humiliation that comes upon us through such an example. Even the dead are not always safe from this critical examination, especially if their example appears inimitable. (*CPR* 202; emphasis in original)

Van's tendency to shunt Lucette to the margins of his life and family memoir suggests that he feels the sting of the reproof leveled against him by her moral conduct ("inimitable" on their "pellet of muck"). And when he does allow himself to dwell on "such moral issues as Lucette's fate," he tries to mitigate his role in her death by deterministic arguments of the kind he used to rationalize his incestuous relationship with Ada.

Van and Ada's attempt to exonerate themselves of any responsibility regarding Lucette turns on a canny misrepresentation of the terms most closely applicable to their situation. In his letter to Ada and her husband in the aftermath of the tragedy, Van makes Lucette's survival dependent upon a contingent feeling beyond the will's reach. Only love, he insists, could have prevented her suicide:

> As a psychologist, I know the unsoundness of speculations as to whether Ophelia would not have drowned herself after all, without the help of a treacherous sliver, even if she had married her Voltemand. Impersonally I believe she would have died in her bed, gray and serene, had V. loved her; but since he did not really love the wretched little virgin, and since no amount of carnal tenderness could or can pass for true love, and since, above all, the fatal Andalusian wench who had come, I repeat, into the picture, was unforgettable, I am bound to arrive, dear Ada and dear Andrey, at the conclusion that whatever the miserable man could have thought up, she would have *pokonchila s soboi* ("put an end to herself") all the same. (*A* 398)

Ada, too, makes love the missing ingredient in their relationship with Lucette:

> Oh, Van, oh Van, we did not love her enough. *That's* whom you should have married, the one sitting feet up, in ballerina black, on the stone balustrade,

> and then everything would have been all right—I would have stayed with you both in Ardis Hall, and instead of that happiness, handed out gratis, instead of all that we *teased* her to death! (*A* 466; emphasis in original)

By referring to their conduct as "teasing," Ada miniaturizes their selfishness and cruelty. More importantly, however, both Van and Ada's separate claims that a lack of love killed Lucette deflect attention from the moral transgression for which they can be rightfully held accountable. Unlike love—a heteronomous feeling which "no amount of carnal tenderness" can replicate—respect can be bestowed freely and without self-degradation (Lucette's courtesy to the Robinsons is appropriately described by Van as a "*free* gift of staunch courtesy" [*A* 392; my emphasis]). By highlighting their lack of love for Lucette while remaining silent on the subject of respect, Van and Ada count on their readers to exonerate them for refusing to sacrifice their own lives for the sake of saving the life of another. The harrowing truth is that they needed to sacrifice very little in order to save her dignity and, by extension, perhaps even her life.

Ada's proposition that Lucette would have been saved had Van married her, and Van's speculation that she would have lived had he loved her, is as demeaning to Lucette as Ada's earlier claim that her sexual infidelities with Philip Rack were driven by pity (*A* 267). Nicholas Berdiaev's contribution to *Problems of Idealism* helps identify the flaws in their reasoning by integrating key principles borrowed from Kant and Nietzsche. "To relate to a human being only with pity and compassion," he writes,

> means to see in him not a human being equal in value to oneself, but a weak and sorry slave; it means, finally, to be oneself a slave to his sufferings and weaknesses. There is a higher morality, which will correspond to a higher level of human development. It is based on the revolt of human strength, not weakness; it demands not pity for the slave, but respect for the human being, relating to him as to "I."

Rejecting the ideal of love for an ideal of respect, Berdiaev presses his moral vision into the service of the liberal struggle for civil freedoms: "Only such a morality corresponds to a high consciousness of human dignity and befits that part of contemporary humanity that is leading the great liberation movement."[40]

In the same essay, Berdiaev sets out to dismantle the traditional association of altruism with moral approbation and of egoism with moral disapproval by invoking Kant's distinction between "the empirical 'I' and the spiritual 'I.'" Berdiaev's reformulation helps expose the opportunism that leads Van and Ada to suggest that only their own martyrdom could have saved Lucette. Locating moral value in the sacrifice of one's happiness for the sake of the happiness of another is "deprived of any ethical meaning whatsoever," Berdiaev argues, because

> every "I" has the same right to happiness as every "thou"; no one has the advantage here, but at the same time both the happiness of the "I" and that of the "other" are equally nonethical concepts. . . . If "altruism" demands that one's spiritual "I" be sacrificed in the name of the happiness of the "other," then this demand is positively immoral, because my spiritual "I" has absolute moral value, while the happiness of the "other" is sometimes an excellent thing, but it has no moral value. If altruism, however, demands that one sacrifice the lower instincts of his empirical nature in the name of the spiritual, moral-rational nature of another human being, that one not infringe on the inalienable rights of another's spiritual nature, that one facilitate another's spiritual development through common work in the creation of human culture, then all this is demanded first of all by one's own spiritual "I." Since this moment enters into the struggle for one's own moral personhood, the word "altruism" does not apply here.[41]

Berdiaev's argument suggests that non-Kantian terms such as "egoism" and "altruism" do not apply to Van and Ada's moral predicament in relation to Lucette. It also undermines their effort to identify happiness as a moral end superseding all others.

In his interpretation of Kant's moral philosophy in the book read by V. D. Nabokov during his incarceration at Kresty, Kuno Fischer explains why happiness cannot serve as a "moral" end in Kant's system. As Fischer notes, happiness is only a "sensuous good"; it is empirically determined and adheres to "pragmatical laws" that are ethically neutral. "Moral laws," by contrast, are independent of circumstances and determined by reason alone. Their end is not happiness, but virtue. In Fischer's summing up of Kant's ethics, the object of morality is "our *deserving* to be happy" or "happiness only as a consequence of worth."[42] The distinction gets at the heart of Van and Ada's failure to accommodate themselves to the happiness that a lasting reunion should afford them. Though they are never forced to part again after Andrey Vinelander's death, their newfound happiness is frequently shot through with the misery of knowing that this happiness is unearned and undeserved. To use Ada's terminology against her, they intuit that happiness ought not to be "handed out gratis" (*A* 466).

Van is clearly protecting himself when he claims that there is nothing he could have done to guarantee Lucette's happiness. But from the delimited number of options available to him on their fateful transatlantic crossing, his assessment is right. A romantic affair between them would most likely have ended in despair and humiliation. The only unequivocally moral option available to Van in this carefully crafted scenario is to have been honest with Lucette, just as he claims to have done in his explanatory letter to Ada and Andrey. Though such a course of action was unlikely to have made Lucette happy or even to have dissuaded her from committing suicide, it would have granted her the respect that Van and Ada had denied her since childhood. Cut off from happiness, Lucette might have yet found sufficient reason to live a life graced by dignity.

In "using the first pretext at hand to keep her away from his bed" (*A* 393), Van allows sexual satiety to turn him into the kind of egoist imagined by Berdiaev. Such an individual privileges "his empirical nature" (his physical comfort, his emotional condition) above his own and other people's "spiritual, moral-rational nature" (the capacity to follow universally valid moral principles such as truth-telling). To be an egoist is to be "trite and cruel," and it is a measure of Lucette's generosity that "she could not accept him as being either" (*A* 394). While Van's moral indolence leads to the kind of self-debasement described by Berdiaev, Lucette's refusal to be complicit in Van's self-debasement reminds him of the "moral-rational nature" he has betrayed by indulging his "lower instincts."

"AESTHETIC BLISS" AND "OBJECTIVE VALUE"

Van and Ada turn upside down Kant's assertion that respect applies only to persons and never to things (*CPR* 202); this inversion enables us to see why Nabokov felt justified to insist upon a connection between art and ethics. Van and Ada's respect for the claims of art does not translate into a respect for others, and their artistic virtues make their lack of social virtues glaringly conspicuous. Their dirty secret is that they refuse to treat human beings with the same scrupulous attentiveness, honesty, and courtesy that they bestow upon the world of things.

Rorty's interest in Nabokov is sparked by the radical disjunction he sees between, on the one hand, Nabokov's insistence on a connection between art and ethics, and, on the other, his tendency to endow his villains with a heightened artistic sensibility. Gerard de Vries echoes Rorty when he, too, concludes that this practice reflects Nabokov's mistrust of his own assertions regarding the ties that bind ethics to aesthetics.[43] But a closer look at the passage from which such discussions proceed suggests a way to reconcile this perceived dilemma. As Nabokov writes in the afterword to *Lolita,* "for me a work of fiction exists only insofar as it affords me what I shall bluntly call aesthetic bliss, that is a sense of being somehow, somewhere, connected with other states of being where art (curiosity, tenderness, kindness, ecstasy) is the norm" (OB 296). Though the passage sets up a correspondence between art and moral virtues (such as curiosity and kindness), it also casts this correspondence into a different dimension. The connection between art and ethics has been severed in our world, and Nabokov's gnomic words recall Van's letter to Ada in the aftermath of Lucette's suicide: "In other more deeply moral worlds than this pellet of muck, there might exist restraints, principles, transcendental consolations, and even a certain pride in making happy someone one does not really love" (*A* 398).

The two formulations resonate with each other in instructive ways. Van insists that moral standards are absent from his planet, but his statement is undercut in advance by his earlier admission that "as a gentleman and an artist" he feels all too keenly the pull of moral claims (*A* 393–94). Nabokov, too, credits "aesthetic bliss" with the power to transport us into an otherworldly dimension where moral virtue is the norm. That art should be endowed with this capacity is a function of its autonomy. Artists are unique for Nabokov because they experience freedom in a more palpable fashion than the rest of us. They embody, to quote from "The Art of Literature and Commonsense," the "capacity to wonder at trifles—no matter the imminent peril—these asides of the spirit, these footnotes in the volume of life [that] are the highest forms of consciousness" (*LL* 374). Rorty is right to note that the artist's tendency "to wonder at trifles" exacts a high ethical price (such as, for example, a disregard for the pain of others), and Nabokov's fiction acknowledges the enormity of these costs. Nonetheless, this same fiction also suggests that freedom is priceless.

Nabokov's celebration of art's non-utilitarian impulse in "The Art of Literature and Commonsense" doubles as a celebration of non-utilitarian ethics. The list of examples he summons up to illustrate the "irrational standards" of his worldview does not acknowledge any distinction between ethical and aesthetic merit: "the hero who dashes into a burning house" and risks "squandering a precious five seconds to find and save, together with the child, its favorite toy" becomes analogous to a chimney sweep depicted in a cartoon "falling from the roof of a tall building and noticing on the way that a sign-board had one word spelled wrong, and wondering in his headlong flight why nobody had thought of correcting it." The analogy turns on their shared rejection of utilitarian calculation, or, in the essay's preferred terminology, "commonsense." In the "divinely absurd world of the mind" embraced by Nabokov, "commonsense is ejected together with its calculating machine" and "statistics pluck up their skirts and sweep out in a huff" (*LL* 373–74).[44]

Nabokov's suggestion that utilitarianism is incompatible with freedom restates the argument made by Kant and Russia's neo-idealist philosophers that ethics and freedom are coextensive. As Novgorodtsev sums up this claim in his contribution to *Problems of Idealism,* "individualism is so much a part of ethics that these two concepts can be taken for synonyms. As the sphere of freedom, ethics first of all supposes the self-determination of the person. The first and basic definition of ethics is the definition of conscious duty, and such duty can have meaning only in relation to the person, as the one source of conscious decisions" (EIPL 304–5).

Like artists who ignore an "imminent peril" for the sake of attending to "trifles," individuals who disregard utility for the sake of acting in accordance with universally binding moral principles showcase their agency by rising above material circumstances. This in no way implies, however, an equivalence between art and moral virtue; to conclude that all morally upright individuals are also artists—or vice versa—would be to fall prey to a faulty syllogism. The compassion, solicitude, and courtesy of characters such as Luzhin's wife in *The Defense* or Albinus's brother-in-law Paul in *Laughter in the Dark* are unaccompanied by a refined aesthetic sensibility. Maximov, Krug's loyal friend in *Bend Sinister,* is a case in point:

> No subtlety of thought tainted his honesty, he was as reliable as iron and oak, and when Krug mentioned once that the word "loyalty" phonetically and visually reminded him of a golden fork lying in the sun on a smooth spread of pale yellow silk, Maximov replied somewhat stiffly that to *him* loyalty was limited to its dictionary denotation. Commonsense with him was saved from smug vulgarity by a delicate emotional undercurrent, and the somewhat bare and birdless symmetry of his branching principles was ever so slightly disturbed by a moist wind blowing from regions which he naïvely thought did not exist. The misfortunes of others worried him more than did his own troubles, and had he been an old sea captain, he would have dutifully gone down with his ship rather than plump apologetically into the last lifeboat. (*BS* 237; emphasis in original)

Maximov is no artist, but his willingness to sacrifice his life for the sake of an abstract moral principle ("he would have dutifully gone down with his ship rather than plump apologetically into the last lifeboat") seems to flow "from regions which he naïvely thought did not exist." That these regions should recall those "other states of being" described by Nabokov as originating in "aesthetic bliss" is fitting given his location of the source of art and ethics in a transcendent domain.

The proliferation of villainous artists in Nabokov's fiction seems to confirm Rorty's claim that Nabokov was haunted by the suspicion that art and ethics are mutually exclusive. But Nabokov's preoccupation with artist-villains can also be read as an inquiry into the ways in which art can serve as an interpretive tool for the moral vision reflected in Kant's evocatively colorful, yet stern, iris. Van and Ada's approach to art and nature showcases the reverence engendered by a recognition of what Allen Wood calls "objective value." Their lovingly precise observations of the natural world and exacting fidelity to the artistic work of others draw attention to their moral omissions in the sphere of human relations.

Ada's description of herself and Van as "a unique superimperial couple" is linked to her sense that they recognize an intense moral connection between themselves and the world they inhabit:

> The song of a Tuscan Firecrest or a Sitka Kinglet in a cemetery cypress; a minty whiff of Summer Savory or Yerba Buena on a coastal slope; the dancing flitter of a Holly Blue or an Echo Azure—combined with other birds, flowers and butterflies: *that* has to be heard, smelled and seen through the transparency of death and ardent beauty. (*A* 60; emphasis in original)

Their appreciation of these details is fashioned as a moral injunction. A similar injunction motivates their attacks on sloppy translations. Careless or inept translations are decried as the product of irresponsible engagements with the external world:

> "Old storytelling devices," said Van, "may be parodied only by very great and inhuman artists, but only close relatives can be forgiven for paraphrasing illustrious poems. Let me preface the effort of a cousin—anybody's cousin—by a snatch of Pushkin, for the sake of rhyme—"
>
> "For the *snake* of rhyme!" cried Ada. "A paraphrase, even my paraphrase, is like the corruption of 'snakeroot' into 'snagrel'—all that remains of a delicate little birthwort." (*A* 196)

Ada's suggestion that non-literal translations are indefensible moral transgressions parallels Nabokov's own approach to the act of translation. "The term 'free translation' smacks of knavery and tyranny," he writes in 1955 in an essay about his labors as translator of Pushkin's *Eugene Onegin.*[45] When asked eleven years later what correlations he found between life and the act of translation, Nabokov suggested that a work of art is an extension of its author and, as such, calls for the same reverence as a human individual:

> There is a certain small Malayan bird of the thrush family which is said to sing only when tormented in an unspeakable way by a specially trained child at the annual Feast of Flowers. There is Casanova making love to a harlot while looking from a window at the nameless tortures inflicted on Damiens. These are the visions that sicken me when I read the "poetical" translations from martyred Russian poets by some of my famous contemporaries. A tortured author and a deceived reader, this is the inevitable outcome of arty paraphrase. The only object and justification of translation is the conveying of the most exact information possible and this can be only achieved by a literal translation, with notes. (*SO* 81)

The "tortures" caused an author by an "arty paraphrase" are incomparable (in scale or kind) to the torments inflicted upon Damiens or the Malayan bird, but this correlation of radically disproportionate moral evils provides an illuminating insight into Nabokov's thinking about ethics. The example of the Malayan bird conveys Nabokov's horror and repugnance when confronted by the fact that art can be used to inflict and justify pain. The same feelings are produced when art claims to be detached from the world's cruelty and suffering. The second example suggests that only a *poshliak,* a vulgar Casanova, can allow his personal pleasures to remain unaffected (or, worse yet, to be heightened) by "the nameless tortures" inflicted upon another. Art, these examples intimate, is not exempt from the ethical considerations that apply to ordinary people but is firmly embedded in the moral matrix of everyday life.

Art, for Nabokov, is not beyond the reach of the moral law, and the art produced by others comes with an added set of moral imperatives. His characteristic identification of "arty paraphrase" with moral delinquencies such as tyranny, cruelty, and deception is revealingly staged in the novel's most sustained account of the responsibilities of translation. As Boyd has painstakingly demonstrated in his monograph on *Ada,* mistranslation is associated with Lucette throughout the novel, but it is here that Ada's denunciation of "English-speaking transmongrelizers" for whom the practice of translation is guided by reasons other than the "artistic and moral" is most conspicuously tied to Lucette (*A* 55). Ada's gloss on Van's quotation from Rimbaud's "Mémoire" ("*Les robes vertes et déteintes des fillettes*") sets up correspondences between Lucette, the color green, and the ethics of translation (*NA* 53–54):

> Well, Larivière allows me to read him only in the Feuilletin anthology. . . . Incidentally, she will come down after tucking in Lucette, our darling copperhead who by now should be in her green nightgown . . . the nuance of willows, and counting the little sheep on her *ciel de lit* which Fowlie turns into "the *sky's bed*" instead of "bed ceiler." (*A* 55–56)

The significance of Rimbaud's "Mémoire" to Van and Ada's romance (the poem provides the key to their coded letters during their first separation) and Lucette's lifelong partiality for the color green tie this discussion about the ethics of translation to the story of Lucette.[46]

DECEPTION AND KANT'S "FORMULA OF HUMANITY"

The radical difference between Nabokov's approach to deception in art and translation turns on a specifically Kantian conception of moral duty. For Nabokov deception is a natural and wholesome ingredient of art, but it is a noxious substance in the realm of translation. His condemnations of "arty" and "poetic" translations on behalf of the "deceived reader" occur frequently in his writings, but it is in his polemical exchange with his critics over the translation of *Eugene Onegin* that he draws the sharpest distinction between art and the act of translation:

> In regard to my novels my position is different. I cannot imagine myself writing a letter-to-the-editor in reply to an unfavorable review, let alone devoting almost a whole day to composing a magazine article of explanation, retaliation, and protest. . . . If, however, adverse criticism happens to be directed not at those acts of fancy, but at such a matter-of-fact work of reference as my annotated translation of *Eugene Onegin* (hereafter referred to as EO), other considerations take over. Unlike my novels, EO possesses an ethical side, moral and human elements. It reflects the compiler's honesty or dishonesty, skill or sloppiness. If told I am a bad poet, I smile; but if told I am a poor scholar, I reach for my heaviest dictionary. (*SO* 241)

The differences that allow Nabokov to distinguish so unambiguously his own art from art produced by others hinge on the second variant of Kant's supreme principle of moral conduct, the categorical imperative. This second variant, the Formula of Humanity, commands that all rational beings be treated as autonomous and deserving of respect: "So act that you use humanity, whether in your own person or in the person of any other, always at the same time as an end, never merely as a means" (*GMM* 80).

The Formula of Humanity's injunction against instrumentalizing others explains why *Ada*'s heated discussions about the ethics of translation bear so intimately on "moral issues such as Lucette's fate." Van's deception of Lucette on the night of her suicide anticipates the conjunction of "good intentions" with "cruelty and deception" articulated by Nabokov in relation to Robert Lowell's adaptation of a famous poem by Osip Mandelstam: "I cannot help feeling that despite the good intentions of adapters something very like cruelty and deception is the inevitable result of their misguided labors" (*SO* 282–83). Van, too, claims that his intentions were good when he lied to his half-sister. But he also knows that in spite of his good intentions, his deception is unforgivably cruel. This cruelty is a function of the nature of deception and has nothing to do with the deceiver's skills or intentions. A more elaborate deception—like an "arty" or "poetic" translation—would have been no less cruel because, as Kant insists, deception always instrumentalizes its target.

Kant's argument that the right to self-determination prohibits all actions that would jeopardize it is the cornerstone of his moral philosophy. Van's deception diminishes Lucette's humanity because it denies that she is, as Kant would have said, an end-in-herself. He justifies his deception on the grounds that it is a necessary strategy for Lucette's protection, but fails to acknowledge that Lucette is capable of determining her own ends. Christine Korsgaard uses Kant's Formula of Humanity to justify his uncompromising (and often criticized) prohibition against deception:

> According to the Formula of Humanity, coercion and deception are the most fundamental forms of wrongdoing to others—the roots of all evil. Coercion and deception violate the conditions of possible assent, and all actions which depend for their nature and efficacy on their coercive or deceptive character are ones that others cannot assent to.[47]

Rae Langton has similarly argued that in Kant's view deception makes a person "thing-like: something that cannot choose what it does."[48] These arguments would make Van's deception morally wrong because it sets up a situation in which Lucette cannot endorse his plans for her welfare.

When Van takes a paternalistic approach to Lucette's infatuation with him by lying to her, he is like the purveyor of paraphrastic translations who takes liberties with someone else's artistic creation. Actions such as these deny the autonomy of rational individuals and the objective value of things. By contrast, the deceptions Nabokov celebrated as the natural idiom of art and nature take dignity and autonomy as their point of departure. They are shared games, or, to invoke a favorite metaphor of Nabokov, a form of play. Unlike Van's deception of Lucette and the deceptions perpetrated by nonliteral translators, the primary function of these deceptions is to be exposed. The human subject's ability to uncover deception is analogous for Nabokov to the birth of consciousness, that elusive ontological entity whose mysteries lie at the heart of human identity and freedom: "It occurs to me that the closest reproduction of the mind's birth obtainable is the stab of wonder that accompanies the precise moment when, gazing at a tangle of twigs and leaves, one suddenly realizes that what had seemed a natural component of that tangle is a marvelously disguised insect or bird" (*SM* 617).

Such deceptions elevate the spirit by making it aware of its unique identity as a bearer of higher-order consciousness. This is a key principle in Godunov-Cherdyntsev's theory of evolution. "The fantastic refinement of 'protective mimicry,'" Fyodor writes in his redaction of his father's monograph, is one of nature's "whims" that

> can be, if not appreciated, at least merely noticed only by a brain that has developed in a related manner, and the sense of these whims can only be that—like a code or a family joke—they are accessible only to the illuminated, i.e., human, mind, and have no other mission than to give it pleasure . . . which,

> in a world lacking an appointed observer endowed with artistic sensitivity, imagination, and humor, would simply be useless (*lost upon the world*), like a small volume of Shakespeare lying open in the dust of a boundless desert. This fact, even taken alone, implies a silent, subtle, charmingly sly conspiracy between nature and the one who alone can understand, who alone has at last achieved this comprehension—a spiritual alliance concluded above and beyond all the seething, the stirring, the darkness of roaming reveilles, behind the back of all the world's organic life. (FB 219)

Whereas deception in social relations makes people thing-like, nature's deceptions are recursive mechanisms that remind the human mind of its special dignity as an entity different from the world of things. The same logic guides art's dishonesty, for it, too, assumes that its audience is equal to the task of seeing through it ("A grateful spectator is content to applaud the grace with which the masked performer melts into Nature's background" [*SO* 153]). The contract underwriting such deceptions, Nabokov suggests, stipulates an emphatically non-instrumentalizing relationship, "an artistic harmonious balance between the reader's mind and the author's mind" (*LL* 4).

In *Speak, Memory,* Nabokov provides an example of interpersonal dishonesty that escapes the kinds of degradation Kant associates with deception. In the chapter devoted to Cécile Miauton, his French-Swiss governess referred to throughout as "Mademoiselle," Nabokov recalls the visit he and a friend paid her in Lausanne many years after she left his family's employ. Finding her almost totally deaf, the two friends bring her a hearing device the day after their initial visit. Mademoiselle's response to the generous gift underscores the speciousness of Van's rationale for his deception of Lucette: "She adjusted the clumsy thing improperly at first, but no sooner had she done so than she turned to me with a dazzled look of moist wonder and bliss in her eyes. She swore she could hear every word, every murmur of mine. She could not for, having my doubts, I had not spoken" (*SM* 457). Recalling this last encounter with Mademoiselle after learning of her death, Nabokov is moved by "the radiant deceit she had used in order to have me depart pleased with my own kindness" (*SM* 458). A species of heightened courtesy, Mademoiselle's deception is, unlike Van's, at once clumsily transparent and strikingly *artistic.* Like the best art according to Nabokov's aesthetic philosophy, it seeks to direct the target's attention to his own kindness, or, what is the same in Nabokov's view about art and ethics, ponder his capacity to act outside a materialist economy of self-interest.

Deception's effects upon autonomy also help untangle the apparent contradictions between Nabokov's epistemological claims. His frequent assertions that reality is intrinsically subjective ("reality is a very subjective affair" [*SO* 10]) are hard to square with his equally forceful insistence upon historical truth and factual precision. The logic that drives this perceived contradiction also moves Nabokov to smile if told that he is a bad poet and reach for his heaviest dictionary if told that he is a poor scholar. His scholarly commitment to an uncompromising objectivism is heard again in the harsh reprimand he directed at the editor of the *Sunday Times* of London for distorting the historical record: "I wish to submit that at a time when in so many eastern countries history has become a joke, this precise beam of light upon a precious detail may be of some help to the next investigator" (*SO* 215). The statement's reference to Soviet propaganda makes it a characteristic example of Nabokov's frequent pleas for historical accuracy. Propaganda, censorship, and all other forms of political dishonesty seek to manipulate, or, to use the language of Kant, to turn autonomous individuals into things. Unlike the enchanting deceptions of art, which seek to expand human consciousness by making it aware of its uniqueness and freedom, political deception drives the human spirit into the ground.

Nabokov's understanding of deception helps us come to terms with the triangulation of his ethics, aesthetics, and politics. His extension of the concept of rights to intellectual property—implicit in his philosophy of translation—is consistent with his liberalism, and his epistemology, like that of Vladimir Vernadskii, is inflected by his liberal commitment to freedom. In *Ada,* he leads us to the source of these links, revealing the core principle that gives rise to the views—on art, translation, science, ethics, politics, jurisprudence, epistemology, and metaphysics—that shape his intellectual universe. That core principle is embedded in Van's poignant assessment of his deception of Lucette on the night of her suicide. As a gentleman, Van knows that human relations should be grounded in the kind of courtesy that Lucette shows the Robinsons at the expense of her own self-interest. As an artist, he knows that Lucette must not be instrumentalized but must be treated with the same kind of scrupulous honesty as a translation. The "gentleman" and the "artist" converge in this instance because they share the same moral insight: one's relations with others must always be guided by respect. Van's "trite and cruel" words to Lucette contrast sharply with her conduct toward the Robinsons, as if in confirmation of Nabokov's and Aikhenvald's pronouncements that goodness and kindness never deceive and therefore can never be tainted by *poshlost'*.

CONSEQUENTIALISM VS. DEONTOLOGY

Although Van feels confident that his deception does not cause Lucette's death, he nonetheless feels culpable, which may be the reason why he claims to have done precisely what his lie prevented him from doing. Only moments before Lucette's telephone call, Van contemplates a much more appropriate way of dealing with the situation:

> He welcomed the thought which suddenly seemed so absolutely true, and new, and as lividly real as the slowly widening gap of the sitting room's doorway, namely, that on the morrow (which was at least, and at best, seventy years away) he would explain to Lucette, as a philosopher and another girl's brother, that he knew how agonizing and how absurd it was to put all one's spiritual fortune on one physical fancy and that his plight closely resembled hers, but that he managed, after all, to live, to work, and not pine away because he refused to wreck her life with a brief affair. (*A* 393)

Though this appeal to Lucette's reason is never made, Van lays claim to it in his explanatory letter to Ada and Andrey. This letter—tellingly—fails to mention Lucette's telephone call and Van's shameful recourse to deception: "The romantic attachment she had formed, the infatuation she cultivated, could not be severed by logic" (*A* 397), he writes them.

In spite of his claim that Lucette would have killed herself even without the intervention of his lie, Van feels guilty about the role his lie plays in her tragedy. The afternoon before their fateful midnight telephone conversation, Lucette accuses Van of being involved with a woman on board. Van is not, but his promise not to deceive her on this count is met by Lucette with skepticism: "You deceived me many, many times when I was a little girl. If you're doing it now *tu sais que j'en vais mourir.*" To Van's reminder that only recently she had promised him a harem, Lucette replies: "Not today, not today! Today is sacred" (*A* 386). Van's claim that he is "not alone" naturally convinces Lucette that he had already deceived her earlier that day, and the structure Van lends to the day's events in his narrative demonstrates that he knows this. The sequence of events must also cause Van considerable pain given that his deception cannot be abstracted from the fulfillment of Lucette's threat (even as this threat is expressed in terms that we usually understand as figurative): she kills herself after Van has lied to her on the day she had begged him to set aside as sacred.

Van's lie and Lucette's threat that she would die if he deceived her seem to insist on an uncanny connection between his deception and her suicide. Van's anxiety about his role in the tragedy is a reminder that the most painful consequences can attend even the most convenient and innocuous lies. His account of the events leading up to Lucette's death unfolds in a way that seems to endorse Kant's twin claims about the moral duty of truth-telling. First, Kant argues that one must under no circumstances or for any purpose tell a lie because lying undermines truthfulness and the contract of reciprocity upon which human relations depend.[49] Van cannot ignore the tragic irony at the heart of his deception: the fictitious betrayal in which he implicates himself during the telephone call casts doubt upon all his other statements to Lucette, including his promise that he would not conceal from her his involvement with other lovers on board. (In setting up these intricately crafted scenarios, Nabokov may have recalled his father's assertion in *The Provisional Government* that "once duplicity appears it is never forgotten" [*PG* 101].) Van's invented betrayal hopelessly negates any possibility of truthfulness between him and Lucette.

Kant's second claim about the duty of truthfulness contends that a liar is responsible for all the consequences that ensue as a result of his deception, even if those consequences were completely unforeseeable.[50] Van's admission that it is impossible to know how Ophelia's life would have unfolded "without the help of a treacherous sliver" acknowledges that his own treachery is ineliminably implicated in the tragedy (*A* 398). His concurrent claim that "whatever the miserable man could have thought up, she would have *pokonchila s soboi* ('put an end to herself') all the same" presumes that decisions, once made, are unalterable and beyond the reach of reconsideration. It makes Lucette "thing-like" by denying her the capacity to change her mind when confronted by new arguments and new circumstances. Van must know that his lie is precisely the kind of deception that would lead her to despair, and that the things he does not say to her (but contemplates saying and claims to have said in his letter to Ada and Andrey) might have had a different effect.

Van's contention that his deception of Lucette was "morally right" because it sought to protect her from his lust deploys the logic of consequentialism, the moral theory whose paradigmatic example is utilitarianism. His profound uneasiness about the extent to which he might be judged responsible for her suicide throws into question consequentialism's reliability as a foundation for ethics. Based on the pursuit of the good, consequentialism rejects the view that actions can be right or wrong in themselves because the rightness or wrongness of an act is always judged by its outcome. By contrast, the deontological tradition associated with Kant privileges the right over the good, and argues that agents must refrain from doing things that are wrong in and of themselves even if they foresee that such actions will have good outcomes. This distinction is best illustrated by a consideration of the ethical value of deception. According to the consequentialist model, deception is acceptable if it leads to a greater good; according to Kant's deontological model, deception is always wrong and should be avoided even if it might lead to a greater good. The circumstances of Lucette's suicide highlight the problems that bedevil ethical theories that privilege potential good over the right. Van's deception, perpetrated in the name of preventing an undesirable consequence, is wrong precisely because he betrays his half-sister in the name of an outcome he can neither predict nor bring about. For Van the philosopher, Lucette's suicide serves as a reminder that to put one's trust in consequentialism is to have the arrogance of thinking that one can foretell the future.

The intellectual descendants of the contributors to *Problems of Idealism* were united in condemning Marxism for its uncritical worship of progress and enslavement of the present to the future. In her assessment of the moral failures that characterized life in Soviet Russia, Nadezhda Mandelstam blames one idea above all others for guiding her country down the path of disaster. "The idea in question," she writes, "was that there is an irrefutable scientific truth by means of which, once they are possessed of it, people can foresee the future, change the course of history at will and make it rational. This religion—or science, as it was modestly called by its adepts—invests man with a god-like authority and has its own creed and ethic." This "creed and ethic," she concludes, was grounded in the seductive consequentialist axiom "that the end justifies the means."[51]

Nabokov was similarly attuned to the connection Nadezhda Mandelstam draws between consequentialism and the moral evils of the Soviet regime. In a letter to Wilson, Nabokov denies the consequentialist's guiding premise (adopted by Chernyshevski, Plekhanov, and the Bolsheviks, and rejected by Russia's neo-idealist philosophers) that the outcomes of actions can be determined in advance. Interestingly, he notes further that this unpredictability turns on nature's deceptiveness: "Such is the artistic deceptiveness of nature's methods that the thing that eventually brings the most evil or the most benefit to most people is an unpredictable casual freak of a thing which could never have been suspected of developing into a general boon or blight. How glum Engels would have looked were he shown some modern factories" (*DBDV* 37).[52] The implications of Nabokov's remark to Wilson are spelled out by Novgorodtsev in his contribution to *Problems of Idealism* when he states that "the task [of moral philosophy] consists in establishing an absolute precept for moral aspirations. Immediate practical success has no bearing on the force of this precept: *fais ce que dois, advienne que pourra* [do what you must, come what may]" (EIPL 292). Without the ability to predict the consequences of one's actions, one must act according to unconditional, universally binding moral principles.

Before Lucette's fatal telephone call, Van tells himself that "on the morrow" he will help her deal with her hopeless infatuation in a rational manner. But his faith in "tomorrow" is cruelly betrayed and Van never has another opportunity to speak with Lucette. It is possible to think of Van's philosophical treatise on time as a response to this betrayal. *The Texture of Time* denies the existence of the future (Van calls it "Sham Time" [*A* 439]), and in doing so retroactively casts doubt on Van's consequentialist defense of his deception. As he writes after his disappointing reunion with Ada at Mont Roux,

> Time is anything but the popular triptych: a no-longer existing Past, the durationless point of the Present, and a "not-yet" that may never come. No. There are only two panels. The Past (ever-existing in my mind) and the Present (to which my mind gives duration and, therefore, reality). If we make a third compartment of fulfilled expectation, the foreseen, the foreordained, the faculty of prevision, perfect forecast, we are still applying our mind to the Present. . . . The future is but a quack at the court of Chronos. (*A* 448)

Nabokov must have been acutely aware of the connection between consequentialism and Marxism because he has Van direct his refutation of the future at those "social thinkers" who "feel the Present as pointing beyond itself toward a not yet realized 'future.'" Van dismisses such thinking as nothing more than "topical utopia, progressive politics" (*A* 448–49). His denial that the future exists is a reminder that without the guarantee of tomorrow, the moral agent must seek to do what is right rather than pursue a probable future good.

But if consequentialism fails to vindicate Van and Ada, it also fails to convict them. To read Lucette's suicide as a consequence of Van and Ada's actions is to deny Lucette the autonomy and integrity due to her as a rational being. A guilty verdict for Van and Ada secured on the basis of a consequentialist ethics replicates their crime against Lucette. A more reliable ethical standard must refuse to sacrifice Lucette's dignity to the ethics that would defend her. A standard of this kind must focus, as Kant's does, on what is right rather than what is good. This distinction also provides a means of coming to terms with the paradoxes engendered by the novel's preoccupation with ethics.

The twin pressures facing the reader of *Ada* emerge from a set of apparently contradictory moral demands. The first of these dictates that readers should not seek to secure a guilty verdict for Van and Ada at the expense of Lucette's autonomy. (As Korsgaard aptly observes, Kantians consider it "inconsistent with respect for others to regard their actions as simply a *consequence* of what *you* do.")[53] The second imperative dictates that Lucette's autonomy should not give others the license to mistreat her or to consider themselves independent of the terms in which she makes decisions. To blame Van and Ada for Lucette's suicide is to suggest that we can track a sequence of actions that led to her death. But the gap between action and consequence (for example, the gap between the cruel schemes devised by young Van and Ada to escape from Lucette's irritating intrusiveness and Lucette's suicide) makes this project impossible. This methodology fails not because Van and Ada are innocent, but because the novel suggests that consequentialism is an inadequate guide for moral action.

Narrative itself abets Van and Ada's effort to acquit themselves of any wrongdoing in relation to their half-sister. By its very nature, narrative affords a delimited view of history and singles out for attention those events that offer a causally determined version of the past. "Destiny is quite often another name for narrative, the order we retrospectively find in scattered events," notes Michael Wood.[54] If Van expects his readers to acquit him and Ada by seeing their love affair as ineluctably determined by external pressures, Nabokov counts on these same readers to see beyond Van's family chronicle by resisting the overdetermined quality of his narrative.[55] Only by refusing to accept Van's seductive narrative determinism can readers begin to perceive that unconditional moral standards apply even on Van's "pellet of muck" (*A* 398). In the non-deterministic world crafted by Nabokov, Van and Ada can be said neither to have caused Lucette's suicide, nor to have been exempted from the moral laws that ought to govern human relations. Those laws make them complicit in, but not the cause of, Lucette's fate.

KANT AND THE ETHICS OF SEX

The novel's ethical model prohibits all actions that diminish another human being's autonomy by making use of her without her free consent. This principle makes it possible to measure, without lapsing into the problems that attend consequentialism, the extent to which Van and Ada are guilty of mistreating Lucette. Van and Ada are guilty of failing to treat Lucette with respect. In relation to her suicide, they are only guilty to the extent that Van's deception makes him responsible for the consequences that arise from it. This ethical standard is complicated, however, by the fact that Lucette frequently consents to, and sometimes even invites, such debasement.[56] Interestingly, it is almost exclusively in those moments that Van is able to act morally. For example, when Lucette implores Van to deflower her, he refuses to indulge her. This scenario recalls one of the most troubling features of *Lolita.* If Dolly's initiation of sex with Humbert is not to absolve him of his brutish crimes against her, it is necessary to explain why Dolly's proposition cannot count as consent. A Kantian framework is especially pertinent here because both *Ada*'s and *Lolita*'s moral rigorism seems to collide with the permissiveness of libertarianism.

The ethical complication that arises from Dolly's and Lucette's sexual desire suggests that Kant's Formula of Humanity is in need of qualification in specific contexts. Kant was aware of this problem, and he regarded sexuality as the one sphere of human activity that mandates a more detailed examination of the moral law. Sexual love, he argues in *Lectures on Ethics,*

> is a degradation of human nature; for as soon as a person becomes an Object of appetite for another, all motives of moral relationship cease to function, because as an Object of appetite for another a person becomes a thing and can be treated and used as such by every one. This is the only case in which a human being is designed by nature as the Object of another's enjoyment.[57]

Kant argues that this sexual debasement can be overcome only in the context of monogamous matrimony. Kant's argument turns on two key ideas, each of which helps untangle the ethical problems that plague both *Lolita* and *Ada*.

The first of these has to do with the proposition that sex cannot be regarded as a service to be bought or sold: "Man cannot dispose over himself because he is not a thing; he is not his own property; to say that he is would be self-contradictory; for in so far as he is a person he is a Subject in whom the ownership of things can be vested, and if he were his own property, he would be a thing over which he could have ownership" (*LE* 165). The second proposition states that only equality between partners can prevent the degradation of the weaker partner's dignity. It is on these grounds that Kant declares concubinage and polygamy morally unacceptable (*LE* 166–68). Only in monogamous matrimony can the dignity of both partners be said to embody Kant's ideal of mutual surrender and repossession:

> If, then, one yields one's person, body and soul, for good and ill and in every respect, so that the other has complete rights over it, and if the other does not similarly yield himself in return and does not extend in return the same rights and privileges, the arrangement is one-sided. But if I yield myself completely to another and obtain the person of the other in return, I win myself back; I have given myself up as the property of another, but in turn I take that other as my property, and so win myself back again in winning the person whose property I have become. (*LE* 167)

According to these propositions, neither Dolly's nor Lucette's sexual desire can provide a moral justification for sexual relations with men who cannot offer them a relationship of perfect mutuality. Statutory rape and pedophilia both diagnose the vast inequality between Humbert and Dolly, an inequality that leads to the most destructive kind of sexual degradation for the young girl.

Kant's moral philosophy offers an especially compelling interpretive tool for reading *Ada*'s preoccupation with the ethics of sex. By making equality the determining factor in the moral judgment of sexual relations, Kant both circumscribes and expands the parameters of what counts as a legitimate sexual encounter. As Korsgaard notes, the most startling consequence of Kant's writings on sex emerges in his statements about incest.[58]

Though Kant argues that incest is dangerous from a reproductive point of view and should therefore be avoided, he also points out that from a purely moral perspective, "the sole case in which the moral grounds against incest apply absolutely is that of intercourse between parents and children." Once again, this restriction rests on inequality: "in sexual intercourse each person submits to the other in the highest degree, whereas between parents and their children subjection is one-sided; the children must submit to the parents only; there can, therefore, be no equal union" (*LE* 168).

Nabokov brackets off the reproductive objections to incest by making Van sterile.[59] Furthermore, by emphasizing the striking similarities between Van and Ada (their physical likeness, exceptional intellectual prowess, sexual voracity), Nabokov suggests that their relationship is almost preternaturally egalitarian. When Demon uncovers their incestuous affair, his insistence that they separate is nothing more, as Demon himself admits, than a feeble invocation of social norms and prohibitions: "You force me to bring up the tritest terms such as 'family,' 'honor,' 'set,' 'law.' . . . All right, I have bribed many officials in my wild life but neither you nor I can bribe a whole culture, a whole country" (*A* 355). Van's surrender to his father's reasoning also fails to provide a coherent argument against the intrinsic immorality of incest. As he writes in a hurried missive to Ada,

> Do what he tells you. His logic sounds preposterous, prepsupposing [*sic*] a vague kind of "Victorian" era, as they have on Terra according to "my mad" [?], but in a paroxysm of [illegible] I suddenly realized he was right. Yes, right, here and there, not neither here, nor there, as most things are. You see, girl, how it is and must be. (*A* 356–57; editorial additions in original)

Van cannot defend his relationship with Ada because his moral integrity has been compromised by his relationship with Lucette. Were he to invoke his right to engage in consensual, non-reproductive sexual relations with his sister, he would have to invoke principles such as human dignity and the right to self-determination, the very principles that he betrayed by his repeated failure to treat Lucette with honesty and respect.

The difficulty of finding unconditional reasons for banning non-reproductive incest among consenting adults contrasts sharply with the novel's critique of all sexual relationships that are not grounded in reciprocity. Demon's cruelty and brutality are obscured during his relationship with the equally ruthless Marina. Those tendencies become painfully evident, however, in his relationships with partners much weaker than himself, such as the helpless Aqua or the "Spanish girls who were getting more and more youthful every year until by the end of the century, when he was sixty, with hair dyed a midnight blue, his flame had become a difficult nymphet of ten" (*A* 313).

Incest, the red herring of the novel's ethical preoccupations, makes visible the novel's investment in a moral philosophy that is at once radically permissive and uncompromisingly rigoristic.[60] This ethical framework also reveals the extent to which Nabokov's three novels about unconventional sexuality—*Lolita, Pale Fire,* and *Ada*—are committed to exploring moral standards that are universally binding and therefore independent of socio-historical conditions. As chapter 2 has shown, Humbert attempts to justify his relationship with Dolly by appealing to the fact that some cultures have cultivated (and some still cultivate) a much more tolerant attitude toward sexual relations with minors (*L* 116, 140), but the novel's overarching concern with the young girl's pain exposes the opportunism of his appeals to moral relativism. By contrast, Charles Kinbote's homosexuality fails to elicit the sharp moral reprobation that accompanies his sexual interest in young boys and his consistent treatment of others as means to his own ends.[61] Nabokov's tendency of exploiting homosexuality for comic effect is regrettable, but he does not seem to have regarded homosexual activity as morally objectionable and certainly not legally punishable. Critics who charge Nabokov with homophobia tend to forget that not all of his gay characters are figures of fun. In *Pnin,* for instance, the homosexual Lake is young Victor's beloved and revered teacher of painting at St. Bart's. Nabokov endows Lake with the talent and dignity associated with his most trustworthy and likable artists (*P* 365–66).[62]

Ada's lack of interest in the ethical dimension of Van and Ada's incestuous relationship (at least relative to its preoccupation with their cruel treatment of Lucette) confirms Rorty's assertion that Nabokov is a political liberal, and that his fiction illustrates the truth of Judith Shklar's contention that cruelty is, in the eyes of the liberal subject, the worst moral failure.[63] The novel also invites readers to distinguish between universally binding moral transgressions and socially contingent prohibitions. The ethical model that emerges from this distinction establishes the novel's peculiar blend of radical libertarianism and strict moral rigorism; it also calls to mind Nabokov's self-description as an "old-fashioned liberal" and "rigid moralist" (*SO* 96, 193). Moreover, it supplies an ideological frame for the novel's suggestion that sexual relations based on equality and consent (like incest and homosexuality, for example, but unlike pedophilia) do not qualify as moral misconduct.

In drawing such fine distinctions Nabokov is following in the footsteps of his father, whose admission that he found homosexuality repugnant did not prevent him from belonging to a minority of Russian jurists who argued that homosexual acts between consenting adults ought to be decriminalized. In her informative account of the legal debates surrounding homosexuality in late-imperial Russia, Laura Engelstein turns to V. D. Nabokov's arguments in favor of repealing the anti-sodomy statutes in Russia's criminal code as exemplary of the efforts made by Russia's liberal jurists to reorient the law in a secular direction and insist on its greater formal recognition of individual rights and personal autonomy.[64] Unlike their conservative critics who refused to acknowledge a distinction between the public and private spheres by arguing that no behavior could avoid having social consequences, these liberal jurists opposed moralistic conceptions of criminal law and insisted on a strict separation between the private and public. Engelstein underscores the connection between legal and political discourse in these debates when she notes that these liberal jurists viewed morality-based legal standards as a vestige of the paternalistic tyranny they opposed in the political arena.[65]

Engelstein describes V. D. Nabokov as "a staunch partisan of privacy" who argued that neither moral standards nor medical norms could be imposed by legal means.[66] "In the eyes of the healthy and normal segment of the population," he writes in his evaluation of the proposed reforms of 1903 to the 1845 Code of Punishments,[67] "sodomy will always and everywhere appear as it really is: an act inspiring profound disgust, perhaps pathological, perhaps merely a vice" (Pp 168).[68] Even so, he insists that there are no justifiable legal reasons for punishing sodomy between consenting adults when it is performed in private.

The qualification is important because V. D. Nabokov seeks to decriminalize only *private* homosexual acts. When sodomy takes place in the public domain, he notes, it offends public morality, and should therefore be open to prosecution:

> Doubtlessly, as far as sodomy offends public morality, it is liable to be prosecuted and punished. The maintenance of brothels for uranists, male prostitution, finally—the performance of the act in the presence of witnesses—all this, understandably, is intolerable precisely in the name of public morality [*neterpimo imenno vo imia obshchestvennoi nravstvennosti*].

Private homosexual activities, however, do not impinge on public morality, and therefore should be regarded as beyond the reach of the law: "But when sodomy is, so to speak, *intra muros*, or secret, there is no need to talk about public morals" (Pp 162). This qualification, however, should not be taken to suggest that V. D. Nabokov drew a sharp distinction between homosexual and heterosexual activities that offended public morality. According to the logic of his arguments, *all* sexual activities conducted in the public's view should be illegal because they infringe upon the core value of liberalism: personal inviolability.

V. D. Nabokov's commitment to this overarching liberal principle explains his refusal to equate morality with the law. He explicitly stated, for example, that the unreformed Code of Punishments erred in confusing "the concepts of criminal and immoral, sinful and criminal [*smeshenie poniatii prestupnago i beznravstvennago, grekhovnago i prestupnago*]" (Pp 132). His unwillingness to subordinate the law to public morality is demonstrated in his objection against the argument that homosexuality should be criminalized because it is more distasteful or harmful than other forms of extramarital sexual relations:

> From the moral point of view, satisfaction of the sexual urge is permissible only within marriage, and even then, only by natural means. Thus *every* extramarital satisfaction and every unnatural one within marriage should be penalized. To claim that homosexuality is more repugnant than other perversions is, in the first place, a matter of subjective judgment. In the second place, such *distinguo* [*sic*] are hardly possible or permissible in this particular domain.[69]

V. D. Nabokov placed these arguments in the service of the decriminalization campaign of the German physician and homosexual rights activist Magnus Hirschfeld. Engelstein notes that V. D. Nabokov omitted what she calls his "decorous" moralistic disapproval of homosexual behavior in the article he contributed to Hirschfield's journal.[70] Though the disclaimer's deletion was most likely a consequence of V. D. Nabokov's scrupulously politic and polite nature, it also makes it possible to imagine that his moral disapproval of homosexuality was less well-defined than the Russian text suggests.

V. D. Nabokov's efforts to decriminalize voluntary adult homosexual intercourse are closely related to his endorsement of provisions for the protection of minors. These decrees, he states, are the reformers' greatest achievement (Pp 134, 189). But although he praises the proposed increases in age-of-consent statutes, he opposes the ways in which the reformers defined the actions covered by age-of-consent legislation. The criminalization of acts identified as "lascivious," he argues, generates significant errors at the level of legal taxonomy. As acts that excite or satisfy sexual lust, he elaborates, so-called "lascivious acts" divert attention away from what should be the guiding criterion for legal punishment: the violation of another's chastity or integrity. As he explains, "I think that both the expression 'lascivious acts [*liubostrastnyia deistviia*]' and the interpretation of this expression by the explanatory note are inexact and incorrect, and propose a different term, in closer conformity to the legal meaning of the given crime, namely 'a shameless act offending (or "violating") chastity [*bezstydnoe deistvie oskorbliaiushchee (ili "narushaiushchee") tselomudrie*].'" By identifying sexual crime with the excitation and satisfaction of lust, he notes further, the reformers open the door for the criminalization of a variety of harmless activities, such as those of the fetishist or the passionate kisser (Pp 140–42).

V. D. Nabokov's critique of the project's inconsistencies show him to be working within the parameters of a legal philosophy that prizes above all other values (as does Kant) human dignity and the individual's right to self-determination. This is especially evident in his remarks on the subject of incest. Setting up "the purity of family relations" as a legal good, he writes, leads the reformers into logical inconsistency, as when they are moved to criminalize incest but not adultery (Pp 133). Furthermore, the reformers' identification of this legal good with the protection of *social* rather than *personal* interests excludes (wrongly, he implies) incest from the list of offenses against the individual.[71] His prioritization of personal interests over collective ones can also be observed in his statement that "the task of protecting the purity of family relations is, of course, first and foremost, a family responsibility. The interference of the state in this matter is quite a delicate and difficult business." He qualifies his support of legislation that would decriminalize incest by noting that "to institute the absolute decriminalization of incest" in Russia's current legal system "would constitute too an abrupt and dangerous departure from tradition" (Pp 172). Taken together, these examples show that V. D. Nabokov's writings on sexual crime were driven by a key overriding principle: namely, that acts should be deemed criminal not when they infringe upon public morality but when they violate another's personal integrity. In Engelstein's elegantly succinct formulation, the critical question guiding V. D. Nabokov's legal reasoning was "how to protect victims against abuse, not participants against their own desires."[72]

Bringing V. D. Nabokov's jurisprudential writings to bear on Nabokov's representation of pedophilia, homosexuality, and incest in the three crowning achievements of his literary career might seem as stiff and chilling as applying the cold-blooded rigor of Kantian moral philosophy to Van and Ada's relationship with Lucette. The views that Van and Ada are guilty of failing to treat their half-sister as an end-in-herself, or that Kinbote's instrumentalization of John Shade replays in a minor key Humbert's exploitation of Dolly, are severe and formal ways of describing the moral delinquencies portrayed in these novels. It may be that what Humbert, Kinbote, Van, and Ada refuse to acknowledge in Dolly, Shade, and Lucette is their "*Humanität*," the humanity that Kant, on the verge of his death, still felt stirring within him as he greeted his physician, and the humanity that Lucette, in her misery and despair, is able to show the Robinsons as her world was collapsing around her.

V. D. NABOKOV AND CULTURE

In the torrent of tributes, telegrams, and obituaries that flooded the Russian émigré press in the immediate aftermath of V. D. Nabokov's murder, a number of words were repeatedly invoked to describe the departed. Close friends, political associates, and strangers referred to him as a "knight" (*rytsar'*) whose "pure" (*chistaia*), "luminous" (*svetlaia*), and "noble" (*blagorodnaia*) life was a measure of his uncompromising personal integrity. Oscar Gruzenberg, the brilliant lawyer who served as defense counsel in the prosecutions of the Vyborg signatories and Mendel Beiliss, referred admiringly to V. D. Nabokov's "rejection of the smallest compromise" (*otkaz ot maleishago kompromissa*) and "wise heart" (*umnoe serdtse*).[73] Taken together, Gruzenberg's words recall the rare blend of warm compassion and self-legislated moral rigorism that comprise Kant and Lucette's "*Humanität.*" Former friends and collaborators linger over the disinterested nature of V. D. Nabokov's political activism and note, further, that he willingly and without regret relinquished the many privileges of his birth in the struggle for freedom and justice. Makletsov underscores the anti-utilitarian orientation of his criminal jurisprudence; Vladimir Tatarinov describes him as a "gentleman from head to toe"; Pasmanik, in his Crimean memoirs, calls him "the knight of Russia's spiritual aristocracy, the bearer of the glory of Russian culture."[74]

Though these ovations paint a full-fledged Kantian sensibility, postmortem appraisals—predictably platitudinous and one-sided—are not always trustworthy. In the case of V. D. Nabokov, however, at least one writer tried to move beyond graveside effusions in order to confront the living man's complicated reputation. By referring to his many detractors, Tatarinov provides an entry into aspects of V. D. Nabokov's life that suggest a decidedly un-Kantian approach to ethics. He notes that V. D. Nabokov was bitterly criticized by those on the left and the right: while socialists thought of him as a secret monarchist and reactionary, conservatives considered him a weak link in the struggle against Bolshevism. A more disturbing contradiction arose in relation to V. D. Nabokov's position on anti-Semitism. While some attacked him for his alleged anti-Semitism, others claimed that "Nabokov sold himself to the Yids [*Nabokov prodalsia zhidam*]."[75]

These conflicting views are perhaps best understood in light of Browder's description of V. D. Nabokov as a man of "strong political convictions" who was nonetheless capable of demonstrating a "refreshing flexibility" during a time of rigid dogmatism and violent factionalism.[76] A similar portrait emerges from the pages of Rosenberg's detailed account of the events surrounding Russia's second revolutionary upheaval and Pasmanik's account of V. D. Nabokov's participation in the Crimean Regional Government. Significantly more vexed is the question of his alleged anti-Semitism. Notwithstanding his scathing attacks on the Kishinev pogroms and the prosecution of Mendel Beiliss, and the fact that many of his closest friends and collaborators were Jewish, some scattered comments in *The Provisional Government* give credence to Pearson's observation that V. D. Nabokov's "covert anti-Semitism" was an open secret among his acquaintances (NP 17–18). He remarks, for instance, that the steering committee of the Provisional Council of the Russian Republic "could frankly have been called the Sanhedrin" as "the predominant portion of its membership were Jews" (*PG* 151). Later, he refers to the Bolshevik leader Moses (Moisei) Uritskii as having an "impudent Jewish face" (*PG* 177). Browder was sufficiently troubled by such traces of anti-Semitism to cite an explanation by his son:

> My father felt so infinitely superior to any accusation of antisemitism (its official brand, or even the more disgusting household variety) that out of a kind of self-confidence and contempt for showcase philosemitism he used to make it a point—and go out of his way to make it—of being as plainspoken about Jew and Gentile as were his Jewish colleagues (such as Joseph Hessen and Grigory Landau) or the Christian but impeccably unprejudiced Miliukov.[77]

Those to whom this explanation seems strained can find support for their doubt in Vinaver's portrait of V. D. Nabokov. Though generally admiring, Vinaver's account paints V. D. Nabokov as an expert in the kind of instrumentalizing deceit so fundamentally at odds with Kantian ethics. Vinaver recalls with resentment the undeserved confidence V. D. Nabokov inspired in his colleagues on the left not only during his participation in the Crimean Regional Government but also during his work in the First State Duma and the Provisional Government. According to Vinaver, V. D. Nabokov's unfailing courtesy and good manners (*blagovospitannost'*) enabled him to become a master in political deception (*NpKv* 69–70).

Profoundly loyal to the Crimean liberal experiment and stung by V. D. Nabokov's retrospective disavowal of their joint enterprise, Vinaver is a biased chronicler. Nonetheless, he refers to a number of less familiar episodes in V. D. Nabokov's career that demonstrate a shrewd pragmatism and a willingness to compromise principle for the sake of utility. For Vinaver, V. D. Nabokov's repudiation of his work in the Crimea was a direct consequence of a notable character flaw: he observes that his colleague frequently fell prey to an "easy skepticism" (*legkii skeptitsizm*) when faced with defeat. Vinaver provides several examples of such changes of heart in his former colleague, the most memorable of which was V. D. Nabokov's response to the Vyborg appeal. According to Vinaver, V. D. Nabokov fully supported the manifesto when he signed it. A year later, however, when the Vyborg signatories prepared for trial, V. D. Nabokov wanted to publicly repudiate the appeal, and it was only with great difficulty that Vinaver and others dissuaded him from such a course of action. Vinaver further recalls that V. D. Nabokov delivered a brilliant speech in the appeal's defense at the trial (*NpKv* 72).

Documentary evidence confirms, in part, Vinaver's version of these events. Zimmerman supports V. D. Nabokov's claim in *The Provisional Government* that he disagreed with the appeal from the very beginning but signed it because he could not think of an acceptable alternative (BRR 294, note 58; *PG* 82). At the trial, however, V. D. Nabokov stated that "at Vyborg, I consciously and with full conviction participated in that action, the last action of the people's representatives."[78] Furthermore, he erected his defense upon arguments that he, an eminent jurist profoundly committed to legality, had opposed time and again both in principle and practice. It is as difficult, for instance, to believe him when he tells the judges that the appeal's "constitutionality" did not enter into his personal deliberations at Vyborg, as it is painful to hear him claim that "there are such moments in the life of private individuals and governments which dictate that *salus publica* be acknowledged as *suprema lex*." His highly individualist streak must have recoiled from his assertion that "there are moments when the highest duty lies in unification, when it is necessary to submit to joint action, when it is necessary to provide people with the example of acting according to one conviction."[79]

V. D. Nabokov's pragmatism becomes visible at other points in his political career. His position on Russia's war aims during the First World War was guided by strictly utilitarian considerations. In *The Provisional Government,* he records his disagreement with Miliukov over the war and his willingness to consider concluding a separate peace with Germany in order to prevent the country from slipping into complete anarchy (*PG* 87, 110–12). During his sojourn in the Crimea, a similar utilitarianism led him to argue in favor of accommodation with Russia's formal enemies after these ousted the Bolsheviks from the peninsula (*Rg* 96). According to Browder, this attempt to form an alliance with the German occupiers against the Bolsheviks had a damaging effect on V. D. Nabokov's reputation.[80]

In arguing for accommodation with the Germans, V. D. Nabokov mobilized his legendary calm, courtesy, and conviction against his Kadet opponents, which included the revered patriarch of Russia's liberal movement, Ivan Petrunkevich (*Rg* 96). Nabokov's reference to these events suggests that he was sensitive to the predicament faced by his father in the Crimea: "Patriotic Russians were torn between the animal relief of escaping native executioners and the necessity of owing their reprieve to a foreign invader—especially to the Germans" (*SM* 570). And though Nabokov seems to have recognized the destructive effects of "fanatical integrity" and the "tragic inability to sink to compromise," he paints a different picture of his father, as if refusing to admit that the sheer force of political circumstances could bend a beloved father's moral compass (*DBDV* 222). In his memoirs, letters, and interviews, Nabokov makes no mention of this episode in his father's career. Instead, he proudly observes that "unswervingly he conformed to his principles in private and public matters" (*SM* 509). No doubt Nabokov would have found it difficult to reconcile the man who, during Russia's war with Japan, whisked away his family from a waterside café in Abbazia after noticing two Japanese officers sitting nearby, with the man who, during Russia's civil war, was willing to negotiate with the Germans in a desperate attempt to rout the Bolsheviks (*SM* 375).

It is possible that Nabokov does not mention the controversial aspects of his father's biography because he wished to remember his father as a man who exemplified the Kantian moral ideals endorsed in *Ada*. But it is just as likely that Nabokov did not see his father's reversals of view as betrayals of Kantian moral principles. The "easy skepticism" criticized by Vinaver can be recast as a commitment to what Kant proudly identified as the defining legacy of the Enlightenment: "the calling of each individual to think for himself."[81] The submission of one's views and actions to constant revaluation and the capacity to think and act independently are manifestations of the same higher-order consciousness mobilized by Nabokov and his father to exempt humanity from the determinism of nature.

The human being's capacity to stand above the instincts of the herd lies at the heart of V. D. Nabokov's all-embracing commitment to culture. As Boyd has recently argued, Nabokov's high artistic standards derived from a broad understanding of cultural progress inherited from his father: "From his father Nabokov imbibed a strong sense of cultural meliorism, a sense that culture had evolved to make humans more humane, and that it could continue to evolve much further, and that art had played and could continue to play a key role."[82] Boyd places great stock in Pasmanik's description of V. D. Nabokov as a "finely cultured human being," a "true spiritual aristocrat" who recoiled from "the smallest display of plebeianism and lack of culture." According to Pasmanik, V. D. Nabokov joined the Kadet Party for cultural rather than political reasons, and it was his fundamental commitment to culture that fueled his aversion toward the anti-Semitism of his own family and the tsarist regime (*Rg* 93; see also *VNRY* 155–56).

Pasmanik's portrait of V. D. Nabokov helps explain why Nabokov may have viewed his father's changes of course as proof rather than challenge of his commitment to Kantian values. Pasmanik notes that V. D. Nabokov was a fierce individualist who refused to be enslaved by party dogma (*Rg* 94). And unlike Vinaver and Petrunkevich, both of whom Pasmanik describes as ineffectual idealists, V. D. Nabokov could be trusted to wed moral principle to practical necessity (*Rg* 93, 113–14). These unique qualities led Pasmanik to seek his counsel when trying to determine what position he should assume toward the Germans in the Crimean-Kadet newspaper *Tavricheskii golos* (*The Tauride Voice*). According to Pasmanik, V. D. Nabokov supported joining forces with the Germans against the Bolsheviks for reasons of culture:

> Insofar as we have become cultured Europeans, it is thanks to the Germans. Our science, our technology, our philosophy are the fruits of German cultural influence. Even economically we are tied to Germany rather than to England or France. As far as Bolshevism is concerned, the Germans have exploited it, . . . but they did not create it. We, the Russian people, our tsars, our bureaucrats and our gentry, our intelligentsia and our unbalanced "third element," our lazy clergy—we have all created Bolshevism. We must make peace with the Germans, if that is still possible. (qtd. in *Rg* 94)

V. D. Nabokov was not alone in representing Bolshevism as the enemy of culture. Describing the litany of horrors unleashed by Lenin's armies, anti-Bolsheviks consistently identified the civil war as a struggle between culture and its antithesis: barbarism (*varvarstvo*), brutality (*zverstvo*), savagery (*dikost'*), cruelty (*zhestokost'*).[83] In supporting collaboration with Russia's formal enemies, V. D. Nabokov was aligning himself with the thousands of Crimeans who greeted the German occupiers as long-awaited liberators that brought peace and order to a land devastated by the Bolsheviks' inhuman ruthlessness.[84]

These historical details cast a different light on those episodes in V. D. Nabokov's life that could be seen as sidetracking him from the path of Kantian rectitude. Whatever dubious pragmatic bargains he may have struck in a lifetime characterized by political catastrophe and defeat were guided by values clustered around the concept of culture. In *Ada* Nabokov celebrates these values—compassion, courtesy, honesty, integrity—as proofs of humanity's capacity to transcend its bestial nature and conduct itself according to principles that spring from "more deeply moral worlds than this pellet of muck."

Vladimir Tatarinov's candid appraisal of V. D. Nabokov's life showcases these values when he notes that the various charges leveled against V. D. Nabokov did not prevent him from inspiring the greatest confidence in friends and foes alike. Tatarinov's description of the "motley group of callers" who came daily "*k Nabokovu* [to Nabokov]" is as moving as it is vivid. These included students, Orthodox Christians, Jews, officers, actors, socialists, and anyone, in general, who sought "help, protection and comforting." Opposing factions solicited his help "not in the role of ordinary participant or representative of a particular side, but in the role of chairman, arbitrator." To the question "Why did everyone trust him?" Tatarinov supplies an answer that merits quotation in full:

> In addition to recognizing his great intellect, vast knowledge, intrinsic culture and tactfulness, no one ever doubted his honesty, selflessness, and impartiality. V. D. always placed his personal interests in last place, and he even

> sacrificed his personal preferences and antipathies for the sake of serving the collective and full interests of that Great Lady—Russia—whom he served so faithfully. Though connected with diverse circles by birth, education, career, and finally by his political convictions, V. D. always and everywhere preserved his spiritual independence and remarkable impartiality that can only be found in the greatest of English judges. . . . People perceived and understood that private and group interests were always alien to him and from here rose the confidence that surrounded him.[85]

Tatarinov's description is borne out by many others. In the commemorative tribute published on the front page of *Rul'* two days after V. D. Nabokov's murder, Joseph Hessen refers to his friend's "deep thoughtfulness, combined with an intellectual honesty and sincerity." He further notes: "He was as reliable as solid rock, and inspired the trust of political friends and enemies alike." In *Gody izgnaniia,* written many years after his friend's death, Hessen recalls how strenuously Avgust Kaminka lobbied to include V. D. Nabokov on the editorial board of *Rul'* not only because he was a faithful and caring friend, but also because he put great stock in V. D. Nabokov's unblemished "moral authority." Gruzenberg echoes these assessments when he notes that though V. D. Nabokov bore the scars of many wounds, not a single stain left its trace on his spirit. In an interview from 1973 Nabokov was laying claim to this legacy when he identified "the term 'responsibility' . . . with moral tradition, with principles of decency and personal honor deliberately passed from father to son."[86]

To read Nabokov's novels as exercises in aesthetic frivolity is to suggest that Nabokov was blind to the rich and complex legacy his father bequeathed him in his capacity as one of Russia's most beloved and revered political figures. It is also to confuse Nabokov with *Ada*'s David van Veen, the eccentric Dutch architect who brings to life a project conceived by his dead grandson. David van Veen resolves to erect a thousand and one "floramors" (glamorous brothels for the enormously wealthy) "all over the world—perhaps even in brutal Tartary, which he thought was ruled by 'Americanized Jews,' but then 'Art redeemed Politics'—profoundly original concepts that we must condone in a lovable old crank" (*A* 278). As is so frequently the case, Van is willing to overlook what his creator cannot. Art, for Nabokov, cannot redeem politics, and his art, in particular, can neither ignore nor condone the views of "a lovable old crank" when they brush up against the harsh political realities of dictatorships such as Tartary, Antiterra's version of the Soviet Union.

Because of its kinship with deception, art often entices us to look past or around such tragedies, distracting us when our attention should be most firm and resolute:

> None could help admiring David van Veen's knack of making his brand-new Regency mansion look like a renovated farmhouse or of producing a converted convent on a small offshore island with such miraculous effect that one could not distinguish the arabesque from the arbutus, ardor from art, the sore from the rose. (*A* 279)

These kinds of seductive deceptions moved Plato to banish poets from his republic. His prohibition should remind us that art is never above suspicion. But if art can disguise vice or suffering as beauty—"the sore" as "the rose"—it does not follow that art cannot be a significant repository of value. Like the subtleties of natural mimicry, art's penchant for dissimulation can serve as a reminder of humanity's unique potential to rise above the vicissitudes of nature. Within Nabokov's special cosmology, a capacity to experience aesthetic pleasure and an attunement to disinterested moral imperatives are twin consequences of human freedom. This freedom, however, is always vulnerable and must be stubbornly guarded against the depredations of those who would violate it (in Nabokov's pantheon of villains, that includes political tyrants, sexual predators, calculating opportunists, and insolent translators). Nabokov knew that Plato was not wrong to insist that art was a form of deception. But he also knew that Hesiod's Muses are not wrong, either, when they come clean at the beginning of the *Theogony:* "We know how to say many false things similar to genuine ones, but we know, when we wish, how to proclaim true things."

Chapter Four

Nabokov's Berkeley: Fantasy, History, and "the Splendor of Lone Thought"

> I admit that the night has been ciphered right
> well
> but in place of the stars I put letters,
> and I've read in myself how the self to
> transcend—
> and I must not be overexplicit.
> —Vladimir Nabokov

> All things belong to the same order of things, for such is the oneness of human perception, the oneness of individuality, the oneness of matter, whatever matter may be. The only real number is one, the rest are mere repetition.
> —Vladimir Nabokov

> Lenin jumped when he heard the words *esse est percipi*. They threw him into a fit of anger.
> —Nikolai Volskii

WHEN ASKED IN A 1969 interview for *Vogue* whether his "aesthetic distance" from the world's events was natural or cultivated, Nabokov offered the following corrective:

> My aloofness is an illusion resulting from my never having belonged to any literary, political, or social coterie. I am a lone lamb. Let me submit, however, that I have bridged the "aesthetic distance" in my own way by means of such absolutely final indictments of Russian and German totalitarianism as my novels *Invitation to a Beheading* and *Bend Sinister*. (*SO* 156)

Nabokov's frequent expressions of indifference toward "social purpose" and "moral message" have fueled numerous misleading assessments of his work.

He is at least partly to blame for this state of affairs. Even here, Nabokov's assertion that he is "a lone lamb" seems calculated to attract more attention than does the ensuing assertion that two of his novels are frankly political. The statement also deflects from a larger truth: *Invitation to a Beheading* and *Bend Sinister* are not isolated testaments to his earnest and sustained engagement with the sociopolitical realities of his world.

A sub-canon of politically inflected work also includes short stories such as "The Leonardo" ("Koroliok," 1933), "Tyrants Destroyed" ("Istreblenie Tiranov," 1938), and "Cloud, Castle, Lake" ("Oblako, ozero, bashnia," 1937), each of which examines the philosophical foundations of totalitarianism. More significantly, the distance separating *Invitation to a Beheading* and *Bend Sinister* from the seemingly apolitical fantasies of *Glory, Pale Fire,* and *Ada* is surprisingly short. All five of these novels work within the parameters of the same political and ideological preoccupations. They also share an interest in testing the metaphysical grounds of Nabokov's own views about the relationship between art and life, mind and matter, history and politics. These novels enable Nabokov to explore his deepest and most cherished intellectual convictions without having to don what he regarded as the coarse and threadbare mantle of engaged literature. To modify Michael Wood's elegant formulation, fantasy makes Nabokov's fiction "consistently philosophical" by enabling him to be "serious and playful, serious because playful" (*MD* 6).

Zoorland, the northern country invented by *Glory*'s protagonist Martin Edelweiss, is initially devised as an expedient of courtship. Like a latter-day Othello, Martin hopes to seduce Sonia Zilanov with tales of exotic adventure. But what begins as a pure act of the imagination, a romantic divertissement, gradually succumbs to historical reality; Zoorland becomes an allegory of Soviet tyranny comparable to those Nabokov will depict in more explicit terms in *Invitation to a Beheading* and *Bend Sinister:*

> The region was rocky and windy, and the wind was recognized as a positive force since by championing equality in not tolerating towers and tall trees, it only subserved the public aspirations of atmospheric strata that kept diligent watch over the uniformity of the temperature. And, naturally, pure arts, pure science were outlawed, lest the honest dunces be hurt to see the scholar's brooding brow and offensively thick books.[1]

Zoorland and the Soviet Union become synonymous in Martin's mind when he decides to cross illegally into Russia for a mere twenty-four hours. Martin's best friend, an Englishman named Darwin, can only deride this preposterous venture, and the novel risks letting its readers slide into sympathy with Darwin's view (*Gl* 199–200). Nabokov, writing about himself in the third person in his foreword to the novel, was later moved to ensure that the ideological significance of Martin's deed would not be lost upon the non-Russian reader:

> "Fulfillment" would have been, perhaps, an even better title for the novel: Nabokov cannot be unaware that the obvious translation of *podvig* is "exploit," and, indeed, it is under that title that his *Podvig* is listed by bibliographers; but if you once perceive in "exploit" the verb "utilize," gone is the *podvig*, the inutile deed of renown. The author chose therefore the oblique "glory." . . . It is the glory of high adventure and disinterested achievement; the glory of this earth and its patchy paradise; the glory of personal pluck; the glory of a radiant martyr. (*Gl* xii–xiii)

As always, Nabokov assigns value to actions and principles that challenge key tenets of Marxist-Leninist ideology. And though Martin "is not necessarily interested in politics" (this is "the first" of the "two mastertricks" to which Nabokov confesses in the same foreword), Sonia's father, a man "intensely active in liberal politics," understands Martin's achievement in precisely the terms set out by Nabokov: "I simply refuse to believe," he tells the baffled Darwin, "that a young man, pretty much removed from Russian political problems and more of a foreign cut I'd say, could prove capable of—well, of a high deed, if you like" (*Gl* xii, 77, 204).[2]

Zilanov is right to view Martin's romantic adventure as an act laden with political significance.[3] Though Zilanov's political "congresses" and "brochures" (*Gl* 77) fail to interest Martin, his "high deed" is nonetheless a subversive political act. Significantly, the impetus for Martin's decision to cross illegally into Russia begins to take form during a conversation with a friend of the Zilanovs. The friend, Mrs. Gruzinov, explains to Martin that Irina, the Zilanovs' niece, suffers from a debilitating "mental deficiency." Having "never paid much attention" to Irina, Martin experiences "a strange shock" when Mrs. Gruzinov refers to Irina as "a permanent living symbol" of recent Russian history.

As a victim of the civil war's violence and brutality, Irina is a haunting reminder of the extent to which all Russian émigrés have been marked by the Russian Revolution.[4] Irina's story hardens Martin's resolve to see his homeland again and enables him to understand his desires in political terms: "The night of Zoorland seemed to him even darker, its wildwood deeper, and Martin already knew that nothing and nobody could prevent him from penetrating, as a free pilgrim, into those woods, where plump children are tortured in the dark, and a smell of burning and of putrefaction permeates the air" (*Gl* 150).

Nabokov speaks approvingly of Martin's "high adventure and disinterested achievement," of his "personal pluck" and "radiant martyr[dom]" (*Gl* xiii). And yet, the fact that Irina is driven into mental illness by Russia's new darkness hints at Nabokov's own darkening vision. Martin, spiritedly disappearing into the wilds of Zoorland never to be heard from again, and Irina, nursing her demons under the protection of a loving family, reappear thirty years later in *Pale Fire* in the form of "Dr. Charles Kinbote," a persona adopted by a man who claims to be the last king of Zembla, a distant northern kingdom fallen into the grip of political tyranny. Driven into exile by a Soviet-sponsored revolution, Zembla's Charles Xavier II seeks refuge in the sleepy college town of New Wye, Appalachia, where he disguises himself as an eccentric professor of literature at Wordsmith University. Zembla's misty castles and azure bays, strange customs and political intrigues are the products of an astonishingly robust imagination, but unwelcome drafts from the real world continually subvert Kinbote's grand delusion.

Pale Fire lacks an instrument of narrative information such as Mrs. Gruzinov, and the source of Kinbote's mental illness is never explicitly identified. However, various clues suggest that both Kinbote and Charles II are alter egos of Vseslav Botkin, an "American scholar of Russian descent," whose "persecution mania" and "hallucinations" are sublimations of Russian history (*PF* 659, 505).[5] As in Irina's case, Botkin's psychic trauma springs from dangers faced in a homeland ravaged by war and revolution. His new life in New Wye fails to provide the sanctuary he seeks: "And when physical exhaustion and the sepulchral cold drove me at last upstairs to my solitary double bed, I would lie awake and breathless—as if only now living consciously through those perilous nights in my country, where at any moment, a company of jittery revolutionists might enter and hustle me off to a moonlit wall" (*PF* 504).[6] Isolated and misunderstood in a country as indifferent to Russian history as it is to Kinbote's ravings about Zembla, Botkin must reinvent himself to live.

Nostalgia, Nabokov writes in his 1970 introduction to the English translation of *Mary* (*Mashen'ka,* 1926), "remain[s] throughout one's life an insane companion."[7] As a fellow refugee, Kinbote seethes with nostalgia for a homeland that abides in the mind alone. "History permitting," Kinbote concludes, "I may sail back to my recovered kingdom, and with a great sob greet the gray coastline and the gleam of a roof in the rain" (*PF* 658). History remained deaf to Nabokov's longing to return to his own lost kingdom, and he was compelled to rely upon other, inalienable possessions—"literature, language, and my own Russian childhood" (*SO* 10)—when trying to appease his "insane companion" with another fictional homecoming.

These are the consolations of *Ada,* a novel conceived and completed above Lake Geneva on the highest floor of the opulent Montreux Palace Hotel. By this time Nabokov's literary reputation and financial independence were secure. His American citizenship, combined with his residence in a country famous for its political neutrality, suggest that he might have been ready to shake old political and ideological obsessions from the folds of his art. *Ada*'s unapologetic self-indulgence seems to bear this out. Nabokov's elitism and aestheticism appear to culminate in a eulogistic encomium to class privilege and social irresponsibility.

If history and politics are sublimated in Nabokov's earlier fiction, they seem to have vanished altogether from the pages of *Ada*. Antiterra's geopolitical structure is scarred by its own version of the Cold War, but *Ada*'s protagonists have no ties to Tartary, the collection of Soviet-type dictatorships huddled behind a "Golden Curtain" (*A* 145).[8] Only on Terra, Antiterra's mythical parallel planet, are "America" and "Russia" separated by "*political*, rather than *poetical*" lines (*A* 19; emphasis added). Van and Ada move freely across Antiterra's charmed landscape as the scions of one of Amerussia's noblest and wealthiest families, speaking a Russo-French version of English and immersing themselves in the poetry of two continents. The suffering and anxiety bred by bad politics are as distant from the Veens' opulent lives as one planet from another.

Ada gives voice to Nabokov's lifelong nostalgia for Russia and his new tenderness for America. But it risks doing so at a cost that no serious writer can afford, and Nabokov must have known that a cure for his nostalgia could not be attained by removing the "political" from the "poetical." Unlike Martin's Zoorland and Kinbote's Zembla, fabricated worlds whose political coordinates emblematize the desires and anxieties of their creators, Antiterra provides a new version of the political fantasies of *Invitation to a Beheading* and *Bend Sinister*. In *Ada*, as in these earlier novels, the very nature of the fantasy is generated by a set of specific ideological preoccupations.

THE METALITERARY AS METAPHYSICS

Nabokov's attraction to innovative metaliterary strategies is well documented, but *Ada* follows that attraction to new extremes. Unlike *Invitation to a Beheading* and *Bend Sinister*, where fictions are exposed as fictions in each novel's final scene, *Ada* pulls back this veil in its opening sentence, a playfully parodic inversion of *Anna Karenina*'s famous opening words. Van's first journey to Ardis Hall is as much a literary journey as it is a spatial one: "At the next turning," he recalls, "the romantic mansion appeared on the gentle eminence of old novels" (*A* 32). His love affair with Ada is punctuated by similar references to its fictional ontology: "Then Van and Ada met in the passage, and would have kissed at some earlier stage of the Novel's Evolution in the History of Literature" (*A* 79; see also 103, 230, 380). These gestures are part of Nabokov's general ambivalence toward literary realism. In *Ada* this ambivalence is part of a complex response to the relationship between literary realism and philosophical materialism.

The narrative's frequent allusions to other Nabokovian offspring can be understood as an aspect of this response. One of Van's dreams conjures up a stray reference to "the Vane sisters"; Ada translates John Shade's poetry into Russian and French; Van and Ada spend a morning "reworking their translation of a passage (lines 569–572) in John Shade's famous poem" describing the emotional dilemmas posed by an anthropomorphic hereafter (*A* 416, 459, 465). Pifer seizes upon Lucette's self-comparison to *Lolita*'s Dolly Haze ("I'm like Dolores—when she says she's 'only a picture painted on air'" [*A* 371]) to observe that "the Veens appear to derive their special status from the very artifice in which they dwell. They are creatures fashioned by art, existing in a world of fabrication."[9]

These conspicuous gestures toward *Ada*'s status as a literary artifact are unrelated to similar strategies employed by postmodernist fiction.[10] Rather, as Vladimir Alexandrov has noted, Nabokov's use of "the metaliterary is camouflage for, and a model of, the metaphysical."[11] In the case of *Ada,* these metaliterary touches contribute, in a radically new way, to Nabokov's longstanding campaign against materialist philosophy. Like Jorge Luis Borges's short story "Tlön, Uqbar, Orbis Tertius," *Ada* is a thought experiment born of a desire to generate a universe of the kind postulated by the most uncompromising of idealist philosophers, the eighteenth-century Anglo-Irish philosopher George Berkeley, Bishop of Cloyne (1685–1753).

During his research for his dissertation titled "Terra: Eremitic Reality or Collective Dream?" Van is led to conclude that Terra is "a green world rotating in space and spiraling in time, which in terms of matter-and-mind was like ours" (*A* 146). *Ada*'s frequent reminders of its own artificiality point to the fallacy of Van's conclusion that his planet's ontological makeup replicates our own. As a self-contained world emanating from Nabokov's imagination, Antiterra is emphatically a product of spirit alone.[12]

Van is vain and cruel, but his intellectual preoccupations connect him to his creator. His "passion for the insane" (comparable, he tells us, to the passion "some have for arachnids or orchids") finds its correlative in Nabokov's own pantheon of fictional madmen and driving passion for butterflies (*A* 270). Van's inquiries into the nature of time and other existential dimensions are obsessions Nabokov shared, and his intellectual daring is something Nabokov must have valued (*SM* 369–70). Above all, Van's willingness to renounce what Konstantin Godunov-Cherdyntsev called "idols or habits of thought" prompts Nabokov to lead Van to the very brink of solving the puzzle of his existential predicament (FB 215).

Van's implicit dualism is a consequence of his cognitive limitations.

Like his forerunner, *Bend Sinister*'s Adam Krug, Van cannot know that he is a character of fiction without forfeiting his sanity. Unlike Krug, however, Van has access to a community of madmen and mystics who provide him with detailed information about Terra, the parallel planet that *Ada*'s readers recognize as their own. His "terrological" studies lead him to speculate that Terra may exist "as a state of mind" or as a form of "inner space" (*A* 211, 270). He derives this curious conclusion from the startling consistency of his patients' visions of Terra:

> He interviewed numerous neurotics, among whom there were variety artists, and literary men, and at least three intellectually lucid, but spiritually "lost," cosmologists who either were in telepathic collusion (they had never met and did not even know of one another's existence) or had discovered, none knew how or where, by means, maybe, of forbidden "ondulas" of some kind, a green world rotating in space and spiraling in time, which in terms of matter-and-mind was like ours and which they described in the same specific details as three people watching from three separate windows would a carnival show in the same street. (*A* 146)

From the vantage point of psychology alone, Van's conclusion that Terra is "a state of mind" or a form of "inner space" is predictable and justifiable. From a metaphysical perspective, however, the collective nature of this phenomenon remains puzzling. This shared "transcendental delirium" (*A* 271) extends the relevance of Van's conclusions beyond the domain of psychology into the domain of philosophy (Van's second area of professional expertise). Considered from a philosophical perspective, Terra's capacity to invade the minds of Antiterra's insane seems like a fictional representation of Berkeley's immaterialist cosmology. When Van speculates that Terra is a world "which in terms of matter-and-mind was like ours," he is astutely (but unknowingly) suggesting that Terra, too, is a world unalloyed by material substance.

RUSSIAN MARXISM AND GEORGE BERKELEY

At the height of Russia's first revolutionary period, Peter Struve wrote in *Osvobozhdenie* that Russia's liberationists "part with the Social Democrats (and revolutionaries in general) not only in tactics and not only in program, but in the very philosophical foundations of world outlook [*v samykh filosofskikh osnovakh mirosozertsaniia*]."[13] Though Struve was calling attention to the Marxists' indifference to liberal rights, his words also adumbrate the ways in which Russian political activism was often self-consciously rooted in philosophical principles established by party authorities. With an urgency unrivaled by their Western counterparts, key members of Russia's political parties were moved to establish party platforms on matters ranging from metaphysics and epistemology to debates concerning the proper theoretical foundations of ethical thought.

Leszek Kolakowski notes that Russia's *intelligenty* were responsive to the turn to idealism characteristic of Silver Age culture. A broad segment of the intelligentsia began to abandon the positivistic, materialistic, and utilitarian modes of thought that had dominated the second half of the nineteenth century.[14] Christopher Read has persuasively argued that the proliferation between 1903 and 1908 of Marxist publications committed to refuting philosophical idealism demonstrates that this trend was a deep source of anxiety for Russia's Social Democrats (*RRRI* 41, 52, 54). For Kolakowski and Read, the revival of idealist political thought heralded by *Problems of Idealism* played a decisive role in the development of Russian Marxist philosophy by pushing Russia's Social Democrats to formulate a philosophical position compatible with Marxism and explicitly opposed to idealism.[15]

The first of the published replies to *Problems of Idealism* was a collection of essays from 1904 titled *Ocherki realisticheskogo mirovozzreniia* (*Sketches on a Realist Worldview*). Leading Bolsheviks contributed to the volume: Anatolii Lunacharskii (Lenin's future commissar for education), Vladimir Bazarov, and Alexander (Aleksandr) Bogdanov, among others. Though the contributors frequently contradicted each other, they were united in supporting epistemological realism—that is, the claim that external reality is independent of perception (*RRRI* 41, 209). Other works followed in quick succession: a collection of essays produced, at Plekhanov's instigation, by Liubov Aksel'rod (under the pseudonym "Ortodoks") entitled *Filosofskie ocherki* (*Philosophical Sketches,* 1906); Bogdanov's three-volume *Empiriomonizm* (*Empirio-Monism,* 1904–06); Paul (Pavel) Yushkevich's *Materializm i kriticheskii realizm* (*Materialism and Critical Realism,* 1908); Nicholas (Nikolai) Valentinov's *Filosofskie postroeniia marksizma* (*The Philosophical Constructions of Marxism,* 1907); Lunacharskii's *Religiia i sotsializm* (*Religion and Socialism,* 1908); the collection of essays *Ocherki po filosofii marksizma* (*Sketches on Marxist Philosophy,* 1908); and Lenin's *Materialism and Empirio-Criticism* (1909) (*RRRI* 41).

Though the contributors to this upsurge in Marxist theoretical writing were all critics of idealism, they diverged in the particulars of their respective philosophical positions. Bitter polemics erupted among these firm epistemological realists, and their attempts to discredit each other were at once remarkably consistent and indicative of the degree to which idealism was an opprobrious term and feared enemy. The most prominent combatants—Plekhanov, Bogdanov, and Lenin—consistently accused one another of being closet idealists. As Read notes, this was "the worst possible slander in their eyes." Soviet philosophers would continue this tradition of labeling their ideological opponents as idealists (*RRRI* 42).

The chief bogeyman in these heated polemics was Berkeley. Nabokov's meticulous research into the intellectual history surrounding Chernyshevski's life and work alerted him to the important role played by Berkeley within the discourses of Russian Marxism. In *The Development of the Monist View of History* (1895), a book celebrated by Lenin as having educated a whole generation of Russian Marxists, Plekhanov retells the history of philosophy as a battle between Berkeley's idealist monism and Holbach's materialist monism.[16] Predictably, the book defends materialism and tries to refute idealism. Lenin proceeded in the same manner in his *Materialism and Empirio-Criticism,* the philosophical magnum opus that would become the official philosophical platform of the Soviet regime. Famous for its philosophical naïveté, coarse style, and personal vitriol, the work sought to restore Russian Social Democracy to orthodox Marxist foundations.[17] Lenin vilifies Bazarov, Bogdanov, Yushkevich, Valentinov, and Viktor Chernov by arguing that their so-called revisionary "Marxism" is in fact a version of Berkeleian idealism. Indeed, the book opens with an extended description of Berkeley's philosophy. This structure is motivated by Lenin's claim that these wayward Marxists have betrayed materialism by embracing empiriocriticism, a philosophical school associated with the work of Ernst Mach and Richard Avenarius. According to Lenin, empirio-criticism is nothing more than a newfangled reincarnation of Berkeleian idealism (*MEC* 10–26).

Bogdanov and Bazarov were unfazed by Lenin's accusations and retaliated in kind. In *Vera i nauka* (*Faith and Science*), Bogdanov argued that Lenin's philosophy is "idealism, clericalism, priestly superstition [*idealizm, klerikalizm, popovshchina*]."[18] In *Na dva fronta* (*On Two Fronts,* 1910), Bazarov heaped scorn on Lenin's naive philosophical pronouncements and argued that Lenin was as much an idealist as Kant (*RRRI* 51–52).

Nikolai Volskii, one of Lenin's protégés in Geneva, broke off relations with his master long before Lenin publicly denounced his philosophical monograph (published under the pseudonym "Valentinov") in *Materialism and Empirio-Criticism.* Volskii concludes his memoir *Encounters with Lenin* by highlighting the same tight connection between theoretical philosophy and political practice observed by Struve half a century earlier. When someone bent on needling him observed that his quarrel with Bolshevism in 1904 had been precipitated by mere "philosophical questions," Volskii offered an instructive response: "Of course, it was not only because of this, but even had this been so is it possible, knowing what happened after 1904, to treat my dispute with Lenin as so unimportant?" As he adds further, Lenin's rabid intolerance toward the philosophical views of others, showcased so vividly in *Materialism and Empirio-Criticism,* had calamitous political consequences. After Lenin's death, *Materialism and Empirio-Criticism* became "holy writ for Communists everywhere." In Stalin's hands, it was used as a deadly weapon against the regime's real or imagined enemies; as Volskii evocatively observes, "a straight, well-bulldozered road" leads from Lenin's philosophical work to the NKVD's show trials and interrogation rooms. This "historical sequel," Volskii admits, is "so bizarre that it looks like some fantasy of a brain deranged by madness."[19]

Nabokov interleaved *Ada* with the shocking trajectory noted by Volskii. He was also deeply pained by—to borrow one of Volskii's phrases—the "deadly, crushing significance" of Lenin's intellectual intolerance.[20] In an interview from 1971, he observes: "I would like to say a lot about my heroic readers in Russia but am prevented from doing so—by many emotions besides a sense of responsibility with which I still cannot cope in any rational way" (*SO* 192). This sense of responsibility is distilled in *Ada* as an artistic refutation of the philosophical beliefs whose entrenchment had guaranteed that only the "heroic" risked reading Nabokov in the Soviet Union.

Berkeley's philosophy must have been congenial to Nabokov for a number of reasons, but the philosopher's status as the Bolsheviks' arch-enemy would have made him immensely attractive. A series of oblique clues establish Berkeley's importance to *Ada*. Many of these clues cluster around Van's adoptive mother Aqua, from whom Van derives his interest in time, insanity, and terrology. As he tells Ada after rereading Aqua's suicide note, "I often think it would have been so much more plausible, esthetically, ecstatically, Estotially speaking—if she were really my mother" (*A* 29). Among the most severe manifestations of Aqua's mental illness, he reports, was her inability to tell time: "The effort to comprehend the information conveyed somehow to people of genius by the hands of a timepiece, or piece of time, became as hopeless as trying to make out the sign language of a secret society or the Chinese chant of that young student with a non-Chinese guitar whom she had known at the time she or her sister had given birth to a mauve baby" (*A* 25). This handicap enables Demon and Marina to deceive Aqua (with only partial success) into accepting Van as her own biological son.

This deception is chronicled in Marina's herbarium, the same herbarium that enables Van and Ada to discover that they are siblings in the novel's first chapter. The "young student" whose "Chinese chant" distresses Aqua is also present in this scene. Two items in the herbarium stand out from the rest by virtue of their artificiality and their connection to Aqua. The first of these items is labeled "artificial edelweiss brought by my new nurse with a note from Aqua saying it came from a '*mizernoe* and bizarre' Christmas Tree at the Home." The second item, added to the herbarium two months later, is identified as a "fancy flower of paper, found in Aqua's purse. Ex, 16.II.1870, made by a fellow patient, at the Home, which is no longer hers" (*A* 11).

Ada seizes upon these two entries to showcase her scientific knowledge and powers of deduction. "The paper flower so cavalierly dismissed," she informs Van in her flashy, pedantic manner, "is a perfectly recognizable reproduction of an early-spring sanicle that I saw in profusion on hills in coastal California last February." She identifies the "artificial edelweiss" as a reproduction of "the *Pied de Lion*" done "by the same hand—possibly belonging to a very sick Chinese boy who came all the way from Barkley College" (*A* 11–12).

Ada's ascription of the artistically reproduced sanicle and edelweiss to a sick Chinese boy from Barkley College seems hopelessly arbitrary until Van's reference—fourteen pages later—to "the Chinese chant of that young student with a non-Chinese guitar" whom Aqua had come to know during her incarceration at the Swiss sanatorium. The clue regarding the second part of Ada's deduction comes from the sanicle's habitat: having seen it grow on the hills of coastal California, Ada plausibly infers that the artist attended a local college, such as the University of California at "Barkley." As a characteristic Antiterran transformation, "Barkley" channels Terra's "Berkeley," the town and institution of higher learning named, significantly, after George Berkeley.[21] The connection is strengthened further by the fact that Antiterra's "Barkley" transcribes the accepted pronunciation of the philosopher's name rather than the pronunciation of the University of California's flagship campus.

Marina's herbarium holds the key to Van and Ada's parentage; it also playfully and mysteriously establishes, very early on, the specific pedigree of the novel's unique metaphysics. The "very sick Chinese boy" from "Barkley College," resurrected by Ada from the pages of Marina's telltale herbarium, is encountered only in a series of deceptively offhand allusions. Taken together, these allusions are part of the puzzle that bedevils Van's philosophical speculations. Time, the mystery that drives Van's academic work, is linked to the Chinese boy by way of Aqua's bewildered response to both time and the boy's Chinese chant. "Barkley College," the boy's alma mater (an Antiterran institution of higher learning that may bear more than a nominal connection to its famous namesake), is the critical clue in this web of allusions. Named after a philosopher who emancipated existence from material substance, "Barkley College" gestures toward a metaphysical model that accommodates Nabokov's yearning for a universe shaped by the playful rules of art rather than the iron laws of mechanical necessity.

"BERKELEY AND BERGSON"

Nabokov admitted that Berkeley was on his mind when he was writing *Ada*. In the preamble to his response to the 1970 *TriQuarterly* issue dedicated to his life's work, he insists that he was driven to such an uncharacteristic exercise by a desire "to eliminate slight factual errors of which such a marvelous gift must be free" (*SO* 284). One such error, he writes, is Jeffrey Leonard's assertion that Borges's essay "A New Refutation of Time" influenced Van's *The Texture of Time.* "Mr. Leonard would have lost less of it had he gone straight to Berkeley and Bergson" (*SO* 290), Nabokov concludes.

It is tempting to view this as yet another example of Nabokov's attachment to playful alliterations,[22] but the remark is too internally consistent to be dismissed. In "A New Refutation of Time," Borges claims to complete the idealist project begun by Berkeley (whom he credits with refuting the existence of space and matter) and continued by Hume (whom he credits with refuting the existence of spirit) by taking their arguments to what he sees as their logical conclusion: "Once matter and spirit, which are continuities, are negated, once space too has been negated, I do not know what right we have to that continuity which is time." "Time," he states, "is a delusion: the difference and inseparability of one moment belonging to its apparent past from another belonging to its apparent present is sufficient to disintegrate it."[23]

When Nabokov claims that Leonard "would have lost less of it" had he gone to Berkeley and Bergson, he is, characteristically, denying an intellectual debt to others. But he is also—and this is out of character—acknowledging a debt to two philosophers whose conception of time was much closer to his own than that of Borges. Moreover, his comment that Leonard should have gone "straight to" Berkeley and Bergson implicitly concedes that at least *some* of "it" is not lost by getting to Berkeley and Bergson by way of Borges.

Van's philosophical aspirations are considerably more modest than those of Borges. Unlike Borges, he does not seek to refute the existence of time altogether but merely to deny its abstract metrical dimension. This aim allies him with both Berkeley and Bergson. As Borges tells us in "A New Refutation of Time," Berkeley defined time as "the succession of ideas in my mind, which flows uniformly, and is participated [in] by all beings."[24] Berkeley's conception of time inspired Bergson, and it bears a striking resemblance to a major component in Van's conception of time.

Like Borges and the sick Chinese boy from Barkley College, Bergson leads readers into the novel's Berkeleian topography. *Ada*'s first reference to Bergson occurs in relation to Van's invocation of Bergson's conception of "duration" ("*la durée*") (*A* 300–301).[25] Bergson used the term to signify an inner understanding of time, but his insistence that time should be considered concretely rather than in abstract mathematical terms had been anticipated by Berkeley two hundred years earlier. Berkeley, too, claimed that time has no intrinsic metrical component, and challenged the mathematical argument that time is infinitely divisible:

> Whenever I attempt to frame a simple idea of *time,* abstracted from the succession of ideas in my mind, which flows uniformly, and is participated by all beings, I am lost and embrangled in inextricable difficulties. I have no notion of it at all, only I hear others say, it is infinitely divisible, and speak of it in such a manner as leads me to entertain odd thoughts of my existence: since that doctrine lays one under an absolute necessity of thinking, either that he passes away innumerable ages without a thought, or else that he is annihilated every moment of his life: both of which seem equally absurd. Time therefore being nothing, abstracted from the succession of ideas in our minds, it follows that the duration of any finite spirit must be estimated by the number of ideas or actions succeeding each other in that same spirit or mind. Hence it is a plain consequence that the soul always thinks: and in truth whoever shall go about to divide in his thoughts, or abstract the *existence* of a spirit from its *cogitation,* will, I believe, find it no easy task.[26]

Van's *The Texture of Time,* written on the eve of his second reunion with Ada at Mont Roux, is speculative rather than definitive. (Punctuated by evasions, retractions, and contradictions, its progress mirrors Van's agitated state of mind.) Berkeley's ghostly presence in the text is as elusive as Van is uncertain about the results of his philosophical endeavor. Nonetheless, Nabokov seems to have been sincere when he identified Berkeley as an influence on Van's meditations on time. Van's "philosophical" definition of time (cited by Nabokov in *Strong Opinions*)[27] echoes Berkeley's twin claims that time is "the succession of ideas in our minds" and that mortal existence is predicated upon cogitation:

> Time is but memory in the making. In every individual life there goes on from cradle to deathbed the gradual shaping and strengthening of that *backbone of consciousness,* which is the Time of the strong. "To be" means to know one "has been." "Not to be" implies the only "new" kind of (sham) time: the future. (*A* 448; emphasis in original)

When Van refers to the past as "an accumulation of sensa" and as "a constant accumulation of images" (*A* 435, 436), he seems to concur not only with Berkeley but also with Nabokov's own observation that "the Past is a constant accumulation of images" (*SO* 186).

Van concedes, however, that time also contains a "physiological" component that is less benevolent than its Berkeleian, "philosophical" counterpart: "Physiologically the sense of Time is a sense of continuous becoming, and if 'becoming' has a voice, the latter might be, not unnaturally, a steady vibration; but for Log's sake, let us not confuse Time with Tinnitus, and the seashell hum of duration with the throb of our blood" (*A* 448). Van cannot escape the ravages of "physiological" time; he pens these lines in the miserable aftermath of his failed reunion with Ada. When he descends the stairs of his hotel and meets the much-changed Ada (corseted, wrinkled, myopic), he comes to realize that time is more than "memory in the making." Only the next day, after Ada's unexpected return, does Van reenter into the kindlier domain of "philosophical" time. Like Nabokov, who nourished his nostalgia by denying time's existence, Van and Ada soothe the pain associated with their separations by an act of temporal compression. The seventeen years of their final separation become a fold in time's carpet. This, at least, is the metaphor Nabokov himself used to describe his own losses: "I confess I do not believe in time," he tells us in *Speak, Memory*. "I like to fold my magic carpet, after use, in such a way as to superimpose one part of the pattern upon another" (*SM* 479). When Nabokov conflates time with memory he does so in an effort to bring time under his authority.

Berkeley's conception of time is an intrinsic component of his idealist metaphysics and epistemology. His idealist monism—that is, his immaterialist metaphysics—is grounded in his claim that matter is not, as postulated by Descartes, a self-sustaining substance extending in space and following the laws of physics. According to Berkeley, material substance is a complex system of sensory impressions continuously transposed into our minds by the mind of God. Berkeley's famous epistemological apothegm, *esse* is *percipi*, refers to his claim that the empirical world consists of sense impressions ("ideas") that are perceived or are perceivable by minds, such as human beings ("finite spirits") and God (the "infinite spirit").

Like Descartes and Locke before him, Berkeley used the term "ideas" to refer to the components of human thought (*PHK* 41). In its complete version, the Latin tag defines both spirits and ideas in relation to the act of perception: the *esse* of ideas is *percipi* (to be perceived [or perceivable]) and the *esse* of spirits is *percipere* (to perceive). This formulation intersects in suggestive ways with Nabokov's emphasis on the creative function of perception. "Average reality begins to rot and stink as soon as the act of individual creation ceases to animate a subjectively perceived texture," he famously stated in an interview from 1968 (*SO* 118). The sentiment also surfaces repeatedly in Nabokov's fiction, as when Demon Veen struggles to come to terms with the incongruity between his romantic past and the drab present. As he examines his former mistress, Marina, across the dinner table at Ardis, he is described as making an effort "to *realize* (in the rare full sense of the word) . . . to *possess* the reality of a fact by forcing it into the sensuous center" (*A* 200; emphasis in original).

Berkeley's efforts to refute the Cartesian definition of material substance amplifies the significance of Nabokov's uncharacteristic acknowledgment of debt to "Berkeley and Bergson." The two paraliterary references to immaterialism Nabokov made at a time when *Ada* was his principal literary preoccupation suggest that his injunction to Leonard may also hold the key to one of Nabokov scholarship's more enduring mysteries. In a 1966 interview at Montreux (four years prior to Nabokov's response to Leonard), Alfred Appel, Jr., asked Nabokov about the role of doubles in his fiction (as compared, for instance, to those in the novels of Andrei Belyi and Thomas Mann). Nabokov's answer seems deliberately mystifying: "Those murky matters have no importance to me as a writer. Philosophically, I am an indivisible monist" (*SO* 85). When asked three years later to elaborate upon this cryptic confession, he offered the following elucidation: "Monism, which implies a oneness of basic reality, is seen to be divisible when, say, 'mind' sneakily splits away from 'matter' in the reasoning of a muddled monist or half-hearted materialist" (*SO* 124).

Scholars interested in Nabokov's metaphysics have focused on the confessional rather than the contextual aspects of this baffling philosophical assertion.[28] Such an approach, however, must ignore the playful tone in which this declaration is made ("Incidentally, your handwriting is very like mine" is the sentence that follows Nabokov's reference to his "indivisible monism" [*SO* 85]), as well as the difficulty of asserting that Nabokov subscribed to a philosophical position as rare and counterintuitive as a brand of monism that rejects categorically the independent existence of matter. (Though his definition of his "indivisible monism" allows for either a monism of mind or matter, even a passing familiarity with his work must dismiss out of hand the possibility that he was endorsing the latter.) A contextual approach avoids these problems by shifting the focus away from Nabokov's personal system of beliefs to the philosophical and aesthetic concerns that preoccupied him at the time he made these statements. The stakes may be lowered by this approach, but the results are nonetheless illuminating.

BERKELEY'S INDIVISIBLE MONISM

Nabokov identified himself as an "indivisible monist" in 1966, the same year he began writing *Ada* at a rapid pace, and *Ada,* now completed, was the main subject of the *Time* interview in which he offered the ontological elaboration cited above.[29] It is highly probable, then, that Nabokov's statements about his monism were inspired by his work on the novel which was his central concern during this period. *Ada*'s idiosyncratic cosmology supports this view. Berkeley, history's most famous and radical idealist "indivisible monist," presides over *Ada*'s universe.

In light of his injunction to Leonard, it is fitting that Nabokov's familiarity with Berkeley's philosophy should be mediated by Bergson, the philosopher Nabokov identified as one of his "top favorites" "between the ages of 20 and 40" (*SO* 43). Berkeley figures prominently as the representative of idealism in three of Bergson's key texts: *Matter and Memory* (*Matière et mémoire,* 1896), *Mind-Energy* (*L'énergie spirituelle,* 1919), and *The Creative Mind* (*La pensée et le mouvant,* 1934). Bergson's references to Berkeley typically revolve around philosophical problems that interested Nabokov his entire life. As Bergson explains, the subject of *Matter and Memory* is "the problem of the relation between soul and body." He attempts to solve this problem by positioning material substance "half way between the place to which Descartes had driven it and that to which Berkeley drew it back."[30] On the second page of this same work, Bergson refers to Berkeley's argument that empirical reality "exists only for mind" ("*n'existe que pour un esprit, comme le voulait Berkeley*"), a comment that is also in tune with Godunov's comment to Fyodor that nature seems to have been "invented by some waggish artist precisely for the intelligent eyes of man."[31] Bergson states further that "philosophy made a great step forward on the day when Berkeley proved, as against the 'mechanical philosophers,' that the secondary qualities of matter have at least as much reality as the primary qualities."[32] This statement resonates with Nabokov's interest in debunking the claims of his own time's "mechanical philosophers," men of enormous cultural and historical influence such as Marx, Engels, Darwin, Freud, Chernyshevski, Lenin, and Plekhanov.

In *The Creative Mind,* Bergson observes that Berkeley's theory of knowledge is based on an auditory model ("matter is a language which God speaks to us") which he renders (now as a visual trope) as "*a thin transparent film* situated between man and God" ("une *mince pellicule transparente* située entre l'homme et Dieu").[33] Four years after the French publication of *The Creative Mind,* Nabokov completed *The Gift,* in which an epiphanic experience suggests to Fyodor that the empirical world is "the reverse side of a magnificent fabric, on the front of which there gradually formed and became alive images invisible to him" (*Gift* 314). One year later, in the 1939 philosophical poem "Oko" ("The Oculus"), the "magnificent fabric" is replaced by "the silent old cinema / of clouds, and grainfields, and vines."[34] Both images bring to mind Bergson's metaphors for Berkeley's vision of the cosmos.

Bergson is mentioned frequently in *Ada* in connection with Van's *The Texture of Time* (*A* 301, 433, 438, 460). By contrast, Berkeley's name appears only once, and not openly but in the guise of a characteristic Antiterran transformation. Even so, *Ada*'s Berkeley is, to borrow from Paul Valéry a digestive metaphor for influence, perfectly assimilated ("*Le lion est fait de mouton assimilé*"). Only a "plagiarist," as Valéry noted elsewhere, "has badly digested what he has got from others; he brings up bits of it that can be recognized."[35]

Time, according to Berkeley, is a product of humanity's cognitive limitations. Ideas must succeed one another in the minds of finite spirits because the human mind cannot apprehend the universe as it exists in the mind of God. The image Van conjures up to express his longing to escape into timelessness recalls Berkeley's vision of a universe that abides in its totality in God's mind. "The irreversibility of Time (which is not heading anywhere in the first place)," Van writes, "is a very parochial affair: had our organs and orgitrons not been asymmetrical, our view of Time might have been amphitheatric and altogether grand, like ragged night and jagged mountains around a small, twinkling, satisfied hamlet" (*A* 430). Nabokov, too, yearned to transcend time in terms that recall Berkeley's cosmology: "For every dimension presupposes a medium within which it can act, and if, in the spiral unwinding of things, space warps into something akin to time, and time, in its turn, warps into something akin to thought, then, surely, another dimension follows—a special Space maybe, not the old one, we trust, unless spirals become vicious circles again" (*SM* 620). In a 1964 interview with Alvin Toffler, Nabokov invokes this metaphysical hierarchy again when he reads from notes compiled and rejected during his work on *Pale Fire:* "Time without consciousness—lower animal world; time with consciousness—man; consciousness without time—some still higher state" (*SO* 30).

As always, art extends Nabokov's yearnings and aspirations beyond the reach of human possibility. The "special Space" in which consciousness is unhindered by temporal constraints is accessible to the artist during moments of creative inspiration. As an artist, Nabokov claims to know his work of art as Berkeley's God is said to know his created universe. This total knowledge, Nabokov explains, is nevertheless fractured by the temporal limitations imposed by the mechanics of writing and reading:

> You might if you choose develop any part of the picture, for the idea of sequence does not really exist as far as the author is concerned. Sequence arises only because words have to be written one after the other on consecutive pages, just as the reader's mind must have time to go through the book, at least the first time he reads it. Time and sequence cannot exist in the author's mind because no time element and no space element had ruled the initial vision. (*LL* 379–80; see also *SO* 31–32)

Nabokov frequently asserted that this type of inspiration originates in a transcendent domain. As he explains in a 1966 interview with Appel, "I am afraid to get mixed up with Plato, whom I do not care for, but I do think that in my case it is true that the entire book, before it is written, seems to be ready ideally in some other, now transparent, now dimming, dimension, and my job is to take down as much of it as I can make out and as precisely as I am humanly able to" (*SO* 69). Like Berkeley's God, the human artist translates a timeless vision into the language of temporality.

The process of literary creation also provided Nabokov with an analogy for a form of existence that has no need for material substance. Krug, Nabokov's most distinguished fictional philosopher, describes the literary achievements of Shakespeare in terms that recall the traditional Judeo-Christian notion that the word of God created the world:

> Nature had once produced an Englishman whose domed head had been a hive of words; a man who had only to breathe on any particle of his stupendous vocabulary to have that particle live and expand and throw out tremulous tentacles until it became a complex image with a pulsing brain and correlated limbs. (*BS* 263)

While holding for the first time Shade's manuscript, Kinbote echoes this tribute to the world-making powers of art in one of *Pale Fire*'s most memorable passages: "We are absurdly accustomed to the miracle of a few written signs being able to contain immortal imagery, involutions of thought, new worlds with live people, speaking, weeping, laughing" (*PF* 648). These reminders that art can conjure up live worlds remain safely metaphorical, but Nabokov also invites us to ponder the metaphysical implications of this cognitive possibility. Berkeley spells out these implications by arguing that the empirical world *is* a linguistic text. Sensory perceptions, he states, connect the human to the divine, for they "constitute an universal language of the Author of nature."[36] Sensory qualities (color patches or sound bites, for example) function like the letters of an alphabet which God combines into bundles of sensations to make up words (such as "apples" or "trees"). These, in turn, he combines into sentences according to established rules of grammar (the patterns we erroneously identify as mechanistic laws of nature). Berkeley's conception of the universe as a divine grammar makes his universe non-mechanistic and non-deterministic.[37] Kinbote's entrancing passage about the miraculous capacity of language to manifest "new worlds with live people" ends in an epiphany that resonates with Berkeley's claim that the material world is a language communicated to us from the beyond: "Solemnly I weighed in my hand what I was carrying under my left armpit, and for a moment I found myself enriched with an indescribable amazement as if informed that fireflies were making decodable signals on behalf of stranded spirits, or that a bat was writing a legible tale of torture in the bruised and branded sky" (*PF* 649).

Berkeley's worldview can be said to be "indivisibly monist" in the terms set out by Nabokov because, as Berkeley states, "there is not any other substance than *spirit*, or that which perceives" (*PHK* 43). In his own efforts to overcome the problems posed by dualism, Descartes also entertained the possibility that matter does not exist, but ultimately rejected it on the grounds that God cannot be a deceiver:

> Although we are all persuaded that material things exist, yet because we have doubted this before and have placed it in the rank of the prejudices of our childhood, it is now requisite that we should inquire into the reasons through which we may accept this truth with certainty. To begin with we feel that without doubt all our perceptions proceed from some thing which is different from our mind. For it is not in our power to have one perception rather than another, since each one is clearly dependent on the object which affects our senses. It is true that we may inquire whether that object is God, or some other different from God. But inasmuch as we perceive, or rather are stimulated by sense to apprehend clearly and distinctly a matter which is extended in length, breadth, and depth, the various parts of which have various figures and motions, and give rise to the sensations we have of colours, smells, pains, etc., if God immediately and of Himself presented to our mind the idea of this extended matter, or merely permitted it to be caused in us by some other object which possessed no extension, figure, or motion, there would be nothing to prevent Him from being regarded as a deceiver. . . . But God cannot deceive us, because deception is repugnant to His nature . . . And hence we must conclude that there is an object extended in length, breadth, and depth, and possessing all those properties which we clearly perceive to pertain to extended objects. And this extended object is called by us either body or matter.[38]

The possibility that God is a deceiver, so repugnant as to be inadmissible to Descartes, would have appealed to Nabokov.[39] The notion that an otherworldly being invents a universe so intricately "real" as to deceive us into thinking that it is constituted of material substance would belong to the category of enchanting tricks that Nabokov ascribes to art and nature:

> The fake move in a chess problem, the illusion of a solution or the conjuror's magic: I used to be a little conjuror when I was a boy. I loved doing simple tricks—turning water into wine, that kind of thing; but I think I'm in good company because all art is deception and so is nature; all is deception in that good cheat, from the insect that mimics a leaf to the popular enticements of procreation. (*SO* 11; see also *SO* 153 and *Gift* 344)

Turning water into wine is the young boy's version of the mature artist's turning word into image. That an infinitely more gifted artist should be able to turn images into things is the logical extension of these evocative analogies.

As Barabtarlo has noted, all of Nabokov's work is "driven by an insatiable love for material detail accessible to any of the five senses."[40] The argument that material substance does not exist seems to collide with Nabokov's passionate appreciation of the physical world and sensory experience. Such a conclusion, however, would be as flawed as Samuel Johnson's famous attempt to refute Berkeley's philosophy by kicking a stone and exclaiming "I refute it *thus*!" As Bryan Magee has written, it "is the crassest possible misunderstanding" of Berkeley "to suppose that he was in any way denying empirical reality. On the contrary, [he was] insisting on it with a specificity that others had not seen the need for, or possibility of."[41] William Butler Yeats, one of many modernist writers fascinated by Berkeley, understood this: "Descartes, Locke and Newton took away the world and give us its excrement instead," he writes in *Pages from a Diary Written in Nineteen Hundred and Thirty*. "Berkeley restored the world . . . Berkeley has brought back to us the world that only exists because it shines and sounds."[42]

Moments before Demon learns about Van and Ada's illicit affair, he indulges in an extended disquisition on the purely aesthetic merits of Bosch's triptych *Garden of Earthly Delights* (see figure 1):

> I mean I don't give a hoot for the esoteric meaning, for the myth behind the moth, for the masterpiece-baiter who makes Bosch express some bosh of his time, I'm allergic to allegory and am quite sure he was just enjoying himself by crossbreeding casual fancies just for the fun of the contour and color, and what we have to study . . . is the joy of the eye, the feel and the taste of the woman-sized strawberry that you embrace *with* him. (*A* 350; emphasis in original)

As in the cases of Humbert and Kinbote, Demon's moral delinquencies do not prevent him from sharing his creator's views about art. His unapologetic appreciation of the sensual (and curt dismissal of "allegory" and "the myth behind the moth") intersects suggestively with Berkeley's claim that appearance *is* reality. The seamless coexistence of the sensuous and the immaterial in Berkeley's philosophy can also serve as a useful heuristic for the otherwise perplexing discontinuity between Nabokov's delight in sensory experience and aversion toward philosophical materialism.

According to Berkeley, the world of experience is neither a distortion of a material prototype nor a degraded copy of a transcendent archetype. Consequently, it demands both our attention and respect. As Philonous, Berkeley's spokesman in *Three Dialogues Between Hylas and Philonous*, summarizes his refutation of skepticism to Hylas (his interlocutor and the spokesman for Locke's representational realism), "every thing that is seen, felt, heard, or any way perceived by the senses, is on the principles I

Figure 1. Hieronymus Bosch, *Garden of Earthly Delights,* triptych with shutters, Museo del Prado, Madrid
Photo credit: Erich Lessing/Art Resource, N.Y.

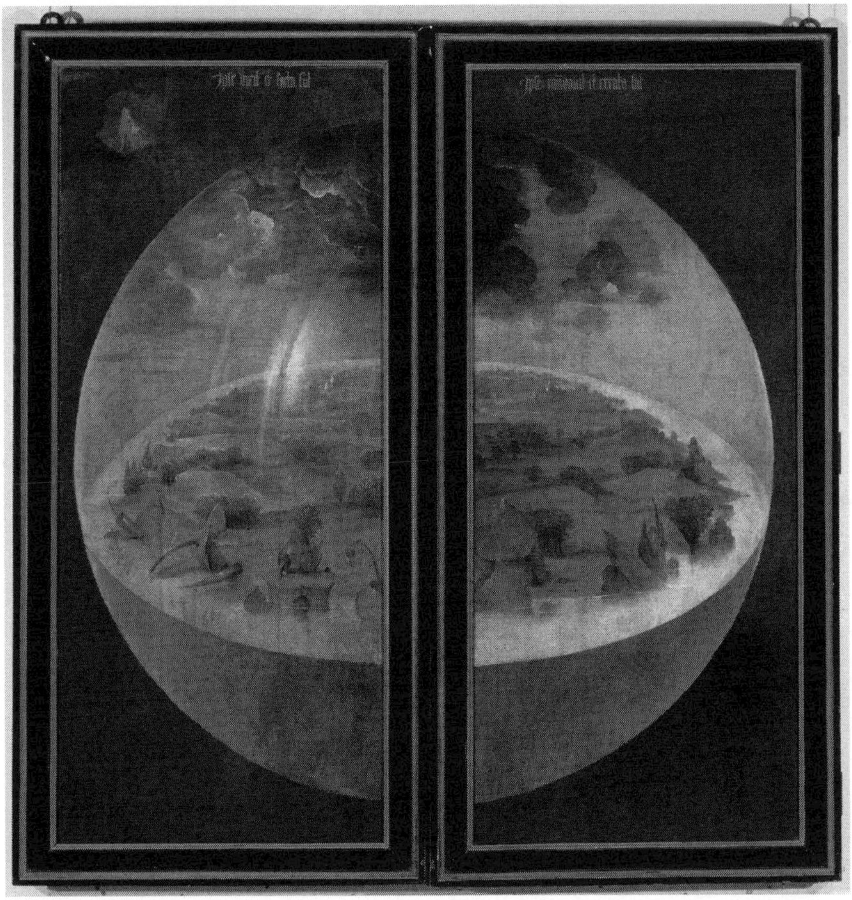

Figure 2. Hieronymus Bosch, *Garden of Earthly Delights,* triptych with shutters (closed wings: *The Creation of the World*), Museo del Prado, Madrid
Photo credit: Erich Lessing/Art Resource, N.Y.

embrace, a real being, but not on yours. Remember, the matter you contend for is an unknown somewhat (if indeed it may be termed *somewhat*) which is quite stripped of all sensible qualities, and can neither be perceived by sense, nor apprehended by the mind."[43]

In a world in which sensory data constitute reality, it makes eminent sense to revel in "the feel and the taste" of Bosch's "woman-sized strawberry." But it also makes sense to probe the depths of this reality, to know the strawberry not merely as a lover of nature but also—to paraphrase Nabokov on the epistemology of lilies—as a botanist specializing in strawberries.

Van's observation that "the only reality" is that which has been "placed under the microscope of reality" recalls Berkeley's assertion that "the microscopical representation is to be thought that which best sets forth the real nature of the thing, or what it is in itself. The colours therefore by it perceived, are more genuine and real, than those perceived otherwise."[44]

Demon's appreciation of the sensual extravagance of Bosch's *Garden of Earthly Delights* invites us to approach *Ada*'s universe with Demon's aesthetic relish. But as Boyd has persuasively argued, *Ada* also invites us to compare its world to Bosch's triptych from another perspective. When the triptych's wings are shut, Boyd reminds us, "their outer sides disclose a picture of the earth in a crystal ball, seen by God" (*NA* 111). This outer picture, Boyd suggests, plays a vital role in establishing the novel's epistemological and metaphysical preoccupations (see figure 2).

Boyd's emphasis on the triptych's outer panels draws attention to a distinguishing feature of Bosch's depiction of Genesis. In the outer panels' upper left-hand corner, God sits in state with a book in his hands, overlooking his creation. Walter Gibson observes:

> In the approximately contemporary frescoes of the Sistine ceiling, Michelangelo represented God as a sort of superhuman sculptor imposing form on the primordial chaos with his own hands. Bosch, on the other hand, followed the more traditional Christian concept in showing God creating through his Word; he is passively enthroned and holds a book, while the divine *fiat* is recorded in an inscription near the upper edge from Psalms 33:9: "For he spake and it was done; he commanded, and it stood fast."[45]

If Nabokov does, indeed, invoke this long-standing Christian tradition, he does so with an eye to the world-making powers of art. These powers are not merely figurative: just as Demon divests Bosch's triptych of myth and allegory in order to immerse himself in the literal, *Ada* bids us consider the possibility of a world created by mind alone.[46]

Berkeley's influence on *Ada* is most powerfully felt in the novel's depiction of material substance. Matter, on Antiterra, is mysterious and unpredictable. It also appears to function as a conduit for interplanetary communication. Van's description of Antiterra begins with an account of "the L disaster," a catastrophe related to electricity "which had the singular effect of both causing and cursing the notion of 'Terra'" (*A* 18). Known as "the Great, and to some Intolerable, Revelation," it "caused more insanity in the world than even an over-preoccupation with religion had in medieval times" (*A* 21). Authorities respond to these events by imposing a general ban on the use of electricity as well as on all language pertaining to it. The ban seems to have been motivated less by politics than by the mass trauma produced by the disaster (*A* 70, 96, 119).

In *Ada,* as elsewhere in Nabokov's writings, electricity is shorthand for material substance. In the commentary to his translation of *Eugene Onegin,* Nabokov suggests that "time, space, and matter" are interconnected. This formulation is anticipated in *Bend Sinister,* and it occurs again (this time "electricity" replacing "matter") in a conversation with Andrew Field: "Electricity. Time. Space. We know *nothing* about these things."[47] In *Pale Fire,* completed five years before Nabokov began *Ada,* electricity is a medium for otherworldly communication. By means of a circlet of light, Aunt Maud conveys a garbled, though ultimately decipherable, message to Hazel (*VNAY* 454). Hazel's research into the paranormal inspires Shade to write a poem titled "The Nature of Electricity." After quoting the poem, Kinbote observes: "Science tells us, by the way, that the Earth would not merely fall apart, but vanish like a ghost, if Electricity were suddenly removed from the world" (*PF* 577). Kinbote's comment and Nabokov's substitution of "electricity" for "matter" in his conversation with Field suggest that Nabokov viewed electricity as the basic component of material substance. Rachel Trousdale has argued that "electricity becomes a metaphor for the spirit" in *Ada, Pale Fire,* and "The Return of Chorb."[48] That electricity, the basic building block of matter, should become linked with spirit is fitting for a writer whose hostility toward materialism never wavered and who playfully identified himself as an "indivisible monist."

As a consequence of Antiterra's ban on electricity, the most important "utilities," such as telephones and motors, are redesigned to run on water (*A* 119).[49] But water, too, behaves strangely on Antiterra, as Aqua's "morbid sensitivity to the language of tap water" attests. She hears conversations, echoes, and fragments of poetry in the rhythms of running water, and these stimuli exacerbate her mental illness (*A* 23–24). Such a response to water, even in one mentally ill, is unsurprising given the way in which water performs the work of electricity on *Ada*'s invented planet. Antiterra's water-based telecommunications technology is at once alarming and unpredictable. The call that interrupts Demon and Marina's dinner with their children is a case in point:

> All the toilets and waterpipes in the house had been suddenly seized with borborygmic convulsions. This always signified, and introduced, a long-distance call. Marina, who had been awaiting for several days a certain message from California in response to a torrid letter, could now hardly contain her passionate impatience and had been on the point of running to the dorophone in the hall at the first bubbling spasm, when young Bout hurried in dragging

> the long green cord (visibly palpitating in a series of swells and contractions rather like a serpent ingesting a field mouse) of the ornate, brass-and-nacre receiver, which Marina with a wild "*A l'eau!*" pressed to her ear. (*A* 208)

Van's long-distance conversation with his typist is rendered nearly incomprehensible by clucking radiators and fizzing soda water set off by the buzz of the "campophone," and his frantic efforts to reach Ardis later that evening "had only resulted in such a violent rhapsody of 'eagre' that finally the basement boiler gave up and there was no hot water" (*A* 300, 311).

During Van's first picnic at Pineglen, Marina shows him and Lucette the tree trunk "where in old, very old days a magnetic telephone nested, communicating with Ardis Hall." After the banning of "currents and circuits," however, Dan's grandmother ("an engineer of great genius") "'tubed' the Redmont rill" by making it "carry vibrational *vibgyors* (prismatic pulsations) through a system of platinum segments" so that messages could be transmitted from Ardis Hall to "a picnicking Veen" (*A* 70). Boyd draws attention to the significance and strangeness of the scene: "The 1884 picnic offers the earliest sign of Lucette's nascent and ultimately fatal attachment to Van. . . . It occurs in the midst of a discussion of the electricity that seems weirdly linked with the 'L disaster' . . . and with the 'water-messages' akin to those Aqua thinks she hears in her madness."[50]

Dan's grandmother's ability to make water do the work of long-distance communication may be nothing more than a testament to her engineering skills and resourcefulness. There is no rational explanation, however, for the strange transformations that take place on the road that runs parallel to the Redmont rill and connects the picnic grounds to the train station and to Ardis Hall. Van offers no comment on the curious metamorphoses that punctuate his first journey to Ardis. The horse that he imagined would be waiting for him at the station is nowhere to be found, so Van avails himself of "a hackney coach" left behind by someone else. By the time Van is seated, the "hackney coach" has silently become an "old calèche," and the "old calèche" becomes, first, an "old clockwork taxi" and, later, a "horse" (*A* 32–33). Van's departure from Ardis at summer's end is accompanied by similar events: Van instructs Bouteillan to stop the car at Forest Fork for a prearranged last tryst with Ada, but upon his return the car and chauffeur have mysteriously become "Morio, his favorite black horse, . . . held by young Moore" (*A* 129). (The transformation is only noted by the reader; Van takes it in stride.)

In his monograph on *Ada,* Boyd notes additional events on this same stretch of road that unsettle our assumption that the physical world is stable and predictable. As Boyd perceptively observes, Van passes twice through the same rural hamlet, suggesting that the "chance crease in the texture of time" (*A* 32) that provided him with the old calèche was more than a figure of speech. Van and his driver first pass through "Torfyanka, a dreamy hamlet consisting of three or four log izbas, a milkpail repair shop and a smithy smothered in jasmine. The driver waved to an invisible friend and the sensitive runabout swerved slightly to match his gesture." A small distance further, "they bounced on the cobblestones of Gamlet, a half-Russian village, and the chauffeur waved again, this time to a boy in a cherry tree" (*A* 32). There is nothing extraordinary about Van's journey unless we notice, as Boyd has, that

> "Gamlet, a half-Russian village" is a repetition in time rather than a neighbor in space of "Torfyanka, a dreamy hamlet" (which, the novel makes clear, is also a half-Russian village). . . . What makes significant the strange duplication of Torfyanka and the driver's wave as Van travels on through Gamlet is that it foreshadows the strange duplication in 1888 of the ride back to Ardis from the 1884 picnic. For during both the 1884 and 1888 rides the children's calèche passes through only one settlement, Gamlet:
>
> > Poor Van shifted Ada's bottom to his right knee. . . . In the mournful dullness of unconsummated desire he watched a row of izbas straggle by as the *calèche* drove through Gamlet, a hamlet. ([*A* 72–73])
> >
> > With the fading of that fugitive flame his mood changed. . . . They were now about to enter Gamlet, the little Russian village . . . ([*A* 226])
>
> On Van's first, metamorphic ride to Ardis, his carriage passes first through "Torfyanka, a dreamy *hamlet*," and then through "Gamlet, a half-Russian *village*" ([*A* 32]); on the first picnic ride back to Ardis, the carriage passes through "Gamlet, a *hamlet*" ([*A* 73]) and on the second through "Gamlet, the little Russian *village*" ([*A* 226]). (*NA* 223–24; Boyd's emphasis)[51]

Like the puzzling behavior of electricity and water, these curious repetitions in time and space suggest that Antiterran matter might be something other than a Cartesian self-sustaining substance that follows predictable laws of physics. The electrical calamity "which had the singular effect of both causing and cursing the notion of 'Terra'" (*A* 18) appears to be connected to the behavior of water and its disquieting effects on a madwoman like Aqua. As sources of otherworldly communication and psychic torment, water and electricity appear to belong to the same ontological category as the scientifically inexplicable "ondulas" that are responsible, according to Van's speculations, for the visions of Terra that invade the minds of Antiterra's insane (*A* 146). The spatiotemporal transformations that attend Van's first arrival at and departure from Ardis suggest further that Antiterra's physical makeup might be governed by rules radically different from those governing its sibling planet.

From a literary perspective, these events and phenomena are part of the vast arsenal of metaliterary devices that establish Nabokov's presence in the text.[52] But from the particular philosophical perspective from which Nabokov is operating, they are records of his interest in exploring the kind of world conjured up by Berkeley. These two perspectives become mutually reinforcing if we see Antiterra as a planet whose history unfolds independently of physical laws and follows instead what Nabokov calls in his introduction to *Bend Sinister* the "whims and megrims" of a creative mind (*BS* 165). The "oneness" of its "basic reality" is never compromised by what Nabokov calls a "sneaky" split between mind and matter (*SO* 124). The only dualism to which Antiterra succumbs is the kind Nabokov described in a lecture from 1941 when he noted that "the only acceptable dualism is the unbridgeable division between ego and non-ego."[53] Berkeley's reputation rests on his daring, quirky, and ultimately irrefutable claim that the empirical world—the world of "non-ego"—is inseparable from mind. (As Borges's narrator aptly observes in "Tlön, Uqbar, Orbis Tertius," "Hume noted for all time that Berkeley's arguments did not admit the slightest refutation nor did they cause the slightest conviction.")[54] As mind's offspring, empirical reality dons "quotes" that it wears "like claws" (*A* 175), and in exchange emancipates itself from the degradation associated with what Berkeley calls "blind unthinking" material substance (*PHK* 110).

LENIN AND THE SICK CHINESE BOY FROM BARKLEY COLLEGE

As Read has observed, the conflict between idealism and materialism constituted one of "the two great philosophical axes at the heart of the debates" that shaped pre-revolutionary Russian intellectual history. (The other, no less important to Nabokov, was collectivism and individualism [*RRRI* 8, 94].) Adam Krug, the first of two professional philosophers in Nabokov's fiction, allies himself with Berkeleian idealism when he observes that "consciousness . . . is the only real thing in the world and the greatest mystery of all" (*BS* 316). Like Krug, Van is drawn to metaphysical idealism, and his longstanding interests in terrology and mental illness (as branches of philosophy and psychiatry, respectively) are functions of that fascination.

As youths, Van and Ada "mutely and shyly believed in" an "ineffable hereafter" (*A* 346). After Lucette's death, Van is more explicitly attracted to the idea that personal immortality may be a feature of this hereafter, and it is possible to argue that he weaves that attraction into his memoir. As Boyd has persuasively argued in his monograph on *Ada,* an intricate web of allusions relating to Lucette indicate that her interest in Van's and Ada's lives has survived her death (*NA* 202–10).

Unlike Van and Ada's previous reunions, their meeting after Andrey's death is initially disappointing. In an attempt to avoid an awkward and perhaps ill-fated reunion, Ada returns to Geneva, and Van returns to his hotel room to complete his treatise on time. Upon waking in the morning, Van is surprised to find Ada standing on the floor below him "engrossed in the view." When she explains that she told her driver to turn back "somewhere near Morzhey" (Ada's punning transformation of the locality "Morges" into the Russian "walruses"), Van suggests that her decision may have been prompted by "a mermaid's message" (*A* 450–51). As Boyd has argued, the "mermaid's message" that seems to have emboldened Ada to return to Mont Roux was timed to coincide with Van's simultaneous reflections on "Lucette, now a mermaid in the groves of Atlantis" (*A* 448). Boyd adduces a number of similarly interconnected allusions to conclude that Lucette's "'mermaid's message' is an action manifesting the generosity that characterized her in life, a free gift of kindness that becomes the basis for the happiness of Van and Ada's lives and so of *Ada* itself" (*NA* 208).

Though it is not entirely clear that Van is aware that these are patterned interventions from the otherworld, he is nevertheless preoccupied by thoughts of the afterlife, and deeply ambivalent about precisely the kind of anthropomorphic afterlife that would make possible the interventions catalogued by Boyd. As a fourteen-year-old, he responded to Ada's suggestion that "the soul is immortal" with a crassly worded objection: "You lose your immortality when you lose your memory. And if you land then on Terra Caelestis, with your pillow and chamberpot, you are made to room not with Shakespeare or even Longfellow, but with guitarists and cretins" (*A* 465). A similar formulation returns to his lips in old age:

> One is free to imagine any type of hereafter, of course: the generalized paradise promised by Oriental prophets and poets, or an individual combination; but the work of fancy is handicapped—to a quite hopeless extent—by a logical ban: you cannot bring your friends along—or your enemies for that matter—to the party. The transposition of all our remembered relationships into an Elysian life inevitably turns it into a second-rate continuation of our marvelous mortality. Only a Chinaman or a retarded child can imagine being met, in that Next-Installment World . . . by the mosquito executed eighty years ago upon one's bare leg. (*A* 465–66)[55]

Van admits that Ada "did not laugh" at these words. Instead, "she repeated to herself" the lines from John Shade's *Pale Fire* that they had been translating from English into Russian. Moments later, Van finds himself reaching for his morphine when Shade's lines prompt Ada to reflect upon their culpability in Lucette's fate (*A* 466).

The lines in question confront the moral and emotional dilemmas posed by the kind of anthropomorphic afterlife Lucette's otherworldy interventions seem to require:

> (. . . We give advice
> To widower. He has been married twice:
> He meets his wives; both loved, both loving, both
> Jealous of one another . . .) (*A* 465)

Van's attacks on anthropomorphic conceptions of the afterlife are fueled by his unwillingness to limit metaphysical possibilities to the scope and capacity of the human intellect. Those attacks, however, are also motivated by the fact that the thought of Lucette still fills him with grief. If he has noticed the otherworldly patterns woven into the text of his life, and if he feels invigorated by such knowledge, he might also feel, like Shade's twice-loved widower, that he is undeserving of Lucette's continued love and generosity.

Such guilt may account for the vituperative language in which Van couches his second objection. (When articulating his first objection to eleven-year-old Ada's musings on the soul's immortality, he admits to being mortally distracted by "other desires" [*A* 465].) But there is also something else to attend to here: namely, Van's allusion—the novel's third—to the mysterious, mad, guitar-playing Chinese boy from Barkley College. Mocking the promise of an afterlife populated by loved ones as a fantasy produced first by "guitarists and cretins" and then by "a Chinaman or a retarded child," Van's declarations lead him to a strange bedfellow. Indeed, his remarks seem to imitate the diction and contemptuous tone of Lenin's famous declaration that philosophical idealism is intuitively rejected by "any healthy person who has not been an inmate of a lunatic asylum or a pupil of the idealist philosophers" (*MEC* 56). *Ada*'s "very sick Chinese boy who came all the way from Barkley College" is a highly condensed allusion to Lenin's pronouncement against idealist philosophy. He is at once "an inmate of a lunatic asylum" (Aqua makes his acquaintance at her first Swiss sanatorium) and a "pupil of the idealist philosophers" (his alma mater is at least nominally associated with philosophical idealism).

The remark originally appeared in Lenin's *Materialism and Empirio-Criticism,* and it reemerged again years later in Volskii's *Encounters with Lenin* (*Vstrechi s Leninym*). The latter was first printed in New York in 1953 with a foreword by Michael Karpovich, and it reappeared, in English translation, one year before *Ada*'s publication as *Encounters with Lenin* (1968).

Describing in meticulous detail his long walks with Lenin through the streets of Geneva, Volskii recalls that he had once driven Lenin to rage by citing the Berkeleian dictum *esse est percipi* during a conversation about the merits of Mach's epistemology. Lenin announced to Volskii that Berkeley "should be put away in a lunatic asylum," adding that Mach "must be a complete fool" not to accept the basic materialist truth that the external world exists "independently of any perceptions and sensations." Later, Lenin is said to have observed one more time that only "an idiot" or the "mentally ill" could fail to draw a sharp distinction between a sensation and its material cause.[56]

Contemporaries and intellectual historians have frequently commented on the philosophical philistinism and personal invective that characterize Lenin's writings in general and *Materialism and Empirio-Criticism* in particular (*RRRI* 49–51). Read notes that Lenin's magnum opus was fueled by his anger over the perceived success of the idealist philosophers in seducing Russia's Social Democrats away from Marxist orthodoxy:

> Since Marxism and positivism had allowed themselves to be pushed by the idealists into a position requiring them to establish their opinions on supernatural problems, Lenin was no longer prepared to tolerate any further dalliance with metaphysics. For him, metaphysics in general was only an attempt to obfuscate the "real" issues, that is, man's terrestrial, material, social life, which was the only legitimate concern of Marxists, positivists and revolutionaries. (*RRRI* 54)

Volskii's memoirs bear out Read's assessment of Lenin's motives. As Volskii reports, Lenin wrote *Materialism and Empirio-Criticism* in a sustained burst of passionate hatred directed at his philosophical opponents.[57] He had been deeply upset, for instance, when Peter Struve and Sergey Bulgakov deserted Marxism and embraced philosophical idealism and political liberalism. Lenin also liked to blame Volskii's impatience with Marxist orthodoxy on the fact that Volskii had once attended a seminar taught by Bulgakov at the Kiev Polytechnical Institute.[58]

Like Lenin, Van is a devotee of what he calls "this our sufficient world" (*A* 21), but, unlike him, he is attracted to idealist metaphysics. It seems likely that Van slips into a set of convictions identified with Lenin not because he shares Lenin's philosophical views, but rather because he frequently allows his rage and intolerance to destroy others. (Van's blinding of Kim Beauharnais, the blackmailing photographer and former kitchen boy at Ardis Hall, makes it easy to imagine what forms of ruthless revenge he would have visited upon Percy de Prey and Philip Rack had fate not beaten him to it.) By linking Van's objections to an anthropomorphic afterlife to Lenin's vituperations through the sick Chinese boy from Barkley College, Nabokov is drawing attention to the uncertainty of all knowledge and, by extension, to the foolishness of dismissing the metaphysical beliefs of others. Whatever our personal convictions, *Ada* enjoins its readers to consider these possibilities from a stance diametrically opposed to that adopted by Van and Lenin. Nabokov certainly counts on this kind of sympathetic tolerance from his readers when he opens *Speak, Memory* with a confession of his own fruitless investigations into the beyond:

> Over and over again, my mind has made colossal efforts to distinguish the faintest of personal glimmers in the impersonal darkness on both sides of my life. . . . I have journeyed back in thought—with thought hopelessly tapering off as I went—to remote regions where I groped for some secret outlet only to discover that the prison of time is spherical and without exits. Short of suicide, I have tried everything. I have doffed my identity in order to pass for a conventional spook and steal into realms that existed before I was conceived. I have mentally endured the degrading company of Victorian lady novelists and retired colonels who remembered having, in former lives, been slave messengers on a Roman road or sages under the willows of Lhasa. (*SM* 369–70)

Van's efforts to demean the possibility of personal immortality are shown to be both arrogant and short-sighted. The allusions that link Van, Lenin, and Berkeley through the Chinese boy perform as a double refutation. Lenin identifies idealist philosophers with lunatics, and *Ada* turns this gambit on its head by granting Antiterra's lunatics an epistemic privilege unavailable to their "sane" peers.[59] *Ada*'s readers recognize that Aqua's visions of Terra provide a strikingly accurate picture of their world: the "alabaster buildings one hundred stories high" and the "giant flying sharks with lateral eyes taking barely one night to carry pilgrims through black ether across an entire continent from dark to shining sea" are poetic renditions of our modern skyscrapers and jet-propelled airplanes (*A* 22). Additionally, Antiterra's "lunatics" experience these visions in ways that corroborate the foundational arguments and convictions of Berkeley, the arch-enemy of Lenin's crusade against idealism.

Van's errors are also highlighted by *Ada*'s frequent metaliterary tropes. He seems to regard these chiefly as clever aesthetic flourishes, but they do establish analogies for the metaphysical structure of the universe inhabited by Nabokov and his readers. *Ada*'s obsessive self-reflexivity reminds its readers of their own world. It bears repeating that the world of the novel's readers has been made, under the name Terra, to serve as a hereafter in which (literary) immortality might yet be extended to the novel's agents.

Van's short-sighted dismissal of an anthropomorphic hereafter has a precedent in two episodes in Nabokov's earlier fiction. In *The Gift,* Fyodor's friend Alexander Yakovlevich dies a skeptic because he puts too much faith in his powers of deduction:

> The following day he died, but before that he had a moment of lucidity, complaining of pains and then saying (it was darkish in the room because of the lowered blinds): "What nonsense. Of course there is nothing afterwards." He sighed, listened to the trickling and drumming outside the window and repeated with extreme distinctness: "There is nothing. It is as clear as the fact that it is raining."

Fyodor seems to derive enormous pleasure from the knowledge that the world was refuting his friend's dying words even as he spoke them: "And meanwhile outside the spring sun was playing on the roof tiles, the sky was dreamy and cloudless, the tenant upstairs was watering the flowers on the edge of her balcony, and the water trickled down with a drumming sound" (*Gift* 312).

Alexander Yakovlevich's deathbed skepticism finds a rich counterpoint in John Shade's metaphysical optimism before his own death. Minutes before he is shot and killed, Shade pens these lines in conclusion to *Pale Fire:*

> I feel I understand
> Existence, or at least a minute part
> Of my existence, only through my art,
> In terms of combinational delight;
> And if my private universe scans right,
> So does the verse of galaxies divine
> Which I suspect is an iambic line.
> I'm reasonably sure that we survive
> And that my darling somewhere is alive,
> As I am reasonably sure that I
> Shall wake at six tomorrow, on July
> The twenty-second, nineteen fifty-nine,
> And that the day will probably be fine. (*PF* lines 971–82)

Though Shade's cautious "reasonably sure" and "probably" acknowledge that one's private fate is not capable of proving any grand cosmological point, his death savagely bursts into his hard-won recovery of the harmonious, spiritualized universe of his childhood.

Painful ironies of this kind are reminders of the ineluctable uncertainty of all human knowledge and of the need for tolerance and humility in the face of such uncertainty. Van's scorn for those "Oriental prophets and poets" who are capable of believing in a "generalized paradise" (*A* 465–66) seems innocuous because he lives on a planet on which the "political" appears (deceptively, as these allusions demonstrate) to have been severed from the "poetical." On Antiterra's sister planet, however, Van's comment loses its innocence if we remember, as Read enjoins us to do, that Lenin's intolerance and instinctive, repeated tendency to view idealist philosophy as a form of lunacy congealed into a terrifying reality. Under the political dispensation Lenin set in place, dissent from the party line was regarded as a psychological malady and not infrequently submitted to psychiatric treatment (*RRRI* 56).

ART/LIFE

Ada's Berkeleian subtext is no key to Nabokov's personal philosophy, and Nabokov was not signing on to the full contours of Berkeley's philosophy when he identified himself, tongue firmly in cheek, as an "indivisible monist." But as Dale Peterson has perceptively noted, "although shy of metaphysics and contemptuous of vulgar spiritualism, Nabokov fully appreciated the need for some recourse to alleviate the pain of early dispossession of a world of remembered harmony and grace."[60] Berkeley's idealist philosophy provides the kind of remedy described by Peterson. Embedded as it is in Nabokov's most flamboyant exercise in fiction-making, it provides a heuristic for his understanding of the connection between art and lived experience. Marina's herbarium exposes the true family relations between Van and Ada; it also exposes, by way of the artificial flowers preserved in it, what Nabokov took to be art's relationship to life. As in the case of Van and Ada, this relationship turns out to be dangerously and inconveniently close.

Marina, a self-involved aspiring actress, compiles a herbarium that also serves as a botanical record of the tumultuous events surrounding her son's birth and subsequent adoption. This "regular little melodrama acted out by the ghosts of dead flowers" is a parody of art (*A* 10). Narcissistic and self-serving, Marina uses it to transform the world into her own image. Such an approach to art is dismissive of a different kind of art, exemplified here by the Chinese boy from Barkley College. "Fancy flower of paper, found in Aqua's purse. Ex, 16.II.1870, made by a fellow patient, at the Home, which is no longer hers," reads the label to one of the two contributions the Chinese boy makes to the herbarium. Ada's feverish passion for accuracy in both art and nature leads her to revolt against her mother's offhand description: "The paper flower so cavalierly dismissed is a perfectly recognizable reproduction of an early-spring sanicle that I saw in profusion on hills in coastal California last February. Dr. Krolik, our local naturalist, . . . has determined the example I brought back from Sacramento to Ardis, as the Bear-Foot." The "artificial edelweiss" that makes up the Chinese boy's second contribution to the herbarium is similarly dignified with a taxonomic identity: "the *Pied de Lion* from that poor little Christmas larch, is by the same hand," Ada observes (*A* 11, 12).

The Chinese boy's ghostly presence in Marina's herbarium serves as a reminder that art is inseparable from life and nature. Two years before Nabokov began writing *Ada,* he drew the following analogy between the world and a work of art:

> A creative writer must study carefully the works of his rivals, including the Almighty. He must possess the inborn capacity not only of recombining but of re-creating the given world. In order to do this adequately, avoiding duplication of labor, the artist should *know* the given world. Imagination without knowledge leads no farther than the back yard of primitive art, the child's scrawl on the fence, and the crank's message in the market place. (*SO* 32; emphasis in original)

The Chinese boy from Barkley College illustrates this kind of educated imagination. His artificial flowers are praised by Ada because they precisely and faithfully transpose the natural world into the medium of art. (Ada's interest in drawing fanciful but plausible hybrids is a reflection of her respect for the given world and its possibilities.) This commitment identifies the Chinese boy as a genuine artist and sets him apart from Marina, whose ego frequently distorts and trivializes what it touches. The Chinese boy's ability to reconstruct in Switzerland "a perfectly recognizable reproduction" of a flower he probably once saw in California suggests that he is, like his creator, an aficionado of the art of memory.

Like the critics who have attacked the perceived triviality of Nabokov's work (Kingsley Amis, Hugh Kenner) or its artifice (Dwight Macdonald, Frank Kermode), Marina draws too sharp a distinction between art and life. According to Marina, the Chinese boy's "artificial edelweiss" and "fancy flower of paper" (unlike the specimens originating on the slopes of Ex such as the "*Ancolie Bleue des Alpes*" and the "*Epervière auricule*") belong too clearly to the world of art to reward any search for their counterparts in nature. But such logic diminishes both life and art, and Nabokov conjures Berkeley's ghost to remind us of the ties that bind art to the world of experience. According to Berkeley, the blood that courses through the veins of life also fills the veins of art. They share the same ontology. In this, art and life are like Van and Ada: siblings who seek to conceal their consanguinity by flaunting their differences.

Van's bold declaration that "there is nothing more splendid than lone thought" (*A* 431) echoes the views of his creator. But to interpret these views apart from the broader circumstances of Nabokov's life is to conclude that he was championing the kind of artistic recklessness represented by Kinbote's uncle Conmal, Zembla's first translator of Shakespeare. Insulated from experience, Conmal's vast scholarly achievements are as droll as they are irresponsible. Having mastered the English language "by learning a lexicon by heart," Conmal spends half of a century translating "the works of him whom he called 'dze Bart'" (*PF* 646). When the faithfulness of his translations is challenged, Conmal defends himself in verse:

> I am not slave! Let be my critic slave.
> I cannot be. And Shakespeare would not want thus.
> Let drawing students copy the acanthus,
> I work with Master on the architrave! (*PF* 647)

A life spent in scholarly isolation is revealed to be as foolish and misguided as a life that scorns the achievements of scholarly seclusion.

Art, for Nabokov, is not, as it is for Conmal and Marina, a diversion from the complications and responsibilities of one's personal life, nor is it an escape from the harrowing reality of history. Nabokov's revulsion toward all forms of tyranny (political, psychological, ontological, epistemological) threatens to obscure his firm commitment to what Van aptly calls "this our sufficient world" (*A* 21). Nabokov's defense of "the scholar's brooding brow" and "offensively thick books" (*Gl* 148) is not an endorsement of Conmal's ivory tower, but a direct response to having witnessed the collapse of his homeland's struggle for liberal values under the pressure of an ideology that disdained and destroyed books and scholars.

For Nabokov, a genuine artist is no mere copy-clerk, faithfully reporting witnessed cruelty and injustice, but a godlike individual who must be willing to accept the burden of evil in a world that is, at least in part, his own creation. Art is central to human life not because it brings us closer to a higher being but because it provides the only means of imposing order and meaning upon a world lacking a visible author. The novelistic touches of Van and Ada's first reunion at Mont Roux are welcomed by Ada "as a frame, as a form, something supporting and guarding life, otherwise unprovidenced on Desdemonia, where artists are the only gods" (*A* 417). Unbeknownst to Ada, life on Desdemonia is emphatically providenced; Nabokov generously interleaves Van's narrative with clues signaling his hidden presence behind the scenes. *Ada*'s readers, enjoying the epistemic privilege denied to characters of fiction, stumble upon these clues and are invited to speculate whether they, too, might be similarly "authored." But should these readers feel as unanchored as Ada, should they feel—as does Sineusov in "Ultima Thule" after losing his wife and unborn child—that their lives "got jammed in the door like a finger," and that the "green armored world" responds by drawing "in its feet so as not to catch the disease," art can still provide refuge.[61]

As Michael Wood has observed in relation to Nabokov's short story "Signs and Symbols," reading fiction is a kind of insanity. The "referential mania" that dooms the story's young protagonist (he labors under the delusion that all natural phenomena contain "a veiled reference to his personality and existence") is also "one of the ways in which we find an author in a text."[62] This story from 1947 dramatizes what its author always maintained: art can never be innocent because it always risks involvement in the deceptions of figurative signification. The "tiny half-dead unfledged bird . . . helplessly twitching in a puddle," the playing cards "that had slipped from the couch to the floor," and the three midnight telephone calls that interrupt the old couple's midnight tea are ominous "signs and symbols" masquerading as life's chance encounters.[63] Like the young boy's "referential mania," art is a form of paranoia, a pathology that makes a silent, indifferent world speak to us. Whether friendly or hostile, such communication establishes that human individuals are significant. This, in turn, tells us that the human individual is worth defending from the depredations of history and ideology. According to Nabokov's "theology for sceptics" (as Wood aptly refers to Nabokov's metaphysical position [*MD* 190]), Berkeley may be as mad as Aqua or the protagonist of "Signs and Symbols" to think that the empirical world is a divine speech act directed at us. Nonetheless, the tenderness Nabokov reserves for Aqua and the young man suffering from "referential mania" is a version of the tenderness he reserves for men like Berkeley, who sought to affirm the dignity of the human individual in a sensually captivating but silent world.

It may be that Nabokov reveals here a personality trait he associated with his father. V. D. Nabokov's letters to his wife from Kresty, written on toilet paper and secretly transmitted to Elena Nabokov by Kaminka, are remarkable in their staunch refusal to succumb to bitterness or complaint. "I am perfectly cheerful, calm, merry, and feel excellent [*ia sovershenno bodr, spokoen, vesel i prekrasno sebia chuvstvuiu*]," he assured his wife as frequently as he wrote.[64] Three weeks after being incarcerated, he tried to console her by reminding her not only that these sacrifices were necessary, but also that others were continually asked to sacrifice much more:

> Always remember the insignificance of the troubles we are going through in comparison with so many terrible sufferings. . . . Our three months will beget us more laurels than thorns. We have everything we want, we live in tranquility, we are busy, we work. Of course I would not want to expose myself to danger for the sake of trifles. But in the panorama of history our imprisonment is a very important and necessary episode.[65]

In the last of his published letters, however, V. D. Nabokov's characteristic expressions of reassurance conclude with an assessment that strikes the reader as a bolt from the blue: "I feel excellent in spite of the heat, exercise daily, eat and sleep well, and cheerfully await the end of this idiotic, shameful, and base comedy [*etoi duratskoi, pozornoi i nizkoi komedii*]."[66] If he continued to think of his colleagues' and his own imprisonment as an "important and necessary episode" in Russia's history of liberation, these words would seem to belie that sunny optimism. His son, who survived his father by many decades and liked to think of him as a "robust and cheerful rebel," knew that there had been no historical compensations for his father's imprisonment (qtd. in *VNRY* 32). Pride became Nabokov's only possible response when he reviewed the many sacrifices his father had endured on the way to his sudden death in a doomed struggle against tyranny.

If, as Wood tells us, "referential mania is one of the ways in which we find an author in a text," the author we find in Nabokov's fiction is a protean figure. He encompasses easily recognized permutations of his personality such as *Mary*'s Ganin, *Glory*'s Martin Edelweiss, *The Gift*'s Fyodor Godunov-Cherdyntsev, *Bend Sinister*'s Adam Krug, *Pale Fire*'s John Shade, and *Look at the Harlequins!*'s Vadim Vadimovich. But he also distills himself into less easily identifiable incarnations. One such incarnation is Botkin-Kinbote, the exile rendered insane by his nostalgia for Russia and rendered a poet by his insanity. An equally unlikely alter ego is Marina, whose herbarium, like Nabokov's fiction, bears the traces of a personal history that belies her most cherished public pronouncements.

Nabokov redistributes himself most radically in Humbert Humbert, the villain who acknowledges during one of his most trenchant moments of self-recrimination that art is a paltry consolation in a world defined by pain:

> Unless it can be proven to me—to me as I am now, today, with my heart and my beard, and my putrefaction—that in the infinite run it does not matter a jot that a North American girl-child named Dolores Haze had been deprived of her childhood by a maniac, unless this can be proven (and if it can, then life is a joke), I see nothing for the treatment of my misery but the melancholy and very local palliative of articulate art. (*L* 266)

Humbert's belated understanding of art's woefully inadequate "palliative" function in the face of human cruelty and suffering allies him with Pnin, Nabokov's most endearing and sensitive fictional alter ego. For this fussy, misunderstood, old-fashioned, exiled Russian liberal, the present is alive with the voices of "Armenian massacres, tortures which Tibet invented, colonists in Africa" and "all the precursors of modern atrocity." For Pnin, these voices are one more reminder that "the history of man" is—tragically, poignantly, unforgettably—also "the history of pain" (*Pnin* 419).

Epilogue

> 28 March [1922]. I returned home about 9 P.M., after a heavenly day. After dinner I sat in the chair by the divan and opened a little volume of Blok. Mother, half-lying, was setting the cards out for patience. It was quiet at home—the girls were already asleep, Sergey was out. I was reading aloud those tender poems about Italy, about damp, resonant Venice, about Florence, like a smoky iris. "How splendid that is," Mother said, "yes, yes, exactly: a smoky iris." And then the phone rang in the hall. There was nothing unusual in its ring, I was simply annoyed that my reading was interrupted. I went to the phone. Hessen's voice: "Who's that?" "Volodya. Hello, Joseph Vladimirovich." "I am ringing because, . . . I wanted to tell you, to warn you . . ." "Yes, go on." "Something terrible has happened to your father."
>
> —Vladimir Nabokov

THERE IS NO REASON TO DOUBT that Nabokov genuinely disliked and mistrusted politically engaged art. In the preface written to accompany the 1963 reissue of *Bend Sinister,* he offers a warning to those who would submit his work to political interpretations: "I am neither a didacticist nor an allegorizer. Politics and economics, atomic bombs, primitive and abstract art forms, the entire Orient, symptoms of 'thaw' in Soviet Russia, the Future of Mankind, and so on, leave me supremely indifferent." Even so, he was ready to acknowledge that the world had refused to indulge his indifference, and that his fiction had been irrevocably shaped by political circumstances:

> There can be distinguished, no doubt, certain reflections in the glass directly caused by the idiotic and despicable regimes that we all know and that have

> brushed against me in the course of my life: worlds of tyranny and torture, of Fascists and Bolshevists, of Philistine thinkers and jack-booted baboons. No doubt, too, without those infamous models before me I could not have interlarded this fantasy with bits of Lenin's speeches, and a chunk of the Soviet constitution, and gobs of Nazist pseudo-efficiency. (*BS* 164)

Nabokov was fortunate to escape these "worlds of tyranny and torture," and his assertion that they had "brushed against" him emphasizes how narrowly he had evaded a darker fate. His art and imagination bear the traces of that encounter and of the pain and horror he experienced when recalling those who had suffered and perished. In the wake of the Second World War, for example, he confessed to his sister: "Much as one might want to hide in one's little ivory tower, there are things that torment too deeply, e.g., the German vilenesses, the burning of children in ovens—children as funny and as strongly loved as our children."[1] His numerous comments on the predicament of Soviet writers are riven by despair at the power with which the state held artists under its thumb. As late as 1965 he could still avow to an interviewer that "when I read Mandelshtam's poems composed under the accursed rule of those beasts, I feel a kind of helpless shame, being so free to live and think and write and speak in the free part of the world" (*SO* 58).

As Michael Wood has noted, "Nabokov never forgot what Pnin scrupulously taught himself never to remember: Buchenwald and all the many other horrors of twentieth-century history."[2] Those horrors weighed heavily upon Nabokov, and in spite of being temperamentally uninterested in political advocacy, he knew that no ivory tower, however inconspicuous and out of the way, could insulate him against the forces of history and politics. He seems to have understood this as early as 1919 when he wrote "Dvoe" ("The Two"), a 430-line riposte to "Dvenadtsat'" ("The Twelve"), a mystical poem written by Blok in celebration of the October Revolution. The protagonists of Nabokov's poem, a charming and cultivated young couple, lead a quiet and contented life on their old estate, but all this comes to a violent end when twelve armed peasants attack them and drive them from their home.[3]

David Bethea is right to argue that the poem is an example of Nabokov's tendency to erect artful hedges against the impositions of history.[4] So is Boyd, who asserts that the poem is as "politically naive" as "the nineteen-year-old who wrote it" (*VNRY* 157). But like so much of Nabokov's work, this early poem is also an earnest attempt to lend dignity to the urge to exempt oneself from the authority of history, politics, and social convention. This urge might, perhaps rightly, be dismissed as socially irresponsible and morally reprehensible. It does, however, also sit at the center of liberalism's commitment to tolerance and civil freedoms. Though sensitive to the high costs of liberalism's public neutrality, Nabokov nevertheless staunchly defended the right to be left alone. Forcefully condemned by critics of liberalism, this right is generally undervalued by those who have always enjoyed it. It is to Nabokov's credit that he never allowed himself to forget its significance. He viewed his self-styled "old-fashioned liberalism" as a sacred inheritance from his father, but it also emerged naturally from his own instinctive nonconformism and from his love for what his most explicitly autobiographical creation calls the "fanciful and rare" (*Gift* 156).

"My pleasures," Nabokov said in an interview from 1962, "are the most intense known to man: writing and butterfly hunting" (*SO* 3). Life taught him that intense pleasures are also intensely vulnerable. He knew, for instance, that even butterflies could get him into trouble. Recalling the time he spent in Crimean exile, he notes in *Speak, Memory:* "On a path above the Black Sea, . . . among shrubs in waxy bloom, in March 1918, a bow-legged Bolshevik sentry attempted to arrest me for signaling (with my net, he said) to a British warship" (*SM* 470). Events such as these reminded him that whatever form they might assume for an individual, one's pleasures, however keen, belonged not to men generally, but to a small and sometimes defenseless minority.

This knowledge lies at the heart of the bright and expansive commitment to liberal values that Nabokov shared with his father. The moral courage and leadership V. D. Nabokov demonstrated when he called for the decriminalization of homosexual practices among consenting adults were natural extensions of his liberalism. So, too, was his advocacy on behalf of Russia's Jewish communities. "In home politics I am strongly anti-segregationist" is a statement that reminds us that his son, too, was not always "on the government's side," and that he was unconditionally loyal—when national security was not at stake—to the liberal identity he so passionately claimed as his own (*SO* 98). He took great pride in the fact that the abolition of Russian serfdom by Alexander II had preceded by two years Lincoln's Emancipation Proclamation (qtd. in *VNAY* 143). He similarly attacked American racism when criticizing the publishing industry's refusal to countenance books about "a Negro-White marriage which is a complete and glorious success resulting in lots of children and grandchildren" (OB 295).

Nabokov preferred to remain on the margins of political events and debates, but he also understood that his desire to be left alone could only be the gift of a particular kind of political arrangement. This bitter irony lies at the heart of his art and carefully crafted public persona. His frequent assertions about the uniqueness of his genius ("no creed or school has had any influence on me whatsoever" [*SO* 3]) is the same kind of "mastertrick" he boasts of when noting that Martin is "not necessarily interested in politics" (*Gl* xii). Like Martin, Nabokov had no interest in politics and valued fiercely his eccentricity,[5] but he knew that his capacity to remain a nonconformist and to exempt himself from politics depended on men like *Glory*'s Zilanov and his own father, Russian liberals whose "intense" political activism was the only means by which such freedoms could be secured.

Nabokov's self-styled "supreme indifference" to politics must be understood in two distinct but mutually reinforcing ways. First, it is a version of the Kadet Party's official commitment to remain "above politics" for the sake of promoting a universal commitment to law independent of class or party interests. For Rosenberg, the party's apolitical nature was ultimately responsible for its inability to play a decisive role in shaping Russia's post-revolutionary future. The high premium the Kadet "party of professors" placed on individual autonomy made it incapable of undertaking the coercive measures that secured Lenin's ultimate triumph (*LRR* 472). Like his father, who upheld to the end the party's founding principles of *nadklassnost'* and *nadpartiinost'* against Miliukov's efforts to politicize it, Nabokov remained loyal to the liberal vision of a world in which the law protects individuals from politics (*LRR* 462).

Nabokov's yearning for a world in which the apolitical individual can flourish provides the second vantage point from which his self-styled indifference to politics must be understood. By deliberately avoiding didacticism and political commentary in his fiction, Nabokov was rebelling against the intellectual coercion that had become such an inseparable component of Russian letters. In a 1968 interview with Martin Esslin, Nabokov explained that the crimes perpetrated by Lenin, Stalin, and their supporters were part of a long tradition of disguising intellectual oppression as a commitment to social relevance and progressive politics:

> A hundred years ago, in Russia, the most eloquent and influential reviewers were left-wing, radical, utilitarian, political critics, who demanded that . . . a literary artist be a "reporter on the topics of the day," a social commentator, a class-war correspondent. That was half a century before the Bolshevist police not only revived the dismal so-called progressive (really, regressive) trend characteristic of the eighteen sixties and seventies, but, as we all know, enforced it. . . . The dreary principles once voiced in the reign of Alexander the Second and their subsequent sinister transmutation into the decrees of gloomy police states . . . come to my mind whenever I hear today retro-progressive book reviewers in America and England plead for a little more social comment, a little less artistic whimsy. (*SO* 111–12)

In a cultural context in which didacticism and political commentary were associated with increasingly entrenched forms of tyranny, a commitment to "aesthetic bliss" can only look like a principled and evocative political manifesto.

In his tribute to the nineteenth-century administrator of Russia's first juvenile shelter, V. D. Nabokov describes Nicholas (Nikolai) Rukavishnikov in terms that could be used to characterize his own resplendent career:

> We see in him that rare and striking example of an individual who unexpectedly experiences his public calling, and wholly taken up by this feeling, without wavering and without turning back, and without a thought to the *sacrifice* of his personal happiness—the word "sacrifice" is inappropriate here—but simply abolishing all personal interests for the sake of that public work on which, from this moment onward, the whole meaning of his life was focused.[6]

Nabokov's life and achievements call for a different order of evaluative criteria than the ones listed here, but there is no need to conclude that he inherited an enfeebled version of his father's moral makeup.

In his autobiography, Nabokov describes his father's decision to enroll him, at the age of eleven, at a school "distinguished by its democratic principles, its policy of nondiscrimination in matters of rank, race and creed, and its up-to-date educational methods" (*SM* 513, 517). According to Nabokov's recollections of his years at the Tenishev School, his teachers resented and railed against his aristocratic foppishness and arrogant disdain for progressive communal activities. "The constant pressure upon me to belong to some group or other," he recalls, "never broke my resistance but led to a state of tension that was hardly alleviated by everybody harping upon the example set by my father" (*SM* 518).

Boyd's research into Nabokov's years at the Tenishev School suggests that this self-portrait is misleading. Boyd provides a radically different image of the future artist by summarizing and citing a detailed report penned by an anonymous schoolmaster who taught Nabokov in 1914. This new portrait begins to emerge in juxtaposition to the teacher's descriptions of Nabokov's classmates:

> One, though "very capable, hardworking, serious," is "painfully fond of himself." Another is "lazy, behind in all his courses. Hundreds of justifications and excuses of all sorts. Bully and tell-tale. Crafty, cunning, deceitful: when up to no good, looks you in the eye all innocent." Nabokov's friend Samuil Kyandzhuntsev, though "a very good worker," has "a dose of cunning, prankishness and overfamiliarity [that] demands constant and attentive supervision." Nabokov's even closer friend Samuil Rosov emerges as the model student: "Very serious, conscientious, capable, restrained, independent boy. Fine pupil." At the other end of the class sits the backward giant Grigoriy Popov: "simple, limited; experienced in life, remote from and even hostile to school studies, coarse in pranks, jokes, witticisms, always ready for a fight,

> Popov makes teaching a trial. In difficult moments of the excursion, despite physical strength, proved very weak-spirited, feeble and near tears."

The schoolmaster's evaluation of the fourteen-year-old Nabokov is utterly at odds with Nabokov's later characterization of his relationship with teachers and peers: "Zealous soccer-player, excellent worker, respected as comrade by both flanks (Rosov-Popov), always modest, serious and restrained (though not averse to a joke), Nabokov creates a most agreeable impression by his moral decency."[7] For Boyd, this extraordinary assessment of young Nabokov's moral character illustrates "how strenuously Vladimir tried to follow the precepts and example set by his father."[8] Certainly, the schoolmaster's words evoke character traits that the Russian émigrés gathered at The Pines, Pnin's "fathers and uncles," would have typically associated with Nabokov's father rather than with Nabokov himself.

Nabokov acknowledged that his father's political activism was an ineluctable—and often charmed—component of his childhood: "My father was, indeed, a very active man, but as often happens with the children of famous fathers, I viewed his activities through a prism of my own, which split into many enchanting colors the rather austere light my teachers glimpsed." The frequent committee meetings hosted by his father were heralded by the doorman's assiduous sharpening of pencils on "a bulky old-fashioned machine" (*SM* 518, 519). The men for whom these pencils had been prepared would arrive at Bol'shaia Morskaia "around eight in the evening." "An accumulation of greatcoats and overshoes" convened patiently in the hall as the guests gathered

> to discuss some phase of their opposition to the Tsar. Above the hubbub of voices, a tall clock in a dark corner would break into Westminster chimes; and beyond the committee room were mysterious depths—storerooms, a winding staircase, a pantry of sorts—where my cousin Yuri and I used to pause with drawn pistols on our way to Texas and where one night the police placed a fat, blear-eyed spy who went laboriously down on his knees before our librarian, Lyudmila Borisovna Grinberg, when discovered. But how on earth could I discuss all this with schoolteachers? (*SM* 519–20)

Though Nabokov refrained from trying to explain to his teachers the intricate relationship between these parallel worlds, the shafts of light cast by his father's political activities are refracted into his fiction.

Mysterious passageways, spies, Cousin Yuri, drawn pistols, and even a befuddled librarian make a comeback in *Pale Fire,* the novel that illustrates with special clarity Nabokov's complex attitude toward this father's political legacy. It is also the first novel that Nabokov composed from a position of complete political and economic security. He bestows this security upon John Shade, an American poet who leads a quiet life in the home of his birth. Shade is protected from the dislocations of history and politics, and his misfortunes are strictly personal. This condition seems like a luxury to his paranoid and narcissistic Russian neighbor. Exiled from his homeland by revolution and civil war, Kinbote sees everything through the lens of the politics of his "distant northern land." When Shade is slain by a bullet that was not meant for him, Kinbote interprets the murder as a bungled political assassination for which he himself was the target. Though it is tempting to view Kinbote as Nabokov's antithesis, the temptation should be resisted. As a deposed king obsessed with political conspiracy, Kinbote is a sublimation of Nabokov's own understanding of the incalculable impact of politics upon his own life. As Boyd has noted, Shade is murdered on the birthday of Nabokov's father, who *was* slain by a political assassin bent on killing someone else (*VNAY* 456). If Shade's life reminds us that misfortune can strike at random even under the most congenial political circumstances, Kinbote's life enjoins us to acknowledge that our lives are always bound up in the lives of others. Though this lesson is general enough to have originated from no one in particular, Nabokov regarded it as a gift forced upon him by his father's brave example. It is a testament to his enduring bond to his dead father that Nabokov labored so long and so patiently to probe in his art a lesson that is too easily dismissed as trite and obvious.

Appendix A

Dar naprasnyi, dar sluchainyi,
Zhizn', zachem ty mne dana?
Il' zachem sud'boiu tainoi
Ty na kazn' osuzhdena?

Kto menia vrazhdebnoi vlast'iu
Iz nichtozhestva vozzval,
Dushu mne napolnil strast'iu,
Um somnen'em vzvolnoval? . .

Tseli net peredo mnoiu:
Serdtse pusto, prazden um,
I tomit menia toskoiu,
Odnozvuchnyi zhizni shum.

—A. S. Pushkin, *Sobranie sochinenii v shesti tomakh* (*Collected Works in Six Volumes*), 1:285–86

Appendix B

V chasy zabav il' prazdnoi skuki,
Byvalo, lire ia moei
Vverial iznezhennye zvuki
Bezumstva, leni i strastei.

No i togda struny lukavoi
Nevol'no zvon ia preryval,
Kogda tvoi golos velichavyi
Menia vnezapno porazhal.

Ia lil potoki slez nezhdannykh,
I ranam sovesti moei
Tvoikh rechei blagoukhannykh
Otraden chistyi byl elei.

I nyne s vysoty dukhovnoi
Mne ruku prostiraesh' ty,
I siloi krotkoi i liubovnoi
Smiriaesh' buinye mechty.

Tvoim ognem dusha palima
Otvergla mrak zemnykh suet,
I vnemlet arfe serafima
V sviashchennom uzhase poet.

In times of diversion or idle boredom,
It so happened that I entrusted
To my lyre the soft sounds
Of madness, laziness, and passions.

But even then, the sound of my sly string
I would interrupt against my will,
When your majestic voice
Would startle me unexpectedly.

I shed streams of unexpected tears,
And to the wounds of my conscience
Your sweet-scented speeches
Served as a comforting balm.

And now from a spiritual height
You extend your hand to me,
And with gentle and loving power,
You subdue my tempestuous reveries.

By your fire my scorched soul
Chased away the gloom of worldly cares,
And, to the seraph's harp,
The poet listens with holy terror.

—A. S. Pushkin, *Sobranie sochinenii v shesti tomakh* (*Collected Works in Six Volumes*), 1:321–22

Notes

INTRODUCTION

The epigraphs for this introduction are from Vladimir Nabokov, *Speak, Memory,* 510; and Karpovich, "Two Types of Russian Liberalism," 130.

1. Boyd, *Vladimir Nabokov: The Russian Years,* 168–69.

2. Nabokov, *Speak, Memory,* 513. Nabokov asserts that the debate took place during the spring of 1920, but his biographer, Brian Boyd, assigns it to an earlier and more specific date of November 28, 1919. Charles Nicol, however, emphasizes that only the later date would seem to have enabled Nabokov to rely so completely upon his father's words. According to Nabokov, his father delivered the speech on January 16, 1920; it was published two weeks later (or, as Nicol observes, "two months too late to have been of use" to Nabokov in November). Nicol, "Politics," 628, note 2.

3. Nabokov, introduction to *Bend Sinister,* 164.

4. Nabokov, foreword to *The Eye,* ii.

5. See also Nabokov, *Strong Opinions,* 103–4.

6. Quoted in Boyd, *Vladimir Nabokov: The American Years,* 143.

7. Nabokov, *Dear Bunny, Dear Volodya,* 246.

8. Nabokov, "Problems of Translation: *Onegin* in English," 137.

9. Ibid., 142, 143.

10. Nabokov, *The Gift,* 175.

11. Vladimir Dmitrievich (Vladimir, son of Dmitri) Nabokov will be referred to as "V. D. Nabokov." His son, the writer Vladimir Vladimirovich (Vladimir, son of Vladimir) Nabokov, will be referred to as "Nabokov."

12. See also Browder, introduction to *V. D. Nabokov and the Russian Provisional Government,* 2. D. N. Nabokov's tenure as minister of justice coincided with Alexander II's short-lived but nonetheless very important era of the "Great Reforms" (these included the emancipation of the serfs in 1861 and a significant modernization of the judicial system in 1864). When reactionary advisors to Alexander III insisted that the judiciary be subordinated once again to the tsarist administration, D. N. Nabokov's resistance led the new tsar to order his resignation (Boyd, *Vladimir Nabokov: The Russian Years,* 19–21).

13. The moniker combines the Russian initials ("K" and "D") of the Constitutional Democratic Party.

14. Read, *Religion, Revolution and the Russian Intelligentsia,* 1–2.

15. Nabokov, *Dear Bunny, Dear Volodya,* 222.

16. Gleb Struve, "The Cultural Renaissance," 180–81. Though there are more up-to-date accounts of this fecund period in Russia's cultural and intellectual history, I have relied on Struve's version because of his connection to Nabokov through friendship and a shared paternal legacy.

17. Schapiro, review of Richard Pipes's *Struve, Liberal on the Left,* 119.

18. See Pipes, *Struve: Liberal on the Right,* xi.

19. Nabokov, *Selected Letters,* 485; emphasis in original.

20. Zemstvos were organs of limited local self-government that owed their existence to the reforms passed by Alexander II in the 1860s. The term "liberal" is commonly applied to two parties that emerged from the zemstvos in 1905: the conservative Octobrists and the more progressive Kadets.

21. Pipes, *Struve, Liberal on the Left,* 369–70.

22. Pipes, introduction to V. D. Nabokov's *The Provisional Government,* xii; Boyd, *Vladimir Nabokov: The Russian Years,* 56. See also Pipes, *Struve, Liberal on the Left,* 369–70; and George Fischer, *Russian Liberalism,* 181–88.

23. Nabokov, *Pnin,* 417.

24. Diment, *Pniniad,* 48–51.

25. Barabtarlo, *Phantom of Fact,* 56–57; Connolly, "A Note on the Name 'Pnin,'" 32–33; Diment, *Pniniad,* 42; Field, *VN: The Life and Art of Vladimir Nabokov,* 295.

26. Walicki, *Legal Philosophies of Russian Liberalism,* 24–25. Diment points out that though Nabokov never identified a link between his invented creature and the historical Pnin, his sister—Elena Sikorskaia—immediately made the connection after reading two chapters of the novel in the *New Yorker.* Diment persuasively reconstructs the circumstances under which Nabokov would have come across a detailed biography of Ivan Pnin (Diment, *Pniniad,* 42–44). More recently, Stanislav Shvabrin has speculated that Nabokov's choice of name for his eponymous protagonist may have been guided by a polemic waged over Ivan Pnin's convictions between early-twentieth-century Russian liberals (such as V. D. Nabokov's colleague Aleksandr Kizevetter) and post-revolutionary Soviet historians. See Shvabrin, "Vladimir Vladimirovich Nabokov, Ivan Petrovich Pnin: An Earlier Encounter?"

27. In an interview from 1966, Nabokov offers the following retrospective speculation: "It is not improbable that had there been no revolution in Russia, I would have devoted myself entirely to lepidopterology and never written any novels at all" (Nabokov, *Strong Opinions,* 100).

28. Joseph Hessen, *V dvukh vekakh,* 154; Zimmerman, "Between Revolution and Reaction," 23, note 56.

29. Peter Struve, "Pamiati Vladimira Dmitrievicha Nabokova" ["In Memory of Vladimir Dmitrievich Nabokov"], 192.

30. Emmons, *The Formation of Political Parties,* 29–30.

31. Nabokov, for instance, was close friends in the emigration with Ilya Fondaminsky and Vladimir Zenzinov, both editors of the influential "thick" journal *Sovremennye zapiski* (*Contemporary Annals*). Both men had been prominent Socialist Revolutionaries. Michael Karpovich, Nabokov's friend in America, had also been a Socialist Revolutionary before joining Boris Bakhmetev's delegation charged by the Provisional Government to set up a Russian embassy in the United States.

32. See also Chernobel, "Vladimir Dmitrievich Nabokov," 427, 431.

33. Rosenberg, *Liberals in the Russian Revolution,* 21.

34. Fischer, *Russian Liberalism,* 46–47; see also Pipes, *Struve, Liberal on the Left,* 284–86.

35. Fischer provides a useful gloss of the term:

> Technically, the term "gentry" is synonymous with "nobility," that is, a landowning class with some hereditary privilege. But in Russia, as elsewhere in Europe, the nobility tended to divide into two parts according to origin and to function. With respect to origin, a more ancient nobility, once sovereign and hence aristocratic, was in early modern times augmented by a service nobility created by the rising monarchs. In terms of function, the service nobility inclined toward military service, local administration, and smaller landowning, while the aristocracy oscillated between high office in the central state and their own large estates. As a result, in common parlance . . . "gentry" refers to the new lesser squirearchy, and "aristocracy" to the numerically slight older and higher nobility. (Fischer, *Russian Liberalism,* 5–6)

36. Nethercott, *Russian Legal Culture,* 13–14.

37. Browder, introduction to *V. D. Nabokov and the Russian Provisional Government,* 10, 11.

38. V. D. Nabokov, *The Provisional Government,* 118.

39. It is worth stressing that it was these men's intense commitment to legality and state-structured order that located them on the party's right flank. Unlike Maklakov, a nobleman with close ties to the tsarist bureaucracy, "conservatives" like Struve and Petrazhitskii espoused social ideals that placed them significantly to the left of the party's center (Emmons, *The Formation of Political Parties,* 74; Walicki, *Legal Philosophies of Russian Liberalism,* 397).

40. Novgorodtsev, "Zakonoproekt o neprikosnovennosti lichnosti" ["Draft Legislation on the Inviolability of Personhood"], 2409.

41. Karpovich, "Two Types of Russian Liberalism," 137.

42. Pearson, "The Vyborg Complex," 77. Prince George (Georgii) Lvov was the only Kadet who did not sign the appeal. Upon his arrival in Finland, Lvov fell

ill and did not leave his room until his departure from Vyborg (V. D. Nabokov, *The Provisional Government,* 82).

43. Zimmerman, "Between Revolution and Reaction," 294, note 58; see also Pearson, "The Vyborg Complex," 75–77.

44. Browder, introduction to *V. D. Nabokov and the Russian Provisional Government,* 5.

45. Schapiro, "The Political Thought of the First Provisional Government," 104. In *The Provisional Government,* V. D. Nabokov dwells at length on the legal difficulties he had to confront when drafting the grand duke's act of abdication (V. D. Nabokov, *The Provisional Government,* 49–55). For a copy of the act, see document 101 in the first volume of Browder and Kerensky's *The Russian Provisional Government 1917,* 116.

46. For a detailed account of the events and tactical decisions that led to the formation of the First Provisional Government and the coalitionist provisional regimes that succeeded it, see Schapiro, "The Political Thought of the First Provisional Government," 100–18; and Rosenberg, *Liberals in the Russian Revolution,* 49–59, 70–74, 111–16, 136–47, 170–85, 191–95, 234–60.

47. Joseph Hessen, *Gody izgnaniia,* 77; and Tatarinov, "V. D. Nabokov i russkaia emigratsiia" ("V. D. Nabokov and the Russian Emigration").

48. See also Pipes, introduction to V. D. Nabokov's *The Provisional Government,* xiii. Though Struve severed his connection with the Kadet Party in 1915, he had maintained a close relationship with many of its leaders. In the emigration, he resumed his traditional role of champion of the liberal-conservative right against the liberal-socialist left (Pipes, *Struve, Liberal on the Right,* 335).

49. Though there is general agreement among various extant accounts of these events, they vary in minor details. As an eyewitness to these events and an intimate friend of V. D. Nabokov's, Joseph Hessen seems the most appropriate source to quote here. See also Boyd, *Vladimir Nabokov: The Russian Years,* 190–91; Chernobel, "Vladimir Dmitrievich Nabokov," 431–32; Miliukov, "Pamiati starago druga" ["In Memory of an Old Friend"]; V. I. Hessen, *V bor'be za zhizn',* 42–46; Pipes, introduction to *V. D. Nabokov and the Russian Provisional Government,* xiii–xiv.

50. Sartre, review of Nabokov's *Despair* in *Europe,* 66.

51. See also Nabokov, *Lectures on Literature,* 6.

52. Karlinsky, "Introduction: Dear Bunny, Dear Volodya," 22. Karlinsky's insights are guided by Nabokov's numerous statements to this effect. In *The Gift,* for instance, Fyodor observes that the insistence of Russia's radical intelligentsia on "civic" relevance in literature was ultimately no different than the insistence of the tsar's censors that aesthetic considerations be subordinated to moral ones (Nabokov, *The Gift,* 202; see also Nabokov, *Strong Opinions,* 111–12).

53. Bishop, "Nabokov at Cornell," 237.

54. Rorty, "The Barber of Kasbeam," 198–99.

55. Quoted and translated, in part, by Nethercott, *Russian Legal Culture,* 128; the remainder of the translation is mine. V. D. Nabokov, "O smertnoi kazni" [untitled], ["On Capital Punishment"], 208.

56. The article was translated into Russian and published on the front page of the April 11, 1922, edition of *Rul'* under the title "Lebedinaia pesn'" ["Swan's Song"]. I have only been able to locate a single, illegible copy of the *Daily Dispatch* piece. As a result, I offer my own translation of the Russian version of the article.

57. V. D. Nabokov, "Lebedinaia pesn'," 1. V. D. Nabokov similarly draws upon the forcefulness of literary example in "Otmena smertnoi kazni," 3; "Soviet Rule and Russia's Future," 4; "Plotskie prestupleniia," 136; and "Soderzhanie i metod," 9, 19.

CHAPTER ONE

The epigraphs for this chapter are from Nabokov, *Speak, Memory,* 439; and Plekhanov, *The Development of the Monist View of History,* 274, note.

1. On *The Gift's* complex afterlife, see Boyd, *Vladimir Nabokov: The Russian Years,* 505–6, 516–20.

2. It is worth recalling, too, that Vladimir, Véra, and their son Dmitri's escape from occupied France was a posthumous gift from his father: their passage to the United States was financed by members of a Jewish refugee charity organization who remembered his father's public defense of Russia's Jewish community (Boyd, *Vladimir Nabokov: The American Years,* 11).

3. Scholars have long acknowledged this fact. Boyd's detailed account of V. D. Nabokov's life and achievements in Nabokov's biography is guided by his recognition that V. D. Nabokov played a pivotal role in shaping the character and personal philosophy of his literary son. This argument also anchors Charles Nicol's essay on Nabokov's politics in *The Garland Companion to Vladimir Nabokov* and, most recently, Maria Malikova's "V. V. Nabokov and V. D. Nabokov: His Father's Voice."

4. In his introduction to *Vladimir Nabokov: The Russian Years,* Boyd reads this passage as emblematic of Nabokov's unique writing style and as key to his personality and philosophical interests (6–12).

5. Nabokov, "Father's Butterflies," 216.

6. Johnson, "Recognizing Vladimir Nabokov's Legacy in Science," 150.

7. When Jacob Bronowski had intended to ask Nabokov in an interview from August 1963 whether he thought "scientists are as deeply and personally involved in their work as the novelist is," Nabokov prepared the following reply: "I think it all depends on what scientists or novelists you have in view. Darwin or Gauss were as deeply and rapturously involved in their work as Brown-

ing or Joyce" (Nabokov, "From Notes for Interview with Jacob Bronowski, August 1963"). Readers of Nabokov will know that this description qualifies as the highest praise in Nabokov's lexicon of values. His admiration for Darwin and his achievements should serve as a reminder of the important differences that distinguished his attitudes to Darwin from his contemptuous dismissals of Marx and Freud. In an interview from 1973 with Mati Laansoo, for instance, he explains that only "true scientists of Darwin's type" should have the privilege of traveling to Mars or the moon. By contrast, he sends "Freud and Marx to the garbage can" (Interview with Mati Laansoo, 44, 42). Lumping these three men into one category is only legitimate when speaking of Nabokov's opposition to the positivist, materialist, and utilitarian schools of thought that drew their inspiration from their work.

8. Boyd, review of Zimmer's *A Guide to Nabokov's Butterflies and Moths 2001,* 219.

9. Nabokov, "Notes on Neotropical Plebejinae," 6.

10. Though it can be argued that Darwinism is not a positivistic theory because it does not depend entirely on observation, its widespread association with positivism in the late nineteenth century was not illegitimate. Darwin developed his theory of evolution by recording and systematizing observable data. And although it is impossible to submit all elements of his theory to empirical verification, the theory itself proceeds on the positivistic principle that sure knowledge is derived from observable phenomena and is therefore, in principle at least, empirically verifiable.

11. As Stephen Blackwell has usefully noted, Nabokov's understanding of mimicry included not only "classical mimicry between species (such as the Viceroy's apparent mimicry of the Monarch)" but also "what is more technically called 'object resemblance' or 'protective coloration.' Thus, in his works, moths can 'mimic' leaves or flowers, and caterpillars can mimic roots (or roots caterpillars!)" (Blackwell, *The Quill and the Scalpel,* 38).

12. Nabokov's argument mobilizes the discourse of "natural theology" famously outlined in the Anglican clergyman and philosopher William Paley's *Natural Theology; or, Evidences of the Existence and Attributes of the Deity, Collected from the Appearances of Nature* (1802).

13. Johnson and Coates, *Nabokov's Blues,* 327–28.

14. Gould, "No Science Without Fancy, No Art Without Facts," 94.

15. Nabokov, "Remarks on F. Martin Brown's 'Measurements and Lepidoptera,'" 76; see also Johnson and Coates, *Nabokov's Blues,* 329–30.

16. Zimmer, "Mimicry in Nature and Art," 54–55.

17. Remington, "Lepidoptera Studies," 282.

18. Boyd, review of Zimmer's *A Guide to Nabokov's Butterflies and Moths 2001,* 219.

19. See Nabokov's letter to Mark Aldanov, October 20, 1941, in Boyd and Pyle, *Nabokov's Butterflies,* 247–48.

20. On May 30, 1942, Nabokov informed Wilson that he had submitted the essay to William DeVane, the editor of the *Yale Review* (Nabokov, *Dear Bunny, Dear Volodya,* 70).

21. Kurt Johnson, "Recognizing Vladimir Nabokov's Legacy in Science," 154–55.

22. Vucinich, *Darwin in Russian Thought,* 372.

23. Poole, "Editor's Introduction" to *Problems of Idealism,* 6, 9.

24. Struve, "O chem dumaet odna kniga?" 311–12. See also Poole, "Editor's Introduction" to *Problems of Idealism,* 58, note 22.

25. See Poole, "Contributor Biographies," in *Problems of Idealism,* 446–55.

26. Although Struve's ties to the Kadet leadership were never completely severed, they were consistently strained. His involvement in the publication of *Vekhi* in 1909 significantly compromised his standing in the party, and his increasingly nationalistic and imperialistic positions led to his resignation from the Kadet Central Committee in 1915. Together with V. D. Nabokov, he assumed a leadership role in Kadet politics after the party's split in the emigration.

27. Dolinin, introductory remarks to "Pis'ma V. V. Nabokova k G. P. Struve: 1925–1931: Chast' pervaia" ["V. V. Nabokov's Letters to G. P. Struve: 1925–1931: Part One"], 116; see also Boyd, *Vladimir Nabokov: The Russian Years,* 26, 55.

28. Peter Struve, "Pamiati Vladimira Dmitrievicha Nabokova," 193.

29. Zimmerman, "Between Revolution and Reaction," 196, 228, 248; Rosenberg, *Liberals in the Russian Revolution,* 456; Browder and Kerensky, *The Russian Provisional Government 1917,* vol. 3, document 1199, 1405–06.

30. A second obituary written by Novgorodtsev appeared in *Russkaia mysl',* immediately after an obituary written by Struve. See Novgorodtsev, "V. D. Nabokov v grobu" ["V. D. Nabokov in His Coffin"]; and Novgorodtsev, "Pamiati Vladimira Dmitrievicha Nabokova" ["In Memory of Vladimir Dmitrievich Nabokov"].

31. See Peter Struve, "Toward Characterization of Our Philosophical Development," 152; Sokolov, *Ob ideiakh i idealakh russkoi intelligentsii* [*On the Ideas and Ideals of the Russian Intelligentsia*], 65ff.; Karpovich, "Two Types of Russian Liberalism," 133, 137; Poole, "Editor's Introduction" to *Problems of Idealism,* 26.

32. Ivanov-Razumnik, *Istoriia russkoi obshchestvennoi mysli* [*History of Russian Social Thought*], 453; Kolakowski, *Main Currents of Marxism,* 2:422; Poole, "Editor's Introduction" to *Problems of Idealism,* 1.

33. Gleb Struve, "The Cultural Renaissance," 184; Rosenthal and Bohachevsky-Chomiak, introduction to *A Revolution of the Spirit,* 20–21.

34. Shatz and Zimmerman, introduction to *Signposts: A Collection of Articles on the Russian Intelligentsia,* xii.

35. See Poole, "Note on the Text and Translation," in *Problems of Idealism,* xxiii–xxiv. On Kant's influential role in the development of Russian idealism, see Poole, "The Neo-Idealist Reception of Kant in the Moscow Psychological Society."

36. Novgorodtsev, "Foreword to the Russian Edition," 83.

37. Novgorodtsev, "O filosofskom dvizhenii nashikh dnei" ["Philosophical Trends of Our Time"], 66; qtd. in Poole, "Editor's Introduction" to *Problems of Idealism,* 29.

38. Emerson, foreword to *Problems of Idealism,* xii.

39. Trubetskoi, "Toward Characterization of the Theory of Marx and Engels," 140.

40. Nabokov, *The Eye,* 27–28.

41. Emerson, foreword to *Problems of Idealism,* x.

42. I am indebted to Stephen Blackwell for directing my attention to Nabokov's connection to Aikhenvald.

43. For Aikhenvald's political writings, see his 1918 collection of essays *Nasha revoliutsiia* [*Our Revolution*]. I am grateful to Olga Voronina for helping me track down the volume.

44. Nabokov adopted this pen name early in his literary career in part to distinguish himself from his father. As the name of a fabled bird of paradise in Russian folklore, the pseudonym might be said to have separated Nabokov from the political overtones of his name and signaled his attachment to art (Boyd, *Vladimir Nabokov: The Russian Years,* 180; see also Nabokov, *Strong Opinions,* 161).

45. See Nabokov, "Pamiati Iu. I. Aikhenvalda" ["In Memory of Iu. I. Aikhenvald"].

46. Blackwell, *Zina's Paradox,* 25–27.

47. Wood, *The Magician's Doubts,* 7.

48. Blackwell, "Reconsidering Iulii Aikhenvald."

49. Aikhenvald, review of *Problems of Idealism,* 335.

50. Ibid., 356; qtd., in part, in Poole, "Editor's Introduction" to *Problems of Idealism,* 50.

51. Aikhenvald graduated from Odessa (Novorossiisk) University in 1894 with a degree in philosophy (Blackwell, "Reconsidering Iulii Aikhenvald").

52. Valliere, "Theological Liberalism and Church Reform in Imperial Russia," 121.

53. Bailes, *Science and Russian Culture,* 81; Boyd, *Vladimir Nabokov: The Russian Years,* 33–34.

54. The idealist orientation of Vernadskii's philosophical sensibilities at this time of his life was not a permanent feature of his worldview. As a student at St. Petersburg University, for instance, he was torn between his rationalist and mystical interests. Though his rationalist streak predominated, his attraction to mysticism remained a mainstay of his life even as he suppressed it in most of his published work. Vernadskii's close association with some of Russia's most prominent neo-idealists made him vulnerable to attacks by Soviet philosophers. In the 1920s and 1930s, he was publicly accused on several occasions of being a vitalist

and criticized for his unwillingness to attack religion and idealist philosophy. See Bailes, *Science and Russian Culture,* 34, 40, 122, 163.

55. Ibid., 18, 197, 81.

56. See cat. no. 2161 in *Sistematicheskii katalog biblioteki Vladimira Dmitrievicha Nabokova* (1904); and cat. no. 2799 in *Sistematicheskii katalog Vladimira Dmitrievicha Nabokova: Pervoe prodolzhenie* (1911).

57. Dolinin, introductory remarks to "Pis'ma V. V. Nabokova k G. P. Struve: 1925–1931," 116–18; see also Boyd, *Vladimir Nabokov: The Russian Years,* 199–200, 401, 435, 506. The latter part of Nabokov's correspondence with Gleb Struve has been published in *Zvezda* 4 (1999): 23–39. The earlier letters were published in two more recent issues, *Zvezda* 11 (2003): 115–50, and 4 (2004): 139–63. For a selection of Nabokov's correspondence to Struve in English, see Nabokov, *Selected Letters,* 288–90, 295–96, 378, 470, 482–83, 535, 548–49. The letters are preserved at the Hoover Institution Archives.

58. Bailes, *Science and Russian Culture,* 147.

59. Makletsov, "V. D. Nabokov—Uchenyi," 1.

60. V. D. Nabokov confirms the defining role of the inaugural lecture in the foreword to his *Sbornik statei po ugolovnomu pravu.* Here he states that the collected essays are informed by the "*profession de foi* expressed by the author eight years ago at the start of his teaching career in criminal law."

61. A. M. Medvedev notes that Tagantsev held the highest rank among the eminent group of criminalists who came of age after Russia's 1864 judicial reform (Medvedev, "Nikolai Stepanovich Tagantsev," 471). For a more detailed discussion of V. D. Nabokov's relationship to Tagantsev, see chapter 2.

62. Tagantsev, *Russkoe ugolovnoe pravo* [*Russian Criminal Law*], 478–89.

63. V. D. Nabokov, "Soderzhanie i metod nauki ugolovnago prava" ["The Science of Criminal Law: Contents and Method"], 2.

64. As Kolakowski points out, Chernyshevski's faith that Russia could avoid the injustices associated with capitalist development did not prevent him from championing "the basic values of liberalism" such as "the 'Europeanization' of Russia, the overthrow of the autocracy, political freedom, universal education, and the emancipation of the peasants" (Kolakowski, *Main Currents of Marxism,* 2:314). Nonetheless, there were significant differences between Chernyshevski's ideological commitments and those of his liberal contemporaries. As N. G. O. Pereira writes, Chernyshevski severely criticized the emphasis placed by intelligentsia liberals on individual freedoms and equality before the law, arguing that civil liberties were meaningless in a country whose majority population struggled for the basic necessities of life (Pereira, "N. G. Chernyshevsky as Architect of the Politics of Anti-Liberalism in Russia," 271–72).

65. Nabokov, *Dar,* 356.

66. Vucinich, *Science in Russian Culture, 1861–1917,* 104, 108. The first Russian translation of *The Origin of Species* appeared in 1864.

67. For a similar account of Darwin's penetration into Russian social thought, see James Allen Rogers's contribution to *The Comparative Reception of Darwinism.*

68. Nabokov, *Pale Fire,* 607; emphasis in original.

69. Kolakowski, *Main Currents of Marxism,* 1:400.

70. Plekhanov, *The Development of the Monist View of History,* 274, note.

71. Shatz and Zimmerman, introduction to *Signposts,* xix. The 1905–06 Revolution and its disastrous aftermath led symposium contributors Struve, Kistiakovskii, Berdiaev, Bulgakov, and Frank to join forces with Michael (Mikhail) Gershenzon and Alexander (Aleksandr) Izgoev and publish a sequel to *Problems of Idealism* in 1909. *Vekhi* (*Signposts* or *Landmarks*) sparked feverish and prolonged debate. It went through five editions within a year and generated hundreds of reviews, commentaries, and analyses. Its authors warned that unless the intelligentsia abandoned its positivist outlook, it would not only fail to attain democracy and social justice but bring to an end civilized life in Russia. They argued that humane political institutions could not survive in the morally relativist climate bred by philosophical materialism and utilitarian ethics. Only belief in a metaphysical world order could uphold the absolute values necessary for the establishment of a free, democratic, and cultured society. The Bolshevik seizure of power and the civil war revived interest in the volume and, in 1918, Struve marshaled the authors of *Vekhi* (with the exception of Gershenzon and Kistiakovskii) and six newcomers (Novgorodtsev, once again, among them) for a new symposium titled *Iz glubiny* (*Out of the Depths*). Though the volume echoed many of the themes articulated in *Vekhi,* its religious content was much more pronounced and its tone was more bitter and personal. The historical forces that were seen to have discredited positivism in Russia also reserved a significant role for *Vekhi* and its companion volumes within the tradition of Soviet dissidence. Several dissidents of note—such as Nadezhda Mandelstam and Aleksandr Solzhenitsyn—regarded *Vekhi* as an important part of their cultural patrimony, and associated Stalinism with the moral relativism nurtured by the intelligentsia's pre-revolutionary commitment to positivism. For this short account of the intellectual afterlife of *Problems of Idealism,* I draw on Read, *Religion, Revolution and the Russian Intelligentsia,* 7, 141–42, 163; and Shatz and Zimmerman's introduction to *Signposts: A Collection of Articles on the Russian Intelligentsia.* See also Read, *Religion, Revolution and the Russian Intelligentsia,* 106–20; and Rosenthal and Bohachevsky-Chomiak's introduction to *A Revolution of the Spirit,* 21–24.

72. Bulgakov, "Basic Problems of the Theory of Progress," 86–87.

73. Vernadskii, "O nauchnom mirovozzrenii" ["On the Scientific Worldview"], 1412–13.

74. Bailes, *Science and Russian Culture,* 18.

75. These correlations between Nabokov's and Vernadskii's philosophies of

science are supported by Blackwell's argument in *The Quill and the Scalpel* that Nabokov's thinking about science can be productively understood in relation to the career of another artist-scientist, Johann Wolfgang von Goethe (1749–1832). Impelled by his awareness of the distortive effects of consciousness upon the act of observation, Goethe's cautionary attitude toward major, abstract theories closely parallels Nabokov's and Vernadskii's insistence on the contingency of science as a correlate of the ineluctable subjectivity of perception (Blackwell, *The Quill and the Scalpel,* 54, 57). According to Blackwell, Nabokov's opposition to Darwinism was motivated by the same principles that drove Goethe's aversion to Newton—that is, "a refusal to accept the universality and comprehensiveness of a partial theory" (ibid., 64).

76. When philosophy became the handmaiden of ideology in Soviet Russia, Vernadskii recalibrated his position without abandoning the core principles that structured his life's work. He met the charge of apostasy leveled against him by Marxist-Leninist philosophers by arguing that a country whose progress depended on scientific growth and development demanded that scientists be protected "from the tutorship of representatives of philosophy" (qtd. in Bailes, *Science and Russian Culture,* 164; see also 180). As Bailes notes, Vernadskii did not shy away from publicly criticizing the validity of dialectical materialism as a guide for science: "While he cooperated with the Soviet industrialization drive and was obviously impressed by the enthusiasm for science and education, he was also just as obviously in conflict with Stalinism regarding the constraints it placed on the free development of science. Not only was he critical of the purges, which directly affected personnel in his laboratory; he also criticized the state of Soviet science and its lack of greater freedom of thought and creativity" (Bailes, *Science and Russian Culture,* 165–66).

77. In an interview from 1962, Nabokov suggested that a work of art contains "a kind of merging . . . between the precision of poetry and the excitement of pure science" (Nabokov, *Strong Opinions,* 10).

78. Vernadskii, *Khimicheskoe stroenie biosfery Zemli i ee okruzheniia,* 205; qtd. in Bailes, *Science and Russian Culture,* 198. Vucinich refers to Vernadskii as "an accomplished philosopher and historian of science" and Russia's "leading codifier of modern views on the intellectual potentiality of science." He uses Vernadskii's finely drawn distinction between scientific facts and the scientific worldview to frame his closing remarks on the political and ideological tensions that plagued Russian science in the six decades before the October Revolution. According to Bailes, Vernadskii's liberal commitment to the fundamental value of freedom of thought for science and for human creativity in general is his most lasting legacy to Soviet culture and the international scientific community. See Vucinich, *Science in Russian Culture, 1861–1917,* 477–88; Bailes, *Science and Russian Culture,* 197.

79. Plekhanov, *N. G. Chernyshevsky,* 313–14.

80. The metaphysical dimensions of Nabokov's work have received extensive and sophisticated scholarly attention both before but especially after Véra Nabokov asserted in her foreword to a posthumously published collection of her husband's poetry that "the otherworld" (*potustoronnost'*) was Nabokov's "main theme" (*glavnaia tema*). See Véra Nabokov, "Predislovie" ["Foreword"], 3. Boyd has written insightfully on the subject of Nabokov's inquiries into the mysteries of consciousness, his intuitions about a multileveled universe, and his struggle to reconcile fate with freedom. Boyd's work has also been instrumental in demonstrating the importance of otherworldly intrusion in Nabokov's fiction, particularly in *The Gift, Pale Fire,* and *Ada.* See Boyd, *Vladimir Nabokov: The Russian Years,* 447–78; Boyd, *Nabokov's "Pale Fire";* and Boyd, *Nabokov's "Ada."* D. Barton Johnson's *Worlds in Regression,* Vladimir Alexandrov's *Nabokov's Otherworld,* and Robert Grossmith's doctoral dissertation "Other States of Being: Nabokov's Two-World Metaphysic" provide detailed accounts of the structure, provenance, and literary character of Nabokov's metaphysical intuitions. Shorter studies include Grossmith's "Shaking the Kaleidoscope: Physics and Metaphysics in Nabokov's *Bend Sinister*"; D. Barton Johnson and Brian Boyd's "Prologue: The Otherworld"; D. Barton Johnson's "Vladimir Nabokov and Walter de la Mare's 'Otherworld'"; and Priscilla Meyer's "Dolorous Haze, Hazel Shade: Nabokov and the Spirits." Zoran Kuzmanovich's "'Splendid Insincerity' as 'Utmost Truthfulness': Nabokov and the Claims of the Real" registers the author's impatience with the "otherworldly" orientation of Nabokov scholarship and seeks to reclaim Nabokov as a writer concerned with the here and now.

81. Karshan, "December 1925: Nabokov Between Work and Play," 2.

82. Nabokov, "Braitenshtreter-Paolino," 749.

83. Scanlan, "Nicholas Chernyshevsky and Philosophical Materialism in Russia," 78, 65.

84. For more on Nabokov's response to *Materialism and Empirio-Criticism,* see chapter 4.

85. Lenin, *Materialism and Empirio-Criticism,* 347, 349; emphasis in original.

86. Volskii, *Encounters with Lenin,* 66, 67.

87. Plekhanov, "Chernyshevski v Sibiri" ["Chernyshevski in Siberia"], 382.

88. Plekhanov, *N. G. Chernyshevsky,* 325–26.

89. Shcherbina, "G. V. Plekhanov's Views of Aesthetics," 12.

90. Plekhanov, "Unaddressed Letters," 326.

91. Ibid., 310–11; emphasis in original.

92. Karshan, "December 1925: Nabokov Between Work and Play," 4.

93. Aikhenvald, "Pokhvala prazdnosti," 6.

94. Ibid., 12.

95. It is worth noting that Aikhenvald's defense of idleness was politically motivated. As he explains, he developed it in support of the socialist demand

for an eight-hour workday. This is in spite of the fact, pointed out by Karshan, that Marxism is clearly "the unnamed adversary of Aikhenvald's essay." See Aikhenvald, "Pokhvala prazdnosti," 5, 16–17; Karshan, "December 1925," 7. Like *Problems of Idealism,* Aikhenvald's "Praise of Idleness" demonstrates how idealist principles were being pressed into the service of social reform.

96. Bailes, *Science and Russian Culture,* 150–51, 152, 167–68.

97. Ibid., 56, 116. In an essay titled "Politics, Universities, and Science," Vucinich quotes Vernadskii, who came to the universities' defense by arguing that "without the universities the Russian society could not develop the much needed respect for pure knowledge." Vernadskii argued further that theoretical exploration was the universities' primary function and that academic freedom was a necessary precondition for scientific inquiry (Vucinich, "Politics, Universities, and Science," 164). Vernadskii's defense of "pure knowledge" and academic freedom quoted by Vucinich appeared in the 1914 yearbook of *Rech'* (*Ezhegodnik gazety 'Rech" na 1914 godu*), the daily liberal newspaper edited between 1906 and 1917 by V. D. Nabokov, Joseph Hessen, and August Kaminka (Nabokov, *Speak, Memory,* 509). Nabokov's familiarity with these ideological conflicts over higher education could have come not only from his father but also from the various tutors responsible for his and his brother's education for almost a full decade beginning in 1906. It is likely that these young men, "most of them graduate students at the capital's university," and, as Nabokov speculates, each one chosen by his father as "a representative of another class or race, so as to expose us to all the winds that swept over the Russian Empire" (*Speak, Memory,* 490), would have mentioned to their pupils the political struggles that characterized university life. Lenski, the tutor who had the greatest influence upon the young Nabokov, is—for instance—described as a man of "strong political opinions" (ibid., 455).

98. Interestingly, the work of explorer-naturalists such as Godunov was valued by the tsarist government as a useful instrument of Russian territorial expansion and a means of collecting administrative information in Asia. The expeditions ventured under the aegis of the Russian Geographical Society enabled the government to gather "economic, ethnographic, and demographic information in the Chinese, Tibetan, and Mongolian areas far beyond the boundaries of the empire" (Vucinich, *Science in Russian Culture, 1861–1917,* 223–24). Such exploitation of scientific knowledge for the sake of empire-building may also account for Godunov's indifference to ethnography (Nabokov, *The Gift,* 113). The accusation during the First World War that he was "more concerned with Asian bugs than with the glory of Russian arms" (ibid., 128) draws attention to the ways in which his commitment to pure science was felt to be at odds with a nationalist agenda.

99. V. D. Nabokov, *Tiuremnye dosugi* [*Prison Reflections*], 1868, note 2.

100. V. D. Nabokov, "Zhizn' i deiatel'nost' N. V. Rukavishnikova" ["The Life and Work of N. V. Rukavishnikov"], 153.

101. Boyd is surely right when he says that Nabokov's metaphysical sensibilities were influenced by his mother (Boyd, *Vladimir Nabokov: The Russian Years,* 153). As Nabokov writes in *Speak, Memory,* his mother's "intense and pure religiousness" was matched by "her healthy distaste for the ritual of the Greek Catholic Church and for its priests" (*Speak, Memory,* 387).

102. Peter Struve, "Pamiati Vladimira Dmitrievicha Nabokova," 192.

103. Boyd, *Nabokov's "Pale Fire,"* 225.

104. Nabokov, *The Real Life of Sebastian Knight,* 73–75.

105. Irina Paperno notes that Nabokov's fictitious Strannolyubski seems to have been based on "the pedagogue-mathematician and public figure A. N. Strannolyubski (1839–1903)," who gave lessons in mathematics to Chernyshevski's son, Aleksandr (Sasha). Nabokov probably encountered Strannolyubski's name in N. A. Pypin's essay about Chernyshevski's sons ("Synov'ia Chernyshevskogo") in *Zven'ia* 1 (1932) (Paperno, "How Nabokov's *Gift* Is Made," 317, note 18).

106. Though the fact that Nabokov never published "Father's Butterflies" can be used to dismiss its relevance to his thinking about science, Blackwell provides a compelling argument against such a move:

> There were a variety of reasons that Nabokov never followed through on his plan to attach two addenda to *The Gift* ("The Circle" and "Father's Butterflies"), not least among them the novel's troubled publication history: its crucial fourth chapter was suppressed by the journal *Sovremennye zapiski* in 1938, and Nabokov had to wait until 1952 to see the complete novel published. The addendum was prepared just before the onset of World War II, at a time when Nabokov was still experiencing the novel's artistic afterglow. By 1952 he had changed countries and languages and was in the final years of his work on *Lolita.* (Blackwell, *The Quill and the Scalpel,* 213, note 59)

107. Novgorodtsev's "philosophers who remained free of positivist prejudices" are Christoph von Sigwart (1830–1904) and Rudolf Christoph Eucken (1846–1926) (Novgorodtsev, "Ethical Idealism in the Philosophy of Law," 320–21, note 53).

108. Chernyshevski, *The Anthropological Principle in Philosophy,* 114, 115.

109. Nabokov, "Vtoroe dobavlenie k *Daru,*" 99; Nabokov, "Father's Butterflies," 219, 220.

110. Fyodor is literally correct when he refers to the *tschumarae* as "an imaginary flower, an impossible flower." In his guide to Nabokov's butterflies and moths, Zimmer identifies *Pseudodemas tschumarae* as "an altogether imaginary lepidopteron" and adds that "there does not seem to be a plant by the name of *Tschumara vitimensis* (or *chumara, tchumara,* etc.)" (Zimmer, *A Guide to Nabokov's Butterflies and Moths 2001,* 248).

111. Godunov's idealist terminology is even more pronounced in the Rus-

sian original, where *"ideia"* stands in for both the English "idea" and "concept" (Nabokov, "Vtoroe dobavlenie k *Daru,*" 97–98).

112. Trubetskoi, "Toward Characterization of the Theory of Marx and Engels," 130.

113. The quotation has been emended to take into account Dmitri Nabokov's later corrections to his translation of "Father's Butterflies." In the document's published version, "by chance" is rendered as "accidental."

114. Boyd, "'The Expected Stress,'" 24.

115. Dolinin, "The Gift," 166, note 29.

116. Nabokov, "Vtoroe dobavlenie k *Daru,*" 108.

117. Grayson, "Washington's Gift," 56. Boyd notes that the grammatical structure of Godunov's Russian supports Grayson's speculation: the masculine adjectives *bezuslovnyi* and *nastoiashchii* ("unconditional/unquestionable" and "authentic") call for a masculine noun such as *dar* (Boyd, "'The Expected Stress,'" 24).

118. Pushkin's lyric was written on May 26, 1828. For the Russian original, see appendix A.

119. Boyd notes that this additional intertextual connection was pointed out to him in a personal communication by Gennady Barabtarlo (Boyd, "'The Expected Stress,'" 25).

120. Metropolitan Philaret's rejoinder appears in Boyd, "'The Expected Stress,'" 25. For a more detailed discussion of the metropolitan's "Reply" to Pushkin's poem, see Felix Raskolnikov, "Pushkin and Religion," 11–12.

121. Boyd, "'The Expected Stress,'" 25. For the Russian original of Puskhin's "V chasy zabav il' prazdnoi skuki" and my English translation, see appendix B.

122. Barabtarlo, "'He Said—I Said': An Afternote," 29, 30. The strongest evidence for Barabtarlo's argument is the unidiomatic effect created in the Russian original if the personal pronoun *ia* (I) is taken to be the understood pronoun of *skazal* (said). According to Barabtarlo, Godunov is referring to Pushkin's words in the literary present, as in "Pushkin writes." Barabtarlo further notes that the first-person construction erroneously suggests that Godunov once shared Pushkin's metaphysical pessimism, and only in recent years has adopted the view he expresses in "Father's Butterflies." Such a reading, Barabtarlo contends, clashes with Nabokov's portrayal of his own father in *Speak, Memory* and Fyodor's portrayal of Godunov in *The Gift* as men of "strong and unalterable conviction" acquired well before their respective sons' births (Barabtarlo, "'He Said—I Said,'" 30, 33–34).

123. Barabtarlo, "'He Said—I Said,'" 33–35. It is curious that Barabtarlo does not mention Darwin's *The Descent of Man* (cat. no. 2286), the immediate neighbor of *The Origin of Species* both in V. D. Nabokov's published catalogue and on his library's bookshelf. See *Sistematicheskii katalog biblioteki Vladimira Dmitrievicha Nabokova* (1904).

124. The anticipation of the word *dar* is also announced in the word *udarenie* (stress). Barabtarlo attributes this observation to Boyd and Dolinin (Barabtarlo, "'He Said—I Said,'" 34).

125. Quoted in Barabtarlo, "'He Said—I Said,'" 35.

126. Nabokov, "The Circle," 254.

127. Ibid., 268.

128. Nabokov, "On a Book Entitled *Lolita*," 298.

129. Dolinin, "Nabokov as a Russian Writer," 50, 51, 53, 62.

CHAPTER TWO

The epigraphs for this chapter are from Nabokov, *Strong Opinions,* 187; Makletsov, "V. D. Nabokov—Uchenyi," 2; and Maklakov, *The First State Duma,* 1.

A shorter version of this chapter has appeared as "*Lolita:* Law, Ethics, Politics," in *Approaches to Teaching Nabokov's "Lolita,"* ed. Zoran Kuzmanovich and Galya Diment (New York: Modern Language Association of America, 2008), 121–27.

1. Nabokov, *Lolita,* 154.

2. Boyd speculates that Nabokov returned to work on Fyodor's biography of Chernyshevski between the first draft and the first revision of *Invitation* (Boyd, *Vladimir Nabokov: The Russian Years,* 408).

3. Ibid., 416; Dolinin, "The Gift," 136–37.

4. Nabokov, *Invitation to a Beheading,* 24.

5. Sergey Hessen, "Problema pravovogo sotsializma" ["The Problem of Rule-of-Law Socialism"], 22:279, 278, and 30:382.

6. Sergey Hessen, "Moe zhizneopisanie," 748, 749. Most of Nabokov's Russian novels were first serialized in *Sovremennye zapiski: Zashchita Luzhina* (*The Defense*), 1929–30; *Sogliadatai* (*The Eye*), 1930; *Podvig* (*Glory*), 1931–32; *Camera obscura* (*Laughter in the Dark*), 1932–33; *Otchaianie* (*Despair*), 1934; *Priglashenie na kazn'* (*Invitation to a Beheading*), 1935–36; and *Dar* (*The Gift*) (without the controversial Chernyshevski chapter), 1937–38. Vladislav Khodasevich, Mark Aldanov, and Ivan Bunin were regular contributors to *Sovremennye zapiski.* Nabokov's dear friend and the editor of *Sovremennye zapiski,* Ilya Fondaminsky, thought very highly of Sergey Hessen's series of essays on "rule-of-law socialism" and encouraged him to publish them as a book. See Sergey Hessen, "Moe zhizneopisanie," 749.

7. In his short autobiography, Sergey Hessen confesses with shame and regret that his conception of a "rule-of-law socialism" had so thoroughly captivated his imagination as to lead him, during the first months of the civil war, to misconstrue the nature of Bolshevik rule. A few pages later, he states that his synthesis of liberal and socialist principles published in *Sovremennye zapiski* was among his most valuable contributions to social philosophy (Sergey Hessen, "Moe zhizneopisanie," 743, 749).

8. It was at Sergey Hessen's home in Prague that Nabokov first met Michael Karpovich. Boyd, "Nabokov's Transition," 15; Boyd, *Vladimir Nabokov: The Russian Years,* 378; see also Joseph Hessen, *Gody izgnaniia,* 104.

9. Sergey Hessen, "Moe zhizneopisanie," 728; see also Walicki, *Legal Philosophies of Russian Liberalism,* 407–8. I am grateful to Professor Walicki for leading me to Sergey Hessen's recollections of his apprenticeship among *Pravo*'s editors.

10. Nabokov, "Pamiati I. V. Gessena" ["In Memory of I. V. Hessen"], 2; qtd. in Boyd, *Vladimir Nabokov: The Russian Years,* 205–6. Boyd notes that Nabokov's tribute to Joseph Hessen in *Speak, Memory* is based on this obituary from 1943 (Boyd, *Vladimir Nabokov: The Russian Years,* 558, note 33; Nabokov, *Speak, Memory,* 600). The obituary appeared in the New York daily *Novoe Russkoe Slovo;* it was recently reprinted in *Zvezda* 4 (1999): 42–47, along with a small selection of Nabokov's letters to Joseph and George (Zeka) Hessen. In the earlier memoir *V dvukh vekakh,* Joseph Hessen praises his "young friend Sirin" as "the most distinguished contemporary Russian writer [*moi molodoi drug Sirin, samyi vydaiushchiisia sovremennyi russkii pisatel'*]" (*V dvukh vekakh,* 314). On the friendship between the two families, see also the essay by V. Iu. Hessen (Gessen) in *Nabokovskii vestnik.*

11. For an elaboration of this statement, see Dragunoiu, "Vladimir Nabokov's *Invitation to a Beheading* and the Russian Radical Tradition."

12. After American publishers rejected the book for fear of prosecution, Nabokov offered *Lolita* to Maurice Girodias, who published it in the Olympia Press's Traveler's Edition, a line consisting mostly of pornographic books directed at English-speaking tourists. The French Ministry of Interior banned *Lolita* in 1956 along with twenty-four other Olympia titles. Girodias won his suit against the ban in January 1958, the same year that *Lolita* was published in the United States. See Boyd, "Chronology," 858–60.

13. Making its first appearance in 1957 in the *Anchor Review* (along with extensive excerpts from the novel), the afterword was included at the end of the 1958 Putnam edition and most subsequent editions and translations of *Lolita.*

14. See Davis, "On the Banks of Lake Leman." For similar expressions of Nabokov's feelings for his adoptive homeland, see Nabokov, *Strong Opinions,* 26–27, 98, 113, 124, 131.

15. See Nabokov, "Translation of the Gettysburg Address."

16. In a letter dated April 7, 1947, Nabokov informed Wilson that he was working on "two things": "a short novel about a man who liked little girls" and "a new type of autobiography" (Nabokov, *Dear Bunny, Dear Volodya,* 215).

17. Quoted in Suchoff, "The Rosenberg Case and the New York Intellectuals," 160.

18. See Suchoff, "The Rosenberg Case and the New York Intellectuals"; and Horwitz, "Jews and McCarthyism: A View from the Bronx."

19. Several scholars have read *Lolita* as a Cold War novel. The current

chapter shares their intuition, but argues that Nabokov's understanding of the events and discourses of this period is ineluctably shaped by the Russian context which defined his worldview. If there is a limitation to the worthy arguments listed below, it is that they do not penetrate the Russian contexts in which Nabokov's political convictions were formed. Paul Giles is chiefly interested in *Lolita*'s refraction and subversion of the mythologies constructed by the early American studies movement, but he also notes that Humbert contributes to the "destabilization of cold war ideology," and that *Lolita* "resembles the spy novel, an immensely popular genre during this cold war era." Within this framework, the foreign-born, foreign-bred Humbert plays the part of a secret agent spying on America (Giles, "Virtual Eden: *Lolita,* Pornography, and the Perversions of American Studies," 50, 56). For Frederick Whiting, "the threat posed by Humbert can be adequately understood only in the context of the complex intersection of Cold War political and sexual fears. . . . In much the same fashion that political enemies threatened to penetrate the government, sexual others threatened to infiltrate the home" (Whiting, "'The Strange Particularity of the Lover's Preference,'" 835, 836). Both Whiting and Margot Henriksen note that Humbert's corruption of family life and American childhood is keyed into contemporary tropes for political subversion and national vulnerability. The general conflation of sexual perversion and political subversion during the period is also the starting point of Steven Belletto's and Steven Bruhm's readings of *Pale Fire.* For Belletto, Kinbote's invention of Zembla and its revolution is a complex response to American homophobia during the Cold War (Belletto, "The Zemblan Who Came in from the Cold"). Bruhm argues that *Pale Fire*'s representation of queer subjectivity (so vulnerable to fragmentation and replication) gives the lie to "the unified, protected, Cold-War self" and to the idea that individuals can stand apart from the political forces that shape their world (Bruhm, "Queer, Queer Vladimir," 303, 301). Most recently, Adam Piette has argued that Humbert's "hush-hush" research trip to the Canadian Arctic is code for a secret military expedition in search of uranium. According to Piette, this mission is Humbert's training ground in the Cold War techniques—"the camouflage, the surveillance, the brainwashing, the paranoia, the Hooverite victimization, the spy shape-shifting, the propaganda, the play with secrets, code names, fake fronts, the nuclear terrorizing of children, the infiltrations and demonizations"—that he will refine and use to control Dolly (Piette, *The Literary Cold War,* 83–84).

20. Dated December 12, 1952, the letter was brought to my attention by Brian Boyd, who transcribed it in the 1980s from papers in Véra Nabokov's possession in Montreux, Switzerland. These materials were subsequently sold to the New York Public Library's Berg Collection. My efforts to locate the letter at the Berg were unsuccessful, and I am grateful to Boyd for providing me with his transcription.

21. See Hofstadter, "The Paranoid Style in American Politics," 77.

22. Lock, "Transparent Things and Opaque Words," 118, note 9.

23. Szeftel, Jakobson, and Nabokov agreed to work together on an English edition of the twelfth-century Russian epic *Slovo o polku Igoreve.* Nabokov ended up translating and publishing the poem on his own in 1960 as *The Song of Igor's Campaign.* In her meticulous account of Nabokov's relationship with Szeftel, Diment describes Nabokov's resentment toward Jakobson in the wake of Nabokov's failed bid for a teaching position at Harvard (Diment, *Pniniad,* 39–40). Boyd refers to these events in *Vladimir Nabokov: The American Years,* 302–3, but does not connect Jakobson's refusal to support Nabokov's candidacy with their subsequent rupture. Instead, Boyd suggests that Nabokov severed his ties with Jakobson because he was "convinced that Jakobson was a Communist agent" (*Vladimir Nabokov: The American Years,* 311). Lock's account of the story suggests that Nabokov may have also blamed Jakobson for betraying their shared political legacy. "Roman Jakobson," Lock writes, "had been in 1917–18 a member of the student section of the Russian Constitutional Democratic (Cadet) Party led by Pavel Miliukov (and assisted by V. D. Nabokov). Like V. D. Nabokov and his family, Jakobson's parents and brothers moved to Berlin in 1918; Roman Jakobson remained in Moscow until he made his dubious 'emigration' in 1920, first as a diplomat to Tallinn, then as a member of the Soviet Red Cross Mission in Prague." Lock also emphasizes the perilous nature of Nabokov's accusations against Jakobson: "Given these manifold links, it is clear that Jakobson had every reason to fear Nabokov as one of the few Russian émigrés in the United States in a position to expose his Soviet connections" (Lock, "Transparent Things and Opaque Words," 118–19, note 10). According to Szeftel's diary entry on the subject, Nabokov did not confine his accusations to his private correspondence, but called Jakobson a "bolshevik agent" when speaking about him to others. Szeftel adds further that such speech posed a grave danger for Jakobson "in Joseph McCarthy times" (qtd. in Diment, *Pniniad,* 40).

24. See Field, *VN: The Life and Art of Vladimir Nabokov,* 303–4; and Boyd, *Vladimir Nabokov: The American Years,* 311. See also in this connection a letter Véra Nabokov penned in 1976 to Joan C. Daly on behalf of her husband: "I would not mind proclaiming from the top of the Empire State building that I consider serving the FBI or the CIA both honorable and patriotic but I refuse to see what this has to do in a book about my husband" (Nabokov, *Selected Letters,* 557).

25. Samuel, *Blood Accusation: The Strange History of the Beiliss Case,* 229–30, 244, 255.

26. Quoted in Makletsov, "V. D. Nabokov, kak uchenyi kriminalist" ["V. D. Nabokov as Scholar of Criminal Law"], 2.

27. Nabokov worked concurrently on these two projects until the completion of *Conclusive Evidence* in June 1950 and of *Lolita* in December 1953 (Boyd, *Vladimir Nabokov: The American Years,* 169, 226). He describes the

highlights of his father's political career in chapter 9 of *Speak, Memory,* but, as Boyd observes, key events in V. D. Nabokov's life are used throughout the memoir as formal and thematic signposts in the life of his son (*Vladimir Nabokov: The American Years,*164).

28. Nabokov, *Lectures on Russian Literature,* 12. The first line of Pushkin's untitled poem reads "Ne dorogo tseniu ia gromkie prava . . ." I am grateful to Galya Diment for helping me identify the Russian original.

29. Schapiro, review of Pipes's *Struve, Liberal on the Right,* 125.

30. Struve, "Zametki o sovremennykh delakh" ["Notes on Contemporary Matters"], 497; qtd. in Pipes, *Struve, Liberal on the Left,* 388. A different section of the same article is quoted by Schapiro in his review of Pipes's *Struve, Liberal on the Left,* 120.

31. Tatarinov, Nabokov, and Peter Struve's son Gleb belonged to the literary circle Bratstvo Kruglogo Stola (Brotherhood of the Round Table). Tatarinov was married to Raisa Tatarinov, who founded, together with Aikhenvald, the informal literary circle in which Nabokov participated more actively than in any other during his years in Berlin (Boyd, *Vladimir Nabokov: The Russian Years,* 200, 256). Dolinin enjoins us to remember that Nabokov's self-styled solitariness as a young man was a cultivated stance. He notes that in the 1920s Nabokov was deeply "immersed in the literary life of Russian Berlin." As a member of the Union of Russian Journalists and Writers in Germany, he often spoke at its meetings and seems not to have missed any of its jubilee celebrations. He also frequented literary salons and was a member of several societies and literary circles. See Dolinin, "Doklady Vladimira Nabokova v Berlinskom literaturnom kruzhke" ["The Talks of Vladimir Nabokov to the Berlin Literary Circle"], 7.

32. Tatarinov, "V. D. Nabokov i russkaia emigratsiia" ["V. D. Nabokov and the Russian Emigration"].

33. Struve, "Zametki o sovremennykh delakh," 497; quoted in Pipes, *Struve, Liberal on the Left,* 387; emphasis in original.

34. Schapiro, "The Importance of Law in the Study of Politics and History," 38.

35. Ibid.

36. For Walicki's account of what he refers to as Russia's "legal nihilism," see *Legal Philosophies of Russian Liberalism,* 9–104.

37. Ibid., 4–5; Poole, "Kantian Foundations of Russian Liberal Theory," 26.

38. As in the case of V. D. Nabokov, Vladimir M. Hessen will be referred to as V. M. Hessen. V. M. Hessen was the cousin of Joseph Hessen; he is not to be confused with Joseph Hessen's son, Vladimir I. Hessen, who authored the memoir *V bor'be za zhizn'.*

39. Sergey Hessen, "Problema pravovogo sotsializma," 22:279; emphasis in original.

40. Kant, *Groundwork of The Metaphysics of Morals,* 80.

41. Peter Struve, "V chem zhe istinnyi natsionalizm?" ["What Is True Nationalism?"], 507; qtd. in Pipes, *Struve, Liberal on the Left,* 302. Pipes praises the essay as "the most ambitious attempt in the history of Russian political thought to formulate a consistent doctrine of democratic and national liberalism" (*Struve, Liberal on the Left,* 301). Struve himself wrote in the February 24, 1908 issue of *Rech',* the liberal paper coedited by V. D. Nabokov, that the essay constituted his farewell to Russia as he was preparing to depart for his voluntary exile in the West (*Struve, Liberal on the Left,* 301, note 41).

42. V. M. Hessen, "Vozrozhdenie estestvennago prava," 11:544.

43. Ibid., 11:546.

44. Ibid., 11:543–45.

45. Walicki, *Legal Philosophies of Russian Liberalism,* 220; see also Joseph Hessen, *Gody izgnaniia,* 153. V. D. Nabokov also attended Joseph Hessen's Sunday *jours fixes* described in detail by his son, Vladimir I. Hessen, in his memoir *V bor'be za zhizn'* [*Fighting to Survive*], 18–19; V. D. Nabokov, *The Provisional Government,* 39.

46. In a pamphlet written in Berlin and dedicated in large part to the social philosophy of Novgorodtsev, Joseph Hessen revisits the turn-of-the-century debates surrounding natural law, especially as they had been formulated by V. M. Hessen and Petrazhitskii. Conceding that natural law has no specific content and can be used to justify not only the democratic principles of the French Revolution but also those of Prussian enlightened autocracy, he nonetheless argues that natural law will always be called upon to restore harmony between a society's positive laws and its conception of justice. Natural law, he commonsensically concludes, "unfailingly becomes the focus of public attention in moments of crisis [*estestvennoe pravo . . . neizmenno vystupaet na avanstsenu v momenty krizisov*]" (Joseph Hessen, *Iskaniia obshchestvennago ideala* [*Searching for the Social Ideal*], 29–32).

47. Friedmann, *Legal Theory,* 21, 24.

48. Makletsov, "V. D. Nabokov, kak uchenyi kriminalist," 2.

49. Chernobel, "Vladimir Dmitrievich Nabokov, zhizn' i tvorchestvo" ["Vladimir Dmitrievich Nabokov, Life and Work"], 427.

50. V. D. Nabokov, *The Provisional Government,* 67; see also V. D. Nabokov's tribute to his teacher and mentor, "N. S. Tagantsev: K 50-ti-letnemu iubileiu" ["N. S. Tagantsev on his Fiftieth Anniversary"].

51. Nabokov, "Remarks on F. Martin Brown's 'Measurements and Lepidoptera,'" 76. For a discussion of Nabokov's response to Brown, see chapter 1.

52. Spasovich, "Novye napravleniia v nauke ugolovnago prava" ["New Directions in the Science of Criminal Law"], 219–20.

53. Tagantsev, *Russkoe ugolovnoe pravo* [*Russian Criminal Law*], 482, 490.

54. Ibid., 489–90; Nethercott, *Russian Legal Culture,* 49, 52.

55. Nabokov, *Lectures on Literature,* 377; V. D. Nabokov, *Tiuremnye dosugi,* 1872.

56. The concept of *sostitutivi penali* (penal substitutes) was developed by Ferri in his magnum opus, *Sociologia Criminale.* On Ferri's influence on Russian criminal law, see Nethercott, *Russian Legal Culture,* 45ff.

57. The 1845 Code of Punishments (Ulozhenie o nakazaniiakh ugolovnykh i ispravitel'nykh) was successively updated in 1866 and 1885. In 1903, a new Criminal Code (containing some of the far-reaching proposals assessed by V. D. Nabokov) was ratified but never fully implemented.

58. V. D. Nabokov, "Plotskie prestupleniia po proektu ugolovnago ulozheniia" ["Carnal Offenses According to the Criminal Code Project"], 154.

59. Kant, *The Metaphysics of Morals,* 391–92.

60. Rauscher, "Kant's Social and Political Philosophy," n.p.

61. Kant, "On the Common Saying: That May Be Correct in Theory, but It Is of No Use in Practice," 291; emphasis in original.

62. Nabokov, *Bend Sinister,* 227–28.

63. Nabokov, "What Faith Means to a Resisting People," 212.

64. Ibid.; emphasis in original.

65. Frederick Hayek's analysis of the differences between liberalism and democracy explains why the distinction is important:

> By the insistence on a law which is the same for all, and the consequent opposition to all legal privilege, liberalism came to be closely associated with the movement for democracy. In the struggle for constitutional government in the nineteenth century, the liberal and the democratic movements indeed were often indistinguishable. Yet in the course of time the consequence of the fact that the two doctrines were in the last resort concerned with different issues became more and more apparent. Liberalism is concerned with the functions of government and particularly with the limitation of all its powers. Democracy is concerned with the question of who is to direct government. Liberalism requires that all power, and therefore also that of the majority, be limited. Democracy came to regard current majority opinion as the only criterion of the legitimacy of the powers of government. (Hayek, *New Studies in Philosophy,* 142–43)

66. Kant states: "A constitution providing for the *greatest human freedom* according to laws that permit *the freedom of each to exist together with that of others* . . . is at least a necessary idea, which one must make the ground not merely of the primary plan of a state's constitution but of all the laws too" (*Critique of Pure Reason,* 397; emphasis in original).

67. Hayek, *New Studies in Philosophy,* 133.

68. Quoted in Miliukov, *Political Memoirs,* 37; and Browder, introduction to *V. D. Nabokov and the Russian Provisional Government,* 3.

69. Haines, *The Revival of Natural Law Concepts,* 54–56, 172–73. Wallace Mendelson eloquently raises this objection:

> Familiarity obscures for us what to outsiders is a marked characteristic of American government: our habit of dressing up the most intricate social, economic, and political problems in legal jargon and presenting them to the courts for "adjudication." . . . Behind and overshadowing our open commitment to the fragmentation of power lies a brooding, inarticulate distrust of popular government. This finds expression in judicial review, or judicial supremacy. . . . Neither Congress nor the President, no administrative agency, no governor, no state court or legislature, not a single city or county functionary is immune from the centralized power of judicial review. (Mendelson, *Justices Black and Frankfurter,* 125–26)

70. The tension between natural-law doctrine and positivist medical discourses informs Lionel Trilling's ambivalent response to *Lolita.* Though he recognizes that "within the range of possible heterosexual conduct," the sexual relationship between an adult male and a girl "is one of the few prohibitions which still seem to us to be confirmed by nature itself," he confesses that he was "plainly not able to muster up the note of moral outrage." He rationalizes his reluctance, at least in part, by seeing in Humbert's obsession with Dolly a modern incarnation of the "passion-love" ideal. Though this ideal is now archaic, Humbert's story remains credible in a contemporary setting because it is compatible with the logic of clinical psychiatry. Trilling concludes: "Pathology naturalises the strange particularity of the lover's preference" (Trilling, Review of *Lolita* in *Encounter,* 93, 94, 96, 100).

71. The history of the sexual age of consent is, indeed, as complicated as Humbert's scholarship suggests. Vern L. Bullough notes that although the sexual age of consent has historically coincided with the age of puberty, it has sometimes been set as early as seven. Before becoming legally codified for the first time in the Greco-Roman period, it remained a family or tribal matter (Bullough, "Age of Consent: A Historical Overview," 25). Deborah Gorham provides a detailed account of the late Victorian social purity movement that succeeded in raising England's age of consent from ten to sixteen. David J. Pivar and Mary E. Odem document the parallel crusade that led to the enactment of similar age-of-consent legislation in the United States. See Gorham, "The 'Maiden Tribute of Modern Babylon' Re-examined"; Odem, *Delinquent Daughters;* and Pivar, *Purity Crusade.* In an essay from 1951, Robert C. Bensing tabulates and interprets the laws governing statutory rape at the time Humbert cohabited with Dolly. See Bensing, "A Comparative Study of American Sex Statutes." Humbert is correct when he notes that—in addition to varying from state to state—these age-of-consent laws do not always correlate with America's marriage laws. In his annotations to *Lolita,* Alfred Appel, Jr., underscores Humbert's combina-

tion of legal accuracy and opportunistic dissembling on this subject by turning to the first volume of Chester G. Vernier's *American Family Laws.* Humbert's claim that some American states have preserved "the stipulation of the Roman law, according to which a girl may marry at twelve" (Nabokov, *Lolita,* 127) is confirmed by Vernier's assertion that, as late as 1931, twelve states continued to allow fourteen-year-old males and twelve-year-old females to marry. By contrast, Humbert's follow-up claim that "fifteen is lawful everywhere" is false. According to Vernier, by 1931 twelve jurisdictions had set the minimum marriageable age for girls at fourteen, eight at fifteen, seventeen at sixteen, and two at eighteen. See Appel, "Notes," 378–79, notes 137/3, 137/4; Vernier, *American Family Laws,* 115–17. Numerous scholars have persuasively argued that age-of-consent laws have been pressed into the service of repressive ideological projects. The most radical critiques of age-of-consent laws come from child liberators such as Richard Farson and John Holt, who argue in favor of a single standard of sexual morals and behavior for children and adults. See Bullough, "Age of Consent"; Ehrlich, "From Age of Consent Laws to the 'Silver Ring Thing'"; Farson, *Birthrights;* Gorham, "The 'Maiden Tribute of Modern Babylon' Reexamined"; Holt, *Escape from Childhood;* Odem, *Delinquent Daughters,* 8–81; Sutherland, "From Jailbird to Jailbait"; Ullman, *Sex Seen,* 28–44; Walkowitz, *Prostitution and Victorian Society.*

72. Makletsov, "V. D. Nabokov—Uchenyi."

73. Makletsov, "V. D. Nabokov, kak uchenyi kriminalist."

74. Engelstein, *The Keys to Happiness,* 67–71.

75. Hayek, *New Studies in Philosophy,* 133.

76. The article was first presented as a paper at a conference held at Harvard in 1954.

77. Maklakov, *The First State Duma,* 1; Schapiro, review of Pipes's *Struve, Liberal on the Left,* 120; Gurko, *Features and Figures of the Past,* 469.

78. Zimmerman, "Between Revolution and Reaction," 127; Schapiro, "The Political Thought of the First Provisional Government," 114–16.

79. Miliukov, *Political Memoirs,* 374; Pearson, *The Russian Moderates,* 171.

80. V. D. Nabokov, "Vnutrenniaia voina" ["The Internal War"], 523.

81. V. D. Nabokov, "Deiatel'nost' partii narodnoi svobody v gosudarstvennoi dume" ["The Work of the People's Freedom Party in the State Duma"], 1600.

82. Makletsov, "V. D. Nabokov—Uchenyi," 2.

83. V. D. Nabokov, "Vnutrenniaia voina," 522.

84. Ibid., 518, 519.

85. Pearson, *"Nashe Pravitel'stvo?"*; Pasmanik, *Revoliutsionnye gody v Krymu* [*The Revolutionary Years in the Crimea*], 176.

86. V. D. Nabokov, "Po povodu 'Krymskikh ocherkov'" ["Apropos of 'Crimean Sketches'"]; Vinaver, *Nashe pravitel'stvo* [*Our Government*], 63; see also Pasmanik, *Revoliutsionnye gody v Krymu,* 120–23; Pearson, *"Nashe Pravitel'stvo?"* 23.

87. V. D. Nabokov kept copies of these laws and other documents pertaining to his Crimean political activities in a folder that is now preserved at the Hoover Institution. This folder includes, among other things, the laws and orders of the Crimean Regional Government, the project for the transformation of Crimea's tribunals, the government's regulations for the nomination of senators, and various statutes of the Ministry of Justice. See Krymskoe kraevoe pravitel'stvo, box 2, folder 18, "Papers of V. D. Nabokov," Hoover Institution Archives, Stanford University. Vinaver acknowledges that his account of these critical months in the Crimea draws extensively on the documents preserved in V. D. Nabokov's folder.

88. Vinaver refers to these events in order to highlight the brutality of the Volunteers who consistently discredited the anti-Bolshevik movement and the Crimean Regional Government in the eyes of the local population. In Vinaver's account, these victims of vigilante justice were merely alleged Bolsheviks (Vinaver, *Nashe pravitel'stvo*, 203).

89. The panoply of crimes and abuses perpetrated by members of the Volunteer Army constitutes an important chapter in the history of the Russian Civil War. Eyewitnesses and historians agree that the efforts of the anti-Bolshevik movement and the Crimean Regional Government were severely handicapped by the ultra-reactionary, anti-Semitic, and anarchical elements in Denikin's army (Pasmanik, *Revoliutsionnye gody v Krymu*, 137, 139–42, 146–50; Vinaver, *Nashe pravitel'stvo*, 141–52, 158–77, 203–5; Rosenberg, *Liberals in the Russian Revolution*, 333–34, 340–41, 374–75, 377–80).

90. Raymond Pearson refers to V. D. Nabokov's change of heart as common knowledge in the emigration (Pearson, "*Nashe Pravitel'svo?*" 18), and Joseph Hessen obliquely supports Pearson's claim (*Gody izgnaniia*, 116). The most explicit reference to V. D. Nabokov's repudiation of his work in the Crimea is made in a letter he wrote to Kaminka on June 15, 1919, from London. In the letter, preserved at the National Archives of Finland, V. D. Nabokov writes as follows: "I have frequently and with the greatest bitterness reproached myself for agreeing to work with Vinaver [*ia mnogo raz s velichaishei gorech'iu koril sebia, chto soglasilsia poiti v kombinatsii s Vinaverom*]. Unfortunately, I could not have done otherwise. I could not say 'no' to S. S. [Solomon] Krym due to our special personal relationship, and Vinaver's invitation . . . was made to me in a completely unexpected form. I can only say this: no considerations will ever make me enter into such a partnership again." Earlier in the letter he explains that although the winter of 1918–19 and his work in the Crimean Regional Government "left only good memories," the end of his Crimean sojourn ["*final nash*"] "constituted one of the darkest and most difficult pages of my life. In this matter I am not referring to the external side [*vneshniaia storona*] of our odyssey, with all of its troubles, difficulties, and anxieties. It was the moral sufferings [*nravstvennye perezhivaniia*] that were terrible, almost unbearable." It is possible that by "*final nash*" V. D. Nabokov was referring exclusively to the terror and chaos

that accompanied his and his family's hasty evacuation. But his emphasis on his "moral sufferings" (as opposed to the more superficial—"external"—aspects of his troubles) suggests that he was also referring to the collection of antecedent political events in which he had played a critical role and that culminated in the misunderstandings, humiliations, and fears that characterized his flight from the Crimea. I am grateful to Evgenii Belodubrovskii for bringing the letter to my attention and for sharing with me its contents. Professor Belodubrovskii was alerted to the letter's existence by Julitta Suomela.

91. Telegram sent by Konstantin Nabokov to V. D. Nabokov, inscribed at the top: "*Nabokov prosit peredat' bratu* [Nabokov requests to be forwarded to his brother]." Krymskoe kraevoe pravitel'stvo, box 2, folder 18, "Papers of V. D. Nabokov (2)," Hoover Institution Archives, Stanford University.

92. For the documents outlining the new wartime legislation, see appendices 5–7 in Vinaver, *Nashe pravitel'stvo,* 232–36. According to Vinaver, V. D. Nabokov took an especially keen interest in the text of these "exceptional" measures and was deeply concerned about their correct interpretation (*Nashe pravitel'stvo,* 186–87).

93. In his account of the Crimean Regional Government, Vinaver recalls that there were far more disagreements between him and V. D. Nabokov than between him and the cabinet's socialist ministers (*Nashe pravitel'stvo,* 63–64).

94. Pifer, "Nabokov's Discovery of America: From Russia to *Lolita,*" 411.

95. According to Woodhouse, two precedent-setting decisions—*Meyer v. Nebraska* (1923) and *Pierce v. Society of Sisters* (1925)—succeeded in protecting "the family unit from destructive state intervention, but at a high price for children" (Woodhouse, "The Constitutionalization of Children's Rights," 29, 8–9). In a landmark decision from 1967 (*In re Gault*), the Supreme Court established that juveniles accused of crimes in delinquency proceedings were entitled to a variety of procedural protections under the Fourteenth Amendment. But as Laurence D. Houlgate explains, this extension of some constitutional rights to children was narrow in scope: "It would be a mistake . . . to conclude from these pronouncements that the Court, having decided in the late 1960s and the 1970s that children are 'persons,' determined that children should have the same set of constitutional rights that we ascribe to adults. If the Court did see children as persons, then it surely saw them as peculiar sorts of persons for purposes of constitutional analysis." According to Houlgate, the thirty-year history of the Supreme Court's rulings on the constitutional rights of children struggled with the following dilemma: "either children are to be regarded as *persons* with fundamental rights that the state must respect, or they are to be regarded as *human beings* who are always in some form of custody" (Houlgate, "Three Concepts of Children's Constitutional Rights," 78–80; emphasis in original).

96. Hayek, *New Studies in Philosophy,* 133.

97. Wald, "Children's Rights: A Framework for Analysis," 276, note 82, 260, note 22.

98. Nabokov, *Lectures on Russian Literature,* 2.

99. Ibid.

100. Humbert's portrayal of the institutional alternatives open to Dolly in the event of their affair's exposure is opportunistic but not inaccurate. His prediction that he will go to jail while Dolly—as a "dependent, neglected, incorrigible and delinquent" child—will be "analyzed and institutionalized" resonates with factual reality (Nabokov, *Lolita,* 140–41). As Odem writes, most young women involved in statutory rape cases were portrayed by the courts as either helpless victims or troubled delinquents. Both groups were sent to state institutions for their protection and rehabilitation. The system of juvenile courts, special police bureaus, detention centers, and reformatories set up by progressive reformers during the first decades of the twentieth century to monitor and regulate the sexuality of young women was firmly in place during Humbert and Dolly's years of cohabitation. See Odem, *Delinquent Daughters,* 95–127. Pifer and Kuzmanovich have written perceptively about Nabokov's keen sensitivity to the vulnerability of children. Though this tender concern for children—so conspicuous in novels such as *Bend Sinister, Lolita, Pale Fire,* and *Ada*—sprang naturally from Nabokov's own parental affections and anxieties, a secondary source may have been his father's scholarly interests. On April 4, 1901, V. D. Nabokov opened the third convention of Russia's chapter of the International Union of Criminalists with an extended tribute to the achievements of N. V. Rukavishnikov, a nineteenth-century philanthropist who dedicated the last five years of his short life to the administration of Russia's first juvenile shelter. V. D. Nabokov describes in close detail not only the far-reaching reforms Rukavishnikov introduced during his inspired administration, but also the paternal love, care, and tenderness he bestowed upon his charges. He further praises Rukavishnikov's insistence on "the necessity for a strict classification system for vicious and criminal children by age" that would enable caregivers to draw meaningful distinctions between the correctional efforts aimed at small children and the more compulsory measures needed for the education of older children (V. D. Nabokov, "Zhizn' i deiatel'nost' N. V. Rukavishnikova," 154–55, 157). Like his evaluation of the proposed reforms to the 1845 Russian Code of Punishments, V. D. Nabokov's speech to his fellow criminalists demonstrates an abiding interest in the relationship between age and vulnerability that his son was to showcase in *Lolita.*

101. Beiner, *What's the Matter with Liberalism?* 36.

102. Though the word "privacy" does not appear in the U.S. Constitution, the document's first ten amendments (the Bill of Rights) guarantee certain freedoms from interference and intrusion that can be understood to embody the concept of privacy. Though the concept of privacy was frequently invoked by the Supreme Court in its interpretations of the Bill of Rights and the Fourteenth Amendment, it was not until the 1960s that the term "privacy" was given a key role in the interpretation of the Fourteenth Amendment. The proliferation of

privacy-related law in the United States has fueled a heated debate between liberals and their communitarian, progressive, and feminist critics who contend that a commitment to privacy interferes with the pursuit of the common good. This overview of privacy-related American jurisprudence draws on Anita Allen's "Privacy in American Law." For the communitarian critique see Etzioni, *The Limits of Privacy;* for the progressive critique, see Kennedy, "The Stages of the Decline of the Public-Private Distinction," and Peller, "The Metaphysics of American Law"; for the feminist critique, see MacKinnon, *Toward a Feminist Theory of the State.*

103. *Lolita*'s celebration of American tolerance is not unequivocal, and several scholars have drawn attention to the novel's critique of American anti-Semitism. In his annotations to *Lolita,* Appel documents what he refers to as the novel's "anti-Semitism theme." See Appel, "Notes," 367, note 77/1; 368, note 81/1; 373, note 120/1; 423–24, note 263/4; 435, note 299/2. Douglas Anderson argues that Humbert's dream of fathering two successive generations upon Dolly serves as "an imaginative equivalent for the insane solipsism of blood and race that the 1935 Nuremberg Laws enacted at the outset of the Nazi policy of extermination" (Anderson, "Nabokov's Genocidal and Nuclear Holocausts in *Lolita,*" 79). Susan Mizruchi argues that *Lolita*'s "holocaust subtext" exposes methodological and doctrinal affinities between Humbert's self-defense and the strategies of self-defense used by Nazi war criminals tried at Nuremberg. Among the "crucial continuities between some of Humbert's most cherished beliefs and Nazi ideology" is Humbert's "positivistic" tendency to see individuals as sociological types (Mizruchi, "*Lolita* in History," 637–38, 640). My reading of *Lolita* as an exploration of the perils of legal positivism is related to these arguments. Schapiro has made a persuasive case that the Nazis' rise to power and ability to entrench themselves in office so successfully was largely due to their exploitation of the legal-positivist traditions that dominated German jurisprudence during the Weimar Republic. See Schapiro, "The Importance of Law in the Study of Politics and History," 32–34, 40.

104. Belknap, *Cold War Political Justice,* 27.

105. *Lolita* has a much earlier precursor in *The Enchanter,* a novella Nabokov wrote in 1939 in Paris under the title *Volshebnik. The Enchanter* also tells the story of a middle-aged man who marries a woman in order to gain access to her young daughter, but, as Dmitri Nabokov observes in his epilogue to his English translation of the novella, "*Lolita* is unquestionably the product of very new and different artistic stimuli" (Dmitri Nabokov, "On a Book Entitled *The Enchanter,*" 107). It is worth noting that *Lolita*'s legal framework and Humbert's invocation of legal positivism in defense of his actions have no precedent in *The Enchanter.* Perhaps even more significant for my argument is the fact that *The Enchanter*'s protagonist fails to have intercourse with his victim. The young girl's screams not only expose his nefarious designs but lead to his death

as he tries to flee the scene. *The Enchanter's* European setting clearly did not provide its protagonist with the same freedoms as the United States bestowed so lavishly upon Humbert.

106. Belknap, *Cold War Political Justice,* 6.

107. Schrecker, *The Age of McCarthyism,* 27.

108. Belknap, *Cold War Political Justice,* 4. Belknap borrows the term from Otto Kirchheimer and Theodore L. Becker, whose individual works show how governments manipulate the legal system to serve political ends.

109. After his landslide victory in the 1936 presidential election, Franklin D. Roosevelt tried to pass the Judiciary Reorganization Bill (the so-called "court-packing" bill) with the intention of appointing a more progressive cohort of justices to the Supreme Court. The scheme's subordination of law to politics stirred anxiety in the American public and the bill failed. Roosevelt was able to reconstitute the Supreme Court by appointing eight new justices to the bench by following established procedure.

110. Friedmann, *Legal Theory,* 142.

111. Ibid., 143–44; Hall et al., *American Legal History,* 490.

112. The long-standing conflict between the claims of judicial activism and restraint in the debates surrounding the proper role of the American judiciary was particularly acute during this period. See Wallace Mendelson, *Justices Black and Frankfurter.*

113. Schrecker quotes Justice Robert Jackson, who explained in 1949 that the Court felt "it would be an unwarranted act of judicial usurpation to strip Congress of its investigatory power or to assume for the courts the function of supervising congressional committees" (Schrecker, *McCarthyism,* 67).

114. Griffith, *Judge Learned Hand and the Role of the Federal Judiciary,* 208; see also Belknap, *Cold War Political Justice,* 127; and *United States v. Dennis.*

115. The *Dennis* ruling opened the floodgates for Communist prosecutions. The federal government relied on the Supreme Court decision to obtain 128 indictments against party leaders and members, of which more than 100 were convicted (Hall et al., *American Legal History,* 534).

116. *Dennis v. United States,* 510–11.

117. Ibid., 539–40.

118. Friedmann, *Legal Theory,* 148.

119. *Dennis v. United States,* 580–81.

120. Ibid., 590–91.

121. V. D. Nabokov, "Vnutrenniaia voina" ["The Internal War"], 519, 520; emphasis in original.

122. Scholars have typically dismissed Ray's "general lesson" as facile, platitudinous, or immaterial to the inner workings of the novel. But Ray's words are no less true for being hackneyed. "In principle and in practice," writes Amitai Etzioni, "there is no escaping the basic tension between our profound desire for

privacy and our deep concern for public safety and public health." When Toker refers to Ray's conclusion as "a comically well-meaning cliché," she defines "cliché" as "a statement that has lost its efficacy but not necessarily its validity." See Etzioni, *The Limits of Privacy,* 3; Toker, *Nabokov: The Mystery of Literary Structures,* 199.

123. Charlotte's violation of Humbert's privacy seems keyed into a biographical event that Nabokov describes in *Speak, Memory.* Coming upon his brother Sergey's diary, the youthful Nabokov not only read its contents, but exposed Sergey's homosexuality to his tutor (Nabokov, *Speak, Memory,* 580). According to Boyd, this invasion of Sergey's privacy came to haunt Nabokov's later life and work: "Perhaps Vladimir's belated self-reproach for that glance at the diary and his unthinking impulse to pass on the information may account in part for his fierce opposition in later years to any infringement of personal privacy" (Boyd, *Vladimir Nabokov: The Russian Years,* 106). Crucially, however, Charlotte discovers not a young man's homosexual desires, but an adult man's sexual designs on a twelve-year-old girl. From the perspective of parents and anti-Communists, it would be difficult to determine whether Charlotte's detective work qualifies as wise vigilance or an inexcusable violation of privacy.

124. Nabokov, foreword to "The Waltz Invention," 8.

125. Arendt, "The Ex-Communists," 597–98.

126. Mandelstam, *Hope Against Hope,* 331.

127. Kuzmanovich, "'Splendid Insincerity' as 'Utmost Truthfulness,'" 41.

128. Berlin, "Two Concepts of Liberty," 214.

129. Arendt, "The Ex-Communists," 599.

130. V. D. Nabokov used the term in an editorial titled "Drugu-protivniku" published in *Rul'* on the occasion of Miliukov's assuming the editorship of the Paris daily *Poslednie novosti* (Joseph Hessen, *Gody izgnaniia,* 122–23).

131. Nabokov's abortive attempt to incinerate the batch of index cards that constituted the first incarnation of *Lolita* is the best-known example of the doubts he entertained about writing a novel on such a controversial subject (Boyd, *Vladimir Nabokov: The American Years,* 170; see also Nabokov, *Strong Opinions,* 105). The same fears made him destroy the novel's manuscript pages and led him to consider publishing it pseudonymously. His fears were validated when *Lolita* was initially turned down by every American publishing house to which it had been submitted (*Vladimir Nabokov: The American Years,* 225, 220–21, 264).

132. Nabokov, *Lectures on Russian Literature,* 5, 12.

CHAPTER THREE

The epigraphs for this chapter are from Chernyshevski, *The Anthropological Principle in Philosophy,* 124; Peter Struve, preface to Berdiaev's *Sub'ektivizm i individualizm v obshchestvennoi filosofii,* 9; and Novgorodtsev, "Ethical Idealism in the Philosophy of Law," 305.

An earlier and shorter version of this chapter appeared as "Vladimir Nabokov's *Ada:* Art, Deception, Ethics," *Contemporary Literature* 46, no. 2 (2005): 311–39.

1. Bobbie Ann Mason and Brian Boyd provide sustained ethical readings of the novel in their monographs on *Ada.* Mason argues that Lucette is central to the novel's action, and that Van and Ada are responsible for her suffering and suicide. She also claims, interestingly, that Van is to blame for Ada's loss of vitality (Mason, *Nabokov's Garden: A Guide to "Ada,"* 22–23; see also 93–120). In *Nabokov's "Ada": The Place of Consciousness,* Boyd argues that Lucette's fate is *Ada*'s principal preoccupation. Boyd demonstrates that a web of symmetries and thematic correspondences underscores Van and Ada's culpability in Lucette's suicide. This chapter extends and revises Mason's and Boyd's pioneering insights.

2. Nabokov, *Ada,* 298.

3. In her influential review of *Pale Fire* for the *New Republic,* Mary McCarthy notes, without elaborating, that Nabokov's "practical morality, like Kant's, seeks to reconcile the Enlightenment with universal maxims of conduct held as axioms" (McCarthy, ["A Bolt from the Blue,"] 136). Kuzmanovich also links Kant and Nabokov when he argues that the connection between ethics and aesthetics in Nabokov's personal philosophy springs from an imaginative empathy similar to that postulated by Kant (Kuzmanovich, "'Splendid Insincerity' as 'Utmost Truthfulness,'" 40). Without naming Kant as an influence, Toker deploys Bakhtin's conception of the carnivalesque to align Nabokov with what is clearly a Kantian moral philosophy:

> The ethical ideology that is evolved in the fictional works of Vladimir Nabokov can be described as an idealistic variety of rational individualism. . . . Ethical idealists are not satisfied with the belief in doing as one would be done by; they respect the individual rights of others not because of a calculation that this conduct would boomerang but because it is (deontologically) right. They dispense with the expectation of reciprocity along with the basic assumption of philosophical egoism, namely, that all ethical motivation ultimately derives from considerations of self-interest. (Toker, "'The Dead Are Good Mixers,'" 92–93)

4. Nabokov, appendix 2 to *Eugene Onegin,* 3:498; Nabokov, *Nikolai Gogol,* 148; Nabokov, *Strong Opinions,* 153.

5. Nabokov, *Nikolai Gogol,* 64.

6. Ibid., 67–68.

7. Nabokov, *Lectures on Russian Literature,* 313. *Poshlism* and *poshlust* are terms of Nabokov's own coinage. Hugh McLean notes that "Philistines and Philistinism" was never a "lecture" but "the draft of an article" that drew heavily

on Nabokov's discussion of *poshlost'* in *Nikolai Gogol* (McLean, "*Lectures on Russian Literature*," 272). John Burt Foster, Jr., provides a fine discussion of Nabokov's evocative transliteration of "*poshlost'*" as "*poshlust*," and Sergej Davydov devotes a short essay to the subject in *The Garland Companion to Vladimir Nabokov.* See Foster, "Poshlust, Culture Criticism, Adorno, and Malraux"; and Davydov, "Poshlost." Nabokov also writes about "*poshlost'*" in *Strong Opinions,* where he includes many of his bêtes noires under the rubric: "Freudian symbolism, moth-eaten mythologies, social comment, humanistic messages, political allegories, overconcern with class or race"; "such concepts as 'America is no better than Russia' or 'We all share in Germany's guilt'"; "listing in one breath Auschwitz, Hiroshima, and Vietnam is seditious *poshlost'*" (Nabokov, *Strong Opinions,* 101).

8. On the relationship between Nabokov and Aikhenvald, see chapter 1. Aikhenvald's essay, published in *Pokhvala prazdnosti,* was first delivered as a lecture for the Free Academy of Spiritual Culture.

9. Aikhenvald, "Bessmertnaia poshlost'" ["Immortal *Poshlost'*"], 19.

10. Ibid., 21–22.

11. "As long as we are part of nature," Aikhenvald writes,

> our state within it remains ambiguous. Yes, the human being is a permanent ambiguity, some sort of hardened blunder of the universe, a creature that has been inopportunely caught in between matter and spirit [*Da, chelovek—permanentnaia dvusmyslennost', kakaia-to zastyvshaia nelovkost' mirozdaniia, sushchestvo, nevpopad popavshee mezhdu materiei i dukhom*]. To overcome *poshlost'* one needs to overcome nature. To escape from nature completely, to depart from it through the gates of death . . . is the only way to shake off from oneself the dust of *poshlost'.* (Ibid., 54–55)

12. Ibid., 44–45.

13. Ibid., 48; Nabokov, *Lectures on Russian Literature,* 313.

14. Panofsky, *Meaning in the Visual Arts,* 1. The original story appears in Wasianski, *Immanuel Kant in seinen letzten Lebensjahren,* 298. It is repeated in Stuckenberg, *The Life of Immanuel Kant,* 443, and (in abridged form) in Kuehn, *Kant: A Biography,* 422.

15. Poole, "Kantian Foundations of Russian Liberal Theory," 1–2.

16. Novgorodtsev, "O filosofskom dvizhenii nashikh dnei" ["Philosophical Trends of Our Time"], 66; qtd. in Poole, "Editor's Introduction" to *Problems of Idealism,* 29.

17. For the many ties that bound Nabokov to the Hessen family, see chapter 2.

18. Sergey Hessen, "Moe zhizneopisanie," 733, 734, 736–37.

19. See *Sistematicheskii katalog biblioteki Vladimira Dmitrievicha Nabokova* (1904).

20. V. D. Nabokov, "Pis'ma V. D. Nabokova," 267, 269.

21. Kant, *Critique of Pure Reason,* 397.

22. Poole, "Utopianism, Idealism, Liberalism," 76.

23. Boyd, *Nabokov's "Ada,"* 145.

24. Kant, *Critique of Pure Reason,* 534-35.

25. For Kant's development of this argument, see *Critique of Pure Reason,* 537–46; and *Groundwork of The Metaphysics of Morals,* 88–9.

26. D. Barton Johnson has persuasively argued that incest, too, is a well-established family tradition: "The incestuous relationship of Van and Ada is but the final episode in a series of incestuous matings among Veens and Zemskis over several generations." Johnson provides compelling evidence that Demon, Aqua, and Marina are more closely related than their family tree would suggest. As the offspring of an incestuous and adulterous affair between Dolly Durmanov and Dedalus Veen, Demon is either the half-brother or full brother of Aqua and Marina (Johnson, "The Labyrinth of Incest in Nabokov's *Ada,*" 238–41). In a similar vein, Lucy Maddox suggests that Dan and Demon may not be cousins, but twin brothers: "it seems suspicious," she notes, "that they were born on the same day and that Demon is said to be of 'Anglo-Irish' ancestry, while the only English name given in the genealogy is that of Dan's mother, Mary Trumbell, and the only specifically Irish name is that of Aqua and Marina's grandmother, Mary O'Reilly." This last observation leads her to speculate further that Dan and Demon might be the twin brothers or half-brothers of Aqua and Marina (Maddox, *Nabokov's Novels in English,* 111).

27. For these and other similar parallels, see Mason, *Nabokov's Garden,* 25; and Boyd, *Nabokov's "Ada,"* 147.

28. Mason argues that Van's reconstruction of his family history is an opportunistic effort to discover "an assurance that incest is a hereditary evil beyond Van's control" (Mason, *Nabokov's Garden,* 24–25).

29. Rorty, "The Barber of Kasbeam," 213–14.

30. Though the explicit reference here is to Kant, the keyhole remembered by Van might also allude to Sartre's famous argument about the painful connection between self and other. The shame experienced by an individual caught looking through a keyhole is emblematic for Sartre of the relational nature of consciousness: "I am for myself," he states, "only as I am a pure reference to the Other" (Sartre, *Being and Nothingness,* 260). Nabokov disliked Sartre (Sartre's Marxism and his negative 1939 review of *Despair* were no doubt partly to blame), and he dismissed existentialism as "a fashionable brand of café philosophy" (Nabokov, *Strong Opinions,* 175, 212, 228–30). Nonetheless, Sartre's use of shame as a key factor in his definition of subjectivity resonates with *Ada*'s study of the moral dimensions of Van and Ada's treatment of Lucette. If Lucette is the superfluous "other" in Van and Ada's idyllic world, Sartre's keyhole scenario provides a way of reinterpreting her marginality as centrality. When Lu-

cette reminds Van that he and Ada used to incarcerate her in a closet in order to engage in sexual intercourse, Van probably experiences the same kind of shame experienced by an individual caught spying through a keyhole. Sartre argues that shame is a sign of our human interdependence: "Shame is by nature *recognition.* I recognize that I *am* as the Other sees me. . . . Thus shame is shame *of oneself before the Other;* these two structures are inseparable" (Sartre, *Being and Nothingness,* 222; emphasis in original).

31. This strategy is also conspicuous in *Lolita,* where Humbert Humbert relies on art's capacity for deception ("You can always count on a murderer for a fancy prose style," he states on the first page of his memoir) to seduce readers into suspending their urge to deliberate on the problems posed by his affair with Dolly. *Lolita* is structured as a dilemma: the aesthetic pleasures to be derived from Humbert's stylistic virtuosity are positioned against the crimes that virtuosity simultaneously describes and occludes. Yet our sense that this is in fact a dilemma may be the novel's most cunning deception in light of Nabokov's insistence that our experience of aesthetic pleasure is tied to our capacity to make ethical judgments, and that our freedom and self-determination originate in that dual enterprise.

32. Kant, *Critique of the Power of Judgment,* 227.

33. Ibid., 96.

34. Kuzmanovich anticipates my argument when he notes: "By situating the ethical impulse in our innate abilities to imagine a situation other than the one we find ourselves in, Nabokov is thoroughly Kantian, for in his own ethical theory Kant also uses imagination as the mental eye on the effect that our actions have on others" (Kuzmanovich, "'Splendid Insincerity' as 'Utmost Truthfulness,'" 40). Leland de la Durantaye arrives at a similar conclusion by way of Hannah Arendt's famous account in *Eichmann in Jerusalem* of the Nazi war criminal's outraged response to *Lolita.* Turning to Kant's *Critique of the Power of Judgment* (to which Arendt turned herself in an effort to formulate a new moral philosophy on the eve of her death), de la Durantaye underscores the significance of intellectual empathy for understanding the moral failures that connect Adolf Eichmann to Humbert Humbert: "What Eichmann the man shares with Nabokov's literary creation is the inability or unwillingness '*to think from the standpoint of somebody else.*'" A few pages later, de la Durantaye returns to Kant's *Critique of Judgment* when he refers to Nabokov's insistence that his students avoid identifying with fictional characters and cultivate a coolness of judgment (Nabokov, *Lectures on Literature,* 4). As de la Durantaye aptly points out, Nabokov's injunction corresponds with Kant's claim that aesthetic judgment is fundamentally disinterested (de la Durantaye, *Style Is Matter,* 5, 9–10; emphasis in original).

35. Scruton, *Kant: A Very Short Introduction,* 104. Nabokov's first encounter with Kant's aesthetic theory may have been mediated by Vladimir Soloviev, Russia's most respected and influential idealist philosopher. Published for the

first time in the Moscow Psychological Society's journal, *Voprosy filosofii i psikhologii,* Soloviev's essay "Beauty in Nature" defines beauty in terms that anticipate Nabokov's views with striking precision:

> Formal beauty always shows itself as pure uselessness, whatever its material elements. . . . And if [formal beauty] cannot be valued as a means for the satisfaction of one or another daily or physiological requirement, then this means it is valued as a goal in itself. In beauty—even with the most simple and primary of its manifestations—we meet up with something *absolute* that exists not for the sake of another but for its own sake, so that, by its very existence, it gladdens and satisfies our soul, which, resting on beauty, becomes tranquil and is liberated from life's strivings and labors. (Soloviev, "Beauty in Nature," 33–34)

Though Soloviev does not single out Kant by name, he admits that his definition of beauty is closely indebted to "the last great representatives of German philosophy." I am grateful to Randall Poole for bringing Soloviev's writings on aesthetics to my attention.

36. Wood, *Kant's Ethical Thought,* 46; emphasis in original.

37. Fischer, *A Commentary on Kant's Critick of the Pure Reason,* 292.

38. Dean, *The Value of Humanity in Kant's Moral Theory,* 134–35.

39. Kant, *Critique of Practical Reason,* 200; emphasis in original.

40. Berdiaev, "The Ethical Problem in the Light of Philosophical Idealism," 181.

41. Ibid., 173–74.

42. Fischer, *A Commentary on Kant's Critick of the Pure Reason,* 292–94; emphasis in original.

43. De Vries, "'Perplex'd in the Extreme,'" 146–47.

44. As Toker perceptively notes, Nabokov's admirable characters "do not excel in utilitarian ethical calculations." The actions of Martin Edelweiss, Fyodor Godunov-Cherdyntsev, Cincinnatus C., Adam Krug, Timofey Pnin, and John Shade "enter into complex relationships with self-interest or personal compulsions, yet the latter merely support rather than dictate the characters' choices. Nabokov's texts discourage skeptical interpretations of his characters' motives in frameworks such as psychological egoism, long-term interest, or neurosis" (Toker, "'The Dead Are Good Mixers,'" 93).

45. Nabokov, "Problems of Translation," 127.

46. Lucette is described as wearing green in *Ada* at 158, 182, 328, and 457.

47. Korsgaard, *Creating the Kingdom of Ends,* 140.

48. Langton, "Duty and Desolation," 489.

49. According to Kant:

> Truthfulness in statements that one cannot avoid is a human being's duty to everyone, however great the disadvantage to him or to another that may result from it; and although I indeed do no wrong to him who unjustly compels me

> to make the statement if I falsify it, I nevertheless do wrong in the most essential part of duty *in general* by such falsification, which can therefore be called a lie (though not in a jurist's sense); that is, I bring it about, as far as I can, that statements (declarations) in general are not believed, and so too that all rights which are based on contracts come to nothing and lose their force; and this is a wrong inflicted upon humanity generally. (Kant, "On a Supposed Right to Lie," 612; emphasis in original)

50. "That is to say, if you have *by a lie* prevented someone just now bent on murder from committing the deed, then you are legally accountable for all the consequences that might arise from it. But if you have kept strictly to the truth, then public justice can hold nothing against you, whatever the unforeseen consequences might be" (Kant, "On a Supposed Right to Lie," 612; emphasis in original). Statements such as these are responsible for the outcry against Kant's inflexible moral rigor.

51. Mandelstam, *Hope Against Hope,* 165, 331.

52. Nabokov asserted his hostility toward historical determinism and his fondness for the unpredictability of chance as early as 1926. In a talk prepared for delivery to the Aikhenvald-Tatarinov literary circle in Berlin and preserved at the New York Public Library's Berg Collection, Nabokov states:

> If every day in a man's life is a sequence of chance occurrences—and this is what invests it with divinity and power—all the more then the history of mankind is only chance. One may connect these chances and tie them up into tidy bouquets of periods and ideas, losing in the process the aroma of the past, and we see things not as they were but as we want them to have been. . . . Why should we imitate those paradoxical enemies of hazard who spend years over the green cloth at Monte Carlo, calculating the odds of red and black stakes in order to find some faultless system? There is no system. The roulette of history knows no laws. (Nabokov, "On Generalities," 12–13; qtd. in Dolinin, "Clio Laughs Last," 209)

For an account of the circumstances surrounding Nabokov's contributions to the Aikhenvald-Tatarinov literary circle, see Dolinin, "Doklady Vladimira Nabokova v Berlinskom literaturnom kruzhke" ["The Talks of Vladimir Nabokov to the Berlin Literary Circle"], 8.

53. Korsgaard, *Creating the Kingdom of Ends,* 388, note 1; emphasis in original.

54. Wood, *The Magician's Doubts,* 133.

55. The fact that Van and Ada are fictional characters does not put them beyond an ethical reading, nor does it diminish their moral accountability within the world of the novel. By stating that his characters are "galley slaves" when asked if his characters were ever known to evade his control and determine

the course of his novels, Nabokov was countering E. M. Forster's "trite little whimsy" with a self-evident ontological truth (Nabokov, *Strong Opinions,* 95). Yet Nabokov also knew that a dogmatic application of this truism would abolish the very conceits that make fiction possible. Though fictional characters are by definition "galley slaves," they must conduct themselves as if their choices matter. As Nabokov illustrates at the end of *Bend Sinister,* Krug's realization that he is a character of fiction is accompanied by madness (*Bend Sinister,* 351–52). To enjoy such an epistemic privilege is to escape metaphysical anguish and moral responsibility, but it also means being permanently exiled from one's fictional world. Ada's explanation of her choice of a theatrical career reflects the incommensurability of the authorial and fictional domains: "In 'real' life we are creatures of chance in an absolute void—unless we be artists ourselves, naturally; but in a good play I feel authored, I feel passed by the board of censors, I feel secure" (*Ada,* 341–42). If Ada's choice of profession can be read as a yearning to live beyond the reach of moral responsibility, Nabokov prevents her from knowing that she is "authored" and "passed by the board of censors." Ada, like all of Nabokov's fictional characters, must bear the burden of her freedom.

56. Lucette's suicide is the most extreme example of such self-debasement. For Kant, suicide is wrong because it leads to a contradiction under the Formula of the Universal Law: the principle of "self-love" whose function is to promote life cannot be used to destroy it (Kant, *Groundwork of The Metaphysics of Morals,* 74). Commentators agree that this argument does not work as stated, partly because it is unclear why self-love should have the function of promoting life, and partly because it is unclear why self-love cannot serve two opposite functions—such as motivating us to stay alive when life is pleasant, and stop living when life becomes insufferable (Feldman, "Kantian Ethics," 295). Korsgaard argues that Kant's prohibition against suicide would pose no problems had he derived it from the Formula of Humanity rather than, as he does, from the Formula of Universal Law: if the human being is the source of all value, it is both immoral and incoherent to act in a way that denies and destroys this repository of value (Korsgaard, *Creating the Kingdom of Ends,* 152). Seeing Lucette's suicide in this framework is to ascribe blame to Van and Ada for instigating the debasement that will prevent Lucette from becoming a responsible caretaker of her own life. Boyd's conclusion that Van and Ada's premature sexual initiation of Lucette leads to her suicide coincides with this reading even if the moral reasoning that leads to it proceeds by a different route.

57. Kant, *Lectures on Ethics,* 163.

58. Korsgaard, *Creating the Kingdom of Ends,* 195.

59. Inbreeding is as risky in the novel's world as it is in ours ("if practiced rigidly incest led to various forms of decline, to the production of cripples, weaklings, 'muted mutates' and, finally, to hopeless sterility"), but legal sanctions against incest began to be imposed only in the wake of the extinction of a prized

species of sheep and the scandal generated by "a certain Ivan Ivanov" who impregnated his five-year-old great-granddaughter and, later, the child his great-granddaughter bore him. Events such as these led to the criminalization of incest in spite of the fact that the new laws were perceived as infringements upon "one of humanity's main rights—that of enjoying the liberty of its evolution, a liberty no other creature had ever known" (Nabokov, *Ada,* 108–9).

60. This argument collides with Mason's thesis that "*Ada* is about incest, and, as incest is treated in the book, it is virtually synonymous with solipsism" (Mason, *Nabokov's Garden,* 13). According to Mason, *Ada* depicts incest as the moral transgression that lies at the root of its principal tragedies, including Lucette's suicide and Ada's unfulfilled life. My argument that the novel does not judge incest, in and of itself, as morally wrong finds indirect support in D. Barton Johnson's detailed overview of *Ada*'s treatment of sibling incest in relation to other novels interested in the same theme. He notes: "In virtually all treatments of the brother-sister incest theme, the relationship, once revealed, leads to grief, separation, and death." Nabokov's novel, by contrast, allows "the reunited sibling-lovers [to] live happily ever after" (D. Barton Johnson, "The Labyrinth of Incest in Nabokov's *Ada,*" 236–37).

61. Kant condemns homosexuality as a vice, and it is therefore difficult to map his arguments onto *Pale Fire.* Kant speaks of a class of "duties to oneself" that he justifies not only on the grounds of the categorical imperative, but also in terms of "nature's purposes" (defined as self-preservation, the preservation of the species, and the preservation of the person's biological capacity to enjoy life). Our duty, Kant argues, is to avoid vices (such as suicide, sexual self-debasement, gluttony, and drunkenness) that compromise these objectives (Kant, *The Metaphysics of Morals,* 545). Kant further differentiates between two kinds of sexual vices, each of which violates one's duty to oneself as an animal and moral being. By being "contrary to sound reason," *crimina carnis secundum naturam* ("natural" vices such as fornication and adultery) must be avoided because they degrade humanity "by placing it on a level with animal nature." *Crimina carnis contra naturam* ("unnatural" vices such as masturbation, same-sex intercourse, and bestiality) are "contrary to natural instinct and to animal nature" and thus place humanity "below the level of animals" (Kant, *Lectures on Ethics,* 164, 169–70). Since these "unnatural" sexual activities are incompatible with the ends of nature, Kant declares them to be wrong in all contexts.

Lara Denis and Alan Soble have convincingly argued that Kant's appeal to nature cannot justify his unconditional rejection of "unnatural" sex. Denis provides eight reasons why nature alone cannot furnish Kant with an argument for self-regarding duties. "Nature's ends," she asserts, "are not equipped to serve as an independent justification for duties to oneself, nor are they a conclusive indication of what [the Formula of Humanity] requires" (Denis, "Kant on the Wrongness of 'Unnatural' Sex," 235–39). As Kant himself admits, only the Formula of Humanity can determine the rightness or wrongness of an act, and as Denis and Soble demonstrate, the Formula of Humanity fails to establish homosexuality as a vice. What is more, Kant's view that monogamous (heterosexual) marriage is the only social configuration that makes sex compatible with the Formula of Humanity can be mobilized in defense of monogamous same-sex marriage. To quote Denis, "there seems to be no support for the view that homosexual sex as such is wrong—that it cannot, like heterosexual sex, be made permissible by being put into a context of a mutually respectful (perhaps contractual) relationship. . . . Homosexual sex should be viewed as only as morally risky as heterosexual sex, and for the same main reason: because of the objectification that is part of sexual desire. The fact that one cannot procreate through homosexual sex does not seem to show, according to [the Formula of Humanity], that there is anything self-regardingly vicious about it" (Denis, "Kant on the Wrongness of 'Unnatural' Sex," 239–40). Like Denis, Soble argues that Kant makes limited use of nature's objectives as an argumentative tool, and that his uncharacteristic appeal to nature when speaking of homosexuality provides him with nothing more than an opportunity to express his personal aversion toward it. See Soble, "Kant and Sexual Perversion," 70–78.

62. Scholars like Steven Belletto and Steven Bruhm have elegantly and persuasively challenged the view that Nabokov's satirical depiction of Kinbote is a record of his homophobia. According to Belletto, *Pale Fire* is a critique of the Cold War political culture that cast homosexuals in the role of political threats on a par with Communists. "Nabokov's emphasis on Kinbote's homosexuality," he writes, "serves to parody the contemporary homophobia of Cold War psychiatrists and social critics: the novel suggests that homophobic narratives are as farfetched as Kinbote's Zembla narrative" (Belletto, "The Zemblan Who Came in from the Cold," 758). In a similar vein, Bruhm argues that *Pale Fire* resists "the psychoanalytic tendency to see the gay man as a 'type,'" and satirizes "the very homogeneity that assumes all gay men are the same, and that they all want the same thing." According to Bruhm, "if Nabokov hated homosexuality, that hatred was self-contested" (Bruhm, "Queer, Queer Vladimir," 294, 302, 295). Belletto and Bruhm dwell on Nabokov's troubled relationship with his brother Sergey, who was imprisoned by the Nazis for his homosexuality. Though Sergey was eventually released, he was returned to prison under suspicion of being a British spy and died in captivity. For Kevin Ohi, the critical tendency to denigrate Kinbote's homosexuality flows from an insensitivity to the "intractable dilemma" posed by narcissism to the enterprise of reading and interpretation. Ohi finds Kinbote morally unobjectionable and claims that *Pale Fire* is invested in unsettling conventional (and often homophobic) models of critical practice (Ohi, "Narcissism and Queer Reading in *Pale Fire*," 163, 166). Boyd responds to Ohi in the same issue of *Nabokov Studies* in which Ohi's essay appears.

63. Rorty, "The Barber of Kasbeam," 199.

64. See Engelstein, *The Keys to Happiness,* 57–71.

65. Ibid., 63, 70.

66. Ibid., 67.

67. Though it is difficult to evaluate Nabokov's attitude toward homosexuality from his brief reference in *Speak, Memory* to his father's study of sexual crime, he seems proud of his father's broad-minded tolerance: "In the same essay he reveals a very liberal and 'modern' approach to various abnormal practices, incidentally coining a convenient Russian word for 'homosexual': *ravnopolïy*" (Nabokov, *Speak, Memory,* 512). Boyd refers to V. D. Nabokov's monograph on sexual crimes and provides a brief account of his contributions to criminal jurisprudence in *Vladimir Nabokov: The Russian Years,* 54.

68. V. D. Nabokov's remark is made in response to the argument that to decriminalize sodomy is tantamount to sanctioning it.

69. V. D. Nabokov, "Plotskie prestupleniia," 163; qtd. in and trans. by Engelstein, *The Keys to Happiness,* 67.

70. Engelstein, *The Keys to Happiness,* 69–70, 70, note 41. See Vladimir Nabokoff, "Die Homosexualität im Russischen Strafgesetzbuch" ["Homosexuality in the Russian Penal Code"].

71. V. D. Nabokov's observations regarding the reformers' resolutions on incest are part of his larger argument about the legal inconsistencies generated by the term "*nepotrebstvo* [obscenity, indecency, depravity]" (V. D. Nabokov, "Plotskie prestupleniia," 132–33). He criticizes the reformers for failing to identify a single legal good that is violated by actions covered by this term and for providing instead a proliferation of such goods. One such good—"the purity of family relations [*chistota semeinykh otnoshenii*]"—is especially harmful because it serves the interests of society at the cost of personal interests. "*The purity of family relations,* protected not on behalf of individual interests but in the interests of society at large," he writes, leads to the exclusion of incest (as an act that destroys such purity) "from the list of offenses against the private individual" (ibid., 133; emphasis in original). The reformers' reliance on a slippery term such as *nepotrebstvo,* he elaborates, generates the same incoherence as the phrase "purity of family relations": "if we say that by the term '*nepotrebstvo*' . . . we must understand any illegal (from the external point of view) satisfaction of sexual lust, then, regardless of the formality of such a construction, which contradicts the fundamental principles of this project, we can pose the following question: why is adultery excluded from it, while incest is included in it?" (ibid., 133). By tracing the shifts in legal meaning associated with the term *nepotrebstvo,* Engelstein shows that V. D. Nabokov was not alone in criticizing the term's lack of clarity and legal usefulness (Engelstein, *The Keys to Happiness,* 40–41).

72. Engelstein, *The Keys to Happiness,* 69.

73. Gruzenberg, "Moia pamiatka o V. D. Nabokove" ["My Memorial to V. D. Nabokov"], 1.

74. Joseph Hessen, "Pamiati druga" ["In Memory of a Friend"]"; Ganfman, "V. D. Nabokov," 1; Makletsov, "V. D. Nabokov, kak uchenyi kriminalist"; Tatarinov, "V. D. Nabokov i russkaia emigratsiia," 8; Pasmanik, *Revoliutsionnye gody v Krymu,* 122.

75. Tatarinov, "V. D. Nabokov i russkaia emigratsiia," 8.

76. Browder, introduction to *V. D. Nabokov and the Russian Provisional Government,* 10–11.

77. Quoted ibid., 9–10.

78. V. D. Nabokov, "Protsess 169 deputatov pervoi gosudarstvennoi dumy" ["The Trial of the 169 Deputies of the First State Duma"], 2116.

79. Ibid., 2121–22.

80. Browder, introduction to *V. D. Nabokov and the Russian Provisional Government,* 6.

81. Kant, "An Answer to the Question: What Is Enlightenment?" 18.

82. Boyd, "Nabokov's Transition from Russian to English," 18.

83. Pasmanik, *Revoliutsionnye gody v Krymu,* 136, 141, 151; Krishevskii, "V Krymu (1916–1918 g.)" ["In the Crimea (1916–1918)"], 108–9.

84. Krishevskii, "V Krymu," 114–15.

85. Tatarinov, "V. D. Nabokov i russkaia emigratsiia," 8.

86. Joseph Hessen, "Pamiati druga"; Joseph Hessen, *Gody izgnaniia,* 115; Gruzenberg, "Moia pamiatka o V. D. Nabokove"; Nabokov, Interview with Mati Laansoo, 41.

CHAPTER FOUR

The epigraphs for this chapter are from Vladimir Nabokov, "Fame," 111, lines 113–16; Vladimir Nabokov, *The Real Life of Sebastian Knight,* 81; Volskii, *Encounters with Lenin,* 208.

1. Nabokov, *Glory,* 148.

2. Sonia's father is a comic figure, but he is also meant to arouse affection and command respect:

> He had done a goodly amount of traveling around in his time, was intensely active in liberal politics, conceived life as a succession of congresses in various cities, had miraculously escaped a Soviet death, and always carried a bulging briefcase. And when someone said meditatively, "What shall I do with these books—it's raining," he would wordlessly, instantly, and extremely skillfully swaddle the books in a sheet of newspaper, rummage in his briefcase, produce some string and, in a flash, tie it crosswise around the neat package, a process which the luckless acquaintance, shifting from foot to foot, watched with apprehensive *attendrissement.* "There you are, sir," Zilanov would say and, after a hasty good-bye, was off to Riga, Belgrade, or Paris. . . . While marveling

> at his inattention to landscapes, comforts, and cleanliness, Martin nevertheless admired Zilanov for that plodding dryish courage of his, and every time he saw him could not help recalling that this seemingly unathletic and unfashionable man . . . had escaped from the Bolshevists by crawling through a drain-pipe, and had once fought a duel with the Octobrist Tuchkov. (Nabokov, *Glory*, 77–78)

Zilanov lends support to Ivan Tolstoy's interesting thesis that Nabokov felt conflicted about his father and his father's political career. According to Tolstoy, V. D. Nabokov figures in his son's fiction not only as an idolized hero, but also as a target of satire, so that he is at once a Godunov and a Chernyshevski (Tolstoy, "Vladimir Dmitrievich, Nikolai Stepanovich, Nikolai Gavrilovich," 181).

3. Dolinin has persuasively argued that Nabokov's *Podvig* (the Russian title of *Glory*) is a riposte to contemporary Soviet literature's crude glorification of Soviet achievements. Dolinin draws special attention to Vladimir Bakhmetev's *The Crime of Martin* (*Prestuplenie Martyna*), whose protagonist fails to realize the "high deeds" (*podvigi*) for which he seems destined because "his lingering individualism, his unerased dream of personal glory" prevents him from subordinating "his will to the 'iron necessity' of the class struggle" (Dolinin, "Clio Laughs Last," 208).

4. This claim is only superficially at odds with the view (well argued by Dolinin and openly endorsed throughout my own work) that Nabokov resisted historically deterministic accounts of human behavior. "It would be a mistake," Nabokov writes in his commentary to *Eugene Onegin*, "to regard Lenski, the lyrical lover, as 'a typical product of his time'" (Nabokov, commentary to *Eugene Onegin*, 2:275). Nonetheless, the view that human beings have choice and that human choices influence the unfolding of history in no way negates the claim that history has an impact on human affairs. If, as Dolinin observes, the central characters of Nabokov's Russian-language novels seem untouched by the Russian Revolution and the civil war, it is not because Nabokov discounted the human cost of such historical events (Dolinin, "Clio Laughs Last," 204–5). Terrorized into permanent infancy and silence by "two rowdies" who physically and verbally abused her during the civil war, Irina is a grim reminder of our inescapable vulnerability to history (Nabokov, *Glory*, 149–50). Characters like her remain on the periphery of the main action in Nabokov's fiction not because their stories are trivial, but because Nabokov is unwilling to entrust them to hackneyed phrases like those employed by Mrs. Gruzinov when she refers to Irina as "a permanent living symbol" of recent Russian history. The same horror and stupefaction are experienced by Pnin when recalling the murder in a Nazi concentration camp of another marginal character, Mira Belochkin. In the cases of Irina and Mira, language and consciousness recoil from speaking and making sense of such events. But Nabokov was also willing to put the victims

of history and ideology at the center of his plots. In *Bend Sinister,* Krug's son David is tortured and killed in a ghastly experiment conducted under the aegis of a political dictatorship. In "Cloud, Castle, Lake," the nonconformist Vasiliy Ivanovich is tortured and mutilated by a group of proto-fascist Germans who refuse to allow the dreamy Russian émigré the pleasures of flight and solitude. Though the tragedies of Irina, David, and Vasiliy Ivanovich might seem accidental or arbitrary, they are the predictable outcomes of particular ideological attitudes or political structures. They horrify and bewilder precisely because they are products of deliberation and ideology. In his assessment of Nabokov's approach to history, John Burt Foster, Jr., has perceptively noted that Nabokov's hostility toward topical art is one aspect of his wider hostility toward "general ideas." Nabokov's work, Foster argues, "does respond to history, but it does so by translating the extremity of its epoch into concrete, individualized situations and images" (Foster, "*Bend Sinister,*" 29).

5. Boyd quotes from diary material Nabokov prepared for possible interviews regarding *Pale Fire:* "I wonder if any reader will notice the following details: 1) that the nasty commentator is not an ex-king and not even Dr. Kinbote, but Prof. Vseslav Botkin, a Russian and a madman" (Boyd, *Vladimir Nabokov: The American Years,* 709, note 4). Boyd also locates the origins of Kinbote's pathology in Russian history: "Kinbote has built up his Zembla to cope with an overwhelming sense of loss—and that it is the loss of Russia emerges irresistibly. *Zemlya* is Russian for 'land,' and Nova Zembla or Novaya Zemlya part of Russia's far north." He provides further evidence for his conclusion by noting the conspicuous repetition of the pair "English and Russian" in Kinbote's gloss of line 615 of Shade's poem (ibid., 434).

In *Pnin,* the novel that immediately preceded *Pale Fire,* Pnin's nightmares appear to set a pattern for Kinbote's flight from Zembla and a reason for concluding that Botkin's delusions are tied to the circumstances of his Russian past: "He had fallen asleep at last, . . . and in the course of one of those dreams that still haunt Russian fugitives, even when a third of a century has elapsed since their escape from the Bolsheviks, Pnin saw himself fantastically cloaked, fleeing through great pools of ink under a cloud-barred moon from a chimerical palace, and then pacing a desolate strand with his dead friend Ilya Isidorovich Polyanski as they waited for some mysterious deliverance to arrive in a throbbing boat from beyond the hopeless sea" (Nabokov, *Pnin,* 375).

6. In *Gody izgnaniia,* Joseph Hessen recalls the fears and horrors that attended flight from Russia after the Bolsheviks came to power. These stories often ended in tragedy (*Gody izgnaniia,* 49–51).

7. Nabokov, *Mary,* xiv.

8. Antiterra's two superpowers clash in the Second Crimean War which breaks out during Van's second sojourn at Ardis (Nabokov, *Ada,* 242, 254). Its consequences for the Veens extend no further than robbing Van of the opportu-

nity to fight a duel with Percy de Prey (who dies in action at Chufutkale shortly after Ada's sixteenth birthday) and preventing Grace Erminin from attending Ada's birthday picnic on account of having to see her boyfriend sail off to Tartary with his regiment (ibid., 257, 213–14). The Allies' victory is noted by way of Demon's observation that "our territorial triumphs, et cetera" have raised the price of stocks and that his "friend Bessborodko" stands "to be installed in Bessarabia" (ibid., 263).

9. Pifer, *Nabokov and the Novel,* 136.

10. On the relationship between Nabokov's fiction and postmodernist writing, see Maurice Couturier's "Nabokov in Postmodernist Land."

11. Alexandrov, *Nabokov's Otherworld,* 18.

12. This conclusion is compatible (with some slight modifications) with Mason's argument that Van invents Antiterra in order to insulate himself and Ada from a world that is unsympathetic toward his emotions and behavior (Mason, *Nabokov's Garden,* 12).

13. Peter Struve, "Zametki o sovremennykh delakh," 497.

14. Kolakowski, *Main Currents of Marxism,* 2:419–20.

15. Ibid., 2: 422–23; Read, *Religion, Revolution and the Russian Intelligentsia,* 40–41.

16. Plekhanov, *The Development of the Monist View of History,* 14. Plekhanov borrows this dichotomy from Engels's *Ludwig Feuerbach and the Outcome of Classical German Philosophy* (1888).

17. Volskii, *Encounters with Lenin,* 248.

18. Bogdanov, *Vera i nauka,* 168; qtd. in Read, *Religion, Revolution and the Russian Intelligentsia,* 51.

19. Volskii, *Encounters with Lenin,* 260, 256–58, 244.

20. Ibid., 257.

21. Two colleges merged in 1868 to found the University of California at Berkeley. The *Encyclopaedia Britannica* reports that the campus was named after the philosopher George Berkeley (see "Berkeley").

22. *Ada* is replete with such alliterations: one page alone yields "the Idea of Dimension & Dementia" and the "Queenston College for Glamorous and *Glupovatïh* ('dumb') Girls" (Nabokov, *Ada, or Ardor,* 291).

23. Borges, "A New Refutation of Time," 221, 226–27; see also 230.

24. Quoted ibid., 230.

25. Boyd, Marina Grishakova, and Toker have insightfully examined the affinities between Nabokov's and Bergson's views on time. See Boyd, *Vladimir Nabokov: The Russian Years,* 294–95; Grishakova, *The Models of Space, Time and Vision in V. Nabokov's Fiction,* 90–91, 108–10, 128–29, 202–3; Toker, "Nabokov and Bergson" and "Nabokov and Bergson on Duration and Reflexivity."

26. Berkeley, *The Principles of Human Knowledge,* 83–84; emphasis in original.

27. Nabokov seems to have vacillated in regard to the ideas Van expresses in his treatise on time. In a 1969 interview, for instance, he quotes Van's definition of time without endorsing it: "This is Van speaking, Van Veen, the charming villain of my book. I have not decided yet if I agree with him in all his views on the texture of time. I suspect I don't" (Nabokov, *Strong Opinions,* 143). Two years later in an interview with Paul Sufrin, however, he seems more willing to agree with Van's conclusions: "My conception of the texture of time somewhat resembles its image in Part Four of *Ada.* The present is only the top of the past, and the future does not exist" (Nabokov, *Strong Opinions,* 184).

28. Toker suggests that the "two world" model of Nabokov's speculative metaphysics ("the world of quotidian reality and the 'otherworld' from which one sometimes gets 'leakings and drafts'" [Nabokov, *Speak, Memory,* 382]) contradicts his claim that he is an "indivisible monist." Toker offers a partial solution via the philosophy of Bergson, in which matter is sometimes transmuted into creative consciousness (Toker, "Nabokov and Bergson," 369). Blackwell has advanced Ernst Mach's *neutral monism* as a way of understanding Nabokov's philosophical confession. He observes that several aspects of Mach's epistemology intersect with those of Nabokov, but he also notes that his aim is "not to confirm Nabokov as an official Monist, but rather to suggest how the term and its baggage can be useful in coming to an understanding of his vision of the world in the broadest sense" (Blackwell, "Nabokov, Mach and Monism," 122). In my doctoral dissertation, I argued that Berkeley's idealism provides the closest analogue for Nabokov's cryptic philosophical declaration and, more generally, for his metaphysical and epistemological intuitions.

29. *Ada* was completed in October 1968 and published by McGraw-Hill on May 5, 1969 (Boyd, "Chronology," 865).

30. Bergson, *Matter and Memory,* x.

31. Ibid., viii; Bergson, *Oeuvres,* 161; Nabokov, *The Gift,* 110.

32. Bergson, *Matter and Memory,* ix.

33. Bergson, *The Creative Mind,* 141, 140; Bergson, *Oeuvres,* 1356; emphasis in original.

34. Nabokov, "The Oculus," 101.

35. Valéry, "Choses Tues," 19; *Analects,* 235.

36. This citation refers exclusively to "objects of vision" (Berkeley, *An Essay Towards a New Theory of Vision,* 231). In this early work, Berkeley claims that only visual perceptions are "in the mind." Only in his later and definitive *Principles of Human Knowledge* does he confer the same status on all objects of sense and make them mind-dependent. As A. A. Luce writes, this distinction between *An Essay Towards a New Theory of Vision* and Berkeley's subsequent philosophy is not motivated by a change of view, but by a strategic unveiling of his radical new theory. Although a convinced immaterialist at the time of writing *An Essay,* Berkeley did not argue his case against matter in this preliminary

work but prepared the way for the *Principles* by working out at the level of visual experience a principle that is intended to be valid for all sense experience (Luce, "Editor's Introduction" to *An Essay Towards a New Theory of Vision*, 148).

37. As in a language system, the relationship between words and the things they denote is not causally determined, and finite spirits learn through experience to associate words with meanings. Fire, for instance, is not the *cause* of pain, but a *sign* of pain: "the connexion of ideas does not imply the relation of *cause* and *effect*, but only of a mark or *sign* with the thing *signified*. The fire which I see is not the cause of the pain I suffer upon my approaching it, but the mark that forewarns me of it" (Berkeley, *The Principles of Human Knowledge*, 69). Berkeley's rejection of causality, however, has no bearing on our daily lives. As in *Ada* ("three elements, fire, water, and air, destroyed, in that sequence, Marina, Lucette, and Demon" [Nabokov, *Ada*, 360]), we live, suffer, and die *as if* we were at the mercy of material substance and mechanical process.

38. Descartes, *The Principles of Philosophy*, 254–55.

39. On the complex role of deception in both *Ada* and Nabokov's moral and aesthetic philosophies, see chapter 3.

40. Barabtarlo, "Nabokov's Trinity," 117.

41. Magee, *The Philosophy of Schopenhauer*, 67. Berkeley's idealist epistemology was conceived as a reaction against what has come to be known in philosophical circles as "the problem of perception." This long-standing problem, elegantly summarized here by Magee, is born of Cartesian dualism:

> If the world consisting of all other material objects apart from my own body exists independently of whether I exist or not, and in dimensions of space and time that are also independent of me; and if my knowledge of that world derives from the fact that those objects impinge on my body's senses in such ways as to cause effects in my brain which might be described as mental states in which the objects are represented; how can I ever know that the representations correspond to the objects, in other words that my perceptions correspond to reality? The only way one can check the accuracy of a copy is to compare it with the original, but in this case we have no independent access to the original, and therefore cannot make the comparison. We have access to the copy alone—indeed it is only from the copy that we infer the existence of the original at all. . . . The question can be radicalized. If all I experience, and all I ever *can* experience, are mental states, what warrant do I have for believing that anything exists other than mental states? (Magee, *Confessions of a Philosopher*, 94–95)

Berkeley argued that the philosophical systems inherited from Descartes and Locke lead to skepticism and that it is unreasonable to expect rational individuals to believe in the existence of a material world to which they have no direct access. The only way to avoid skepticism about the existence of a "real" empirical world, he concluded, is to conceive of physical objects as mind-dependent collections of sensory impressions. Accordingly, an apple is a collection of the sensory qualities that we experience during the act of perception (which includes the sensation of eating it). When things are not being perceived by us, they are said to exist either in the secondary sense that they would become perceivable if we took the appropriate steps to see them, smell them, or touch them, or in the sense that they are being constantly perceived by God (Sprigge, "Idealism," 663).

42. Yeats, *Pages from a Diary,* 41–42.

43. Berkeley, *Three Dialogues,* 260; emphasis in original.

44. Nabokov, *Strong Opinions,* 10–11; Nabokov, *Ada,* 175; Berkeley, *Three Dialogues,* 185.

45. Gibson, *Hieronymus Bosch,* 88–92.

46. According to Berkeley, Cartesian dualism undermines God's omnipotence: "How therefore can you suppose, that an all-perfect spirit, on whose will all things have an absolute and immediate dependence, should need an instrument in his operations, or not needing it make use of it?" (Berkeley, *Three Dialogues,* 219). Berkeley's rejection of material substance on the ground of its redundancy correlates with Nabokov's celebration of economy and scorn for dual solutions in chess problems. In *The Gift,* Fyodor's composition of chess problems illustrates this guiding principle: "Pondering the alternatives, thus and thus excluding cumbrous constructions, the blots and blanks of support pawns, struggling with duals, he achieved the utmost accuracy of expression, the utmost economy of harmonious forces" (Nabokov, *The Gift,* 171). In a review of Frederick Woodbridge's *An Essay on Nature,* Nabokov draws an explicit parallel between chess problems and metaphysics when he correlates "a chess-problem composer's attitude toward 'duals'" to "what has been dubbed in philosophy 'dualism'" (Nabokov, "Prof. Woodbridge in an *Essay on Nature*"). A world in which material substance exists unnecessarily would be analogous to a chess problem designed by a composer who did not heed what Shade calls the "interdiction of dual solutions" (Nabokov, *Pale Fire,* 602).

47. Nabokov, commentary to *Eugene Onegin,* 2.353; Nabokov, *Bend Sinister,* 306; qtd. in Field, *Nabokov: His Life in Part,* 87.

48. Trousdale, "'Faragod Bless Them,'" 119.

49. Van's long life enables him to witness the introduction and banning of various electricity surrogates (Nabokov, *Ada,* 376, 377, 393, 455).

50. Boyd, "Annotations to *Ada,*" 74–75.

51. Similar transformations in *Invitation to a Beheading* and *Pale Fire* are associated with characters who irresponsibly fail to attend to details. See Nabokov, *Invitation to a Beheading,* 17–18, 28, 30, 38–39, 43–44, 99, and Kinbote's commentary to line 408 in *Pale Fire.* I have argued elsewhere that the inconsistencies that unsettle *Invitation*'s narrative originate in Fyodor's critique

of Chernyshevski's general indifference to detail and specialized knowledge. See Dragunoiu, "Vladimir Nabokov's *Invitation to a Beheading* and the Russian Radical Tradition." *Ada*'s metamorphoses call for a different explanation, however, as Van, unlike Jakob Gradus of *Pale Fire* and the regime's minions in *Invitation to a Beheading,* is very much alive to his surroundings. Eighty years after his first journey to Ardis, Van can still recall: "Sunflecks and lacy shadows skimmed over [the driver's] legs and lent a green twinkle to the brass button deprived of its twin on the back of the coachman's coat" (Nabokov, *Ada,* 32). The fact that Van's memory of this day is dazzlingly accurate is confirmed by his recollection that Ada arrived at Ardis wearing "a white frock with a black jacket" (ibid., 34). Ada maintains that he must have imagined her wearing a black jacket on such a hot day, but Kim's photos retrospectively reveal that Van's recollection was correct (ibid., 318).

52. For discussions of Nabokov's various strategies of self-encoding, see Connolly, *Nabokov's Early Fiction,* 157–60; Dolinin, "The Caning of Modernist Profaners"; Guy, "Les anagrammes cosmopolites de l'auteur dans son oeuvre"; Shapiro, "Setting His Myriad Faces in His Text"; and Tammi, *Problems of Nabokov's Poetics,* 314–59.

53. Nabokov, "Playwriting," 321.

54. Borges, "Tlön, Uqbar, Orbis Tertius," 8.

55. *Transparent Things* proposes that the soul is immortal and that memory is not exactly "lost" after death. Once spirits are freed from the constraints of time, they have access to the past without having to rely on memory.

56. Volskii, *Encounters with Lenin,* 208, 218. In an interview with Douglas Davis from 1964, Nabokov explained that the Montreux Palace Hotel was an ideal seminary for *Ada.* "I am working on a novel which 'happens' on Lake Leman," he explained, adding further that Switzerland "is the most pleasant and poetical country in Europe. Gogol, Tolstoy, Byron, Dostoevski walked here. Gogol wrote *Dead Souls* here. Dostoevski found himself penniless here. Tolstoy caught a good case of venereal disease here. As I say, it is a poetical country." See Davis, "On the Banks of Lake Leman." Though Lenin's long residence in Geneva would have detracted from Switzerland's poetical nature in Nabokov's estimation, it is unlikely that Nabokov was blind to the Soviet dictator's associations with Lake Leman and its surroundings. Lenin walked its shores, and he seems also to inhabit the first novel Nabokov wrote there.

57. Volskii, *Encounters with Lenin,* 245.

58. Ibid., 182, 183, 206–7, 220, 242.

59. Madness often attends metaphysical insight in Nabokov's fiction. Krug, for instance, loses his sanity the moment he discovers the true nature of his existence. In "Ultima Thule," Adam Falter discovers "the essence of things" at the cost of his social and emotional bearings. As he tells Sineusov, "the shock of Truth" is so intense that it "can no longer be 'absorbed,'" and it is only "by chance

that it did not kill me." Upon being initiated into this Truth, Doctor Bonomini "died of astonishment" (Nabokov, "Ultima Thule," 508, 509, 513, 515).

60. Peterson, "Nabokov and Poe," 470–71.

61. Nabokov, "Ultima Thule," 501.

62. Nabokov, "Signs and Symbols," 599; Wood, *The Magician's Doubts,* 73.

63. Nabokov, "Signs and Symbols," 599, 602.

64. V. D. Nabokov, "Pis'ma V. D. Nabokova iz Krestov k zhene" ["V. D. Nabokov's Letters to His Wife from Kresty Prison"], 266, 269, 270, 271, 272, 273, 275.

65. Ibid., 270–71.

66. Ibid., 275.

EPILOGUE

The epigraph for the epilogue is from Elena Nabokov's transcript of Vladimir Nabokov's diary preserved at the New York Public Library's Berg Collection. I cite it from Boyd, *Vladimir Nabokov: The Russian Years,* 191.

1. Nabokov, *Perepiska s sestroi* [*Correspondence with Sister*], 41. I quote Leona Toker's translation of the passage in her *Nabokov: The Mystery of Literary Structures,* 177–78.

2. Michael Wood, "The Politics of Zembla," 1.

3. Unpublished to this day, Nabokov's "Dvoe" is preserved at the New York Public Library's Berg Collection. See Boyd, *Vladimir Nabokov: The Russian Years,* 156–57 and 552, note 67.

4. Bethea, "Nabokov and Blok," 376–79.

5. In "Eccentric Modernism: Nabokov and Yeats," John Burt Foster, Jr., emphasizes the importance of eccentricity in Nabokov's life and art.

6. V. D. Nabokov, "Zhizn' i deiatel'nost' N. V. Rukavishnikova," 149–50; emphasis in original.

7. Quoted in Boyd, "New Light on Nabokov's Russian Years," 6. These findings are also reported in the Russian translation of the first volume of Boyd's biography of Nabokov, *Vladimir Nabokov: Russkie gody,* 129–30.

8. Boyd, *Vladimir Nabokov: Russkie gody,* 129.

Bibliography

Aikhenvald, Iulii. "Bessmertnaia poshlost'" ["Immortal *Poshlost'*"]. In *Pokhvala prazdnosti: Sbornik statei,* 18–56. Moscow: Kostry, 1922.

———. *Nasha revoliutsiia* [*Our Revolution*]. Moscow: Revoliutsiia i kultura, 1918.

———. "Pokhvala prazdnosti" ["Praise of Idleness"]. In *Pokhvala prazdnosti: Sbornik statei,* 5–17. Moscow: Kostry, 1922.

———. Review of *Problems of Idealism* [under "Obzor knig"]. *Voprosy filosofii i psikhologii* 14:2, no. 67 (1903): 333–56.

———. *Siluety russkikh pisatelei.* Vol. 1. Berlin: Slovo, 1929.

Akselrod, Liubov (Ortodoks). *Filosofskie ocherki: Otvet filosofskim kritikam istoricheskogo materializma* [*Philosophical Sketches: Response to the Philosophical Critics of Historical Materialism*]. St. Petersburg, 1906.

Alexandrov, Vladimir E., ed. *The Garland Companion to Vladimir Nabokov.* New York: Garland, 1995.

———. "Nabokov and Bely." In *The Garland Companion to Vladimir Nabokov,* 358–66.

———. *Nabokov's Otherworld.* Princeton, N.J.: Princeton University Press, 1991.

Allen, Anita L. "Privacy in American Law." In *Privacies: Philosophical Evaluations,* edited by Beate Rössler, 19–39. Stanford, Calif.: Stanford University Press, 2004.

Amis, Kingsley. Review of *Lolita,* by Vladimir Nabokov. *Spectator,* November 6, 1959, 635–36. Reprinted in Page, *Nabokov: The Critical Heritage,* 102–7.

Anderson, Douglas. "Nabokov's Genocidal and Nuclear Holocausts in *Lolita.*" *Mosaic: A Journal for the Interdisciplinary Study of Literature* 29, no. 2 (1996): 73–90.

Appel, Alfred, Jr. "Notes." In *The Annotated Lolita,* by Vladimir Nabokov. Edited by Alfred Appel, Jr. New York: McGraw-Hill, 1970.

Arendt, Hannah. "The Ex-Communists." *The Commonweal* 57, no. 24 (1953): 595–99.

Bailes, Kendall E. *Science and Russian Culture in an Age of Revolutions: V. I.*

Vernadsky and His Scientific School, 1863–1945. Bloomington: Indiana University Press, 1990.

Barabtarlo, Gennady. "'He Said—I Said': An Afternote." *The Nabokovian* 45 (2000): 29–36.

———. "Nabokov's Trinity (On the Movement of Nabokov's Themes)." In Connolly, *Nabokov and His Fiction,* 109–38.

———. *Phantom of Fact: A Guide to Nabokov's "Pnin."* Ann Arbor, Mich.: Ardis, 1989.

Becker, Theodore L. *Political Trials.* Indianapolis, Ind.: Bobbs-Merrill, 1971.

Beiner, Ronald. *What's the Matter with Liberalism?* Berkeley: University of California Press, 1992.

Belknap, Michael R. *Cold War Political Justice: The Smith Act, the Communist Party, and American Civil Liberties.* Westport, Conn.: Greenwood, 1977.

Belletto, Steven. "The Zemblan Who Came in from the Cold, or Nabokov's *Pale Fire,* Chance, and the Cold War." *ELH* 73 (2006): 755–80.

Bensing, Robert C. "A Comparative Study of American Sex Statutes." *Journal of Criminal Law, Criminology, and Police Science* 42, no. 1 (1951): 57–72.

Berdiaev, Nikolai A. "The Ethical Problem in the Light of Philosophical Idealism." In Poole, *Problems of Idealism,* 161–97.

Bergson, Henri. *The Creative Mind.* Translated by Mabelle L. Andison. New York: Philosophical Library, 1946.

———. *Matter and Memory.* Translated by Nancy Margaret Paul and W. Scott Palmer. London: George Allen & Unwin, 1911. Reprint, Edinburgh: Riverside, 1929.

———. *Mind-Energy: Lectures and Essays.* Translated by H. Wildon Carr. New York: Henry Holt, 1920.

———. *Oeuvres.* Edited by André Robinet. Paris: Presses Universitaires de France, 1970.

"Berkeley." *Encyclopaedia Britannica.* 2009. *Encyclopaedia Britannica Online* 24 (2009). http://www.search.eb.com/eb/article-9078781.

Berkeley, George. *An Essay Towards A New Theory of Vision.* Edited by A. A. Luce. In volume 6 of *The Works of George Berkeley, Bishop of Cloyne,* edited by A. A. Luce and T. E. Jessop, 159–239. London: Nelson, 1948; rpt. 1964.

———. *The Principles of Human Knowledge.* Edited by J. E. Jessop. In volume 2 of *The Works of George Berkeley, Bishop of Cloyne,* edited by A. A. Luce and T. E. Jessop, 21–113. London: Nelson, 1949; rpt. 1964.

———. *Three Dialogues Between Hylas and Philonous.* Edited by T. E. Jessop. In volume 2 of *The Works of George Berkeley, Bishop of Cloyne,* edited by A. A. Luce and T. E. Jessop, 165–263. London: Nelson, 1949; rpt. 1964.

Berlin, Isaiah. "Two Concepts of Liberty." In *Liberty,* edited by Henry Hardy, 166–217. Oxford: Oxford University Press, 2002. Originally published in 1958.

Bethea, David M. "Nabokov and Blok." In Alexandrov, *The Garland Companion to Vladimir Nabokov*, 374–82.

Bishop, Morris. "Nabokov at Cornell." In *Nabokov: Criticism, Reminiscences, Translations, and Tributes,* edited by Alfred Appel, Jr., and Charles Newman, 234–39. Evanston, Ill.: Northwestern University Press, 1970.

Blackwell, Stephen H. "Nabokov, Mach and Monism." In Grayson, McMillin, and Meyer, *Nabokov's World, Volume 1: The Shape of Nabokov's World,* 121–31.

———. *The Quill and the Scalpel: Nabokov's Art and the Worlds of Science.* Columbus: Ohio State University Press, 2009.

———. "Reconsidering Iulii Aikhenvald." Paper presented at the 56th Annual Kentucky Foreign Language Convention, University of Kentucky, Lexington, April 24–26, 2003.

———. *Zina's Paradox: The Figured Reader in Nabokov's "Gift."* New York: Peter Lang, 2000.

Bogdanov, Aleksandr A. *Empiriomonizm: Stat'i po filosofii* [*Empirio-Monism: Philosophical Essays*]. 3 vols. 2nd ed. St. Petersburg, 1905.

———. *Vera i nauka: O knige V. Il'ina "Materializm i empiriokrititsizm"* [*Faith and Science: On V. Il'in's book "Materialism and Empirio-Criticism"*]. Moscow, 1910.

Borges, Jorge Luis. *Labyrinths: Selected Stories and Other Writings,* edited by Donald A. Yates and James E. Irby. New York: New Directions, 1964.

———. "A New Refutation of Time." Translated by James E. Irby. In *Labyrinths,* by Jorge Luis Borges, 217–34.

———. "Tlön, Uqbar, Orbis Tertius." Translated by James E. Irby. In *Labyrinths,* by Jorge Luis Borges, 3–18.

Bowers, Fredson. Introduction to *Lectures on Russian Literature,* by Vladimir Nabokov, edited by Fredson Bowers, vii–xvii. San Diego: Harvest, Harcourt, Bruccoli Clark, 1981.

Boyd, Brian. "Annotations to *Ada.*" *The Nabokovian* 42 (1998): 40–76.

———. "Chronology." In Boyd, *Vladimir Nabokov: Novels 1955–1962,* by Vladimir Nabokov, 837–68.

———. "'The Expected Stress Did Not Come': A Note on 'Father's Butterflies.'" *The Nabokovian* 45 (2000): 22–29.

———. *Nabokov's "Ada": The Place of Consciousness.* Christchurch, N.Z.: Cybereditions, 2001. Originally published in 1985.

———. *Nabokov's "Pale Fire": The Magic of Artistic Discovery.* Princeton, N.J.: Princeton University Press, 1999.

———. "Nabokov's Transition from Russian to English: Repudiation or Evolution?" *Nabokov Studies* 11 (2007/2008): 1–29.

———. "New Light on Nabokov's Russian Years." *Cycnos* 10, no. 1 (1993): 3–9.

———, ed. *Novels and Memoirs 1941–1951.* By Vladimir Nabokov. New York: Library of America, 1996.

———, ed. *Novels 1955–1962.* By Vladimir Nabokov. New York: Library of America, 1996.

———, ed. *Novels 1969–1974.* By Vladimir Nabokov. New York: Library of America, 1996.

———. "Reflections on Narcissus." *Nabokov Studies* 5 (1998/1999): 179–83.

———. Review of *A Guide to Nabokov's Butterflies and Moths 2001,* by Dieter E. Zimmer. *Nabokov Studies* 6 (2000/2001): 215–20.

———. *Vladimir Nabokov: Russkie gody* [*Vladimir Nabokov: The Russian Years*]. Translated by Galina Lapina. St. Petersburg: Nezavisimaia gazeta/ Symposium, 2001.

———. *Vladimir Nabokov: The American Years.* Princeton, N.J.: Princeton University Press, 1991.

———. *Vladimir Nabokov: The Russian Years.* Princeton, N.J.: Princeton University Press, 1990.

———, and Robert Michael Pyle, eds. *Nabokov's Butterflies: Unpublished and Uncollected Writings.* By Vladimir Nabokov. Boston: Beacon, 2000.

Browder, Robert P. Introduction to *V. D. Nabokov and the Russian Provisional Government, 1917.* Edited and translated by Virgil D. Medlin and Steven L. Parsons, 1–11. New Haven, Conn.: Yale University Press, 1976.

———, and Alexander F. Kerensky, eds. *The Russian Provisional Government 1917: Documents.* 3 vols. Stanford, Calif.: Stanford University Press, 1961.

Bruhm, Steven. "Queer, Queer Vladimir." *American Imago* 53, no. 4 (1996): 281–306.

Bulgakov, Sergey N. "Basic Problems of the Theory of Progress." In Poole, *Problems of Idealism,* 85–123.

Bullough, Vern L. "Age of Consent: A Historical Overview." *Journal of Psychology and Human Sexuality* 16, nos. 2/3 (2004): 25–42.

Chernobel, G. T. "Vladimir Dmitrievich Nabokov, zhizn' i tvorchestvo" ["Vladimir Dmitrievich Nabokov, Life and Work"]." In *Istoriia Russkoi pravovoi mysli: Biografii, dokumenty, publikatsii* [*A History of Russian Legal Thought: Biographies, Documents, and Publications*], edited by V. P. Kashepov, A. V. Mitskevich, and S. A. Piatkina, 425–43. Moscow: Ostozh'e, 1998.

Chernyshevski, N. G. [Nikolai Gavrilovich]. *The Anthropological Principle in Philosophy.* In *Selected Philosophical Essays,* edited by M. Grigoryan, 49–135. Moscow: Foreign Languages Publishing House, 1953.

Connolly, Julian W., ed. *Nabokov and His Fiction: New Perspectives.* Cambridge, Eng.: Cambridge University Press, 1999.

———. *Nabokov's Early Fiction: Patterns of Self and Other.* Cambridge, Eng.: Cambridge University Press, 1992.

———. "A Note on the Name 'Pnin.'" *Vladimir Nabokov Research Letter* 6 (1981): 32–33.

Couturier, Maurice. "Nabokov in Postmodernist Land." *Critique: Studies in Contemporary Fiction* 34, no. 4 (1993): 247–60.

Davis, Douglas M. "On the Banks of Lake Leman: Mr. Nabokov Reflects on 'Lolita' and 'Onegin.'" *National Observer,* June 29, 1964, 17.

Davydov, Sergej. "Poshlost." In Alexandrov, *The Garland Companion to Vladimir Nabokov,* 628–33.

Dean, Richard. *The Value of Humanity in Kant's Moral Theory.* Oxford: Clarendon, 2006.

Denis, Lara. "Kant on the Wrongness of 'Unnatural' Sex." *History of Philosophy Quarterly* 16, no. 2 (1999): 225–48.

Dennis v. United States. 341 U.S. 494 (1951).

Descartes, René. *The Principles of Philosophy.* In volume 1 of *The Philosophical Works of Descartes,* translated by Elizabeth S. Haldane and G. R. T. Ross, 201–302. Cambridge, Eng.: Cambridge University Press, 1931.

Diment, Galya. "The Nabokov-Wilson Debate: Art Versus Social and Moral Responsibility." In Larmour, *Discourse and Ideology in Nabokov's Prose,* 15–23.

———. *Pniniad: Vladimir Nabokov and Marc Szeftel.* Seattle: University of Washington Press, 1997.

Dolinin, Alexander. "The Caning of Modernist Profaners: Parody in *Despair.*" Online at http://www.libraries.psu.edu/nabokov/doli1.htm.

———. "Clio Laughs Last: Nabokov's Answer to Historicism." In Connolly, *Nabokov and His Fiction: New Perspectives,* 197–215.

———. "Doklady Vladimira Nabokova v Berlinskom literaturnom kruzhke" ["The Talks of Vladimir Nabokov to the Berlin Literary Circle"]. *Zvezda* 4 (1999): 7–11.

———. "*The Gift.*" In Alexandrov, *The Garland Companion to Vladimir Nabokov,* 135–69.

———. Introduction to "Pis'ma V. V. Nabokova k G. P. Struve: 1925–1931: Chast' Pervaia" ["V. V. Nabokov's Letters to G. P. Struve: 1925–1931: Part One"]. Published by E. B. Belodubrovskii and A. A. Dolinin. *Zvezda* 11 (2003): 115–50.

———. "Nabokov as a Russian Writer." In *The Cambridge Companion to Nabokov.* Edited by Julian W. Connolly, 49–64. Cambridge, Eng.: Cambridge University Press, 2005.

———. "Nabokov i Blok" ["Nabokov and Blok"]. In *Tezisy dokladov nauchnoi konferentsii "A. Blok i russkii postsimvolizm,"* 36–44. Tartu, Estonia: Tartu University, 1991.

———. "Primechaniia [k *Daru*]" ["Notes to *The Gift*"]. In volume 4 of *Vladimir Nabokov (V. Sirin): Sobranie sochinenii russkogo perioda v piati tomakh: 1935–1937* [*Vladimir Nabokov (V. Sirin): Collected Russian-Language Works in Five Volumes: 1935–1937*], edited by M. V. Kozikova, 634–768. St. Petersburg: Symposium, 2000.

Dragunoiu, Dana. "'The Universe Embraced by Consciousness': Vladimir Nabokov's Philosophical Domain." Ph.D. dissertation, University of Toronto, 2000.

———. "Vladimir Nabokov's *Invitation to a Beheading* and the Russian Radical Tradition." *Journal of Modern Literature* 25, no. 1 (2001): 53–69.

Durantaye, Leland de la. *Style Is Matter: The Moral Art of Vladimir Nabokov.* Ithaca, N.Y.: Cornell University Press, 2007.

———. "Vladimir Nabokov and Sigmund Freud, or a Particular Problem." *American Imago* 62, no. 1 (2005): 59–73.

Ehrlich, J. Shoshanna. "From Age of Consent Laws to the 'Silver Ring Thing': The Regulation of Adolescent Female Sexuality." *Health Matrix* 16, no. 1 (2006): 151–81.

Emerson, Caryl. Foreword to *Problems of Idealism,* edited by Poole, vii–xviii.

Emmons, Terence. *The Formation of Political Parties and the First National Elections in Russia.* Cambridge, Mass.: Harvard University Press, 1983.

Engelstein, Laura. *The Keys to Happiness: Sex and the Search for Modernity in Fin-de-Siècle Russia.* Ithaca, N.Y.: Cornell University Press, 1992.

Ernst, Morris L., and David Loth. *Report on the American Communist.* New York: Henry Holt, 1952.

Etzioni, Amitai. *The Limits of Privacy.* New York: Basic Books, 1999.

Farson, Richard. *Birthrights.* New York: Macmillan, 1974.

Feldman, Fred. "Kantian Ethics." In *Ethical Theory: Classical and Contemporary Readings.* 2nd ed. Edited by Louis P. Pojman, 288–301. Belmont, Calif.: Wadsworth, 1995.

Ferri, Enrico. *Criminal Sociology.* Edited by William W. Smithers. Translated by Joseph I. Kelly and John Lisle. Introduction by Charles A. Ellwood and Quincy A. Myers. New York: Agathon, 1967.

Field, Andrew. *Nabokov: His Life in Part.* New York: Viking, 1977.

———. *VN: The Life and Art of Vladimir Nabokov.* New York: Crown, 1986.

Fink, Hilary L. *Bergson and Russian Modernism: 1900–1930.* Evanston, Ill.: Northwestern University Press, 1998.

Fischer, George. *Russian Liberalism, from Gentry to Intelligentsia.* Cambridge, Mass.: Harvard University Press, 1958.

Fischer, Kuno. *A Commentary on Kant's Critick of the Pure Reason.* Introduction, explanatory notes, and appendices by John Pentland Mahaffy. London: Longmans, Green, 1866.

Foster, John Burt, Jr. "*Bend Sinister.*" In Alexandrov, *The Garland Companion to Vladimir Nabokov,* 25–36.

———. "Eccentric Modernism: Nabokov and Yeats." In Grayson, McMillin, and Meyer, *Nabokov's World, Volume 2: Reading Nabokov,* 141–55.

———. "Poshlust, Culture Criticism, Adorno, and Malraux." In Connolly, *Nabokov and His Fiction,* 216–35.

Friedmann, W. *Legal Theory.* New York: Columbia University Press, 1967. Originally published in 1944.

Ganfman, M. I. [Maksim Ippolitovich]. "V. D. Nabokov." *Rul'* 417 (March 30, 1922): 1–2.

Gibson, Walter S. *Hieronymus Bosch.* London: Thames and Hudson, 1973.

Giles, Paul. "Virtual Eden: *Lolita,* Pornography, and the Perversions of American Studies." *Journal of American Studies* 34, no. 1 (2000): 41–66.

Gorham, Deborah. "The 'Maiden Tribute of Modern Babylon' Re-examined: Child Prostitution and the Idea of Childhood in Late-Victorian England." *Victorian Studies* 21 (1978): 353–79.

Gould, Stephen Jay. "No Science Without Fancy, No Art Without Facts: The Lepidoptery of Vladimir Nabokov." In Sarah Funke et al., *Véra's Butterflies: First Editions by Vladimir Nabokov Inscribed to His Wife,* 84–114. New York: Glenn Horowitz, 1999.

Grayson, Jane. "Washington's Gift: Materials Pertaining to Nabokov's *Gift* in the Library of Congress." *Nabokov Studies* 1 (1994): 21–67.

———, Arnold McMillin, and Priscilla Meyer, eds. *Nabokov's World, Volume 1: The Shape of Nabokov's World.* New York: Palgrave, 2002.

———, Arnold McMillin, and Priscilla Meyer, eds. *Nabokov's World, Volume 2: Reading Nabokov.* New York: Palgrave, 2002.

Gregor, Mary J., ed. and trans. *Practical Philosophy.* By Immanuel Kant. Cambridge, Eng.: Cambridge University Press, 1996.

Griffith, Kathryn. *Judge Learned Hand and the Role of the Federal Judiciary.* Norman: University of Oklahoma Press, 1973.

Grishakova, Marina. *The Models of Space, Time and Vision in V. Nabokov's Fiction: Narrative Strategies and Cultural Frames.* Tartu, Estonia: Tartu University Press, 2006.

Grossmith, Robert. "Other States of Being: Nabokov's Two-World Metaphysic." Ph.D. dissertation, University of Keele, 1987.

———. "Shaking the Kaleidoscope: Physics and Metaphysics in Nabokov's *Bend Sinister.*" *Russian Literature Triquarterly* 24 (1991): 151–61.

Gruzenberg, Oskar O. "Moia pamiatka o V. D. Nabokove" ["My Memorial to V. D. Nabokov"]. *Rul'* 420 (April 2, 1922): 1.

Gurko, V. I. [Vladimir Iosifovich]. *Features and Figures of the Past: Government and Opinion in the Reign of Nicholas II.* Edited by J. E. Wallace Sterling, Xenia Joukoff Eudin, and H. H. Fisher. Translated by Laura Matveev. Stanford, Calif.: Stanford University Press, 1939.

Guy, Laurence. "Les anagrammes cosmopolites de l'auteur dans son oeuvre, ou l'identité renversée de Vladimir Nabokov." *Cahiers du monde russe* 37, no. 3 (1996): 337–48.

Haines, Charles Grove. *The Revival of Natural Law Concepts.* New York: Russell & Russell, 1965. Originally published in 1929.

Hall, Kermit L., William M. Wiecek, and Paul Finkelman. *American Legal History: Cases and Materials.* New York: Oxford University Press, 1991.

Hayek, F. A. *New Studies in Philosophy, Politics, Economics and the History of Ideas.* Chicago: University of Chicago Press, 1978.

Henriksen, Margot A. *Dr. Strangelove's America: Society and Culture in the Atomic Age.* Berkeley: University of California Press, 1997.

Hesiod. *Theogony, Works and Days, Testimonia.* Edited and translated by Glenn W. Most. Loeb Classical Library, 2006.

Hessen [Gessen], Iosif [Joseph] V. *Gody izgnaniia: Zhiznennyi otchet* [*The Years of Exile: An Autobiographical Account*]. Paris: YMCA, 1979.

———. *Iskaniia obshchestvennago ideala* [*Searching for the Social Ideal*]. 2nd ed. Berlin, 1922.

———. "Pamiati druga" ["In Memory of a Friend"]. *Rul'* 417 (March 30, 1922): 1.

———. *V dvukh vekakh: Zhiznennyi otchet* [*Two Centuries: An Autobiographical Account*]. Berlin: Speer & Schmidt, 1937.

Hessen [Gessen], Sergey I. "Bor'ba utopii i avtonomii dobra v mirovozzrenii F. M. Dostoevskago i Vl. Solov'eva" ["The Struggle Between Utopia and the Autonomy of the Good in the Worldview of F. M. Dostoevsky and Vl. Soloviev"]. *Sovremennye zapiski* 45–46 (1931): 271–305, 321–51. Reprinted in Sergey Hessen, *Izbrannye sochineniia,* 609–77.

———. *Izbrannye sochineniia.* Edited by Andrzej Walicki and N. Chistiakova. Moscow: ROSSPEN, 1999.

———. "Moe zhizneopisanie." In *Izbrannye sochineniia,* 723–82.

———. "Problema pravovogo sotsializma" ["The Problem of Rule-of-Law Socialism"]. *Sovremennye zapiski* 22 (1924): 257–92; 23 (1925): 313–41; 27 (1926): 382–429; 28 (1926): 299–341; 30 (1927): 380–408; 31 (1927): 328–57.

Hessen [Gessen], V. I. [Vladimir Iosifovich]. *V bor'be za zhizn' (Zapiski emigranta)* [*Fighting to Survive (Memories of an Émigré)*]. New York: Rausen, 1974.

Hessen [Gessen], V. Iu. "Gesseny i Nabokovy—Sotrudnichestvo i druzhba" ["The Hessens and the Nabokovs—Collaboration and Friendship"]. *Nabokovskii vestnik* 1 (1998): 182–92.

Hessen [Gessen], V. M. [Vladimir Matveevich]. "Vozrozhdenie estestvennago prava" ["The Revival of Natural Law"]. *Pravo* 10, 11 (1902): 475–84, 533–47.

Hofstadter, Richard. "The Paranoid Style in American Politics." *Harper's Magazine* 229, no. 1374 (1964): 77–86.

Holt, John. *Escape from Childhood.* New York: Dutton, 1974.

Horwitz, Morton J. "Jews and McCarthyism: A View from the Bronx." In *Secret Agents: The Rosenberg Case, McCarthyism, and Fifties America,* edited by Marjorie Garber and Rebecca L. Walkowitz, 257–63. New York: Routledge, 1995.

Houlgate, Laurence D. "Three Concepts of Children's Constitutional Rights:

Reflections on the Enjoyment Theory." *University of Pennsylvania Journal of Constitutional Law* 2, no. 1 (1999): 77–94.

In re Gault. 387 U.S. 1 (1967).

Ivanov-Razumnik, R. V. *Istoriia russkoi obshchestvennoi mysli* [*The History of Russian Social Thought*]. Vol. 2. 2nd ed. St. Petersburg: 1908.

Johnson, D. Barton. "Belyj and Nabokov: A Comparative Overview." *Russian Literature* 9, no. 4 (1981): 379–402.

———. "The Labyrinth of Incest in Nabokov's *Ada*." *Comparative Literature* 38, no. 3 (1986): 224–54.

———. "Vladimir Nabokov and Walter de la Mare's 'Otherworld.'" In Grayson, McMillin, and Meyer, *Nabokov's World, Volume 1: The Shape of Nabokov's World*, 71–87.

———. *Worlds in Regression: Some Novels of Vladimir Nabokov*. Ann Arbor, Mich.: Ardis, 1985.

———, and Brian Boyd. "Prologue: The Otherworld." In Grayson, McMillin, and Meyer, *Nabokov's World, Volume 1: The Shape of Nabokov's World*, 19–25.

Johnson, Kurt. "Recognizing Vladimir Nabokov's Legacy in Science: Where We Are Today, Where We Go From Here." *Nabokov Studies* 6 (2000/2001): 149–61.

———, and Steve Coates. *Nabokov's Blues: The Scientific Odyssey of a Literary Genius*. Cambridge, Mass.: Zoland Books, 1999.

Kaminka, Avgust, and V. D. Nabokov. *Vtoraia Gosudarstvennaia Duma* [*The Second State Duma*]. St. Petersburg, 1907.

Kant, Immanuel. "An Answer to the Question: What Is Enlightenment?" In Gregor, *Practical Philosophy*, by Immanuel Kant, 11–22. Originally published in 1784.

———. *Critique of Practical Reason*. In Gregor, *Practical Philosophy*, by Immanuel Kant, 133–271. Originally published in 1788.

———. *Critique of Pure Reason*. Translated and edited by Paul Guyer and Allen W. Wood. Cambridge, Eng.: Cambridge University Press, 1998. Originally published in 1781 and 1787.

———. *Critique of the Power of Judgment*. Translated by Paul Guyer and Eric Matthews. Edited by Paul Guyer. Cambridge, Eng.: Cambridge University Press, 2000. Originally published in 1790.

———. *Groundwork of The Metaphysics of Morals*. In Gregor, *Practical Philosophy*, by Immanuel Kant, 37–108. Originally published in 1785.

———. *Lectures on Ethics*. Translated by Louis Infield. Foreword by Lewis White Beck. New York: Harper & Row, 1963. Originally published in 1930.

———. *The Metaphysics of Morals*. In Gregor, *Practical Philosophy*, by Immanuel Kant, 363–603. Originally published in 1797.

———. "On a Supposed Right to Lie from Philanthropy." In Gregor, *Practical Philosophy*, by Immanuel Kant, 605–15. Originally published in 1797.

———. "On the Common Saying: That May Be Correct in Theory, but It Is of

No Use in Practice." In Gregor, *Practical Philosophy*, by Immanuel Kant, 273–309. Originally published in 1793.

Karlinsky, Simon. "Introduction: Dear Volodya, Dear Bunny; or, Affinities and Disagreements." In Nabokov and Wilson, *Dear Bunny, Dear Volodya*, 1–25.

Karpovich, Michael. "Two Types of Russian Liberalism: Maklakov and Miliukov." In *Continuity and Change in Russian and Soviet Thought*, edited by Ernest J. Simmons, 129–43. New York: Russell & Russell, 1967. Originally published in 1955.

Karshan, Thomas. "December 1925: Nabokov Between Work and Play." *Nabokov Studies* 10 (2006): 1–25.

Kennedy, Duncan. "The Stages of the Decline of the Public-Private Distinction." *University of Pennsylvania Law Review* 130 (1982): 1349–57.

Kenner, Hugh. *A Homemade World: The American Modernist Writers*. London: Marion Boyars, 1977.

Kermode, Frank. Review of *Pale Fire*, by Vladimir Nabokov. *New Statesman*, November 9, 1962, 671–72. Reprinted in Page, *Nabokov: The Critical Heritage*, 144–48.

Kirchheimer, Otto. *Political Justice: The Use of Legal Procedure for Political Ends*. Princeton, N.J.: Princeton University Press, 1961.

Kolakowski, Leszek. *Main Currents of Marxism*. 3 vols. Translated by P. S. Falla. Oxford: Clarendon, 1978.

Korsgaard, Christine M. *Creating the Kingdom of Ends*. Cambridge, Eng.: Cambridge University Press, 1996.

Krishevskii, N. "V Krymu (1916–1918 g.)" ["In the Crimea (1916–1918)"]. In *Arkhiv russkoi revoliutsii*, edited by I. V. Hessen [Gessen], 71–124. Vol. 13. Berlin: Slovo, 1924. Reprinted in *Slavistics Printings and Reprintings*, edited by C. H. Van Schooneveld. The Hague: Mouton, 1970.

Kuehn, Manfred. *Kant: A Biography*. Cambridge, Eng.: Cambridge University Press, 2001.

Kuzmanovich, Zoran. "'Splendid Insincerity' as 'Utmost Truthfulness': Nabokov and the Claims of the Real." In Grayson, McMillin, and Meyer, *Nabokov's World, Volume 1: The Shape of Nabokov's World*, 26–46.

Langton, Rae. "Duty and Desolation." *Philosophy* 67 (1992): 481–505.

Larmour, David H. J., ed. *Discourse and Ideology in Nabokov's Prose*. London: Routledge, 2002.

Lenin, V. I. *Materialism and Empirio-Criticism: Critical Comments on a Reactionary Philosophy*. Moscow: Progress, 1973.

Leonard, Jeffrey. "In Place of Lost Time: *Ada*." *TriQuarterly* 17 (1970): 136–46.

Levine, Peter. "*Lolita* and Aristotle's Ethics." *Philosophy and Literature* 19, no. 1 (1995): 32–47.

Lock, Charles. "Transparent Things and Opaque Words." In Grayson, McMillin, and Meyer, *Nabokov's World, Volume 1: The Shape of Nabokov's World*, 104–20.

Luce, A. A. "Editor's Introduction" to *An Essay Towards A New Theory of Vision,* by George Berkeley, edited by A. A. Luce. Vol. 1 of *The Works of George Berkeley, Bishop of Cloyne,* edited by A. A. Luce and T. E. Jessop, 143–57. London: Nelson, 1948; rpt. 1964.

Lunacharskii, A. *Religiia i sotsializm* [*Religion and Socialism*]. 2 vols. St. Petersburg, 1908, 1911.

Macdonald, Dwight. Review of *Pale Fire,* by Vladimir Nabokov. *Partisan Review* (Summer 1962): 437–42. Reprinted in Page, *Nabokov: The Critical Heritage,* 137–40.

MacKinnon, Catharine A. *Toward a Feminist Theory of the State.* Cambridge, Mass.: Harvard University Press, 1989.

Maddox, Lucy. *Nabokov's Novels in English.* Athens: University of Georgia Press, 1983.

Magee, Bryan. *Confessions of a Philosopher.* London: Weidenfeld & Nicolson, 1997.

———. *The Philosophy of Schopenhauer.* Oxford: Oxford University Press, 1997.

Maklakov, Vasilii. *The First State Duma: Contemporary Reminiscences.* Translated by Mary Belkin. Bloomington: Indiana University Press, 1964.

Makletsov, Aleksandr. "V. D. Nabokov, kak uchenyi kriminalist: K 10-letiiu so dnia konchiny" ["V. D. Nabokov as Scholar of Criminal Law: On the 10th Anniversary of His Death"]. *Rossiia i slavianstvo,* April 23, 1932, 2.

———. "V. D. Nabokov—Uchenyi" ["V. D. Nabokov—Scholar"]. *Rul'* 425 (April 8, 1922): 1–2.

Malikova, Maria. "V. V. Nabokov and V. D. Nabokov: His Father's Voice." In Grayson, McMillin, and Meyer, *Nabokov's World, Volume 2: Reading Nabokov,* 15–26.

Mandelstam, Nadezhda. *Hope Against Hope: A Memoir.* Translated by Max Hayward. New York: Modern Library, 1999. Originally published in 1970.

Mason, Bobbie Ann. *Nabokov's Garden: A Guide to "Ada."* Ann Arbor, Mich.: Ardis, 1974.

McCarthy, Mary. ["A Bolt from the Blue."] Review of *Pale Fire,* by Vladimir Nabokov. *New Republic,* June 4, 1962, 21–27. In Page, *Nabokov: The Critical Heritage,* 124–36.

McLean, Hugh. "*Lectures on Russian Literature.*" In Alexandrov, *The Garland Companion to Vladimir Nabokov,* 258–73.

Medvedev, A. M. "Nikolai Stepanovich Tagantsev, Zhizn' i tvorchestvo (1843–1923)." In *Istoriia russkoi pravovoi mysli: Biografii, dokumenty, publikatsii,* edited by V. P. Kashepov, A. V. Mitskevich, and S. A. Piatkina, 465–77. Moscow: Ostozh'e, 1998.

Mendelson, Wallace. *Justices Black and Frankfurter: Conflict in the Court.* Chicago: University of Chicago Press, 1961.

Meyer, Priscilla. "Dolorous Haze, Hazel Shade: Nabokov and the Spirits." In

Grayson, McMillin, and Meyer, *Nabokov's World, Volume 1: The Shape of Nabokov's World,* 88–103.

Meyer v. Nebraska. 262 U.S. 390 (1923).

Miliukov, Paul N. [Pavel Nikolaevich]. "Pamiati starago druga" ["In Memory of an Old Friend"]. *Rul'* 417 (March 30, 1922): 2.

———. *Political Memoirs, 1905–1917.* Edited by Arthur P. Mendel. Translated by Carl Goldberg. Ann Arbor: University of Michigan Press, 1967.

Mizruchi, Susan. "*Lolita* in History." *American Literature* 75, no. 3 (2003): 629–52.

Nabokov, Dmitri. "On a Book Entitled *The Enchanter.*" In *The Enchanter,* by Vladimir Nabokov. Translated by Dmitri Nabokov, 81–109. New York: Vintage, 1991. Originally published in 1986.

Nabokov, V. D. [Vladimir Dmitrievich]. "Deiatel'nost' partii narodnoi svobody v gosudarstvennoi dume" ["The Activity of the People's Freedom Party in the State Duma"]. *Vestnik partii narodnoi svobody* 30 (October 1, 1906): 1595–1603.

———. "Die Homosexualität im Russischen Strafgesetzbuch" ["Homosexuality in the Russian Penal Code"] [under Vladimir Nabokoff]. *Jahrbuch für sexuelle Zwischenstufen* 2 (1903): 1159–71.

———. "Kishinevskaia krovavaia bania" ["The Kishinev Bloodbath"]. *Pravo* 18 (April 27, 1903): 1281–85.

———. "Krovavyi god" ["The Bloody Year"]. *Poliarnaia zvezda* [*The Polar Star*] 5 (January 12, 1906): 315–23.

———. "Lebedinaia pesn'" ["Swan's Song"]. *Rul'* 427 (April 11, 1922): 1–2.

———. "Letter to Avgust Kaminka." National Archives of Finland. Russian emigrants 8: copy of Vladimir Nabokov's letter to Professor Kaminka. London, June 15, 1919.

———. "N. S. Tagantsev: K 50-ti-letnemu iubileiu." *Pravo* 12 (1913): 738–41.

———. ["O smertnoi kazni"]. Untitled. In *Smertnaia kazn': Mneniia russkikh kriminalistov* [*On Capital Punishment: The Views of Russian Criminalists*], edited by M. N. Gernet. Moscow, 1913. Reprinted in *Smertnaia kazn': Za i protiv* [*On Capital Punishment: Pro et Contra*], edited by O. F. Shishov and T. S. Parfenova, 206–9. Moscow: Iuridicheskaia literatura, 1989.

———. "Otmena smertnoi kazni" ["On the Abolition of the Death Penalty"]. *Rech'* 66 (March 18, 1917): 3.

———. "Pis'ma V. D. Nabokova iz Krestov k zhene. 1908 g." ["V. D. Nabokov's Letters to His Wife from Kresty Prison. 1908."]. *Vozdushnye puti* 4 (1965): 265–75.

———. "Plotskie prestupleniia po proektu ugolovnago ulozheniia" ["Carnal Crimes According to the Criminal Code Project"]. *Vestnik prava* [*Law Bulletin*] 32, nos. 9–10 (1902): 129–89. Reprinted in V. D. Nabokov, *Sbornik statei po ugolovnomu pravu,* 86–146.

———. "Po povodu 'Krymskikh ocherkov'" ["Apropos of 'Crimean Sketches'"]. *Golos Rossii* [*The Voice of Russia*] 221 (September 30, 1920): 2.

———. "Protsess 169 deputatov pervoi gosudarstvennoi dumy: Rech' V. D. Nabokova" ["The Trial of the 169 Deputies of the First State Duma: The Speech of V. D. Nabokov"]. *Vestnik partii narodnoi svobody,* December 18, 1907, 2116–23.

———. *The Provisional Government.* In *V. D. Nabokov and the Russian Provisional Government, 1917,* edited and translated by Virgil D. Medlin and Steven L. Parsons. New Haven, Conn.: Yale University Press, 1976.

———. *Sbornik statei po ugolovnomu pravu* [*A Collection of Articles on Criminal Law*]. St. Petersburg: Tipografiia Tovarishchestva "Obshchestvennaia Pol'za," 1904.

———. "Soderzhanie i metod nauki ugolovnago prava" ["The Science of Criminal Law: Contents and Method"]. In V. D. Nabokov, *Sbornik statei po ugolovnomu pravu,* 1–23.

———. "Soviet Rule and Russia's Future." Supplement to *New Commonwealth* 15 (January 23, 1920): 2–8.

———. "Sovremennoe polozhenie i takticheskiia zadachi konstitutsionno-demokraticheskoi partii." *Pravo* 41 (October 25, 1905): 3404–7.

———. *Tiuremnye dosugi* [*Prison Reflections*]. *Pravo* 34 (August 24, 1908): 1812–21; 35 (September 2, 1908): 1867–78; 36 (September 7, 1908): 1914–27; 38 (September 21, 1908): 2012–20.

———. "Vnutrenniaia voina" ["The Internal War"]." *Poliarnaia zvezda* [*The Polar Star*] 8 (February 3, 1906): 515–23.

———. "Zhizn' i deiatel'nost' N. V. Rukavishnikova" ["The Life and Activity of N. V. Rukavishnikov"]. In V. D. Nabokov, *Sbornik statei po ugolovnomu pravu,* 147–58.

Nabokov, Vladimir V. *Ada or Ardor: A Family Chronicle.* In Boyd, *Novels 1969–1974,* by Vladimir Nabokov, 1–485. Originally published in 1969.

———. "The Art of Literature and Commonsense." In *Lectures on Literature,* 371–80.

———. *Bend Sinister.* In Boyd, *Novels and Memoirs 1941–1951,* by Vladimir Nabokov, 161–358. Originally published in 1947.

———. "Braitenshtreter-Paolino." In volume 1 of *Vladimir Nabokov (V. Sirin): Sobranie sochinenii russkogo perioda v piati tomakh: 1918–1925* [*Vladimir Nabokov (V. Sirin): Collected Russian-Language Works in Five Volumes, 1918–1925*], edited by M. E. Malikova, 749–54. Saint Petersburg: Symposium, 1999.

———. "The Circle." In *A Russian Beauty and Other Stories,* by Vladimir Nabokov, 253–68. New York: McGraw-Hill, 1973.

———. *Dar.* New York: Izdatel'stvo Imeni Chekhova, 1952.

———. *The Defense.* Translated by Michael Scammell in collaboration with the author. New York: Vintage, 1990. Originally published in 1930.

———. *The Enchanter.* Translated by Dmitri Nabokov. New York: Vintage, 1991. Originally published in 1986.

———, trans. *Eugene Onegin: A Novel in Verse.* By Aleksandr Pushkin. 4 vols. Bollingen Series 72. New York: Bollingen, 1964.

———. "Evening on a Vacant Lot." In *Poems and Problems,* by Vladimir Nabokov, 68–73.

———. *The Eye.* Translated by Dmitri Nabokov in collaboration with the author. New York: Vintage, 1990. Originally published in 1965.

———. "Fame." In *Poems and Problems,* by Vladimir Nabokov, 102–13.

———. "Father's Butterflies: Second Addendum to *The Gift.*" Translated by Dmitri Nabokov. In Boyd and Pyle, *Nabokov's Butterflies,* 198–234.

———. Foreword to *The Eye.* Translated by Dmitri Nabokov in collaboration with the author, i–v. New York: Vintage, 1990. Originally published in 1965.

———. "From Notes for Interview with Jacob Bronowski, August 1963." In Boyd and Pyle, *Nabokov's Butterflies,* 566.

———. *The Gift.* Translated by Michael Scammell with Vladimir Nabokov. New York: Vintage, 1991. Originally published in 1963.

———. *Glory.* Translated by Dmitri Nabokov with Vladimir Nabokov. New York: McGraw-Hill, 1971.

———. Interview with Anne Guérin. *L'Express* (Paris), January 26, 1961, 26–27.

———. Interview with Mati Laansoo. *The Nabokov Research Newsletter* 10 (1983): 39–48.

———. Introduction to *Bend Sinister.* In Boyd, *Novels and Memoirs: 1941–1951,* 163–69. Originally published in 1947.

———. *Invitation to a Beheading.* Translated by Dmitri Nabokov with Vladimir Nabokov. New York: Vintage International, 1989. Originally published in 1959.

———. *King, Queen, Knave.* Translated by Dmitri Nabokov with Vladimir Nabokov. New York: Vintage International, 1989. Originally published in 1968.

———. *Lectures on Literature.* Edited by Fredson Bowers. San Diego: Harvest, Harcourt, Bruccoli Clark, 1980.

———. *Lectures on Russian Literature.* Edited by Fredson Bowers. San Diego: Harvest, Harcourt, Bruccoli Clark, 1981.

———. *Lolita.* In Boyd, *Novels 1955–1962,* by Vladimir Nabokov, 1–298. Originally published in 1955.

———. *Look at the Harlequins!* In Boyd, *Novels 1969–1974,* 563–747. Originally published in 1974.

———. *Mary.* Translated by Michael Glenny with Vladimir Nabokov. New York: Vintage International, 1989. Originally published in 1970.

———. "The Nearctic Members of the Genus *Lycaeides* Hübner." *Bulletin of the Museum of Comparative Zoology* 101 (1949): 479–541.

———. *Nikolai Gogol.* Corrected edition. New York: New Directions, 1961. Originally published in 1944.

———. "Notes on Neotropical Plebejinae (Lycaenidae, Lepidoptera)." *Psyche* 52, nos. 1–2 (1945): 1–61.

———. "The Oculus." In *Poems and Problems,* by Vladimir Nabokov, 100–101.

———. "On a Book Entitled *Lolita.*" In Boyd, *Novels 1955–1962,* 293–98.

———. "On Generalities." *Zvezda* 4 (1999): 12–14.

———. *Pale Fire.* In Boyd, *Novels 1955–1962,* 437–667. Originally published in 1962.

———. "Pamiati I. V. Gessena" ["In Memory of I. V. Hessen"]. *Novoe Russkoe Slovo,* March 31, 1943, 2.

———. "Pamiati I. V. Gessena" ["In Memory of I. V. Hessen"]. *Zvezda* 4 (1999): 46–47.

———. "Pamiati Iu. I. Aikhenvalda" ["In Memory of Iu. I. Aikhenvald"]. In volume 2 of *Vladimir Nabokov (V. Sirin): Sobranie sochinenii russkogo perioda v piati tomakh, 1926–1930* [*Vladimir Nabokov (V. Sirin): Collected Russian-Language Works in Five Volumes, 1926–1930*], edited by M. V. Kozikova, 667–68. Saint Petersburg: Symposium, 1999. Originally published in *Rul'* 2457 (December 23, 1928): 4.

———. *Perepiska s sestroi* [*Correspondence with Sister*]. Ann Arbor, Mich.: Ardis, 1985.

———. "Pereshel ty v novoe zhilishche . . ." ["You Have Moved to a New Home"]. *Nashe nasledie* 2 (1988): 112.

———. "Pis'ma k Glebu Struve" ["Letters to Gleb Struve"]. Published by Evgenii B. Belodubrovskii. *Zvezda* 4 (1999): 23–39.

———. "Pis'ma V. V. Nabokova k Gessenam" ["V. V. Nabokov's Letters to the Hessens"]. Foreword, translated and edited by V. Iu. Hessen. *Zvezda* 4 (1999): 42–45.

———. "Pis'ma V. V. Nabokova k G. P. Struve: 1925–1931: Chast' pervaia" ["The Letters of V. V. Nabokov to G. P. Struve: 1925–1931: Part One"]. Published by E. B. Belodubrovskii and A. A. Dolinin. *Zvezda* 11 (2003): 115–50.

———. "Pis'ma V. V. Nabokova k G. P. Struve: Chast' vtoraia (1931–1935)" ["The Letters of V. V. Nabokov to G. P. Struve: Part Two (1931–1935)"]. Published by E. B. Belodubrovskii and A. A. Dolinin. *Zvezda* 4 (2004): 139–63.

———. "Playwriting." In *The Man from the U.S.S.R. and Other Plays,* by Vladimir Nabokov, translated by Dmitri Nabokov, 315–22. New York: Harcourt Brace Jovanovich, Bruccoli Clark, 1984.

———. *Pnin.* In Boyd, *Novels 1955–1962,* 299–435. Originally published in 1957.

———. *Poems and Problems.* New York: McGraw-Hill, 1970.

———. "Postscript to the Russian Edition of *Lolita.*" Translated by Earl D. Sampson, 188–93. In *Nabokov's Fifth Arc: Nabokov and Others on His Life's Work,* edited by J. E. Rivers and Charles Nicol. Austin: University of Texas Press, 1982.

———. "Problems of Translation: *Onegin* in English." In *Theories of Translation: An Anthology of Essays from Dryden to Derrida,* edited by Rainer Schulte and John Biguenet, 127–43. Chicago: University of Chicago Press, 1992. Essay originally published in 1955.

———. "Prof. Woodbridge in an *Essay on Nature* Postulates the Reality of the World." *New York Sun,* December 10, 1940, 15.

———. *The Real Life of Sebastian Knight.* In Boyd, *Novels and Memoirs 1941–1951,* 1–160. Originally published in 1941.

———. "Remarks on F. Martin Brown's 'Measurements and Lepidoptera.'" *The Lepidopterists' News* 4 (1950): 75–76. Reprinted in Boyd and Pyle, *Nabokov's Butterflies,* 458–462.

———. *Selected Letters, 1940–1977.* Edited by Dmitri Nabokov and Matthew J. Bruccoli. San Diego: Harcourt, Brace, Jovanovich, 1989.

———. "Signs and Symbols." In *The Stories of Vladimir Nabokov,* 598–603. New York: Vintage International, 1997.

———. *Speak, Memory: An Autobiography Revisited.* In Boyd, *Novels and Memoirs 1941–1951,* 359–635. Originally published in 1967.

———. *The Stories of Vladimir Nabokov.* New York: Vintage International, 1997.

———. *Strong Opinions.* London: Weidenfeld and Nicolson, 1974. Originally published in 1973.

———. "Translation of the Gettysburg Address (with correspondence)." *The Nabokovian* 24 (1990): 8–14.

———. *Transparent Things.* In Boyd, *Novels 1969–1974,* 487–562. Originally published in 1972.

———. "Ultima Thule." In *The Stories of Vladimir Nabokov,* 500–522. New York: Vintage International, 1997.

———. "Vtoroe dobavlenie k *Daru*" ["Second Addendum to *The Gift*"]. *Zvezda* 1 (2001): 85–109.

———. *The Waltz Invention.* New York: Pocket Cardinal, 1967. Originally published in 1966.

———. "What Faith Means to a Resisting People." *Wellesley Magazine* 26, no. 4 (1942): 212.

———, and Edmund Wilson. *Dear Bunny, Dear Volodya: The Nabokov-Wilson Letters, 1940–1971.* Revised and expanded edition. Edited by Simon Karlinsky. Berkeley: University of California Press, 2001.

Nabokov, Véra. Predislovie [foreword] to *Stikhi,* by Vladimir Nabokov, 3–4. Ann Arbor, Mich.: Ardis, 1979.

Nethercott, Frances. *Russian Legal Culture Before and After Communism: Criminal Justice, Politics, and the Public Sphere.* London: Routledge, 2007.

———. *Une rencontre philosophique: Bergson en Russie, 1907–1917.* Paris: L'Harmattan, 1995.

Nicol, Charles. "Politics." In Alexandrov, *The Garland Companion to Vladimir Nabokov,* 625–28.

Nol'de, B. E. [Boris Emmanuilovich]. "V. D. Nabokov in 1917." In V. D. Nabokov, *The Provisional Government,* 13–31.

Novgorodtsev, Paul [Pavel]. "Ethical Idealism in the Philosophy of Law (On the Question of the Revival of Natural Law)." In Poole, *Problems of Idealism,* 274–324.

———. "Foreword to the Russian Edition." In Poole, *Problems of Idealism,* 81–83.

———. "O filosofskom dvizhenii nashikh dnei" ["Philosophical Trends of Our Time"]. *Novyi put'* 10 (1904): 59–67.

———. "Pamiati Vladimira Dmitrievicha Nabokova" ["In Memory of Vladimir Dmitrievich Nabokov"]. *Russkaia Mysl'* 4 (1922): 194–96.

———. "V. D. Nabokov v grobu" ["V. D. Nabokov in His Coffin"]. *Rul'* 422 (April 5, 1922): 1.

———. "Zakonoproekt o neprikosnovennosti lichnosti" ["Draft Legislation on the Inviolability of Personhood"]. *Pravo* 29 (1906): 2409–18.

Ocherki po filosofii marksizma: Filosofskii sbornik [*Sketches on Marxist Philosophy: Philosophical Collection*]. St. Petersburg, 1908.

Ocherki realisticheskogo mirovozzreniia: Sbornik statei po filosofii, obshchestvennoi nauke i zhizni [*Sketches on a Realist Worldview: Collection of Essays on Philosophy, Social Science and Life*]. St. Petersburg, 1904.

Odem, Mary E. *Delinquent Daughters: Protecting and Policing Adolescent Female Sexuality in the United States, 1885–1920.* Chapel Hill: University of North Carolina Press, 1995.

Ohi, Kevin. "Narcissism and Queer Reading in *Pale Fire.*" *Nabokov Studies* 5 (1998/1999): 153–78.

Page, Norman, ed. *Nabokov: The Critical Heritage.* London: Routledge & Kegan Paul, 1982.

Paley, William. *Natural Theology; or, Evidences of the Existence and Attributes of the Deity, Collected from the Appearances of Nature.* Oxford: J. Vincent, 1828. Originally published in 1802.

Panofsky, Erwin. *Meaning in the Visual Arts.* Garden City, N.Y.: Doubleday, 1955.

Paperno, Irina. "How Nabokov's *Gift* Is Made." *Stanford Slavic Studies* 4, no. 2 (1992): 295–324.

Pasmanik, Daniil S. *Revoliutsionnye gody v Krymu* [*The Revolutionary Years in the Crimea*]. Paris: Imprimerie de Navarre, 1926.

Pearson, Raymond. "*Nashe Pravitel'stvo?* The Crimean Regional Government of 1918–19." *Revolutionary Russia* 2, no. 2 (1989): 14–30.

———. *The Russian Moderates and the Crisis of Tsarism, 1914–1917.* London: Macmillan, 1977.

———. "The Vyborg Complex." *Irish Slavonic Studies* 1 (1980): 73–91.

Peller, Gary. "The Metaphysics of American Law." *California Law Review* 73 (1985): 1151–1290.

Pereira, N. G. O. "N. G. Chernyshevsky as Architect of the Politics of Anti-Liberalism in Russia." *Russian Review* 32, no. 3 (1973): 264–77.

Peterson, Dale E. "Nabokov and Poe." In Alexandrov, *The Garland Companion to Vladimir Nabokov*, 463–72.

Pierce v. Society of Sisters. 268 U.S. 510 (1925).

Piette, Adam. *The Literary Cold War, 1945 to Vietnam*. Edinburgh: Edinburgh University Press, 2009.

Pifer, Ellen. *Nabokov and the Novel*. Cambridge, Mass.: Harvard University Press, 1980.

———. "Nabokov's Discovery of America: From Russia to *Lolita*." In *The American Columbiad: "Discovering" America, Inventing the United States*, edited by Mario Materassi and Maria Irene Ramalho de Sousa Santos, 407–14. Amsterdam: VU University Press, 1996.

Pipes, Richard. Introduction to *The Provisional Government*, by V. D. Nabokov, ix–xiv. Edited by Andrew Field. St. Lucia, Australia: University of Queensland Press, 1970.

———. *Struve, Liberal on the Left, 1870–1905*. Cambridge, Mass.: Harvard University Press, 1970.

———. *Struve, Liberal on the Right, 1905–1944*. Cambridge, Mass.: Harvard University Press, 1980.

Pivar, David J. *Purity Crusade: Sexual Morality and Social Control, 1868–1900*. Westport, Conn.: Greenwood, 1973.

Plekhanov, George V. (N. Beltov). "Chernyshevski v Sibiri." In volume 6 of *Sochineniia*, edited by D. Riazanov, 371–88. 24 vols. 2nd ed. Moscow: Gosudarstvennnoe izdatel'stvo, 1923–27.

———. *The Development of the Monist View of History*. Translated by Andrew Rothstein. Moscow: Foreign Languages Publishing House, 1956.

———. *N. G. Chernyshevsky*. In volume 4 of *Selected Philosophical Works in Five Volumes*, translated by K. M. Cook and S. N. Syrovatkin, edited by K. M. Cook, 169–367. Moscow: Progress, 1980. Originally published in 1909.

———. "Unaddressed Letters." In volume 5 of *Selected Philosophical Works in Five Volumes*, translated by K. M. Cook and A. Fineberg, 263–359. Moscow: Progress, 1981. Originally published serially in 1899–1900.

Poole, Randall A. "Contributor Biographies." In Poole, *Problems of Idealism*, 445–56.

———. "Editor's Introduction: Philosophy and Politics in the Russian Liberation Movement." In Poole, *Problems of Idealism*, 1–83.

———. "Kantian Foundations of Russian Liberal Theory: Human Dignity, Justice, and the Rule of Law." Paper presented at The Weimar Moment: Liberalism, Political Theology, and Law Interdisciplinary Conference, University of Madison, Wisconsin, October 24–26, 2008.

———. "The Neo-Idealist Reception of Kant in the Moscow Psychological Society." *Journal of the History of Ideas* 60, no. 2 (1999): 319–43.

———. "Note on the Text and Translation." In Poole, *Problems of Idealism,* xxi–xxiv.

———, ed. and trans. *Problems of Idealism: Essays in Russian Social Philosophy.* Foreword by Caryl Emerson. New Haven, Conn.: Yale University Press, 2003.

———. "Religion, War, and Revolution: E. N. Trubetskoi's Liberal Construction of Russian National Identity, 1912–20." *Kritika: Explorations in Russian and Eurasian History* 7, no. 2 (2006): 195–240.

———. "Utopianism, Idealism, Liberalism: Russian Confrontations with Vladimir Solov'ev." *Modern Greek Studies Yearbook* 16–17 (2000–2001): 43–87.

Pushkin, Aleksandr S. Volume 1 of *Sobranie sochinenii v shesti tomakh* [*Collected Works in Six Volumes*]. Moscow: Pravda, 1969.

Rampton, David. "The Art of Invocation: The Role of Apostrophe in Nabokov's Early Poetry." *Russian Literature Triquarterly* 24 (1991): 341–54.

———. *Vladimir Nabokov: A Critical Study of the Novels.* Cambridge, Eng.: Cambridge University Press, 1984.

Raskolnikov, Felix. "Pushkin and Religion." *Russian Studies in Literature* 42, no. 1 (2005–2006): 7–35.

Rauscher, Frederick. "Kant's Social and Political Philosophy." In *The Stanford Encyclopedia of Philosophy* (Fall 2007 edition), edited by Edward N. Zalta. http://plato.stanford.edu/archives/fall2007/entries/kant-social-political/.

Read, Christopher. *Religion, Revolution and the Russian Intelligentsia, 1900–1912: The Vekhi Debate and Its Intellectual Background.* London: Macmillan, 1979.

Remington, Charles Lee. "Lepidoptera Studies." In Alexandrov, *The Garland Companion to Vladimir Nabokov,* 274–83.

Rogers, James Allen. "Russia: Social Sciences." In *The Comparative Reception of Darwinism,* edited by Thomas F. Glick, 256–68. Austin: University of Texas Press, 1974.

Rorty, Richard. "The Barber of Kasbeam: Nabokov on Cruelty." In *The Ordering Mirror: Readers and Contexts,* 198–220. New York: Fordham University Press, 1993.

Rosenberg, William G. *Liberals in the Russian Revolution: The Constitutional Democratic Party, 1917–1921.* Princeton, N.J.: Princeton University Press, 1974.

Rosenthal, Bernice Glatzer, and Martha Bohachevsky-Chomiak. Introduction to *A Revolution of the Spirit: Crisis of Value in Russia, 1890–1918,* edited by Martha Bohachevsky-Chomiak and Bernice Glatzer Rosenthal, 1–

40. Translated by Marian Schwartz. Newtonville, Mass.: Oriental Research Partners, 1982.

Samuel, Maurice. *Blood Accusation: The Strange History of the Beiliss Case.* New York: Alfred A. Knopf, 1966.

Sartre, Jean-Paul. *Being and Nothingness: An Essay on Phenomenological Ontology.* Translated by Hazel E. Barnes. London: Methuen, 1966.

———. Review of Nabokov's *Despair* in *Europe* (June 15, 1939), 240–49. In Page, *Nabokov: The Critical Heritage,* 65–66.

Scanlan, James P. "Nicholas Chernyshevsky and Philosophical Materialism in Russia." *Journal of the History of Philosophy* 8 (1970): 65–86.

Schapiro, Leonard. "The Importance of Law in the Study of Politics and History." In Schapiro, *Russian Studies,* 29–44.

———. "The Political Thought of the First Provisional Government." In Schapiro, *Russian Studies,* 100–118.

———. Review of Richard Pipes's *Struve, Liberal on the Left.* In Schapiro, *Russian Studies,* 119–21.

———. Review of Richard Pipes's *Struve, Liberal on the Right.* In Schapiro, *Russian Studies,* 122–27.

———. *Russian Studies,* edited by Ellen Dahrendorf. London: Collins Harvill, 1986.

Schrecker, Ellen. *The Age of McCarthyism: A Brief History with Documents.* 2nd ed. Boston: Bedford, St. Martin's, 2002.

Scruton, Roger. *Kant: A Very Short Introduction.* Rev. ed. Oxford: Oxford University Press, 2001.

Shapiro, Gavriel. "Setting His Myriad Faces in His Text: Nabokov's Authorial Presence Revisited." In Connolly, *Nabokov and His Fiction,* 15–35.

Shatz, Marshall S., and Judith E. Zimmerman. Introduction to *Signposts: A Collection of Articles on the Russian Intelligentsia,* vii–xxv. Translated and edited by Marshall S. Shatz and Judith E. Zimmerman. Irvine, Calif.: Charles Schlacks Jr., 1986.

Shcherbina, V. "G. V. Plekhanov's Views of Aesthetics (Introduction)." In volume 5 of Plekhanov's *Selected Philosophical Works in Five Volumes,* translated by K. M. Cook and A. Fineberg, 7–34. Moscow: Progress, 1981.

Shvabrin, Stanislav. "Vladimir Vladimirovich Nabokov, Ivan Petrovich Pnin: An Earlier Encounter?" Paper presented at the V. V. Nabokov Museum's International Vladimir Nabokov Symposium, St. Petersburg, July 15–19, 2002. http://www.nabokovmuseum.org/PDF/Shvabrin.pdf.

Sistematicheskii katalog biblioteki Vladimira Dmitrievicha Nabokova. St. Petersburg: Tovarishchestvo khudozhestvennoi pechati, 1904.

Sistematicheskii katalog biblioteki Vladimira Dmitrievicha Nabokova: Pervoe prodolzhenie. St. Petersburg: Tovarishchestvo khudozhestvennoi pechati, 1911.

Soble, Alan. "Kant and Sexual Perversion." *The Monist* 86, no. 1 (2003): 55–89.

Sokolov, N. M. *Ob ideiakh i idealakh russkoi intelligentsii* [*On the Ideas and Ideals of the Russian Intelligentsia*]. St. Petersburg: Tipografiia M. M. Stasiulevicha, 1904.

Soloviev, V. S. "Beauty in Nature." In *The Heart of Reality: Essays on Beauty, Love, and Ethics,* edited and translated by Vladimir Wozniuk, 29–66. Notre Dame, Ind.: University of Notre Dame Press, 2003.

Spasovich, V. D. "Novye napravleniia v nauke ugolovnago prava" ["New Directions in the Science of Criminal Law"]. In volume 8 of *Sochineniia V. D. Spasovicha: Poslednie raboty v devianostykh godakh,* 211–300. St. Petersburg: N. Findeizen, 1896.

Sprigge, T. L. S. "Idealism." In volume 4 of the *Routledge Encyclopedia of Philosophy,* edited by Edward Craig, 662–69. London: Routledge, 1998.

Struve, Gleb. "The Cultural Renaissance." In *Russia Under the Last Tsar,* edited by Theofanis George Stavrou, 179–201. Minneapolis: University of Minnesota Press, 1969.

———. *Russkaia literatura v izgnanii* [*Russian Literature in Exile*]. 2nd ed. Paris: YMCA, 1984. Originally published in 1956.

Struve, Petr. "O chem dumaet odna kniga?" ["Reflections of a Certain Book"]. [Signed P. S.] *Osvobozhdenie* 1, no. 18 (March 2, 1903): 311–12.

———. "Pamiati Vladimira Dmitrievicha Nabokova" ["In Memory of Vladimir Dmitrievich Nabokov"]. *Russkaia Mysl'* 4 (1922): 192–93.

———. Preface to Nikolai A. Berdiaev's *Sub'ektivizm i individualizm v obshchestvennoi filosofii* [*Subjectivism and Individualism in Social Philosophy*], 5–78. Moscow: Kanon, 1999. Originally published in 1901.

———. [Signed P. G.] "Toward Characterization of Our Philosophical Development." In Poole, *Problems of Idealism,* 143–60.

———. "V chem zhe istinnyi natsionalizm?" ["What Is True Nationalism?"]. *Voprosy filosofii i psikhologii* 12, no. 59 (1901): 493–528. Originally signed "P. Borisov."

———. "Zametki o sovremennykh delakh" ["Notes on Contemporary Matters"]. *Osvobozhdenie* 3, nos. 78–79 (October 12/15, 1905): 495–98.

Stuckenberg, J. H. W. *The Life of Immanuel Kant.* Bristol: Thoemmes, 1990. Originally published in 1882.

Suchoff, David. "The Rosenberg Case and the New York Intellectuals." In *Secret Agents: The Rosenberg Case, McCarthyism, and Fifties America,* edited by Marjorie Garber and Rebecca L. Walkowitz, 155–69. New York: Routledge, 1995.

Sutherland, Kate. "From Jailbird to Jailbait: Age of Consent Laws and the Construction of Teenage Sexualities." *William and Mary Journal of Women and the Law* 9 (2003): 313–49.

Szeftel, Marc. "Personal Inviolability in the Legislation of the Russian Absolute Monarchy." *American Slavic and East European Review* 17 (1958): 1–24.

Tagantsev, N. S. [Nikolai Stepanovich]. From *Russkoe ugolovnoe pravo* [*Russian Criminal Law*]. In *Istoriia Russkoi pravovoi mysli: Biografii, dokumenty, publikatsii* [*A History of Russian Legal Thought: Biographies, Documents, and Publications*], edited by V. P. Kashepov, A. V. Mitskevich, and S. A. Piatkina, 478–512. Moscow: Ostozh'e, 1998.

Tammi, Pekka. *Problems of Nabokov's Poetics: A Narratological Analysis.* Helsinki: Suomalainen Tiedeakatemia, 1985.

Tatarinov, Vladimir. "V. D. Nabokov i russkaia emigratsiia" ["V. D. Nabokov and the Russian Emigration"]. *Golos emigranta* 12 (April 1922): 8.

Toker, Leona. "'The Dead Are Good Mixers': Nabokov's Versions of Individualism." In Connolly, *Nabokov and His Fiction,* 92–108.

———. "Nabokov and Bergson." In Alexandrov, *The Garland Companion to Vladimir Nabokov,* 367–73.

———. "Nabokov and Bergson on Duration and Reflexivity." In Grayson, McMillin, and Meyer, *Nabokov's World, Volume 1: The Shape of Nabokov's World,* 132–40.

———. *Nabokov: The Mystery of Literary Structures.* Ithaca, N.Y.: Cornell University Press, 1989.

Tolstoy, Ivan. "Vladimir Dmitrievich, Nikolai Stepanovich, Nikolai Gavrilovich." *Zvezda* 11 (1996): 181–91.

Trilling, Lionel. *The Liberal Imagination.* New York: Viking, 1950.

———. Review of *Lolita* in *Encounter,* October 1958. In Page, *Nabokov: The Critical Heritage,* 92–102.

Trousdale, Rachel. "'Faragod Bless Them': Nabokov, Spirits, and Electricity." *Nabokov Studies* 7 (2002/2003): 119–28.

Trubetskoi, Evgenii N. "Toward Characterization of the Theory of Marx and Engels on the Significance of Ideas in History." In Poole, *Problems of Idealism,* 124–42.

Ullman, Sharon R. *Sex Seen: The Emergence of Modern Sexuality in America.* Berkeley: University of California Press, 1997.

United States v. Dennis. 183 F.2d 201 (2d Cir. 1950).

Valentinov, N. V. [N. V. Volskii]. *Filosofskie postroeniia marksizma: Dialekticheskii materializm, empiriomonizm, i empiriokriticheskaiia filosofiia* [*The Philosophical Constructions of Marxism: Dialectical Materialism, Empirio-Monism, and Empirio-Critical Philosophy*]. Moscow, 1907.

Valéry, Paul. *Analects.* Translated by Stuart Gilbert. Princeton, N.J.: Princeton University Press, 1970.

———. "Choses Tues." In *Tel Quel,* vol. 1. Paris: Gallimard, 1941.

Valliere, Paul. "Theological Liberalism and Church Reform in Imperial Russia." In *Church, Nation and State in Russia and Ukraine,* edited by Geoffrey A. Hosking, 108–30. Edmonton, Can.: Canadian Institute of Ukrainian Studies Press, 1990.

Vernadskii, Vladimir I. *Khimicheskoe stroenie biosfery Zemli i ee okruzheniia* [*The Chemical Structure of the Earth's Biosphere and its Surroundings*]. Moscow: Nauka, 1965.

———. "O nauchnom mirovozzrenii" ["On the Scientific Worldview"]. *Voprosy filosofii i psikhologii* 65 (1902): 1409–65.

———. "Vysshaia shkola v Rossii" ["University Education in Russia"]. In *Ezhegodnik gazety "Rech'" na 1914 godu*, 308–25. Petrograd, 1914.

Vernier, Chester G. *American Family Laws: A Comparative Study of the Family Law of the Forty-Eight American States, Alaska, the District of Columbia, and Hawaii (to Jan. 1, 1931)*. Vol. 1. Stanford, Calif.: Stanford University Press, 1931.

Vinaver, Maksim M. *Nashe pravitel'stvo (Krymskiia vospominaniia 1918–1919 g.g.)* [*Our Government (Crimean Reminiscences 1918–1919)*]. Paris: Imprimerie d'Art Voltaire, 1928.

Volskii, Nikolai V. [N.V. Valentinov]. *Encounters with Lenin*. Translated by Paul Rosta and Brian Pearce. Foreword by Leonard Schapiro. London: Oxford University Press, 1968. Originally published as *Vstrechi s Leninym* in 1953.

Vries, Gerard de. "'Perplex'd in the Extreme': Moral Facets of Vladimir Nabokov's Work." *Nabokov Studies* 2 (1995): 135–52.

Vucinich, Alexander. *Darwin in Russian Thought*. Berkeley: University of California Press, 1988.

———. "Politics, Universities, and Science." In *Russia Under the Last Tsar*, edited by Theofanis George Stavrou, 154–78. Minneapolis: University of Minnesota Press, 1969.

———. *Science in Russian Culture: 1861–1917*. Vol. 2. Stanford, Calif.: Stanford University Press, 1970.

Wald, Michael S. "Children's Rights: A Framework for Analysis." *University of California, Davis Law Review* 12 (1979): 255–82.

Walicki, Andrzej. *A History of Russian Thought from the Enlightenment to Marxism*. Translated by Hilda Andrews-Rusiecka. Stanford, Calif.: Stanford University Press, 1979.

———. *Legal Philosophies of Russian Liberalism*. Oxford: Clarendon, 1987.

Walkowitz, Judith R. *Prostitution and Victorian Society: Women, Class, and the State*. Cambridge, Eng.: Cambridge University Press, 1980.

Wasianski, E. A. C. *Immanuel Kant in seinen letzten Lebensjahren*, in *Immanuel Kant: Sein Leben in Darstellungen von Zeitgenossen*, 215–306. Edited by Felix Gross. Darmstadt: Wissenschaftliche Buchgesellschaft, 1968.

Whiting, Frederick. "'The Strange Particularity of the Lover's Preference': Pedophilia, Pornography, and the Anatomy of Monstrosity in *Lolita*." *American Literature* 70, no. 4 (1998): 833–62.

Wood, Allen W. *Kant's Ethical Thought*. Cambridge, Eng.: Cambridge University Press, 1999.

Wood, Michael. *The Magician's Doubts: Nabokov and the Risks of Fiction*. London: Pimlico, 1994.

———. "The Politics of Zembla." Paper presented at the V. V. Nabokov Museum's International Vladimir Nabokov Symposium, St. Petersburg, July 15–19, 2002. http://www.nabokovmuseum.org/PDF/Wood.pdf.

Woodhouse, Barbara Bennett. "The Constitutionalization of Children's Rights: Incorporating Emerging Human Rights into Constitutional Doctrine." *University of Pennsylvania Journal of Constitutional Law* 2, no. 1 (1999): 1–52.

Yeats, William Butler. *Pages from a Diary Written in Nineteen Hundred and Thirty*. Dublin: Cuala, 1944.

Yushkevich, Pavel S. *Materializm i kriticheskii realizm: O filosofskikh napravleniiakh v marksizme* [*Materialism and Critical Realism: Philosophical Directions in Marxism*]. St. Petersburg, 1908.

Zimmer, Dieter E. *A Guide to Nabokov's Butterflies and Moths 2001*. Hamburg: Privately published, 2001.

———. "Mimicry in Nature and Art." In Grayson, McMillin, and Meyer, *Nabokov's World, Volume 1: The Shape of Nabokov's World*, 47–57.

Zimmerman, Judith Elin. "Between Revolution and Reaction: The Russian Constitutional Democratic Party. October, 1905 to June, 1907." Ph.D. dissertation, Columbia University, 1967.

Index

About the Author

Dana Dragunoiu is an associate professor of English at Carleton University in Ottawa, Canada.

green press
INITIATIVE

Northwestern University Press is committed to preserving ancient forests and natural resources. We elected to print this title on 30% post consumer recycled paper, processed chlorine free. As a result, for this printing, we have saved:

2 Trees (40' tall and 6-8" diameter)
767 Gallons of Wastewater
1 Million BTUs of Total Energy
49 Pounds of Solid Waste
170 Pounds of Greenhouse Gases

Northwestern University Press made this paper choice because our printer, Thomson-Shore, Inc., is a member of Green Press Initiative, a nonprofit program dedicated to supporting authors, publishers, and suppliers in their efforts to reduce their use of fiber obtained from endangered forests.

For more information, visit www.greenpressinitiative.org

Environmental impact estimates were made using the Environmental Defense Paper Calculator. For more information visit: www.papercalculator.org.